OXFORD ESSAYS IN JURISPRUDENCE

OXFORD ESSAYS IN JURISPRUDENCE

Fourth Series

Edited by

JEREMY HORDER

OXFORD
UNIVERSITY PRESS

OXFORD
UNIVERSITY PRESS
Great Clarendon Street, Oxford OX2 6DP

Oxford University Press is a department of the University of Oxford.
It furthers the University's objective of excellence in research, scholarship, and education by publishing worldwide in

Oxford New York
Athens Auckland Bangkok Bogotá Buenos Aires Calcutta Cape Town Chennai Dar es Salaam Delhi Florence Hong Kong Istanbul Karachi Kuala Lumpur Madrid Melbourne Mexico City Mumbai Nairobi Paris São Paulo Singapore Taipei Tokyo Toronto Warsaw
and associated companies in Berlin Ibadan

Oxford is a registered trade mark of Oxford University Press in the UK and in certain other countries

Published in the United States by Oxford University Press Inc., New York

First published 2000

British Library Cataloguing in Publication Data
Data available

Library of Congress Cataloging in Publication Data
Data available

ISBN 0–19–826858–0

1 3 5 7 9 10 8 6 4 2

Typeset in Garamond
by Hope Services (Abingdon) Ltd.
Printed in Great Britain
on acid-free paper by
T.J. International Ltd.
Padstow, Cornwall

Preface

It has always been the underlying purpose of the *Oxford Essays in Jurisprudence* series to give the wider world an insight, once every decade or so, into the kind of scholarship in which members of the Faculty of Law at Oxford are engaged. That remains the purpose of this, the Fourth Series, although it has a special theme. The Fourth Series is devoted to furthering understanding of the philosophical foundations of the common law, a subject that has been central to research and teaching within Oxford's Law Faculty since the late Herbert Hart, and Tony Honoré, effectively invented the subject through their ground-breaking work in the 1950s and 1960s. Unusually, the contributors on this occasion are linked more by their past than by their present membership of the Faculty of Law.They have, however, been asked to write essays because they have all made substantial contributions, whether as members of the teaching group or as invited speakers, to the teaching of the course entitled Philosophical Foundations of the Common Law. This course was offered from 1983 until its (with luck, only temporary) suspension in 1998, as a part of the postgraduate degree of Bachelor of Civil Law at Oxford. The idea for such a course was that of Joseph Raz, who considered that such a course would fulfil a scholarly need that could not be fully met within the confines of the Jurisprudence and Political Theory course already offered on the BCL. The 'Philosophical Foundations' course developed into an excellent proving ground for many scholarly ideas that were, subsequently, to make an important contribution to the flourishing of the subject.

One of the founding members of the 'Philosophical Foundations' teaching group was Tony Honoré, Fellow of All Souls College, and formerly Regius Professor of Civil Law at Oxford. His classes on causation, enjoyed by students ensconced in the comfortable armchairs in his rooms at All Souls, were one of the highlights of the course. Furthermore, he not only contributed one essay each—both still much admired and discussed—to the First and Second Series of *Oxford Essays in Jurisprudence* ('Ownership', 1961, and 'Groups, Laws and Obedience', 1973), but has also generously acted as a consultant to the editors of, and to the contributors to, both the Third and, now, the Fourth Series. I know that all the editors and contributors, myself very much included, have profited a great deal from his wise counsel, as, no doubt, will the editor(s) and contributors when the Fifth Series is in preparation in the next millennium.

JEREMY HORDER

St. Margaret's Day, July 1999.

Contents

Contributors

Roderick Bagshaw is a Fellow and Tutor in Law, Mansfield College, University of Oxford.

Peter Cane is a Professor and Head of the Law Program in the Research School of Social Sciences, Australian National University, and was, formerly, a Tutorial Fellow in Law, and Professor of Law, Corpus Christi College, University of Oxford.

Timothy Endicott is a Fellow and Tutor in Law, Balliol College, University of Oxford.

John Finnis is Professor of Law and Legal Philosophy, University of Oxford, a Fellow and Tutor, University College, University of Oxford, and Biolchini Professor of Law, University of Notre Dame, Indiana.

John Gardner is a Reader in Legal Philosophy, King's College London, and a Fellow of All Souls College, University of Oxford. He was, formerly, a Fellow and Tutor in Law, Brasenose College, University of Oxford.

Jeremy Horder is a Porjes Foundation Fellow and Tutor in Law, Worcester College, and Reader in Criminal Law, University of Oxford.

Nicola Lacey is Professor of Criminal Law, London School of Economics. She was, formerly, a Fellow and Tutor, New College, University of Oxford.

Nicholas McBride is a Fellow and Tutor in Law, Pembroke College, University of Cambridge. He was, formerly, a Fellow of All Souls College, University of Oxford.

Stephen Perry is John J. O'Brien Professor of Law and Professor of Philosophy, University of Pennsylvania.

Stephen Shute is a Senior Lecturer in Law, University of Birmingham. He was, formerly, a Fellow and Tutor in Law, Corpus Christi College, University of Oxford.

A.P. Simester is a Reader in Criminal Law Theory, University of Birmingham.

Stephen Smith is an Associate Professor and Member of the Institute of Comparative Law, Faculty of Law, McGill University. He was, formerly, a Tutorial Fellow in Law, St Anne's College, University of Oxford.

Jane Stapleton is a Professor, Research School of Social Sciences, Australian National University. She was, formerly, a Fellow, Tutor and Reader in Law, Balliol College, University of Oxford, where she remains a Fellow.

The Priority of Persons

John Finnis

So, since all law is made *for the sake of human beings*, we should speak first of the status of persons.[1]

Justinian, *Digest* 1. 5. 2

Knowledge of law amounts to little if it overlooks the *persons for whose sake* law is made.[2]

Justinian, *Institutes* 1. 2. 12

What it is to be a person, and why it matters that one is, are issues no longer thematic in general accounts of law. But the very concept of law, of an existing and projected reality profoundly, and deliberately, different from both anarchy and tyranny is shaped by the recognition that (i) we human beings are all persons and each other's equals in that respect even if in no other; (ii) persons of sufficient maturity and health can understand and communicate what they and other persons mean, and can intend and choose many other ways of behaving, too; and (iii) persons, their well-being, and their intentions matter in ways that nothing else in our environment does. This essay outlines some reasons for bringing these issues, rather neglected in modern jurisprudence, back into focus.

I LAW IS 'FOR THE SAKE OF . . .'

Hart's rejection of 'the positivist thesis that "law may have any content" ' appealed to the 'natural necessity' of 'the minimum forms of protection for persons, property, and promises which are . . . indispensable features of municipal law', 'if it is to serve the minimum purposes of beings constituted as men are'.[3] A 'natural' necessity of this kind is in the first instance a *rational* necessity. As Hart himself remarks, his discussion of the minimum content of law[4] is trying to identify 'the distinctively *rational*

[1] '*Cum* . . . hominum causa *omne ius constitutum sit, primo de personarum statu* . . . *dicemus*' (emphasis added, here and elsewhere unless otherwise indicated).

[2] '*Nam parum est ius nosse si* personae quarum causa *statutum est ignorentur.*'

[3] H.L.A. Hart, *The Concept of Law* (Oxford University Press, Oxford, [1961], 2nd edn. 1994) 199. The word omitted is 'similarly', referring to the same 'setting of natural facts and aims, which make sanctions both possible and necessary in a municipal system' (ibid.). The Postscript, ibid. 248–9, seems to retreat from the book's clear and well argued rejection of the above-described 'positivist thesis': '[l]ike other forms of positivism my theory makes no claim to identify the point or purpose of law and legal systems as such . . . In fact I think it quite vain to seek any more specific purpose which law as such serves beyond providing guides to human conduct and standards of criticism of such conduct.' But ibid. 251 reverts to speaking of 'aims [besides certainty] which law should cherish'.

[4] He called it 'the minimum content of natural law' but meant, rather, the minimum content of positive law (content which, being necessary, one can call natural law).

connection between natural facts and the content of legal and moral rules'.[5] And this 'connection' is 'rational' given the 'minimum purposes' or 'natural aims' of 'beings constituted as men are'. The rationality, then, is that of practical reasoning—reasoning along the following lines (for example): we want to survive; but, given that we are vulnerable and the altruism of others is limited, we cannot survive without rules prohibiting the free use of violence; *so* such rules are necessary and other rules are worthless without these.

Though Hart spoke often enough of human beings' natural aims, plural, his official list of them famously admitted only the aim just mentioned: 'survival'.[6] Fortunately for jurisprudence, his real list of the minimum purposes which give law and legal system their complex, shaping point tacitly went wider. It included the aims or purposes relative to which people—not least Hart and the readers he anticipated—count certain aspects of 'pre-legal' conditions as 'defects', defects to which the minimally adequate response is, as Hart argues, the 'amenity' of power-conferring rules and the 'remedy' of 'secondary rules', the amenities and remedies which make law what it essentially is.[7]

Law, then, is for the sake of serving certain purposes of 'beings constituted as men are', and Hart speaks of serving these purposes as law's *point.* For Ronald Dworkin, on the other hand, 'the most abstract and fundamental *point* of legal practice' is: 'to guide and constrain the power of government [by insisting that] force not be used or withheld . . . except as licensed or required by individual rights and responsibilities flowing from past political decisions about when collective force is justified'.[8] And Dworkin favours a specific conception of that point, 'law as integrity'; 'law insists', he holds, that collective force be licensed by rights and responsibilities 'flowing from' past decisions, in order that the law will thereby benefit 'society' precisely 'by securing a kind of equality among citizens'.[9] And rights and responsibilities only 'flow from' a political community's decisions if that community's practices 'show not only concern but an *equal* concern for all members'.[10]

So law's point, on Dworkin's conception, is to serve the interests of 'citizens' or (equivalently, it seems) 'members of the group'—and if it fails to try to do so, it lacks legitimacy, authority, and obligatory force, and fails to justify the coercion it pretends to justify. Dworkin's restriction of the point to citizens or members of the community seems deliberate. True, one of his summaries of the equality condition says that

[5] Ibid. 193, where the treatment of the minimum content begins: 'it is important to observe that in each case the facts mentioned afford a *reason* why, given survival as an aim, law and morals should include a specific content' (Hart's emphasis).

[6] Ibid. 191. On his argument here, see my *Natural Law and Natural Rights* (Oxford University Press, Oxford, 1980) 30–1, 82.

[7] See *The Concept of Law*, n. 3 above, 28, 41–2, 196–7 (on the 'huge and distinctive amenity' conferred by the institution of power-conferring rules, 'one of the great contributions of law to social life' and 'a step forward as important to society as the invention of the wheel'); 91–9 (on the remedies required to overcome the defects of a social structure of primary rules of obligation restricting the free use of violence, theft and deception); and 155 (on the union of primary and secondary rules as 'the "essence" of law').

[8] Ronald Dworkin, *Law's Empire* (Harvard University Press and Fontana Press, 1986) 93.

[9] Ibid. 95–6.

[10] Ibid. 200 (Dworkin's emphasis).

the 'command of integrity assumes that each *person* is as worthy as any other, that each must be treated with equal concern',[11] and there is mention of the concept of 'general duties [a group's] members owe equally to persons outside it'.[12] But no such general duty is affirmed as having a place in the account of law's empire, and in its context the summary's reference to 'persons' seems to be no more than shorthand for 'members'. Moreover, membership is said to be a matter of 'genetic or geographical or other historical conditions identified *by social practice*'.[13] (Some elements of American legal history which I recall in section IV make these restrictions noteworthy.)

Thus there are telling differences in the conceptions of law's point proposed by Hart and Dworkin as internal to the very idea of law. For Dworkin, 'securing' an equality understood as incompatible with counting 'some members as inherently less worthy than others'[14] is central to law's point and idea. For Hart, concern for any such kind of equality, though 'deeply embedded in *modern* man'[15] and '*now* generally accepted as a statement of an ideal of obvious relevance in the criticism of law',[16] is extrinsic to the concept of law, and the question whether such concern or criticism is warranted 'cannot be investigated'[17] in his book on that concept. But the contrast between these two theorists is softened by Dworkin's noticeable unwillingness to affirm that the equality intrinsic to law's point is the equality of all human beings or of all persons or of any other class of beings identifiable prior to a social practice—a practice, such as the law's, of defining the membership whereby moral and legal rights are 'given'.[18]

II ON LAW AS FOR THE SAKE OF ALL

To the thought that the primary element in law's point is not merely promoting 'survival' but respecting and appropriately promoting the survival of *all* human beings within its jurisdiction, Hart has a simple response, tirelessly deployed throughout his work. Legal systems, he reminds us, 'have long endured though they have flouted these principles of justice'.[19] Moreover, 'it is conceivable that there might be a moral outlook which did not put individuals on a footing of reciprocal equality'.[20] Well, neither the facts nor the logical possibilities are in doubt. But Hart's own strategy of displaying law as a kind of *reason* apt for being counted as a *common standard* for action undercuts this response. Just as fallacious arguments earn a place in a treatise

[11] Ibid. 213. [12] Ibid. 199. [13] Ibid. 201. [14] Ibid. 201.

[15] *The Concept of Law*, n. 3 above, 162. [16] Ibid. 206.

[17] Ibid. 206. Notice that in his book *Punishment and Responsibility* (Oxford University Press, Oxford, 1968) he is willing to say things like (at 22): '[j]ustice simply consists of principles . . . which (i) *treat all alike as persons* by attaching special significance to human volutary action and (ii) forbid the use of one human being for the benefit of others except in return for his voluntary actions against them.'

[18] See Ronald Dworkin, *Life's Dominion* (Alfred A. Knopf, London; Harper Collins, London, 1993) 23

[19] *The Concept of Law*, n. 3 above, 206. [20] Ibid. 165.

on argumentation only as instances of what, despite appearances and popularity, is really *not an argument*, so unreasonable kinds of law and legal system should be attended to in legal theory precisely as instances of law diluted with the effluents of what law *essentially opposes*: the arbitrary exercise of one person's or group's power over other persons and groups. Dworkin is right to hold that 'any full theory of law'[21] will go beyond Hart's explicit and tacit accounts of the benefits which differentiate law from the commands of powerful people, and will include a reference to equality and its moral entailments, 'principles of justice, fairness, and procedural due process'.[22] But, as we have seen, he leaves in shadow the question *who* is equal, and should be treated as equal, to whom.

Roman law, which long endured though flouting some of the principles of justice, gave its students and practitioners a better account of law's point. The opening sentence of the *Institutes* directs us towards it: justice, understood precisely as a disposition to act for a certain kind of purpose: 'Justice is the stable and lasting willingness *to give to each his right*'.[23] 'Each' who? The Birks translation quite properly renders this object as 'to acknowledge all men's rights'. For the closing words of the introductory sections (titles 1–3 of book 1) tell us that law exists 'for the sake of persons', and the following sentence, opening the whole treatise on the law of persons, stakes out the essential position: all men are persons.[24] Slavery is bluntly defined as the subjection of 'someone' to another's ownership and mastery 'contrary to nature',[25] indeed, more precisely, 'contrary to natural law/right'.[26] 'For by natural law/right, from the beginning, all human beings are born free.'[27]

The requirements of justice-for-persons are thus affirmed and flouted in almost the same breath. No attempt is made to deny that slaves are persons and are their owners' equals in human nature. The institution is presented not as justified but as a fact of life and a product of the arbitrament of war—of sheer power. The frankness, to be sure, has its limits; the fact is here veiled that slavery as an institution of the law is maintained by sheer power, long after any war or war-captivity, and is imposed upon persons who were never party to war. Law's point is stated by Roman law's self-interpretative doctrines, but its implications are not pursued with undeflected practical reasonableness.

Law's point—what, or better, whom it is for the sake of—is identified in the opening words of Article 1 of the Universal Declaration of Human Rights (1948), adopting the phraseology of the Roman jurists: '*[a]ll human beings* are born free and equal in dignity and rights'. Article 1's subject, 'all human beings', is equated with the preamble's 'all members of the human family' and 'the human person', so that the

[21] See *Law's Empire*, n. 8 above, 110.
[22] See ibid. e.g. 225.
[23] *Digest* 1. 1. pr.; *Institutes* (*Inst.*) 1. 1. pr.
[24] *Inst.* 1. 2. 12; 1. 3. 1: '[t]he main classification in the law of persons is this: all men are either free or slaves' (*summa itaque divisio de iure personarum haec est, quod omnes homines aut liberi sunt aut servi*).
[25] *Inst.* 1. 3. 2.
[26] *Inst.* 1. 2. 2.
[27] Ibid.: '*servitutes . . . sunt iuri naturali contrariae—iure enim naturali ab initio omnes homines liberi nascebantur.*'

reference of the remaining articles,[28] 'everyone', 'all', and 'no one', is clear. So it is all human beings who are 'equal before the law' and entitled to its 'equal protection' (Article 7); and 'everyone' has the 'right to recognition everywhere as a person before the law' (Article 6).

III ON RULES AS RELATIONSHIPS OF THE DELIBERATING PERSON TO OTHER PERSONS

What is a rule of law? It is certainly not well defined as an 'assemblage of signs declarative of a volition', as Bentham supposed. It is not, indeed, to be defined as any kind of assemblage of signs, for rules of law are no more than evidenced and, in some instances, performatively *effected* by the assembling of such signs. Nor is it, ultimately, the meaning of a set of signs or of an act of signifying, for, while meaning remains constant, validity and obligatoriness may come and go. In my general account of law, I tried to answer the question:

> legal thinking (i.e. the law) brings what precision and predictability it can into the order of human interaction by a special technique: the treating of (usually datable) past acts (whether of enactment, adjudication, or any of the multitude of exercises of public and private 'powers') as giving, *now*, sufficient and exclusionary reason for acting in a way *then* 'provided for'. In an important sense the 'existence' or 'validity' of a legal rule can be explained by saying that it simply is this relationship, this continuing relevance of the 'content' of that past juridical act as providing reason to decide and act in the present in the way then specified and provided for.[29]

The explanation is, I think, sound. But we will get still closer to the bottom of the matter if we say that a rule is a relationship between persons. To say that a rule of positive law exists is to say (i) that its subjects (those upon whom it imposes duties or confers powers, etc.) stand in a certain relationship to the class of person who—whose interests—would be served by the rule-subjects' adherence to their duties or exercise of their powers, etc., and (ii) that those rule-subjects stand in that relationship to persons of that class because they (and in some way also the persons whose interests are thus to be served) stand in a certain relationship to the person(s) whose 'past juridical act' therefore provides 'reason to decide and act in the present in the way then specified and provided for'.

Why give explanatory priority, thus, to the relationship between persons? Well, nothing short of an acknowledgement of the reality and value ('dignity') of other persons, as my equals in reality and value, will suffice to make sense of law's most elementary claims on my attention: its claim to *direct* certain choices of mine, to *override* my self-interest in certain respects, to stipulate *conditions* for lending me its assistance in pursuing my purposes, and so forth.

[28] There is one exception, Art. 16, which has as its subject 'men and women of full age', to signify that marriage is between persons of opposite sex (gender).

[29] *Natural Law and Natural Rights*, n. 6 above, 269 (emphases in original).

The history of jurisprudence since Bentham is, in some important respects, the history of failure and regression. The Benthamite strategy of describing, analysing, expounding law as a kind of mechanism supposed to be fully intelligible by reference exclusively to its origin in a 'volition'—excluding, that is to say, all reference to its point (i.e. its rationale)—was pursued with unsurpassable pertinacity and ingenuity, across more than half the twentieth century, by Kelsen. Its *dénouement* was the spectacular debacle in which Kelsen, rightly acknowledging the failure of his legal philosophy from 1911 to 1960[30] to explain or even coherently describe law's validity, its normativity, its elementary particle (the norm), and its coherence, severed all links between law and practical reasonableness, embraced even the most open contradiction between legal norms,[31] denied the possibility of legal reasoning even by subsumption of an uncontroversial instance under the corresponding norm,[32] and proposed an admitted fiction as the 'scientific' explanation of validity.[33] Kelsen's lifelong aversion from any resort or reference to practical reasonableness to understand, describe, and interpret law became, in the end, a headlong flight. It was, in the last analysis, an aversion from understanding law as a set of implications of one's seeing the point of serving—respecting and promoting—other persons, and so their interests or well-being, as equal in dignity and value to oneself and one's own. But there is, I am suggesting, no other way of understanding law's claims and directives, their grounds and origins, their force, their limits, and their pathological forms.

IV CONSEQUENCES OF CONSIDERING LAW WITHOUT ACKNOWLEDGING PERSONS AS ITS POINT

Kelsen's refusal to treat human persons and their interests and well-being as the point of law, a refusal generally shared by analytical jurisprudence from Bentham on, is plainest in his treatment of persons in the law, in the first instance 'physical (natural) persons'.[34] To say that a human being A has a right 'means only that certain *conduct of* the individual A is the object of a legal right . . . that certain conduct of the individual A is, in a specific way, the contents of a legal norm'.[35] Likewise, of course, with

[30] On the phases of Kelsen's work, see e.g. Stanley L. Paulson, 'Four Phases in Hans Kelsen's Theory? Reflections on a Periodization' (1998) 18 *Oxford Journal of Legal Studies* 154–66 at 161.

[31] Hans Kelsen, *General Theory of Norms* (trans. Michael Hartney, Oxford University Press, Oxford, 1991) 214 ('[a]s far as conflicts between general norms are concerned, it is not the case—as I claimed in my *Pure Theory of Law*—that a conflict of norms which cannot be resolved by the principle *Lex posterior derogat legi priori* makes no sense . . . Each of the two general norms makes sense and both are valid.'), 223–5.

[32] Ibid. 232–8.

[33] Ibid. 256 ('the assumption of a Basic Norm—for instance, . . . the Basic Norm of a legal order, "Everyone is to behave as the historically first constitution specifies"—not only contradicts reality, since there exists no such norm as the meaning of an actual act of will, but is also self-contradictory. . . . The cognitive goal of the Basic Norm . . . can be attained only by means of a fiction.')

[34] Hans Kelsen, *General Theory of Law and State* (trans. Anders Wedberg, Harvard University Press, Cambridge, Mass., 1945) 95.

[35] Ibid. 94.

A's duties. Hence: '[i]n juristic considerations we are concerned with man only insofar as his *conduct* enters into the contents of the legal order.'[36] 'The person exists only insofar as he "has" duties and rights' (these rights pertaining, remember, only to that same person's own conduct); 'apart from them the person has no existence whatsoever.'[37] So:

> That man and person are two entirely different concepts may be regarded as a generally accepted result of analytical jurisprudence. . . . the physical (natural) person is the personification of a set of legal norms which by constituting duties and rights containing the conduct of one and the same human being regulate the conduct of this being. The relation between the so-called physical (natural) person and the human being with whom the former is often erroneously identified consists in the fact that those duties and rights which are comprehended in the concept of the person all refer to the behavior of that human being.[38]

In short: juristic thought as such knows nothing of any human person save that person's conduct as specified in legal norms, and does not have as its primary or any concern the interests and well-being of this or any other person.

In the decades of Kelsen's greatest influence, judges confronted by the practical problems of identifying law and rights after revolution turned to Kelsen's account of revolutionary transition. They found no guidance, but some material for rationalizing conclusions reached on other grounds.[39] So too, Kelsen's treatment of the person has been called upon to rationalize judicial abdication from such disciplined and critical concern with the interests and well-being of real people.

Of course, such an abdication can and has, from time to time, occurred without the aid or encouragement of analytical jurisprudence. Among the most striking examples is the justly infamous judgment of the Supreme Court of the United States in *Scott* v. *Sandford* (1857), holding that members of 'the African race' imported into or born in the United States (whether or not they had become free) were not citizens of the United States, and could never be made citizens by Congress even under its undoubted power of naturalization.[40] The decision rested on the fact that, at the time of the Declaration of Independence (1776) and the founding of the Constitution (1789), public opinion—real enough though the Court vastly exaggerates its unanimity—considered that 'the negro might justly and lawfully be reduced to slavery' as 'beings of an inferior order'.[41] At the time of the framing and adoption of the Constitution, 'neither the class of persons who had been imported as slaves, nor their descendants, whether they had become free' had any 'rights or privileges but such as those who held the power and the Government might choose to grant them'.[42] And 'the duty of the court is . . . to administer [the instrument they have framed] as we find it, according to its true intent and meaning when it was adopted.'[43] The Court's radical failure, then, was to approach its duty of doing justice according to law

[36] Ibid. [37] Ibid. [38] Ibid. 94–5.

[39] See Finnis, 'Constitutional Law', in *Annual Survey of Commonwealth Law* [1967] at 83, 91–5, [1968] 75, 112, [1969] 76–7.

[40] 60 US 393 at 417, 420, *per* Taney CJ for the Court (7: 2).

[41] 60 US at 407, *per* Taney CJ. [42] 60 US at 405, *per* Taney CJ. [43] Ibid.

without recognizing that law, the whole legal enterprise, is for the sake of persons, and that the founders' intentions were therefore to be interpreted—not, as the Court did, so as to promote their background prejudices (from which the Court dissociated itself) against the people they wished to treat as mere property, but rather—in favour of the basic interests and well-being of every person within the jurisdiction so far as was possible without contradicting the Constitution's provisions.

A post-Kelsenian version of *Dred Scott* can be found in the judgment of the New York Court of Appeals in *Byrn* v. *New York City Health and Hospitals* (1972). Discussing the status of children before birth, the Court says:

> What is a legal person is for the law, including, of course, the Constitution, to say, which simply means that upon according legal personality to a thing the law affords it the rights and privileges of a legal person (e.g. Kelsen, General Theory of Law and State, pp. 93–109; Paton, Jurisprudence [3d ed.], pp. 349–356, esp. pp. 353–354 as to natural persons and unborn children; Friedmann, Legal Theory [5th ed.], pp. 521–523; Gray, The Nature and Sources of the Law [2d ed.] ch. II). The process is, indeed, circular, because it is definitional. Whether the law should accord legal personality is a policy question which in most instances devolves on the Legislature, subject of course to the Constitution as it has been 'legally' rendered. . . . The point is that it is a policy determination whether legal personality should attach and not a question of biological or 'natural' correspondence.[44]

The judgment concludes: '[t]here are, then, real issues in this litigation, but they are not legal or justiciable. They are issues outside the law unless the Legislature should provide otherwise.'[45] Like the Supreme Court's presumptionless positivism in *Dred Scott*, this New York judgment foreshadows the Supreme Court's holding, six months later, in *Roe* v. *Wade* (1973), that children *en ventre sa mère* are not persons 'within the meaning of the Fourteenth Amendment'.[46] The Court's reasoning to this holding simply recites the uses of 'person' in the Constitution, remarks that 'none indicates, *with any assurance*, that it has any possible pre-natal application', adds (quite misleadingly)[47] that 'throughout the major portion of the 19th century prevailing legal abortion practices were far freer than they are today', and then simply says that these two facts 'persuade us' of the conclusion.[48]

What we see in these cases is a notable failure of judicial reasoning, of intellectual and moral responsibility in face of the law's most fundamental point and meaning: the service of persons. Here, where juristic thought should be most fully and carefully deployed, we find abrupt ukase. The failure and the abruptness are not peculiar to the court's dealings with the unborn. In 1886 the Supreme Court was asked to settle the question whether the 14th Amendment's provision forbidding any state to deny

[44] 286 NE 2d 887 at 889, *per* Breitel J for the Court (5: 2).

[45] 286 NE 2d at 890.

[46] 410 US 113 at 157, *per* Blackmun J (7: 2). At 162 Blackmun J quotes verbatim, though without acknowledgement, a whole sentence from *Byrn* at 888.

[47] See Finnis, ' "Shameless Acts" in Colorado: Abuse of Scholarship in Constitutional Cases', *Academic Questions*, Fall 1994, 10–41 at 1–18, 36–7.

[48] 410 US at 157–8.

the equal protection of the laws to any *person* within its jurisdiction applies to corporations. Its judgment in *Santa Clara County* v. *Southern Pacific Railroad Co.* is prefaced by the answer: '[t]he court does not wish to hear argument on the question. . . . We are all of opinion that it does.'[49] As Justices Black and Douglas observed in 1949, 'there was no history, logic, or reason given to support that view. Nor was the result so obvious that exposition was unnecessary.'[50] But though this dissenting judgment of Black and Douglas JJ deploys powerful reasons against that 'result', developing the reasons deployed many years earlier in another dissent by Black J,[51] neither the Court itself nor any Justice supporting the result has ever added even a single sentence of justification to the ukase of 1886. Perhaps we should not be surprised, though we are entitled to be dismayed, that no Justice has ever tried to reconcile the 'conclusion' in *Roe* with the 'result' in *Santa Clara.*

As Black and Douglas JJ remark, after demonstrating the arbitrariness of the Court's checkerboard rulings about the application to corporations of the 14th Amendment's several uses of 'person' and 'citizen', and the good sense of a finding that the Amendment's protection is of human beings, natural not artificial persons: '[h]istory has gone the other way'. To which they add, however, that it is not too late for the Court to overrule its error on 'a question of vital concern to the people of the nation'.[52] It is increasingly accepted, by legislative and judicial authorities in most US states,[53] that the unborn child is entitled to protection and remedies in tort even if born dead, and likewise to the protection of the criminal law. These developments, though restricted rather arbitrarily by the constitutional maternal rights declared by the Supreme Court in *Roe,* mark a retreat from simple refusal to take account of the realities of personal existence before birth.

V ON NATURAL AND ARTIFICIAL PERSONS IN LAW

In a realistic moral, political, or legal analysis of human associations and their actions, 'personality' is a distracting metaphor. For it is a metaphor always tugged between its two historic sources. On the one hand, there is *persona* as mask; to this corresponds the law's carefree attribution of legal personality to *anything* that figures as subject (topic) of legal relations, particularly of property and/or litigious relationships: idols, funds, parcels of property on the quayside, the Crown, and so forth. On the other hand, there is *persona* as individual substance, of a rational nature;[54] to this corresponds nothing (save metaphorically) in the many orderings of human interaction and association

49 118 US 394 at 396.

50 *Wheeling Steel Corporation* v. *Glander* 337 US 563 at 577.

51 *Connecticut General Legal Insurance Co.* v. *Johnson,* 303 US 77 (1938) at 85–90.

52 337 US at 580, 581.

53 See e.g. Clark D. Forsythe, 'Human Cloning and the Constitution' (1998) 32 *Valparaiso University Law Review* 469 at 497–502.

54 '*Persona est rationalis naturae individua substantia*': Boethius, *De Duabus Naturis* c. 3 (Migne, *Patrologia Latina* 64, 1343); see Aquinas, *Summa Theologiae* I q. 29 a. 1.

which we call groups[55]—nothing except the people who are members. Still, there is a link between these two sources and poles of meaning of 'person'. For the actor's mask is or creates an assumed identity. But a being of a rational nature can, with sufficient health and maturity, make choices (because understanding different kinds of benefit and different ways to one and the same benefit), and by making choices one shapes one's character/identity—one comes to have, and in that sense assumes, a personal identity (one's character). A day-old baby has—*radically*, albeit not yet in actually usable form—this capacity to choose (with such self-determining, intransitive effects). A mouse, whether day-old or mature, lacks that radical capacity, though even as a day-old embryo it has the radical capacity, unlike an acorn or an oak seedling, to run.

Hart recommended that we 'put aside the question "What is a corporation?", and ask instead "Under what types of conditions does the law ascribe liabilities to corporations?" ', since this would, he thought, clarify 'the precise issues at stake' in 'extension to corporate bodies of rules worked out for individuals'.[56] The advice to look for the truth conditions of propositions, to understand analogies, and to seek for the principle upon which rules are extended from one context to another was sound. But it was mistaken to assume that such techniques of analysis would dissolve the underlying question whether corporations are entities in the same plane of reality as the human persons whom Hart referred to by his term 'individuals'. The suppression of that question, a suppression implicitly defended if not proposed by Hart, opens the way to the agnosticism, arbitrariness, and consequent injustice of cases such as *Byrn* v. *New York City Health and Hospitals.*

Without doubting or challenging the legal rules which distinguish a corporation's rights and liabilities from those of its members, one can make more progress in understanding the relevant realities and interests by first going beyond and behind Hart, to Hohfeld's masterly demonstration that 'transacting business under the forms, methods, and procedure pertaining to so-called corporations is simply another mode by which *individuals* or *natural persons* can enjoy their property and engage in business'.[57] One does not well understand corporate[58] liability (or rights, duties, etc.)

[55] Here and elsewhere in this essay I use 'group' in the second, more specified sense of that highly ambiguous term, whose two basic poles of meaning are (i) class or category, regardless of cohesiveness, co-operation or interaction, e.g. all women in Pakistan (held to be a 'particular social group' for the purposes of the Art. 1A(2) of the Convention relating to the Status of Refugees (1951): *R.* v. *Immigration Appeal Tribunal, ex parte Shah* [1999] 2 WLR 1015), and (ii) a number of persons who co-ordinate their activity over an appreciable span of time by interactions with a view to a shared objective (see Tony Honoré, 'What is a Group?' in his *Making Law Bind: Essays Legal and Philosophical* (Oxford University Press, Oxford, 1987), Finnis, *Natural Law and Natural Rights*, n. 6 above, 150–3).

[56] 'Definition and Theory in Jurisprudence' (1953) in Hart, *Essays in Jurisprudence and Philosophy* (Clarendon Press, Oxford, 1983) at 43, also 45, 47.

[57] Wesley Newcombe Hohfeld, 'Nature of Stockholders' Individual Liability for Corporation Debts' (1909) 9 *Columbia Law Review* 285 at 288, reprinted in Hohfeld, *Fundamental Legal Conceptions as Applied in Judicial Reasoning and other Legal Essays* (ed. W.W. Cook, Yale UP, Princeton, NJ, 1923) 194 at 197. Hart's partly critical remarks about Hohfeld's account of corporations ('Definition and Theory in Jurisprudence', n. 56 above, at 42 n. 22) seem beside the point.

[58] Note that, as Hohfeld incidentally makes clear, the distinction between bodies formally incorporated and unincorporated associations is in many respects much less clear-cut than is often supposed. There is

until one understands how the liabilities etc. of human persons, such as shareholders, directors, employees and other agents, are implicated and affected. The same will be true of the rights and liabilities of other juristic entities such as idols, parcels of goods, etc.; these rights and liabilities are not well understood until one can point, directly or through corporate intermediaries, to individuals with control over ascertainable funds, and so forth.

Hohfeld's more famous analysis of jural relations, though making possible (with a few further specifications) a complete analysis of such relations between persons at any given moment, still leaves something to be explained in terms of the continuity and rationale of rights.[59] Similarly, his demonstration that a corporation's rights etc., as they exist at any moment, are analysable without remainder into individuals' rights etc. should not be understood as showing that a group of persons has no reality. A human group or community has all the reality of group action, as well as of the group's members'—human persons'—acts and dispositions to act, dispositions which are manifested in the members' readiness to participate in, and emotional responsiveness to, the group's action, for the sake of the good(s) which give(s) point to that action. That is to say, the reality of a group is the reality of an order of human, truly personal acts, an order brought into being and maintained by the choices (and dispositions to choose, and responses to choices) *of persons.* A group's act is defined by its 'public' proposal—i.e. by the form in which it is proposed to members of the group, for them to participate in or not. Social acts, though irreducible to the acts of people in the acting group, are constituted exclusively by those acts—acts of individual human persons.[60]

VI ON PERSONS AS PRIMARY BEARERS OF MEANING AND OBJECTS OF INTERPRETATION

Interpretation is primarily and focally a matter of trying to understand the person or persons whose utterance or other significant performance is under consideration.

Decided entirely by Oxford members of the House of Lords, *Mannai Investment Co. Ltd.* v. *Eagle Star Life Investment Co.*[61] might be deemed an Oxford essay in jurisprudence. Does '12th' mean 13th? At large, it clearly does not. But someone who uses the word '12th' may in fact mean 13th, and a proper interpretation of that

evidence of this in the provisions of the Interpretation Act 1978, s. 5 and Sched. (adapted from the Interpretation Act 1889 s. 19): '[i]n any Act, unless the contrary intention appears . . . "Person" includes a body of persons corporate or unincorporate.' Notice also that this definition would be mired in an infinite regress but for the fact that the term 'person' also 'includes' individual persons such as those who are the paradigmatic members of bodies, corporate or unincorporated, of persons.

[59] See e.g. Finnis, *Natural Law and Natural Rights*, n. 6 above, 201–2.

[60] See Finnis, 'Persons and their Associations', *Proceedings of the Aristotelean Society*, Supplementary Vol. 43 (1989) 267–74.

[61] [1997] AC 749, [1997] 3 All ER 352. The Lords divided 3:2, with the two University College judges in the majority (supported by a Scot from Corpus Christi College).

person's use of the word, in the relevant and properly admissible circumstances of the utterance, may determine that that, being what the person meant to convey and would reasonably have been understood to mean to convey, was the utterance's real meaning, properly construed. As Lord Hoffmann says, 'It is a matter of constant experience that people can convey their meaning unambiguously although they have used the wrong words.' It is true, he adds, that:

> the law is not concerned with the speaker's subjective intentions. But the notion that the law's concern is therefore with the 'meaning of his words' conceals an important ambiguity. The ambiguity lies in the failure to distinguish between the meaning of words and the question of what would be understood as the *meaning of a person* who uses words. . . .
>
> When . . . lawyers say that they are concerned, not with subjective meaning but with the meaning of the language which the speaker has used, what they mean is that they are concerned with what he would objectively have been understood to mean. This involves examining not only the words and the grammar but the background as well. So, for example, in *Doe d. Cox* v. *Roe* (1802) 4 Esp 185, 170 ER 685 the landlord of a public house in Limehouse gave notice to quit 'the premises which you hold of me . . . commonly called . . . the Waterman's Arms'. The evidence showed that the tenant held no premises called the Waterman's Arms; indeed, there were no such premises in the parish of Limehouse. But the tenant did hold premises of the landlord called the Bricklayer's Arms. By reference to the background, the notice was construed as referring to the Bricklayer's Arms. The meaning was objectively clear to a reasonable recipient, even though the landlord had used the wrong name. . . .There was no need to resort to subjective meaning.[62]

In an academic essay in jurisprudence, there is no need to employ the rather misleading lawyers' jargon of 'subjective' and 'objective'. But Lord Hoffmann's meaning emerges clearly despite that lawyerly opacity. As he put it later: 'words do not in themselves refer to anything; it is people who *use* words to refer to things'.[63] And again: '[i]n this area [commercial contracts] we no longer confuse the meaning of words with the question of what meaning the use of the words was intended to convey'.[64] The decision of the House was that, similarly, a notice to terminate a lease 'on 12 January 1995' unambiguously conveyed, in all the circumstances of the giving of the notice (including such circumstances as the terms of the lease itself)—as they would have been apparent to and considered relevant by a reasonable bystander at the time—the intention to terminate the lease on 13 January 1995. For that was what a reasonable person aware of the relevant background would have understood to have been the intention and therefore the meaning of the person giving the notice.

Since the law is for the sake of persons, and its rules are fundamentally relationships between persons, it is a mistake to try to understand legal interpretation on the

[62] At 376. Lord Goff, dissenting, accepts that *Doe d. Cox* v. *Roe* was rightly decided—i.e. that the court in that case 'properly construed' the notice—and he does not succeed in explaining satisfyingly why the majority's construction of the notice in *Mannai* itself is not equally 'proper'.

[63] At 378 (his emphasis).

[64] At 380. On interpreting commercial contracts, see also *Investors' Compensation Scheme Ltd* v. *West Bromwich Building Society* [1998] 1 WLR 896, [1998] 1 All ER 98 at 114e–116f, *per* Lord Hoffmann.

model of the creation and representation, recital, or rendering of works of art.[65] So, if jurists seeking to understand the place of interpretation in law were obliged to choose between 'conversational' and 'artistic' models, they would be well advised to choose the conversational. But the alternatives are not exhaustive.

Like participants in conversation, legal interpreters seek to understand the author who, in making some statement, has exercised a private power or public authority. But legal interpreters are entitled and required to treat that statement, especially when made in the exercise of the public powers of legislation or adjudication, as taking its place in the legal system as a whole—in a complex of persons and their institutions, as well as of principles and rules, including techniques and conventions of drafting and interpreting, all presumptively oriented towards justice and common good. Dworkin has proposed that the political, legally organized community be personified, so that such cohering with a larger whole, like integrity of personal character, be taken as axiomatically required.[66] The proposal shows vividly enough that his general assimilation of legal with artistic rather than conversational interpretation is a choice of the less fitting of the two models he puts forward as the alternatives. True, in legal interpretation as in conversation the intent of the author really matters, as the very concept of authority to make or declare law entails.[67] But a properly juridical interpretation will not be as ready to consider authoritative an unjust as it will a just meaning. Thus it differs from sensible conversationalists, who like good historians are quick to detect, and not too ready to overlook, their interlocutors' perhaps vicious purposes and deficiencies of personal character.

VII ON THE NATURE OF PERSONS AND THE GROUND OF THEIR RADICAL EQUALITY

What, then, are the 'natural facts' which should inform juristic thought about the persons whom law exists to serve? What is this human nature, which in its bodiliness is known to lawyers as injured in crimes and torts, and sustained by the resources always somehow disposed of in property rights (howsoever artificial); and which in its irreducible intellectuality is known to us as the maker of signs, signatures, and meanings, and subject of intentions? Here jurisprudential reflection can helpfully go back to its origins, perhaps in Plato's reflections on the trial and execution of Socrates.

In the act of (say) speaking to my partner in discourse—perhaps, the court I am addressing as advocate, or the client I am advising as jurisconsult—I understand my utterance as the carrying out of a choice *which I made*, and in the same act I am aware

[65] See Finnis, 'Natural Law and Legal Reasoning' in Robert P. George (ed.), *Natural Law Theory* (Oxford University Press, Oxford, 1992) 134–57 at 139–43.

[66] *Law's Empire*, n. 8 above, 167–75; see also e.g. 225: '[t]he adjudicative principle of integrity instructs judges to identify legal rights and duties, so far as possible, on the assumption that they were created by a single author—the community personified—expressing a coherent conception of justice and fairness.'

[67] See Joseph Raz, 'Intention in Interpretation' in Robert P. George (ed.), *The Autonomy of Law* (Oxford University Press, Oxford, 1996) 249–86 at 268.

of my audible uttering, see the hearers register their comprehension, feel (say) confidence or anxiety, remember a past misunderstanding, and hope my statement will make my point. This experience of the *unity (including continuity)* of my being—as a feeling, willing, observing, remembering, understanding, physically active and effective mover or cause of physical effects and equally an undergoer and recipient of such effects—is a datum which philosophical exploration of human and other natural realities can adequately account for only with great difficulty and many a pitfall. Still, prior to all accounts of it, this intelligible presence of my many-faceted acting self to myself is a datum of *understanding*; one and the same I—this human being—who am understanding and choosing and carrying out my choice and sensing, etc., is a reality I already truly understand, albeit not yet fully (explanatorily, with elaboration). (Indeed, it is only given this primary understanding of one's understanding, willing, and so forth, that one can and typically does *value* such understanding, freedom, voluntariness, unity of being, and so forth.)

So, as Aristotle and (plainly) Aquinas argue more or less explicitly,[68] any account proposing to explain these realities must be consistent with the complex data it seeks to explain, data which include the proposer's performance, outward and inward, in proposing it. It will not do to propose (as many today propose) an account of personhood such that spirit-person and mere living body are other and other, for 'spirit-person' and 'mere living body' are philosophical constructs neither of which refers to the unified self, the person who had set out to explain his or her own reality. Both of these constructs purport to refer to realities which are other than the unified self yet somehow, inexplicably, related to it.[69]

The only account which meets the condition of consistency with the explainer's own reality and performances will be an account along the lines argued for by Aristotle and Aquinas: the very *form* and lifelong *act(uality)* by which the matter of my bodily make-up is constituted the unified and active subject (me myself) is a factor, a reality, which Aristotle (after Plato) calls *psychē* and Aquinas calls soul (*anima*). In the human animal—the very same animal whose interests in every individual case are to be taken equally into account, in Plato's as in present-day ethics aspiring to be 'postmetaphysical'—from the very outset of his or her existence as human, it is this one essentially unchanging factor, unique to each individual, which explains (1) the unity and complexity of the individual's activities, (2) the dynamic unity in complexity—in one dimension, the programme—of the individual's growth as embryo, foetus, neonate, infant . . . and adult, (3) the relatively mature individual's understanding of universal (e.g. generic) immaterial objects of thought (e.g. classes of entities, or truth and falsity of propositions, or soundness/unsoundness in reasoning), and (4) this unique individual's generic unity with every other member of the species. In members of our species the one factor unifying and activating the living reality of each individual is at once vegetative, animal (sentient and self-locomotive), and intel-

[68] See Aquinas, *De Unitate Intellectus* III.3 [79]; Finnis, *Aquinas: Moral, Political, and Legal Theory* (Oxford University Press, Oxford, 1998), 177–9.

[69] See Finnis, '*Bland*: Crossing the Rubicon?' (1993) 109 *Law Quarterly Review* 329–37 at 333.

lectual (understanding, self-understanding, and, even in thinking, self-determining by judging and choosing). Of course, the manifold activations of these bodily and rational powers are variously dependent upon the physical maturity and health of the individual. But the essence and powers of the soul seem to be given to each individual complete (as wholly undeveloped, *radical* capacities) at the outset of his or her existence as such. And this is the root of the dignity we all have as human beings. Without it claims of equality of right would be untenable in face of the many ways in which people are unequal.

This metaphysics of the activity of discourse, advocacy, adjudication, lecturing, and writing[70] enables jurisprudence to stabilize its most fundamental concepts: the good which, because it is the good of members of a group who all are persons, can and should be a *common* good, and the rights which justice essentially consists in respecting and promoting unyieldingly.

[70] On personal unity and identity as actuated in the activity of writing, see Finnis, 'Persons and their Associations', n. 58 above, at 267–8.

'Philosophical Foundations of the Common Law': Social not Metaphysical

Nicola Lacey*

In *The Concept of Law*,[1] H.L.A. Hart claimed to provide a theory of law based on two distinct methodologies: analytical jurisprudence and descriptive sociology. Yet little more than a decade later, Tony Honoré, in his contribution to the Second Series of the *Oxford Essays in Jurisprudence*, was able to portray the jurisprudential scene as a contest between positivists and natural lawyers, with sociologists of law merely watching from the sidelines.[2] In Honoré's ironic observation, legal theory was a game the rules of which the sociologists had never managed to learn.

This conception of the sociology of law as engaged in a fundamentally different—external rather than internal—form of legal theory now commands a wide consensus among legal theorists. Just as Honoré's sociologists watch the game from the spectators' gallery, Dworkin's social scientists observe law's empire from beyond its frontiers. What is more controversial is the implication of such metaphors—and a claim which might be thought to be implicit in Hans Kelsen's assertion that the sociology of law inevitably presupposes normative jurisprudence[3]—that analytical legal philosophy enjoys a certain intellectual priority. In the image of the sports stadium it is, after all, the spectators who have an interest in watching the players: while the players may enjoy the applause or wince at the jeers of the spectators, they do not need to pay close attention to them. In Dworkin's imperial vision, it seems not unduly tendentious to suggest that sociologists of law are implicitly represented as inhabitants of underdeveloped colonies. For while Dworkin sometimes writes as if historical or social-scientific insights into legal practices provide a perspective complementary to

* I should like to thank Tony Honoré and Jeremy Horder for their comments on an earlier draft of the essay; and John Braithwaite, Simon Bronit, Peter Cane, Hugh Collins, Roger Cotterrell, John Gardner, Ngaire Naffine, James Penner, David Soskice, Jane Stapleton, and Celia Wells for very helpful discussion of its argument. I should also like to record my gratitude to colleagues at the LSE Law Department, whose responses to a presentation of an early draft of the essay had a decisive influence on the development of its argument; and at the Law Program of the Research School of Social Sciences, Australian National University, where a period visiting as Adjunct Professor provided me with the ideal environment in which to work on the essay.

[1] (2nd edn., Clarendon Press, Oxford, 1994; first published 1961).

[2] 'Groups, Laws and Obedience', in A.W.B. Simpson (ed.), *Oxford Essays in Jurisprudence* (Second Series, Oxford University Press, Oxford, 1973) 1, reprinted in Tony Honoré, *Making Law Bind* (Clarendon Press, Oxford, 1987) chap. 2.

[3] 'The sociology of law cannot draw a line between its subject—law—and the other social phenomena; it cannot define its special object as distinct from the object of general sociology—society—without in doing so presupposing the concept of law as defined by normative jurisprudence': *What is Justice?* (University of California Press, Berkeley, Cal., 1971) 270; however, on the previous page, Kelsen refers more even-handedly to 'sociological jurisprudence stand[ing] side by side with normative jurisprudence: neither is able to replace the other because each deals with different problems' (269).

that of internal legal philosophy,[4] he is dismissive of its intellectual contributions to date:

It was Oliver Wendell Holmes who argued most influentially, I think, for this kind of 'external' legal theory; the depressing history of social-theoretic jurisprudence in our century warns us how wrong he was.[5]

At its most general level, this essay examines the implications and merits of the view of analytical jurisprudence as self-standing as against Hart's purportedly more even-handed vision of the relative contributions of sociology and analytical philosophy to the project of theorizing law. I shall raise questions not only about the still controversial intellectual imperialism of analytical, internal jurisprudence but also about the more widely accepted view that internal and external approaches to legal theory may be separated from one another. On closer inspection, the internal/external distinction appears highly problematic.[6] Sociological legal theorists accept that they are bound to attend to the distinctive qualities of law as a social practice—its doctrinal system, its institutional structure, its methods of reasoning, and so on.[7] Hence the sociological approach clearly takes seriously the 'internal' logic of law.[8] But does this, as Kelsen asserts, amount to a presupposition of normative jurisprudence?

[4] Indeed at one or two points he implies a closer link: [p]hilosophers, or perhaps sociologists, of justice can also do useful work in identifying the paradigms that play the role in arguments about justice that I said paradigms would play in arguments about courtesy': *Law's Empire* (Fontana, London, 1986) 75.

[5] Ibid. 14.

[6] For excellent discussion of this question, see Roger Cotterrell, 'Law and Community: A New Relationship' (1998) 51 *Current Legal Problems* 367, at 369–71 and 'Why Must Legal Ideas Be Interpreted Sociologically?' (1998) 25 *Journal of Law and Society* 171: '[s]ociological insight is simultaneously inside and outside legal ideas, constituting them and interpreting them; sometimes speaking through them and sometimes speaking about them. . . . Thus a sociological understanding of legal ideas does not reduce them to something other than law. It expresses their social meaning *as law* in its rich complexity' (181).

[7] See also Roger Cotterrell's *Law Community* (Clarendon Press, Oxford, 1995), which places considerable emphasis on both the specificity and the primacy of legal doctrine as a focus for sociological jurisprudence. Conversely, analytical theorists certainly vary in their view of the strictness of the philosophy/sociology divide: e.g. MacCormick and Weinberger (*An Institutional Theory of Law: New Approaches to Legal Positivism* (Reidel, Dordrecht, 1986)) regard legal positivism as, to a significant degree, located within the social sciences. For further discussion of the relationship between analytical and empirical aspects of legal theory, see Gerald Postema, *Bentham and the Common Law Tradition* (Clarendon Press, Oxford, 1986); P.M.S. Hacker, 'Hart's Philosophy of Law', in P.M.S. Hacker and J. Raz (eds.), *Law, Morality and Society* (Clarendon Press, Oxford, 1977) 1; Pierre Bourdieu, 'The Force of Law: Toward a Sociology of the Juridical Field' (transl. Richard Terdiman) (1987) 38 *Hastings Law Journal* 805; Jürgen Habermas, *Between Facts and Norms* (transl. W. Rehg, Cambridge University Press, Cambridge, 1996); David Nelken, 'The Truth about Law's Truth', in A. Febbrajo and D. Nelken (eds.) [1993] *European Yearbook of the Sociology of Law* 87.

[8] Probably for this reason, sociological and analytic theories sometimes display striking structural similarities. A good example would be legal autopoiesis—the idea of law as a self-referential system—which relates closely to the legal closure asserted by legal positivism (see Gunther Teubner, *Law as an Autopoietic System* (Blackwell, Oxford, 1993)). Autopoietic systems are cognitively open at the same time as they are normatively closed, just as positivist adjudicators are open to features of the social, moral or political environment which bear on the exercise of their interpretive discretion (Hart, n. 1 above, chap. 7). On this positivist view, the boundaries between analytic and either normative or social-scientific theories of law begin to blur. This, of course, is the point made long ago by Lon Fuller ('Positivism and Fidelity to Law: A Reply to Professor Hart' (1958) 71 *Harvard Law Review* 630): and it is precisely what Dworkin's

What distinguishes the sociological approach is not so much a strict sociological methodology but rather a general commitment to theorizing law as a *social* phenomenon.[9] This commitment brings with it a focus upon the historical development of legal orders and their interaction with their social, cultural, political, and economic context. In this essay, I argue that analytical or normative jurisprudence can itself not dispense with these insights: that it makes no sense, to put it in Kelsen's terms, to try to 'discover the specific principles of a sphere of meaning'[10] independently of the socio-historical context in which that sphere exists. Hence, as Cotterrell puts it, 'the enterprise of sociological interpretation of legal ideas is not a desirable supplement but an essential means of legal understanding'.[11]

Hart's own position on the relationship between analytical jurisprudence and descriptive sociology has been challenged from two quite different directions. On the one hand, the grounding of his theory in genuinely sociological insight has been questioned.[12] On the other, his commitment to a 'social fact' theory of law has been criticized on the basis of its reductive tendency—a tendency which, it is argued, obscures the special nature of law and legal reasoning which provides the rationale for distinctively legal theory.[13] There can be no doubt, however, that Hart's vision of the dual, empirical and conceptual aspects of legal theory finds significant expression in the recent development of the discipline. Indeed, twenty-five years after Honoré's wry observation, the diverse and flourishing fields of socio-legal studies, feminist legal theory, some forms of 'critical' legal theory, and law and economics might all be said to exemplify in one way or another the commitment to drawing on not only philosophical analysis but also the insights of the social sciences in constructing theoretical understandings of law.

Yet Honoré's doubt about whether the sociologists of law and the analytical legal theorists are playing by the same rules expresses a continuing puzzle about the methodology of jurisprudence: about the relative contributions of philosophy, social

superficially more porous but at root stringently closed conception of the legal sphere denies (R.M. Dworkin, *Taking Rights Seriously* ([Illegible], London, 1977), chaps. 2–4), Neither positivist nor autopoietic closure is complete. Yet the negotiation of the law/non-law, system/environment boundaries is an uneasy one, and this underpins the difficulty of achieving a clear division between internal and external legal theory.

[9] As Cotterrell has argued: see 'Why Must Legal Ideas be Interpreted Sociologically?', n. 6 above, 183ff.

[10] See Hans Kelsen, *An Introduction to the Problems of Legal Theory* (trans. of the 1st edn. of *The Pure Theory of Law*, trans. by Bonnie Litschewski Paulson, Clarendon Press, Oxford, 1992) 481. For further discussion of the relationship between normative and sociological jurisprudence, see Kelsen's 'The Pure Theory of Law: Its Methods and Fundamental Concepts' (1934) 50 *Law Quarterly Review* 474 at 480–1.

[11] See Cotterrell, 'Why Must Legal Ideas Be Interpreted Sociologically?', n. 6 above, 192, 188ff. It follows that the metaphor of the stadium must be revised; for it is only legal actors, and not legal theorists, who can be seen as 'players' with a fully 'internal' perspective: the internal or normative point of view is, as Hart argued, a crucial object of jurisprudential study, but the theorist's perspective upon it is different from that of a legal actor. This is not to imply that all theoretical perspectives are external in just the same way. Theorists examine the normative social practice of law to different ends, and some jurisprudential arguments aspire to influence legal practices such as the conduct of judicial reasoning or the development of legal concepts.

[12] See e.g. Roger Cotterrell, *The Politics of Jurisprudence* (Butterworths, London, 1989) chap. 4.

[13] G.P. Baker, 'Defeasibility and Meaning', in Hacker and Raz (eds.), n. 7 above, 26.

theory, and the social sciences to our understanding of law. This puzzle about the relationship between conceptual and empirical, philosophical and social-scientific approaches to law arises in particularly intriguing form in the project to which this volume seeks to contribute: the analysis of the 'philosophical foundations of the common law'. As its name attests, the idea of philosophical foundations is rooted firmly in the tradition of analytical jurisprudence.[14] Yet its commitment to analysing 'the common law'—indeed, in many of its manifestations,[15] to analysing specific aspects of the common law—implies a vision of law as the sort of spatially and historically specific phenomenon which is susceptible of social-scientific inquiry. The values and ideals of a political society change over time; conceptions of conduct, agency, and responsibility shift; geo-political and economic circumstances change; the implications of these and many other factors for not only the substance, but also the conceptual framework and even the idea, of law are evidently an interesting object of research.

This idea of legal systems as developing over time and within complex social, economic, cultural, and political environments is well captured by Joseph Raz's idea of the 'non-momentary legal system'.[16] Raz's argument is that the identity of the non-momentary system is determined primarily by its content rather than by its criteria for the identification of valid legal standards. It is the latter—the normative conditions under which a momentary legal system exists—which is the proper object of analytical jurisprudence: this object can be theorized independently of any consideration of the non-momentary system to which it belongs. Hence Raz may be taken to imply that the social-theoretic analysis of law can be neatly bracketed off from the analytic; that in tracing the philosophical foundations of, say, English criminal law, we have no need of any broad understanding of the social functions or meaning of criminalization understood as a connected sequence of practices, of the historical development of the values informing those practices, or of the conceptual frameworks in terms of which they have been carried forward. This resolute distancing of social and historical context is reproduced in analyses of philosophical foundations which

[14] In associating 'philosophical foundations' with a focus on analytical rather than sociological jurisprudence, I am concerned in the first instance with descriptive or interpretive aspects of the project. The persuasiveness of straightforwardly prescriptive claims will generally also depend upon social factors, but the relationship in which I am primarily interested is the one implied by the ways in which theories present themselves as characterizations of the legal world as it is, or proceed on the basis of assumptions about that world. The nature of the relationship between 'descriptive', 'interpretive', and 'prescriptive' aspects remains, of course, one of the central issues of legal theory, not least because—as many 'descriptive' theorists acknowledge—the criteria for selection among legal phenomena to be theorized are inevitably shaped by the theorist's values or point of view. See, variously, J.M. Finnis, *Natural Law and Natural Rights* (1980) chap. 1; Michael S. Moore, *Placing Blame* (Oxford University Press, Oxford, 1997) chap. 1; Jules Coleman, *Risks and Wrongs* (Cambridge University Press, Cambridge, 1992) 1–13 (and see reviews by Peter Cane (1993) 13 *Legal Studies* 396 and George Fletcher (1993) 106 *Harvard Law Review* 1658); Joseph Raz, 'Two Views of the Nature of the Theory of Law: A Partial Comparison' (1998) 4 *Legal Theory* 249.

[15] Notably in the Third Series of the *Oxford Essays in Jurisprudence* (J. Eekelaar and J. Bell (eds.), Oxford University Press, Oxford, 1986).

[16] *The Concept of a Legal System* (Clarendon Press, Oxford, 1970) chap. VIII.

are concerned with the moral coherence of particular common law doctrines. The result is that law is implicitly represented as founded—actually or ideally—on a metaphysics: a moral or conceptual structure whose validity transcends space and time.[17]

Dworkin's influential conception of legal theory as interpretive might be thought to imply a concern with the history of these conceptual foundations.[18] Interestingly, one commentator, Jim Harris, has suggested that Dworkin's rejection of a social fact understanding of law in favour of an assertion of the inevitably evaluative nature of arguments from legal principle implies a concern with the 'non-momentary legal system' characterized by Raz.[19] Yet in fact Dworkin distances himself from any such implication.[20] The 'interpretive' project of 'law as integrity' as much as the 'descriptive' project of legal positivism is severed from all but a small sample of questions about the historical development of legal principles, and these questions are selected on the basis of criteria generated within the interpretive theory itself. I shall suggest that the criteria by which both 'descriptive' and 'interpretive' theories are held answerable to actual legal doctrines and practices remain imperfectly understood. Furthermore, I shall argue that writers exploring 'philosophical foundations' of particular practices, such as attributions of legal responsibility, can neither stay true to 'descriptive' or 'interpretive' aspirations nor present convincing normative arguments unless they temper their philosophical method with a conception of law as a social practice.

THE GENESIS OF CORPORATE CRIMINAL LIABILITY

In the rest of this essay, I shall defend my contention that conceptual questions of legal theory only make sense within a (prior) social analysis of law by considering the contemporary debate about corporate criminal liability for offences against the person. The genesis of the corporation as a recognized subject of such offences in England and Wales is a remarkable one, and poses a fascinating case study for jurisprudence. In 1927, the Court of Appeal held in *R.* v. *Cory Brothers*[21] that there

[17] This feature of much legal theory may be compared with a certain style of doctrinal scholarship: e.g. compare the conceptually oriented approach of Glanville Williams' *Criminal Law: The General Part* (Stevens, London, 1953) with the historically situated approach of George Fletcher's *Rethinking Criminal Law* (Little Brown & Co., Boston, Mass. and Toronto, 1976).

[18] And hence a link with some of the projects developed within 'critical legal studies': see e.g. Robert W. Gordon, 'Historicism in Legal Scholarship', (1981) 90 *Yale Law Journal* 1017; 'Critical Legal Histories' (1984) 36 *Stanford Law Review* 57.

[19] J.W. Harris, *Law and Legal Science* (Clarendon Press, Oxford, 1979) 65–9, 157–8; John Finnis's natural law theory takes a similarly inclusive view of the terrain of legal philosophy: J.M. Finnis, 'Revolutions and the Continuity of Law' in Simpson (ed.), n. 2 above, 44.

[20] See e.g. *Law's Empire*, n. 4 above, 12–14, 273.

[21] *R.* v. *Cory Bros* [1927] 1 KB 810. For an extended and illuminating discussion of corporate manslaughter, see Celia Wells, *Corporations and Criminal Responsibility* (Clarendon Press, Oxford, 1993); on more recent developments, see Nicola Lacey and Celia Wells, *Reconstructing Criminal Law* (Butterworths, London, 1998) chap. 5.II.c.

was no offence of corporate homicide known to law: in 1994, a corporation, OLL,[22] was convicted of corporate manslaughter. What makes the story interesting from a theoretical point of view is the stark fact that in the intervening sixty-seven years there had been no material and relevant change in the law of homicide. There had, it is true, been a significant change in the law governing corporate criminal liability.[23] But this change—the creation of the 'identification doctrine'—itself took place half a century before the developments which concern us here.

What does this tell us about how far 'external'—historical, cultural, and other—factors are implicated in the development of 'internal' ideas about conceptual and normative issues such as responsibility and subject status in criminal law, or about the power of legal concepts autonomously to shape legal reasoning? These are lively issues in contemporary jurisprudence, in which analytic scholars tend to emphasize the role of legal reasoning in developing a refined and coherent set of concepts or legal principles, whereas those taking a variety of 'critical' or sceptical (e.g. Realist) positions, have tended to dismiss conceptual or 'principled' arguments as smokescreens of policy or judicial preference.

The corporate manslaughter story suggests that we have to steer a line between these two extremes: on the one hand, the conceptual framework of manslaughter has inhibited the criminalization of corporations: on the other, the developing role of corporations and the emerging social recognition of corporations as potentially harmful institutions (or even actors) has gradually shifted public, prosecutors', and courts' normative perspectives and led to a re-reading of the relevant concepts so as to encompass at least some cases of corporate homicide. Conceptually, *Cory* decided that corporations could not be indicted for serious offences against the person because they could not have the requisite *mens rea*. While the reasoning in recent cases such as *P & O European Ferries*[24] demonstrates that this problem is still highly relevant to the outcome of corporate manslaughter cases, it also shows that extra-legal, social developments are capable of influencing legal interpretation in ways which make a real difference to the meaning of the conceptual structure of the common law, *as seen from an internal point of view*. The corporate manslaughter story therefore provides an ideal case study for examining the interaction between doctrinal and socio-economic or cultural factors in the development and interpretation of the common law. It raises questions about how far the criminal law as a dynamic system can be analysed in terms of underlying philosophical foundations whose power in underpinning the criteria of legal validity may be understood independently of their historical and social context.

This does not, however, exhaust the interest of the corporate manslaughter story for the theoretical project of this essay. At least three further issues of importance to

[22] *R.* v. *Kite and others*, *The Independent*, 9 Dec. 1994.

[23] *DPP* v. *Kent and Sussex Contractors* [1944] KB 146; *R.* v. *ICR Haulage* (1944) 30 Cr.App.Rep. 31. For further discussion, see text at n. 52.

[24] *R.* v. *P & O European Ferries Ltd.* (1990) 93 Cr.App.R 72; see also *R.* v. *Coroner for East Kent, ex p. Spooner* (1989) 88 Cr.App.R 10.

legal and social theory arise from the development from *Cory* to *OLL*. First, the story connects with a very old debate about law's philosophical foundations: about the nature of legal subjectivity and responsibility and in particular about the place of corporations within general accounts of legal personality. In this context, I shall return to Hart's discussion of corporations in his inaugural lecture, 'Definition and Theory in Jurisprudence'.[25] In particular, I want to examine the implication that human subjects of criminal law are more 'real' or 'natural' than corporations. But in pursuing this question I also want to explore the links between legal and social theory, by tracing the close analogies between the debate about corporate personality in legal theory[26] and the debates in organization theory and in philosophy about competing theories of the firm as a 'real entity' whose identity has some metaphysical status; as an aggregated individual or contractual phenomenon whose collective identity is a convenient fiction; or as a system of communications, distinguished by its capacity for collective action and hence with an identity underpinned by its social *modus operandi*.[27] I shall suggest that by tracing the analogies between these debates we can shed light both on the dynamic or constitutive aspects of legal discourse and on the significance of particular conceptual constructs.

Secondly, the corporate manslaughter story raises some interesting theoretical questions about the relationship between different areas of the common law. In what follows, I shall analyse some recent case-law developments which suggest that specific areas of legal doctrine may be driven by distinctive, and sometimes competing, logics.[28] In particular, the imperatives of commercial or corporate law regulatory frameworks and of criminal law's doctrinal conception of responsibility appear to be at

[25] (1954) 70 *LQR* 37; reprinted in H.L.A. Hart, *Essays in Jurisprudence and Philosophy* (Clarendon Press, Oxford, 1983) chap. 1.

[26] This debate has not, of course, been confined to corporations; it has encompassed, at various times, institutions such as towns, the nation state, churches and the Crown: see Ernst H. Kantorowicz, *The King's Two Bodies* (Princeton University Press, Princeton, NJ, 1957).

[27] There is a vast literature on this topic; much of it is reviewed in Gunther Teubner's 'The Many-Headed Hydra: Networks as Higher-Order Collective Actors', in J. McCahery, S. Picciotto, and C. Scott (eds.), *Corporate Control and Accountability* (Clarendon Press, Oxford, 1993) chap. 3 and 'Enterprise Corporatism: New Industrial Policy and the "Essence" of the Legal Person' (1988) XXXVI *American Journal of Comparative Law* 130; 'the social substratum of the legal person is neither an assemblage of people nor a pool of resources nor a mere organizational structure. Nor is it adequately characterised as an action system or as a formal organization. The substratum is conceived properly as a "collectivity" or "corporate actor", i.e., the self-description of a (usually formally) organized social action system that brings about a cyclical linkage of self-referentially constituted system identity and system elements' (139–40). For classic statements of the aggregate/contractual view, see F. Easterbrook and D. Fischel, 'The Corporate Contract' (1989) 89 *Columbia Law Review* 1416 and Oliver Williamson, 'Corporate Governance' (1984) 93 *Yale Law Journal* 1197. For a different view—presented as 'social' though sometimes interpreted as metaphysical or idealist—see P. French, 'The Corporation as a Moral Person' (1979) 16 *American Philosophical Quarterly* 207; and *Collective and Corporate Responsibility* (University of Columbia Press, New York, 1984); and M. Dan-Cohen, *Rights, Persons and Organisations: A Legal Theory for Bureaucratic Society* (University of California Press, Berkeley, Cal., 1986). For a classic sociological analysis of firms as 'corporate actors', see James Coleman, *Power and the Structure of Society* (W.W. Norton & Co., New York, 1974).

[28] *Meridian Global Funds etc.* v. *Securities Commissioner* [1995] 2 AC 500; see also *Re Supply of Ready Mixed Concrete (no. 2)* [1995] 1 AC 456; *R.* v. *Associated Octel Co. Ltd.* [1996] 1 WLR 1543.

odds. I examine the question whether this is a clash of 'internal' philosophical foundations or rather a contest between underlying social imperatives expressed in legislation.

Finally, although its complexity takes any full analysis beyond the scope of this essay, I shall advert to a third theoretical issue raised by the corporate manslaughter story. This is what we might call a comparative question, in both cultural and historical terms. In thinking about the construction of corporate liability—the available regulatory possibilities and the appropriateness of attributing criminal responsibility—I shall argue that we are constrained by the differing institutional structure of corporations, and by the differing socio-economic and political environments in which corporations operate. For example, basic questions such as the employment tenure of corporate managers, the incentives structuring managerial and employee careers, the accountability structure within the corporation itself and the longer- or shorter-term attitude to profits and financing will all affect regulatory possibilities.[29] This sort of comparative analysis is often ignored in criminal law theory. There has been in the UK a baffling reluctance to investigate the relevance of an intriguing literature in corporate governance about the impact of changes in corporate structures for practices of legal attribution. This is perhaps because it is assumed that the attribution of criminal responsibility is at root a non-consequentialist normative question, independent of the contingencies of particular corporate arrangements.[30] Yet the social facts about corporate structure are of importance to the moral, as much as the practical, appropriateness of imposing criminal liability, for reasons which are analogous to the relevance of empirical understandings about human agency and psychology to individual criminal responsibility. Whatever the dimensions of our moral aspiration, we must believe that it is consistent with a plausible interpretation of the world. Hence, as I shall argue throughout this essay, there is overwhelming reason to think that legal theorists' debates about the future of corporate criminal responsibil-

[29] See e.g. Paul Windolf and Jürgen Beyer, 'Co-operative Capitalism: Corporate Networks in Germany and Britain' (1996) 47 *British Journal of Sociology* 205; John Kay and Aubrey Silberston, 'Corporate Governance' [1995] *National Institute Economic Review* 84. For a useful general assessment of the relevance of theoretical models in the social sciences for socio-legal studies, see Julia Black, 'New Institutionalism and Naturalism in Socio-Legal Analysis' (1997) 19 *Law and Policy* 51. The interaction between possibilities for criminal liability and corporate structure has been most effectively addressed in the work of John Braithwaite and Brent Fisse (see in particular Fisse and Braithwaite, 'The Allocation of Responsibility for Corporate Crime; Individualism, Collectivism and Accountability' (1988) 11 *Sydney Law Review* 468; Braithwaite and Fisse, 'Varieties of Responsibility and Organisational Crime' (1985) 7 *Law and Policy* 315; Fisse and Braithwaite, *Corporations, Crime and Accountability* (Cambridge University Press, Cambridge, 1993)), and in a recent book by Mark Bovens (*The Quest for Responsibility: Accountability and Citizenship in Complex Organisations* (Cambridge University Press, Cambridge and New York, 1998) Part III): see also McCahery, Picciotto and Scott (eds.), n. 27 above; Coleman, n. 27 above, chaps. 3 and 4. On one specific regulatory difficulty flowing from the development of complex corporate networks made up of legally separate collectivities, see Hugh Collins, 'The Ascription of Legal Responsibility to Groups in Complex Patterns of Economic Integration' (1990) 53 *Modern Law Review* 731.

[30] A point which is central to the argument of G.R. Sullivan, 'The Attribution of Culpability to Limited Companies' (1996) 55 *Cambridge Law Journal* 515: I shall consider this argument in more detail below.

ity should be informed not only by normative political and moral theory but also by both theoretical and empirical work in the social sciences.[31]

CORPORATIONS AS PENUMBRAL SUBJECTS OF CRIMINAL LAW

In both jurisprudential scholarship and legal doctrine, the subject of modern systems of criminal law in and beyond the common law world is generally assumed to be a human individual. The elaborated notions of conduct and responsibility, as suggested by the (admittedly misleading) Latin tags *actus reus* and *mens rea*, have been worked out in relation to assumptions about individual human beings, their agency and responsibility, the scope and limits of their capacities for voluntary conduct, and in relation to a moral theory which builds out from these basic assumptions about human being. Much the same is true of the typical subject of criminology: though criminologists have since the publication of Sutherland's pioneering work[32] typically taken a greater interest in corporate crime than have academic criminal lawyers, the framework within which they have done so—that of 'white collar crime'—implicitly sets up the individual offender as the primary analytic focus. Criminology moves between what might be called organizational and occupational conceptions of corporate crime, and in both Sutherland's work and much subsequent research it is the occupational conception which has dominated.[33] This occupational focus—usually on managers—is reflected in, for example, the nature of public debate about the notorious cases of financial wrongdoing in the corporate sector in Britain during the latter part of the 1980s. Interestingly, however, this implicit methodological individualism seems gradually to have been displaced in relation to fatal disasters such as the sinking of the *Herald of Free Enterprise* and the Clapham rail crash, in which a discourse more closely focused on the corporation as a collectivity with its own legal and moral identity appears to be emerging.

The individual human being remains, however, the paradigmatic subject of criminal law. This means that in both doctrinal scholarship and legal theory, the debate about the liability of corporations is marked by a sustained use of metaphors, contrasts, images which depend upon the analogies and disanalogies between 'corporate' and 'human' persons. In the criminal law sphere, sometimes the analogies—action, conduct, agency, effects in the world—are emphasized so as to argue in favour of liability;[34] at other times, the disanalogies—lack of 'soul', 'mind', or 'intentions'; lack of moral capacity; lack of physical body—are emphasized to the opposite effect or in favour of a distinct regulatory scheme.[35]

[31] This is, of course, a different argument from my broader contention about the need to theorize law sociologically.

[32] E. Sutherland, *White-Collar Crime* (Yale University Press, 1983; first published 1949).

[33] See J. Hagan, *Crime and Disrepute* (Pine Forge Press, Thousand Oaks, Cal., 1994).

[34] See e.g. C.V. Clarkson, 'Kicking Corporate Bodies and Damning their Souls' (1996) 59 *Modern Law Review* 557; Pamela H. Bucy, 'Corporate Ethos: A Standard for Imposing Corporate Criminal Liability' (1991) 75 *Minnesota Law Review* 1095.

[35] See e.g. Sullivan, n. 30 above, P. Arenella, 'Convicting the Morally Blameless: Reassessing the Relationship between Legal and Moral Responsibility' (1992) 39 *UCLA Law Review* 1511.

My focus here is an assumption which underlies both analogies and disanalogies. This is the idea that the legal 'personality' of 'individual human persons' is 'real', or rather 'not fictitious' in a sense that corporate personality is. Does this assume that at least some legal concepts reflect invariable—logical or moral—'truths' about the world? This view was, of course, one of the main targets of Hart's (as we might now put it) constructionist argument about legal concepts in 'Definition and Theory'.[36] Though Hart's argument makes it clear that even if some legal concepts apparently have more straightforward 'counterparts in the world of fact' than do others, this is of at most indirect relevance to their constitution as legal persons. For legal personality is not straightforwardly descriptive: rather, it makes reference to the conditions under which it is true to say that some social phenomenon—human, corporate, or other—may be held liable in law.[37] Few legal theorists today would admit to holding the position taken by Michael Moore, whose legal philosophy asserts that legal concepts are built out of a bedrock of 'natural kinds' which, for the purposes of criminal responsibility, include human beings and exclude corporations.[38]

In analysing the philosophical foundations of corporate legal personality, Hart therefore stepped neatly around *metaphysical* questions about the 'reality' of corporate entities. But can such an analysis avoid with equal astuteness *social* questions about the operation of, and attitudes towards, corporate bodies? In emphasizing the construction of corporate legal personality by analogy with individual human personality, Hart sometimes appears to have assumed that the project of seeking a 'counterpart in the world of fact' is *more* misconceived for corporations than for humans as subjects of criminal law. And of course there is an important sense in which this is true. But it is true for historical—and therefore contingent—reasons: it is a persuasive *interpretation of modern criminal law* because, as a matter of history, English criminal law categories have been constructed primarily with human beings and with moral ideas about human responsibility in mind. The so-called 'general principles of criminal law' respond to a particular legitimacy problem in liberal polities: the justification of state punishment of individuals. Yet Hart shows little interest in the relationship between those legal conceptions and the social or moral or economic environment in which they have developed. Hence the implication appears analytic rather than interpretive. This part of 'Definition and Theory' provides a good illustration of his inclination towards the analytical jurisprudence as opposed to descriptive sociology pole of his dual method. Hart's focus is the 'internal' theory of the legal person rather than the social developments which provide the environment (and

[36] This is an argument which is, significantly, almost exactly reproduced in Lord Hoffmann's conception of the company as 'rules', and of rules as the distinctively legal mode of existence in the *Meridian Global Funds* case: see text following n. 55 below.

[37] 'Definition and Theory', n. 25 above, 23; cf. Dworkin's robustly anti-metaphysical approach to group personification: *Law's Empire*, n. 4 above, 168–75, which recognizes the corporation as having a form of moral agency, while asserting that it is a 'creature of the practices of thought and language in which it figures' rather than having any 'independent metaphysical existence' (171).

[38] Moore, n. 14 above, 18–23, 623 and see generally chap. 15. See also John Finnis, 'The Priority of Persons' in this volume.

often impetus) for that legal conception, and he assumes that the two are quite separate. Indeed, there are moments when Hart comes close to the 'logical' or metaphysical view about corporations which it is his purpose to reject. Probably the most vivid example is his reference to 'corporate spirit' as a 'secret of success and not a criterion of identity'.[39] In fact, as we shall see, reform proposals in several jurisdictions have now adopted something close to corporate spirit as a central element in the construction of corporate criminal liability.

The assumption that individual human beings are the obvious or typical subjects of criminal law must be understood, then, as historically specific and as grounded in social practices. Moreover, it must be so understood if it is to be consistent with Hart's approach to corporate responsibility. It is tied up with an interpretation of criminal law as a social practice geared to making judgements about blame, responsibility, and wrongdoing which are closely articulated with the idea of moral agency: a humanist discourse. Within this vision of criminal law, the imposition of corporate liability involves, as Sullivan has argued, a form of anthropomorphism.[40] But, from a social science point of view, this is only one aspect of twentieth- (or indeed nineteenth-)century criminal law. Criminal law's meaning as a system of quasi-moral judgement exists alongside its status as a regulatory or even administrative system, and the relationship between these two aspects of criminal law is arguably one of the most important keys to understanding its operation and development.[41]

Sullivan's position on corporate liability is of particular interest, in that it relies explicitly upon an argument about the philosophical foundations of criminal law to found its claim that corporations cannot appropriately be construed as among criminal law's subjects.[42] The argument is that criminal law is essentially a system of—as it were—blaming and shaming which has its philosophical roots in a conception of agency and responsibility which simply cannot be extended, by metaphor or analogy, to corporations. Yet this argument itself draws upon the fund of 'social' insight the relevance of which it denies. For unless Sullivan's is another version of the extreme, metaphysical argument to which few writers now pay (explicit) allegiance, or a version of the rigid conceptual or 'logical' position rejected by Hart in 'Definition and Theory', it must be based on some social understanding both of criminal law as a social practice and of how individuals and collectivities operate in the social world. In effect, Sullivan elides an argument about what is technically possible in criminal law with one about what is normatively desirable. For though his argument against corporate 'personality' depends on a retributive view, he gives no convincing argument for a retributive *interpretation of* (as opposed to *prescription for*) criminal law.

[39] N. 25 above, 30.

[40] N. 30 above, 531–3.

[41] For development of this argument, see Lacey and Wells, n. 21 above, chap. 1; Nicola Lacey, 'Contingency, Coherence and Conceptualism', in R.A. Duff (ed.), *Philosophy and the Criminal Law: Principle and Critique* (Oxford University Press, New York, 1998); see also Alan Norrie, *Crime, Reason and History* (Butterworths, London, 1993) (with particular reference to corporations, chap. 5). On the development of regulatory criminal laws in the nineteenth century, see also Lindsay Farmer, *Criminal Law, Tradition and Legal Order* (Cambridge University Press, Cambridge, 1997) chaps. 3 and 4.

[42] N. 30 above.

Prescriptively, his argument in favour of a civil, regulatory scheme may have strong recommendations (though this will turn on empirical evidence). But it cannot be supported merely on the basis that corporate liability is inconsistent with the philosophical foundations of criminal law. For those philosophical foundations, as a matter of interpretation, are divided between what we may crudely call retributive and consequentialist principles. The ease with which corporations can be accommodated within criminal law's consequentialist, regulatory schema is amply illustrated by the large numbers of statutory offences which can be committed *only* by a 'corporate body'—a legal attribution of responsibility which sidesteps methodological individualism as neatly as it does metaphysics.

The co-existence of (and tension between) different aspects and social roles of criminal law is rarely confronted in doctrinal analyses or in criminal *law* theory,[43] which tend to marginalize the 'regulatory' offences which focus on the enforcement of a (valued) standard at the expense of ensuring that the conditions for attribution of blame in breaching that standard are fulfilled. This marginalization is facilitated by the way in which analytic criminal law theory draws its boundaries—excluding evidence about patterns of enforcement or even numbers and types of offence on the statute book. This, I suggest, is one strong reason to think that theories of criminal law distort the practices which they purport to illuminate unless they are informed by a historical and contextualized understanding of criminal law.

There are many further ways in which the self-imposed boundaries of 'internal' legal theory distort our understanding of criminal law in ways which undermine the claim to descriptive or even interpretive status, and where jurisprudence needs to be informed by a social perspective. For example, the assumption that *individuals conceived as criminal law conceives them today* are somehow the 'natural' subjects of criminal law is unsettled by historical and anthropological evidence which shows that human persons have been multifariously construed and represented in various spheres of law. Indeed, the very idea of what constitutes a human person varies across cultures, just as human beings' sense of themselves is shaped by their relationships with others and with their social environment.[44] The self-standing, autonomous legal subject defined in terms of a set of cognitive and volitional capacities is a product of post-enlightenment thinking; while the subject of, for example, medieval law was defined to a far greater extent in terms of community norms and membership.[45] Legal subjects (or 'persons') in other systems may be defined in terms of characteristics or contexts which look exotic to us, yet which merely reflect a certain cultural conception of responsibility, human being, and social or community life. To dismiss these arrangements as philosophically incoherent suggests a moral realism which leads back to just the assumptions against which Hart argued in 'Definition and Theory':

[43] As opposed to criminology or penal philosophy.

[44] See e.g. Clifford Geertz, *Local Knowledge* (Basic Books, New York, 1983) 59–63. For a general review of the literature on the social construction of the individual, see Elizabeth Frazer and Nicola Lacey, *The Politics of Community* (Harvester, Hemel Hempstead, 1993).

[45] Tim Murphy, *The Oldest Social Science?* (Clarendon Press, Oxford, 1997) chap. 2.

to metaphysical claims about law's (proper) reflection of (moral) truths. Even in our contemporary system, a careful study of both substantive law and criminal evidence shows that the legal system shifts between different ways of framing human individuals in different contexts, moving, for example, between broader and narrower views of the relevant time frame within which offences and offenders are conceptualized.[46] Descriptive or interpretive legal theory cannot write these movements off as incoherent or unprincipled without either making metaphysical claims or moving to fully fledged prescriptive mode. The wresting of interpretive analysis from its historical and social context constantly suggests a metaphysical implication which contemporary legal theorists are concerned to deny.

Of course, this does not show that such legal frameworks never relate to, or indeed produce, 'truths', but rather that they are social or legal rather than 'metaphysical' truths. This implies a dialectical relationship between the corporation as social and as legal phenomenon. Though the corporation is a legal creation, it has a social being, and the genesis of the corporation as a significant social actor might be expected gradually, other things being equal, to produce a legal framework adequate to explicating the role of corporations in the fields in which they are influential: various forms of economic production; contracting; harmful practices; and, perhaps, wrongdoing. If we are interested in the 'philosophical foundations' of law and of other social institutions, we must surely be concerned with accounts of how these social institutions operate—their structure and dynamics—and hence (potentially) with literature in political science, sociology, and economics, as well as with the more obviously relevant interdisciplinary literature on corporate governance.

If, then, we agree with Hart that attributions of criminal liability are a legal or political matter and not a matter of logic, we should not follow him in holding that practices (or indeed conceptions) of attribution can be analysed without adverting either to the circumstances in which questions about holding collectivities socially responsible are raised or to details about the actual workings of the relevant collectivities.[47] This is because it is a mistake to think that law can afford to ignore insights into the operation of the institutions whose practices it seeks to shape, or that the structure of those practices places no constraints on the development of adequate legal policy.[48] Hence a radical separation between the supposedly 'internal' and 'external' will in fact occlude our understanding of law. If this is persuasive, a further set of questions moves on to the agenda of criminal law theory: questions about how criminal law should respond to the fact that corporations are organized in different

[46] Cf. Mark Kelman, 'Interpretive Construction in the Substantive Criminal Law' (1981) 33 *Stanford Law Review* 591. Another example, which I am grateful to John Seymour for pointing out, is criminal law's construction of liability for secondary parties involved in 'joint enterprises'.

[47] There is a strong resonance between Hart's view on this point and that of Teubner: '[t]here are no fixed objective relationships between pre-legal structures and legal construction. There is no sociological natural law of the legal person' (n. 27 above, 140): the relatively autonomous, if not entirely autopoietic, nature of social institutions not only makes for regulatory difficulties but also renders the idea of a total 'fit' between legal conceptions of social institutions and the 'social substratum' implausible. See further n. 8.

[48] See on this point Collins, n. 29 above; Braithwaite and Fisse (1985), n. 29 above.

ways and operate in very different social, institutional, and economic contexts. Is the variation in corporate structure and agency significantly greater than that of human agency and, if so, what does this imply for criminal law's aspiration to embody general and universally applicable standards and methods of attribution?[49]

INTERPRETING THE LEGAL DEVELOPMENTS

In order to assess more closely the theoretical implications of the corporate manslaughter story, it is worth reviewing the legal developments in a little more depth. The conceptual barriers to corporate criminal liability for offences against the person lie deep in the framework of criminal law doctrine. One problem has to do with the way in which criminal law conceptualizes conduct. If the typical *actus reus* requirement is to be understood as a 'voluntary act', it fits much better with modern ways of conceptualizing individuals than with our social understanding of corporations, whose 'conduct' is more easily conceived in terms of rules, systems, practices, procedures, or even effects. Stretching the 'human' analogy seems an inherently limited exercise. Criminal law can get round the *actus reus* problem by imposing omissions liability on the basis of pre-existing duties to act, but only if it can develop a conception of the distinctive duties of corporations.[50]

It seems, therefore, that the usual notion of *actus reus* as 'conduct' is potentially as limiting as, if not more limiting than, *mens rea*, and that devising a specifically corporate account of conduct itself poses a conceptual challenge. However, the main conceptual problem thought by the court in *Cory* to block corporate liability for offences against the person was the requirement of *mens rea.*[51] In *Cory*, the principal argument was that, since corporations have nothing approaching an individual human mind, the requirements of mental responsibility encapsulated in *mens rea* were impossible to apply. In offences of strict liability, this barrier is removed, and criminal law also imposes vicarious liability on corporate employers for the acts of employees. Given that offences against the person generally require proof of *mens rea*, this is of no assistance to the recognition of corporate homicide. The one possibility derived from the creation, in the 1940s,[52] of the identification doctrine, which equates an individual human mind *with* the corporation for the purposes of criminal

[49] This aspiration to universality appears to sit unhappily with the kind of pragmatism advocated by Teubner's work on the corporate governance of diffuse corporate networks: Teubner, 'The Many–Headed Hydra', n. 27 above. However, for an illuminating discussion of the possibility of tailoring criminal justice to corporate structure and compliance record, see Braithwaite and Fisse (1985; 1993), n. 29 above.

[50] This arguably implies greater co-ordination between criminal law and company law than has so far been attempted. The application of such liability would also entail some complex questions of causation.

[51] The fact that the *actus reus* problem did not arise in *Cory* may be explained by the fact that the conduct requirement for homicide is 'causing death'—something which is far easier to apply to corporate practices than are, for example, the concepts of assault or battery.

[52] *DPP* v. *Kent and Sussex Contractors* [1944] KB 146; *R.* v. *ICR Haulage* (1944) 30 Cr.App.Rep. 31; see Wells, n. 21 above, 103–11. The social genesis of this legal development is itself an interesting topic, though one which lies beyond the scope of this essay.

law. The identification doctrine is, however, of narrow application,[53] for it can only be applied to those sufficiently highly placed—typically managing directors—to be 'identified' with the company as its 'directing mind and will'.

In the context of the increasing power of large corporations in which managerial responsibility is diffuse (or even, as in the case of franchising, in part contracted out to legally separate entities) the restrictiveness of the identification doctrine is problematic. And the impetus for interpretive legal change appears to have come primarily from a number of widely publicized catastrophes in the 1980s, in which managerial failures within just such large and structurally diffuse corporations led to significant loss of life.[54] These incidents were widely argued to underline a need for a regime of corporate criminal liability capable of reflecting the distinctive *modus operandi* of corporations. The most important legal cases arose out of the sinking of the *Herald of Free Enterprise* at Zeebrugge in 1987, in which 189 people died.[55] Yet the legal decisions which followed in fact represent a rather modest extension of the identification doctrine. In *P&O European Ferries*, for example, it was accepted that a corporation could be liable for manslaughter if it could be shown that the systematic failings identified by the Inquiry following the disaster implied that senior management were involved in taking risks which would have been obvious to a reasonably prudent mariner. This case (and its precursor, *ex parte Spooner*) was important in recognizing that corporate liability for manslaughter was in principle possible, and in accepting that evidence about working systems and policies might be relevant in establishing recklessness or negligence. But it made no distinctive conceptual advance. This was because it specifically rejected the idea of aggregating states of mind across numbers of employees and managers so as to construct composite *mens rea*. Hence it is not surprising that the first successful prosecution of corporate manslaughter was of a very small corporation, OLL: this made it easy to apply the identification doctrine and meant that aggregation of individual instances of negligence by different employees was not at issue. Far more difficult is the case of the diffuse, larger corporation—whose power to harm is, ironically, far greater than that of the small corporations which it is easier to draw within the net of criminal liability.

[53] *Tesco Supermarkets Ltd.* v. *Nattrass* [1972] AC 171.

[54] On the causal complexities of the attribution of collective social responsibility, see G. Teubner, 'The Invisible Cupola—From Causal to Collective Attribution in Ecological Liability' in G. Teubner, L. Farmer, and D. Murphy (eds.), *Environmental Law and Ecological Responsibility* (1994) 17. One might argue in relation to Zeebrugge or similar disasters, for example, that the primary cause is the market order, which sets up powerful incentives to cut costs (and hence safety corners). For an analysis of the normative judgments underlying legal attributions of causation, see Jane Stapleton's 'Perspectives on Causation' in this volume.

[55] These and subsequent developments have aroused a wealth of academic comment, much of which appears in earlier notes. See also James Gobert, 'Corporate Criminality: New Crimes for the Times' [1994] *Crim.LR* 722; Gary Slapper, 'Corporate Manslaughter: An Examination of the Determinants of Prosecutorial Policy' [1993] *Social and Legal Studies* 423; Celia Wells, 'Corporate Liability and Consumer Protection: Tesco v. Nattrass Revisited' (1994) 57 *Modern Law Review* 817. For a more general assessment of legal, procedural, and penal issues, see Gary Slapper and Steve Tombs, *Corporate Crime* (Longman, London, 1999).

This was firmly grasped by Lord Hoffmann in a fascinating case which shows a company law analysis cutting through the *mens rea* problem, and which therefore touches on our second theoretical question about the existence of distinctive subsystems within the common law. In *Meridian Global Funds* (1995), the Privy Council held that a corporation could be held liable for breaches of securities and investments regulations by its investment managers. From a criminal law point of view, the decision is problematic: the relevant offence required proof of *mens rea*, and the investment managers were not so highly placed as to be identifiable with the corporation: yet the decision purports to apply *Tesco* v. *Nattrass*. The nub of Lord Hoffmann's argument is socio-economic: in the context of a regulatory regime oriented to reducing a mischief in the operation of fast-moving financial markets, a strict application of criminal law's identification doctrine would defeat the purpose of the legislation because it would give companies an incentive to find out as little as possible about what their middle managers were doing.[56]

Meridian also speaks to our first theoretical question about the autonomy of legal reasoning. The decision assumes that the legislative articulation of regulatory frameworks is always informed by a particular context and that judicial interpretation should itself take into account both that context and the specific structure of the corporation whose conduct is under consideration. This implies that the application of general common law doctrines, such as the stringently limited vicarious liability and identification doctrines in criminal law, must itself be contextualized. The changing institutional structure of commercial practices—not least the emergence of networks less integrated than the conventional firm—poses questions not only for government policy but also for legal theory. Is Lord Hoffmann's argument about the effects of the decision on the operation of commerce converted into a legal argument by the context of the legislative purpose? If so, this suggests that the autonomy of legal argument is somewhat fragile. Yet any other conclusion appears to marginalize legislation in favour of case law.

Though *Meridian* is not concerned with offences against the person, given the rationale of the argument there seems no reason, from the point of view of criminal law theory, to confine it to certain offences. To put the point more cautiously, such an argument would need to be advanced, and would have to be premised on the idea that certain doctrines usually taken to be of general application in criminal law apply in fact only to certain categories of offences. There are, however, interesting implications here for the capacity of doctrinal analysis to grasp a distinction obvious to sociologists and criminologists, and arguably central to an adequate understanding of the nature and development of criminal law: i.e. that between 'quasi-crimes' such as regulatory offences concerning the operation of financial markets and 'real crimes' such

[56] *Meridian*, n. 26 above, at 927. Whether this argument is correct is an empirical question, and it raises an important issue concerning the kind of evidence which should be available to courts. It also raises the question of how rational decisions are to be made if the relevant evidence is unavailable: for an analysis of this intriguing question, see Peter Cane's 'Consequences in Judicial Reasoning' in this volume.

as manslaughter.[57] To apply this to the case at hand, the obvious question arises whether the courts will extend the Privy Council's flexible approach to the identification doctrine into the terrain of 'real crime'. An analysis of philosophical foundations supplemented by the insights of a socio-legal perspective suggests that those foundations vary across, or even within, the various 'subsystems' of the common law. Implicit in Lord Hoffmann's argument for a case-by-case approach based on statutory interpretation is a judicial confrontation with the uneven combination of quasi-moral and instrumental, regulatory impulses in criminal law—a combination fostered by what Dworkin might describe as 'checkerboard' legislation.[58] Can legal theorists dismiss this as an aberration destroying the integrity of law while still asserting their descriptive or 'interpretive' credentials?

SOCIAL/CULTURAL DYNAMICS IN THE JOURNEY FROM *CORY* TO *SPOONER*

As we have seen, the conceptual structure of criminal law doctrine as usually interpreted has indeed constrained the development of corporate manslaughter. Nonetheless, it is certainly not the case that these conceptual problems entirely explain the slow development of corporate homicide law. Given the lack of doctrinal development, they simply cannot explain, for example, why the owners of the *Herald of Free Enterprise* were ultimately prosecuted for (and might well have been convicted of) manslaughter, while the corporations responsible for the design and operation of the *Titanic* or—more recently—the Piper Alpha oil platform or King's Cross Station were not. So what are the other influential factors here? How is it that the judicial decision to hold two named workers on the Piper Alpha platform responsible as the main instigators of the fatal disaster could be described in 1998 as 'indicative of legal bias which allows society to attribute a major incident to human error of specific workers when it originated from corporate misconduct and neglect',[59] when a similar finding thirty years earlier would probably have been regarded (at least in Britain) as perfectly appropriate?

Four main cultural arguments have been advanced to explain the recent steps towards recognition of corporate manslaughter.[60] The first argument has to do with technological change: the growth of technology is argued to have increased the scope for huge disasters which cause so much harm that there is bound to be a strong social reaction. This change is reinforced, secondly, by developments in mass communications: where such disasters occur, everyone knows about them. Perhaps partly as a

[57] On the indeterminacy of principles governing the displacement of the common law presumption in favour of *mens rea* requirements, see Lacey and Wells, n. 21 above, chaps. 1.II. and 5.

[58] Dworkin, n. 4 above: on his view, legislation following no consistent policy thread or unconstrained by individual rights would be unlikely to generate a body of doctrine susceptible of interpretation as coherent. The implications for criminal law are, however, uncertain, given that Dworkin does not see this field as essentially concerned with rights: *Taking Rights Seriously*, n. 8 above, chap. 2.

[59] *Labour Research*, Apr. 1998, 15: my thanks go to Julian Fulbrook for this reference.

[60] This brief account is mainly drawn from that of Celia Wells, n. 21 above.

result of these two factors, sociologists have also noted a change, thirdly, in attitudes to both risk and responsibility. In the modern world, we are unwilling to ascribe tragedies to fate, chance, the gods; our scientific world view makes us look for causes, and in particular for causal agencies to which we can attribute responsibility—notably human beings. We assume that where such causes can be found, this implies that disasters were avoidable; and this makes us willing to attribute blame. This has led some sociologists to argue that in the late modern world, we become increasingly aware of and oriented to risk, yet also increasingly intolerant of it.[61] Finally, both the growing social significance of corporations and increasing public knowledge of their operations, as reflected by, for example, levels of media reporting, have engendered a willingness to blame collectivities as well as individuals.[62] Hence we seem to be witnessing the emergence of (or perhaps a return to) a social construction of corporations as bodies who can be genuinely blameworthy, and whom it is both fair and appropriate to hold directly responsible for crime. The close analysis of how disasters such as the *Herald* sinking occur tend to illuminate the diffusion of responsibility and—as in the case of Sheen J's inquiry[63]—single out not only individual failings which are proximate to the event but also systemic failings in the corporation's rules and procedures developed over a period of time.

In cases such as the *Herald* sinking, it is then argued that the relative importance of these systemic failings as compared with reckless or negligent individual acts or omissions proximate to the event renders the exclusive prosecution of junior employees who are often most directly involved unfair. Significantly, the Crown Prosecution Service recently proceeded against not only the train driver but also Great Western Trains in pursuing a manslaughter prosecution following the 1997 Southall rail disaster in which seven people were killed. Notwithstanding the fact that the corporate manslaughter charge was dismissed by the trial judge, the Crown Prosecution Service decision, as well as public reaction to the charge's dismissal, appear to signify the emergence of a social sense of corporate responsibility which is not a derivative of individually blameworthy acts. This development does not, of course, determine the normative question whether corporations *should* be held liable in criminal law. But it directly raises the question whether law *could* develop a conceptual framework for corporate liability presupposing a model of the firm which, though avoiding the metaphysical and anthropomorphic mystifications of the 'real entity' theory, goes beyond the 'aggregate/contractual' model to recognize both firms' distinctive capac-

[61] See e.g. Anthony Giddens, *Modernity and Self-Identity* (Polity Press, Oxford, 1991).

[62] On the developing social role of corporations, see Coleman, n. 27 above, chap. 1; Bovens, n. 29 above, 11–15. Coleman argues that the growing power of corporate actors in the 19th and 20th centuries has disempowered individuals both materially and psychologically (chap. 2): his call for the restitution of individuals' power via regulatory regimes or changes in property rights (chap. 3) may also shed some light on the contemporary demand for corporate legal (including criminal) accountability. Bovens emphasizes the growing social importance of corporations in the lives of individuals, as measured by increases in the total numbers of corporations; the amount of litigation about corporate activities; and proportionate media reporting of individual and corporate issues.

[63] *MV Herald of Free Enterprise: Report of the Court No. 8074* (Dept. of Transport, London, 1987).

ity for collective action and citizens' interpretation of firms as autonomous and distinctive collectivities operating in the social world.

CORPORATE LIABILITY AND THE IDEOLOGY OF CRIMINAL LAW DOCTRINE

These social explanations taken alone, however, fail to provide a convincing explanation of recent legal developments, for the simple reason that most of them have been firmly in place for several decades. Yet an exclusively legal analysis is equally unpersuasive.

Just as the social explanations, taken alone, fail to provide a convincing explanation of recent developments, an exclusively legal analysis is unpersuasive. The legal concepts which have facilitated the development of corporate responsibility—'objective' recklessness and gross negligence—are themselves hardly new. Their empirical and conceptual importance has, however, been obscured in criminal law theory by a narrow focus on the aspects of criminal law fitting better with a 'quasi-moral' than with a 'regulatory' conception of the social practice of criminalization—a focus which is driven primarily by normative rather than interpretive concerns.

The (at first sight) puzzling flexibility of legal doctrine can be explained, however, if we bridge our cultural and legal explanations with a social interpretation of the internal logic of criminal law. Such a perspective illuminates a wide and significant gap in criminal law thinking between the vaunted subjectivist framework of much doctrine—the idea that 'real' crimes can only be committed with subjective intent or recklessness—and the pluralist reality of criminal law—the fact that a large proportion of crimes can be committed through negligence: a much easier form of *mens rea* to apply to a corporation.[64] Once again, the demands posed on quasi-descriptive interpretive theory by the empirical balance of criminal offences as well as the social patterns of criminal enforcement emerge as raising intriguing theoretical questions.

The idea that subjective forms of *mens rea* do and should predominate in criminal law has undoubtedly underpinned resistance to corporate liability because of the close association between subjective *mens rea* and the human mind. But the reality of pluralism—the co-existence of subjective, objective, and constructive principles of liability, and in particular, in this context, the pervasiveness of negligence, even for an offence as serious as manslaughter[65]—meant that corporate liability could be accommodated once social demands were sufficiently strong. There is an obvious link here with the way in which the co-existence of criminal law as a system of quasi-moral judgement and as an instrumental system of regulation tends to be obscured in criminal law doctrine and theory. For though—as Hart argued[66]—negligence liability *could* be

[64] The gap, of course, widens when we take into account the vast number of 'regulatory' offences of strict liability—many of which apply specifically to corporations: see n. 67 below.

[65] For an excellent study of the pervasiveness of offences of strict liability and negligence in contemporary criminal law, see Andrew Ashworth and Meredith Blake, 'The Presumption of Innocence in English Criminal Law' [1996] *Crim. LR* 306.

[66] 'Negligence, Mens Rea and Criminal Responsibility', *Punishment and Responsibility* (Clarendon Press, Oxford, 1968), 136–57; see also Andrew Simester's 'Can Negligence Be Culpable?' in this volume.

construed in a way which would be consistent with the principles of individual fairness generally taken to underpin the legitimacy of criminal law, the *actual* interpretation of negligence in stringently objective terms is inconsistent with those principles. By vaunting subjectivism but practising widespread objectivism (or even, in some instances, constructive liability), criminal law discourse draws upon the generally legitimizing force of moral constraints which it observes only in a minority of cases.

As we have seen, criminal law continues to take the individual human subject as the model out of which it constructs corporate criminal responsibility. But certain reform proposals and inchoate case-law developments are now gesturing towards the more radical development presaged in the social discourse considered in the previous section: a development which would construe the corporation as a distinctive social, even if not metaphysically 'real', entity. I shall now review these two approaches before going on to examine whether their differences are significant. Again, my purpose in doing so is to demonstrate the interdependence of theoretical tasks often conceived as occupying radically separate spheres in the jurisprudential stadium.

The first approach to corporate criminal liability operates by expanding the conditions under which the 'persons' analogy can be deployed. This can be achieved either by broadening the conditions under which the identification doctrine applies or by widening the range of crimes for which a corporation may be held vicariously liable. A converse development, also in the area of regulatory, 'quasi-crime' is the gradual expansion of individual officer liability for a company's crimes.[67] Another version of this first approach is the somewhat more innovative doctrine of aggregation, which would operate to cumulate individual failings on the part of company employees so as to construct a composite state of negligence or recklessness.[68] Each of these developments retains a methodological individualism, either anthropomorphizing the corporation or assuming that, though essentially a contractual or aggregate entity, liability may on occasion be attributed to the firm for pragmatic reasons. These approaches sit well with an individualistic approach to criminal responsibility, and they concentrate on addressing the *mens rea* bar to corporate criminal liability.

The second approach consists in the construction of corporations as distinctive subjects of criminal law. This addresses *actus reus* as much as *mens rea*, and equates with the organization theorist's view of the firm as an entity with distinctive social capacities and one which social actors interpret and respond to in ways which recognize this distinctiveness. One example here would be the Law Commission's Report on involuntary manslaughter,[69] which recommended an offence of corporate killing.

[67] This approach pierces the corporate veil by, for example, using a relatively modest view of what is implied by a statutory requirement of 'consent', regarding ignorance of law as no excuse, and hence holding the officer liable if he or she knows of the material circumstances which underpin the company's breach: *A-G's Reference (No. 1 of 1995)* [1996] 1 WLR 970. For an excellent discussion, see Joanna Gray, 'Company Law and Regulatory Complexity', in Ross Grantham and Charles Rickett (eds.), *Corporate Personality in the 20th Century* (Hart Publishing, Oxford, 1998) 149.

[68] Questions still arise, of course, about how to identify which actions of corporate employees should be within scope of attribution: should criminal law depend here on employment or company law? See Teubner, 'Enterprise Corporatism', n. 27 above, 151.

[69] *Legislating the Criminal Code: Involuntary Manslaughter* (LC 237, 1996).

This offence would be committed where management failure by the corporation is the cause or one of the causes of a person's death and that failure constitutes conduct falling far below what can reasonably be expected of the corporation (whether or not that failure is an act or omission of an individual).[70] The government has expressed its intention to adopt the Commission's proposals, but has not yet taken any steps in that direction.

A yet more decisive commitment to this second approach is represented by the Australian Model Criminal Code.[71] On this model, corporate liability for crimes of subjective *mens rea* on the basis of fault may be attributed to a corporate body that expressly, tacitly, or impliedly authorized or permitted the commission of the offence. Such authorization or permission can be based not only on a (relatively generous) practice of identification, including high managerial agents, but also on 'corporate culture', defined as an 'attitude, policy, rule, course of conduct or practice within the corporate body generally or in the part of the body corporate where the offence occurred'. In other words, a corporation could be liable because its unwritten rules tacitly authorized non-compliance or even failed to create a culture of compliance.

The Australian Commonwealth Model Code approach therefore allows for a situation where the 'real' fault lies with corporate culture. Yet the Australian model also works in terms of agency: 'authorization' or 'permission'. It builds on a (partial) recognition of systems of work as bases for findings of criminal responsibility or conduct, and arguably sets out in general criminal law doctrine a principle already recognized in the enactment of a wide range of offences specific to corporations in most modern legal systems.[72] Legally, a similar outcome can be achieved *via* the first route—most obviously in terms of the existing conceptual framework of gross negligence, related to a corporate standard of reasonableness. But the second approach demonstrates that the conceptual categories of criminal law *can in principle* be constructed so as to accommodate corporations as directly responsible legal subjects. Such an approach would also have some symbolic significance in shifting the criminal subject status of corporations from penumbra to core, and hence in further diversifying the nature of criminal law as a social practice.

[70] Sullivan (n. 30 above, 531) criticizes the Commission's approach as professing to recognize the firm as a 'merely' legal entity but in fact treating it as a metaphysically 'real' entity. The implication of my argument (as of Hart's) is that this is a false dichotomy: legal concepts may construct corporate liability in a way which responds to the distinctive social capacities and effects of corporations without making metaphysical assumptions. Whether or not they *should* do so is a further question, and one on which I am much in sympathy with Sullivan's consequentialist approach. See also Bovens' persuasive argument—based on available evidence about the impact of different regulatory regimes, and distinguishing in an exemplary manner between normative arguments and arguments about conceptual propriety—for a regulatory system based on individual rather than collective or corporate accountability: Bovens, n. 29 above, chap. 8.

[71] For text and commentary, see Criminal Law Officers' Committee of the Standing Committee of the Attorneys-General, *Model Criminal Code: Final Report* (Australian COD, Canberra, 1993) chap. 2, 'General Principles of Criminal Responsibility', 104–13; see also Australian Criminal Code (1995) Part 2.5. The Australian approach follows closely that advocated by Bucy, n. 34 above.

[72] In English law, see e.g., the duty of disclosure under s.733(2) of the Companies Act 1985, breach of which renders the body corporate itself 'guilty of an offence'.

CONCLUSIONS

What, then, are the principal implications for legal theory which may be drawn from the case study of corporate manslaughter? We have seen that it is impossible to explain the development of this area of law without paying close attention to the interaction of legal-conceptual and social factors. This interaction illustrates the impossibility of drawing any radical line between broadly 'analytic' and 'sociological' attempts to theorize the common law. Whichever route to law reform we follow, we can easily broaden corporate criminal responsibility: as positivism recognizes in its most consistent forms, law is contingent and constructive. Yet underlying assumptions which are obscured by analytic legal theory—for example assumptions about corporations as 'logically' penumbral and humans as 'naturally' paradigmatic criminal legal persons—remain crucial to an adequate understanding of legal developments. How any legal reforms will be interpreted—from within the legal system—will depend on factors outwith the scope of 'internal', analytical legal theory. Furthermore, in banishing to another discipline the socio-historical perspective which explains the current marginality of corporations as criminal law subjects, legal philosophers constantly risk making, or appearing to make, transcendent metaphysical claims which they do not (usually) intend.

Much more difficult than the interpretive question about corporate criminal liability is a prescriptive question on which I have hardly touched in this essay. This is the question whether we *ought* to expand corporate liability for crime: the moral, practical, and political questions bearing on what kind of corporate regulation and what form of sanction would be desirable.[73] A battery of consequentialist arguments is available here: deterring harms, strengthening the hand of regulatory agencies and prosecuting authorities by increasing the scope for plea-bargaining, deterring the formation of companies and dampening relevant economic activities, promoting social responsibility, increasing costs which will be passed on to consumers (and the risk of which are, in the case of unlimited fines, difficult for companies to predict). The upshot of these arguments is evidently and directly dependent upon evidence which, if available at all,[74] can only be supplied by the social sciences.

A different, non-consequentialist argument is that for attributing moral (and quasi-moral, criminal) blame to corporations. Though it seems incontestable that a social discourse of corporate blameworthiness and wrongdoing has emerged, whether we ought fully to equate it with other blaming discourses, or institutionalize it in criminal law, seems far less clear. The debate about corporate criminal liability is

[73] See e.g. Brent Fisse, 'The Attribution of Criminal Liability to Corporations' (1991) 13 *Sydney Law Review* 277, and 'Recent Developments in Corporate Criminal Law and Corporate Liability to Monetary Penalties' (1990) 13 *University of New South Wales Law Journal* 1; John Braithwaite, *Crime, Shame and Reintegration* (Cambridge University Press, Cambridge, 1989) chap. 9.

[74] Again, see Cane's argument (this volume). An important question arising from Cane's analysis is that whether rational consequentialist decision-making has to be based on empirical data or whether it can be based upon models developed within, for example, economics or organization theory.

implicitly driven, like the white-collar crime debate in criminology, by a moral(ist) and political concern about the marginalization of crime in corporate contexts. But we need to think critically, in the light of an adequate understanding of the social practice of criminalization, about the 'blaming culture' from which this concern partly proceeds. Is the ambiguous framework of criminalization appropriate here, or should we take a more straightforwardly regulatory approach? If the latter, does this imply that all the regulatory offences should be removed from the ambit of criminal law? Is it either legitimate or sensible to use a centralized and coercive system to give corporations, in effect, greater incentives to regulate themselves, and does it make sense to frame a general principle of corporate criminal liability given the immense diversity of corporate structure? None of these normative questions can be resolved by the social sciences. But a further argument of this essay is that none of them can be resolved *without* the insights which the social sciences can offer.

In the theoretical contest to assimilate corporations into the liability system of criminal law, it is all too easy to confuse a complicated and fragile normative argument for liability with a far more powerful argument rebutting the claim of conceptual impropriety. It is this latter argument which has been my focus, and in relation to which I hope to have established three theoretical propositions. First, criminal law can be framed so as to construct corporations (or indeed other social phenomena) as subjects without making either metaphysical assumptions or moral/philosophical mistakes. Secondly, the practical decision about how (as much as the normative decision about whether) to construct corporations as subjects of criminal law must be informed both by a rich empirical understanding of the (varying) structure and social significance of corporations and by a conception of criminal law which is clear-headed about its current ambiguity as between regulatory and quasi-moral dimensions. Thirdly, this broad and crucially necessary vision of criminal law as a social practice is obscured by analytic legal theories because of the way in which they draw their boundaries.

These propositions imply that legal philosophers are indeed intellectually dependent on sociologists of law. To the extent that sociological legal theorists are indeed committed to 'learning the rules', the distinctive normativity, methods of reasoning, and relatively autonomous character of law which have provided the focus for analytical jurisprudence are themselves key objects of sociological legal theories: hence the supposed distinction between internal and external legal theory collapses. Philosophers of law are no more or less participants in the law game than are legal sociologists. The real difference is that, without the sociologists, the philosophers would be unable to locate the stadium. As for the game of legal theory, it is time for analytical jurists to recognize that, if their play is to be meaningful, it must be grounded in a social theory of law.

Consequences in Judicial Reasoning

Peter Cane*

INTRODUCTION

In his book *Legal Reasoning and Legal Theory*[1] Neil MacCormick argues that in cases where deductive arguments[2] cannot justify judicial decisions, courts do, and may properly, deploy non-deductive arguments, based on the ideas of consistency, coherence, and consequences, in fashioning a rule or principle of law to resolve the case. MacCormick gives various examples of 'consequence-based reasoning'. One involves reference to decisions which would have to be given in other cases if a particular ruling were given in the instant case.[3] For instance, the 'where-will-it-all-end' argument points out that if liability is imposed in this case, logic or justice will require that liability be imposed in all sorts of other cases as well. A second example given by MacCormick is the argument used by Marshall CJ in *Marbury* v. *Madison* to the effect that not to allow judicial review of statutes would be to 'subvert the very foundation' of the Constitution.[4] Thirdly, MacCormick cites the argument that making a particular ruling would lead the court outside the proper bounds of the judicial function.[5] Yet another example would be the argument that abandoning a 'bright-line' rule in favour of a more flexible principle would generate undesirable uncertainty in the law.

Judicial appeals to the ideas of consistency and coherence rest on widely held views about certain characteristics of sound reasoning. By contrast, judicial appeals to consequences rest on (implicit) assertions about the aims, goals, or purposes which judges think it proper to pursue through their legal decision-making. For instance, the 'where-will-it-all-end' argument implies that the law should treat like cases alike; Marshall CJ's argument implies that courts should uphold the constitution; and the 'bright-line' argument implies that the courts should aim to render legal rights and obligations certain (the principle of 'legal certainty').

The sort of consequence-based reasoning with which MacCormick is concerned may be dubbed 'single-factor reasoning'; and it may be contrasted with 'aggregative reasoning' about consequences. Aggregative reasoning is of the 'all-things-considered' variety, which assesses the desirability of a ruling or a rule by reference to the overall costs and benefits of the ruling. Single-factor reasoning refers to some specific

* Research School of Social Sciences, Australian National University, Canberra. Tony Honoré, Niki Lacey, Aurora Plomer, Jane Stapleton and Andrew von Hirsch made very helpful comments on earlier drafts of this essay.

1 (Revised edn., Clarendon Press, Oxford, 1994).

2 The premises of which are recognized rules of law and established propositions of fact.

3 MacCormick, n. 1 above, 105.

4 Ibid. 129.

5 Ibid. 132–3.

expected consequence of a ruling or a rule. The subject of this essay is single-factor consequence-based reasoning. Such reasoning is a common feature of judicial decision-making, often appearing in the guise of 'policy considerations'. Policy considerations typically concern the expected effects of legal rules. Many single-factor, consequence-based arguments involve assertions about consequences which are, in principle at least, empirically testable by observation of the world around us and by experiment. The focus of this essay is on single-factor, consequence-based arguments which are, in principle at least, empirically testable.

A species of single-factor, empirically testable, consequence-based reasoning not explicitly mentioned by MacCormick refers to the expected impact of judicial rulings and legal rules on the behaviour of those to whom the rulings and rules are addressed. Such reasoning rests on the widely-held view that one of the functions of legal rules is to encourage certain types of behaviour and to discourage certain other types of behaviour. This aim of the law is often put in terms of 'deterrence'; although, of course, read literally, this term only captures the negative motivational goal of discouraging unacceptable behaviour, and not the positive motivational goal of encouraging acceptable behaviour. This essay is primarily concerned with reasoning about the behavioural consequences of legal rules. Reliably predicting the likely impact of legal rules on human behaviour is extraordinarily problematic. There are two main reasons for this. One is that human rule-following has an internal (i.e. a mental) aspect.[6] Another is the difficulty of establishing the generalizations about human behaviour necessary for such predictions. Even if courts were more receptive to empirical data,[7] the high cost and the methodological difficulty of generating such data and their inherent limitations mean that predicting the impact of laws on human behaviour would remain tricky. In fact, while single-factor, empirically testable consequence-based arguments are much used by courts, the judges who deploy such arguments typically do not support them by reference to empirical data, but rest them largely on untested speculation and intuition.[8] The aim of this essay is to examine the implications of this observation. What are the criteria for the truth or validity or authority of a single-factor, consequence-based argument which is (in principle, at

[6] For a discussion of this point see A. Ryan, *The Philosophy of the Social Sciences* (Macmillan, London, 1970) 139ff, esp. 141–2.

[7] At this stage, I make no assumption about whether they should be or not.

[8] A self-professed enthusiast for taking account of what he calls 'the economic consequences' of imposing tort liability is Kirby J of the High Court of Australia: 'Comparativism, Realism and the Economic Factor—Fleming's Legacies' in N.J. Mullany and A.M. Linden (eds.), *Torts Tomorrow: A Tribute to John Fleming* (LBC Information Services, North Ryde, NSW, 1998), 12–15. The following passage deserves quotation: 'at the borderline, judges everywhere . . . are referring to the cost, insurance and other implications of their decisions. They do so *although the evidence rarely (or never) permits them anything approaching an accurate assessment.* Just as other lawmakers would not dream of now performing their functions in disregard of the economic factor, so courts in their function of declaring, clarifying and extending legal principle must take seriously the economic consequences of what they are doing' (emphasis added). See also D. Robertson, *Judicial Discretion in the House of Lords* (Clarendon Press, Oxford, 1998), 400. Judges occasionally acknowledge their ignorance of the likely behavioural consequences of their rulings. A well known example is *Launchbury* v. *Morgans* [1973] AC 127, 136–7, *per* Lord Wilberforce; 142–3, *per* Lord Pearson; 151, *per* Lord Salmon.

least) empirically testable but which is, in fact, based on untested speculation? To what extent is the appeal to consequences designed to lend a spurious air of objectivity to subjective value-judgements? Can appeal to consequences ameliorate the controversiality of much judicial reasoning which is not consequence-based?

My basic contention is that, to the extent that sound empirical support is lacking for arguments about the likely impact of legal rules on human behaviour (to the extent, in other words, that we are ignorant of the likely behavioural consequences of legal rules), we need to develop criteria of good decision-making which do not depend upon knowledge of likely consequences.

A PRELIMINARY WORD ABOUT CONSEQUENTIALISM AND CONSEQUENCE-BASED REASONING

In order to avoid unnecessary misunderstanding, it is important at the outset to distinguish between consequentialism and consequence-based reasoning. As an ethical theory (that is, a theory about how we ought to behave in our relations with others), consequentialism says that people ought to behave in such a way as to maximize the overall achievement of whatever states of the world they consider valuable or good. It might seem to follow from the fact that MacCormick gives only a subsidiary place to reasoning based on consequences in his account of judicial reasoning, that he would reject consequentialism as the ethical theory which ought to inform judicial decision-making. It would, however, be a mistake to conclude that MacCormick is committed to judicial non-consequentialism in this way. It is certainly possible to argue that incessant attention to consequences is not obviously the best way to promote valued objectives;[9] and it would not be too difficult to suggest a consequentialist explanation of the entire judicial reasoning procedure which MacCormick describes. Rule-following, which lies at the core of judicial decision-making, undeniably has its uses. On the other hand, those who reject consequentialism as a comprehensive ethical theory are not committed to a position which would prohibit attention to consequences in any and all circumstances.[10] It is not incoherent to hold that consequences may be ethically important at the same time as denying that they are all-important.

In this essay I take no position in relation to consequentialism as an ethical theory or about whether or not consequentialism is the ethical theory which ought to inform judicial decision-making and reasoning. My concern is to examine the logic and validity of judicial arguments which appeal to some expected consequence of a legal rule or principle as a reason for or against adopting that rule or principle.

[9] P. Pettit, 'Consequentialism' in P. Singer (ed.), *A Companion to Ethics* (Blackwell, Oxford, 1991), chap. 19.

[10] N. (A). Davis, 'Contemporary Deontology' in ibid., chap. 17.

A SINGLE-FACTOR CONSEQUENCE-BASED ARGUMENT

In order to make the following discussion less abstract, I will focus on a widely used single-factor consequence-based argument, which is commonly referred to as 'the overkill argument'. The overkill argument is an argument against the imposition of liability. It is found in many different contexts, but all instances of the argument share something like the following content:

> If the court finds in the plaintiff's favour in this case, the defendant and others similarly placed will be encouraged in future to engage in defensive behaviour, that is, behaviour designed not to conform with the rule or principle which would support a finding in favour of the plaintiff, but rather to minimise the risk of their being held liable in any circumstances to persons like the plaintiff.

In other words, the overkill argument says that holding the defendant liable in the circumstances of the case at hand will cause potential defendants to take precautions against the risk of incurring liability in a range of circumstances not covered by the ruling in this case. The vice of defensive behaviour is that it serves no purpose other than to minimize the perceived risk of incurring legal liability in the future. Defensive behaviour is unduly cautious behaviour;[11] and judicial decisions which provoke such behaviour are said to generate 'over-deterrence'. Underlying the overkill argument is an assumption that one of the functions of the law is deterrence—that is to discourage and reduce the incidence of undesirable behaviour, and to encourage desirable behaviour. In such terms, over-deterrence consists in the encouragement of undesirable behaviour (undue caution). Achievement of the law's goal of deterrence can be compromised by over-deterrence as well as by under-deterrence.

The overkill argument[12] is popular in the medical negligence context. A classic statement is that of Lord Denning MR in *Whitehouse* v. *Jordan*.[13] It was alleged that negligence of a doctor in delivering a baby had caused the child devastating brain damage. Both the Court of Appeal and the House of Lords held unanimously that on the facts, the defendant had not failed to take reasonable care. Lord Denning also justified his decision by drawing a distinction between negligence and 'error of judgement', but several of the Law Lords rejected this approach. Lord Denning rounded off his judgment in this way:

[11] In economic terms, defensive behaviour involves the taking of precautions the cost of which outweighs the benefit they are likely to produce in terms of reduction of adverse outcomes.

[12] Note that the word 'overkill' as used in this context has a different meaning from the way it is used when people say, for instance, that in deference to public opinion, criminal courts sometimes go in for 'overkill' by imposing heavier sentences than they might otherwise do if they were influenced only by accepted principles of sentencing. An analogy in tort law to this phenomenon might be very large awards of damages by juries in defamation cases. Such awards could be seen as having an 'excessive' punitive element. Steps have been taken to prevent such awards being made; and the rules about quantum of damages in tort are designed to avoid overkill in this sense. In the sentencing context, 'overkill' refers to the decision of the court, whereas in the present context it refers to the consequences of the court's decision.

[13] [1980] 1 All ER 650. The decision of the CA was affirmed by the HL [1981] 1 WLR 246.

> If [doctors] are to be found liable whenever they do not effect a cure, or whenever anything untoward happens, it would do a great disservice to the profession itself. Not only to the profession but to society at large. Take heed of what has happened in the United States. 'Medical malpractice' cases there are very worrying . . . The damages are colossal. The doctors insure but the premiums are very high: and these have to be passed on in fees to the patients. Experienced practitioners are known to have refused to treat patients for fear of being accused of negligence. Young men [*sic*] are even deterred from entering the profession because of the risks involved. In the interests of all, we must avoid such consequences in England. Not only must we avoid excessive damages. We must say, and say firmly, that in a professional man [*sic*], an error of judgment is not negligent.

The overkill argument has also been used in the context of actions against other types of professional person; and it has been found attractive as a justification for refusing to impose tort liability on public authorities, as well as for refusing to widen grounds of judicial review of administrative action (such as estoppel). A classic statement in this context is that of Lord Keith of Kinkel (on behalf of the Privy Council) in *Rowling* v. *Takaro Properties Ltd.*[14] It was alleged that a minister had caused the plaintiff company economic loss by negligently failing to take legal advice before (illegally) refusing a licence for the purchase of shares in the company by a Japanese corporation. In discussing the question whether the Minister owed a duty of care to the plaintiff, Lord Keith said:

> It is to be hoped that, as a general rule, imposition of liability in negligence will lead to a higher standard of care in the performance of the relevant type of act; but sometimes not only may this not be so, but the imposition of liability may even lead to harmful consequences . . . There are reasons for believing that this may be so in cases where liability is imposed upon local authorities whose building inspectors have been negligent in relation to the inspection of foundations . . . because there is a danger that the building inspectors of some local authorities may react to that decision by simply increasing, unnecessarily, the requisite depth of foundations, thereby imposing a very substantial and unnecessary financial burden upon members of the community. A comparable danger may exist in cases such as the present, because, once it became known that liability in negligence may be imposed on the ground that a minister has misconstrued a statute and so acted ultra vires, the cautious civil servant may go to extreme lengths in ensuring that legal advice, or even the opinion of the court, is obtained before decisions are taken, thereby leading to unnecessary delay in a considerable number of cases.

The overkill argument is problematic in several ways. One is that the distinction between defensive and non-defensive behaviour is sensitive to attitudes to risk. Conduct which may seem unduly cautious to a person who enjoys risk-taking may be judged reasonable by a person who is more risk-averse. In practice, the *prima facie* standard of 'defensiveness' used by the courts is tied to opinions about desirable behaviour which are (more or less) prevalent in the relevant group to which the defendant belongs. A second problem with the overkill argument is that it gives normative weight to what appear to be illogical reactions to legal liability rules. Since the law

[14] [1988] AC 473, 502.

never imposes an obligation to behave defensively, a person could never incur liability for failing to do so. However, the whole point of defensive behaviour is to avoid legal liability. Of course, defensive behaviour may be a reasonable reaction to uncertainty in the law about the limits of liability.[15] However, the overkill argument is not concerned with the effects of uncertainty about the limits of liability, but with the effect of rules assumed to be sufficiently certain to tell those to whom they are addressed what is required for compliance.

Problems such as these are important, but they are not the subject of this essay. For present purposes I will assume that the notion of 'defensiveness' is (or can be rendered) uncontroversial, and that the overkill argument is normatively acceptable.

THE LOGIC OF THE OVERKILL ARGUMENT

The overkill argument is concerned with two possible future states of the world, one in which the defendant and others like the defendant engage in defensive behaviour as a response to the court's decision, and one in which they do not. The argument involves no assumption or assertion about the amount of relevant defensive behaviour which is engaged in by the defendant and people like the defendant in the world in which the court's decision falls to be made. It only asserts that if the court were to find in favour of the plaintiff, there would be an unacceptable future increase in the amount of relevant defensive behaviour engaged in by the defendant and people like the defendant. Underlying the overkill argument is the idea of an optimum balance between the scope of liability, on the one hand, and the amount of defensive behaviour, on the other. The argument does not assume that the balance at the time of the court's decision is optimum, but only that a decision in favour of the plaintiff would take the balance further away from the optimum (in the direction of excess of defensive behaviour) than it currently is.

The overkill argument can take one of two forms. The first, stronger, form asserts that imposition of liability in the case at hand *will* be met by an increase in defensive conduct. The second, weaker, form asserts that there is a *risk* that imposition of liability in the case at hand will be met by an increase in defensive behaviour.[16] In order to assess the force of both forms of the argument it is useful to look more closely at the structure of human decision-making.

THE STRUCTURE OF DECISIONS

Both versions of the overkill argument are examples of what might be called 'practical reasoning'; that is, reasoning directed at deciding what to do. As a piece of

[15] D. Dewees, D. Duff, and M. Trebilcock, *Exploring the Domain of Accident Law: Taking the Facts Seriously* (Oxford University Press, New York, 1996), 106.

[16] Lord Denning perhaps deploys the stronger form in the above quotation from *Whitehouse* v. *Jordan*, while Lord Keith deploys the weaker form in the above quotation from *Rowling* v. *Takaro Properties Ltd.*

practical reasoning, is the overkill argument a good one? To answer this question, we need a criterion of good practical reasoning. In the rest of this section, I will outline a model of practical reasoning which provides such a criterion. In this model, practical reasoning has several components. The *objective* specifies the effect which the decision-maker aims to achieve. The *strategy* is the means, method, or technique which the decision-maker chooses to achieve the objective. By definition, the strategy is under the decision-maker's control. The path from the strategy to the objective is strewn with factors outside the decision-maker's control which may help or hinder the achievement of the objective. These uncontrolled factors can be divided into two broad groups: *states of nature* and *strategic behaviour*. Strategic behaviour is conduct of people, other than the decision-maker, which occurs as a response or reaction to the decision-maker's objective-seeking strategy. Strategic behaviour may be co-operative or non-co-operative.[17] States of nature are non-human events and non-strategic human behaviour.

The idea of making a decision implies choice. Choosing an objective is an exercise in non-empirical value judgement. To choose one objective to the exclusion of other possible objectives is to express a preference for one state of the world over others.[18] By contrast, the basic criterion for the choice of strategy is efficiency—which strategy is most likely to secure the objective at least cost? This criterion can, in principle at least, be subjected to empirical testing and verification.

In order to assess the efficiency of any available strategy, the decision-maker must be able to predict the likely impact of uncontrollable factors on the operation of the strategy. The more we know about the probability of states of nature and strategic behaviour which may affect the achievement of our chosen objectives, the better able we are to determine whether particular objectives are achievable, and to choose the most efficient strategies for achieving our desired objectives. Conversely, the less information a decision-maker has relevant to judging the likely operation of uncontrollable factors which may affect the achievement of desired objectives, the less able will they be to assess the efficiency of any particular strategy, and the harder it will be for them to make a good decision about what to do. Suppose, for instance, that the objective is to reduce violent crime, and that the proposed strategy is to increase the rates and terms of imprisonment of persons convicted of crimes of violence. In order to assess the likely efficacy and efficiency of that strategy, we need to be able to predict, amongst other things, how potential offenders are likely to react to the strategy of increased rates and terms of imprisonment.[19]

A prediction of what will happen in the future expresses or implies a judgement of probability on a scale from 0 to 1 (where 1 represents certainty and 0 represents impossibility). Such judgements of probability express the degree of belief or level of

[17] Defensive behaviour seems to fall into the latter category.

[18] Of course, people typically have multiple objectives which may conflict with one another. I address this issue in the next section.

[19] For a review of recent relevant research see A. von Hirsch, A.E. Bottoms, E. Burney, and P-O. Wikström, *Criminal Deterrence and Sentence Severity* (Hart Publishing, Oxford, 1999).

conviction on the part of the person making the judgement that the predicted event will occur. If a decision-maker assigns a probability of 1 to a future event, we can say that the decision-maker is certain that the event will occur. If the decision-maker assigns a probability to the event of between 0 and 1, they can be said to believe that there is a risk that the event will occur. If the decision-maker cannot assign a probability to the event, we can say that they are uncertain whether the event will occur or not. In terms of practical reasoning, we can say that decisions about what to do may fall to be made under conditions of certainty, conditions of risk, or conditions of uncertainty, depending on the decision-maker's judgement of the probabilities of the various uncontrollable factors which may have an impact on the strategy chosen to achieve the desired objective.

Ability to predict the future effect of uncontrollable factors is a function of knowledge about the past operation of such factors. Knowledge about the past may be acquired in a variety of ways, ranging from 'rigorous' scientific experimentation, in which all factors (or 'variables') in a process which may contribute to the outcome, except one, are held constant, while the operation of that one factor, and the outcome, are observed; through less rigorous historical, anthropological, or sociological research techniques which seek to isolate the operation of one contributing factor, without holding all other contributing factors constant, by making allowances for the operation of those other factors; to simple observation of contributing factors as, and in whatever context, they occur. In general, the more rigorous the technique by which we acquire our knowledge of the past, the more reliable will that knowledge be as a basis for predicting the future, and the more confident we can be in making such predictions. It does not follow that less rigorous techniques of observation may not generate sound predictions.[20] But the more contributing factors there are involved in the process being examined, the more rigorous our methods of observation need to be in order to generate reliable predictions. Consider again the example of adopting the strategy of increasing rates and terms of imprisonment with the objective of reducing the incidence of violent crime. To the extent that our knowledge of the past does not enable us to isolate the effects of the strategy of increasing rates and terms of imprisonment from the effects of other factors in the process which might have contributed to any decrease in violent crime, any judgement of the likely efficacy of the chosen strategy will be unreliable. Unfortunately, it is typically the case that many factors contribute to the sort of processes to which consequence-based judicial policy arguments refer; and such processes are rarely amenable to rigorous scientific methods of observation. To the extent that our predictions about the future lack support in relevant and reliable knowledge about the past, they will be speculative and intuitive.

The idea of judging the probability of future events in the light of knowledge of the past presupposes a distinction between unique events and events which occur, or

[20] The predictions that the sun will rise tomorrow, and that no human being will ever consume an adult elephant at one sitting, provide examples of good predictions supported by simple observation (concerning the latter see R.A. Posner, 'The Jurisprudence of Scepticism' (1988) 86 *Michigan LR* 827, 839, citing P. Klein, *Certainty: A Refutation of Scepticism* (Harvester, Brighton, 1981), 122).

can be made to occur, repeatedly ('repetitive events'). The classic example of a repetitive event is the toss of a coin. The probability of the various possible outcomes of a repetitive event (heads or tails in the case of a coin-toss) can be assessed by repeatedly observing the event. The more times the event occurs, and the more often the relative frequency of the various possible outcomes is observed, the more confident we can be in our assessment of the probability of those various outcomes. This is because the assessment is more rooted in 'objective' evidence.

In real life, we often want to assess the relative probability of the various outcomes of unique events. To a considerable extent, the art of politics is being able to persuade people that particular novel (and effectively non-repetitive) governing strategies will (probably) have particular outcomes. People can have varying degrees of confidence about the relative probabilities of the various possible outcomes of unique events. The important point to note is that such judgements, by definition, cannot be based on knowledge about the past occurrence of such events. This is important for practical reasoning because unless our chosen strategy is one which can be repeated, any judgement of the likely impact on the strategy of uncontrollable factors will be speculative and intuitive.

To summarize, under the model I have outlined, sound practical reasoning involves choosing the most efficient strategy for achieving desired objectives in the light of what is known about the likely operation of uncontrollable factors. The more we know about the past operation of relevant uncontrollable factors, the better our practical reasoning is likely to be. In circumstances where our knowledge of the past operation of uncontrollable factors is insufficient to enable us to predict their likely future operation, any such prediction will be speculative and intuitive and will, for that reason, provide an unreliable basis for deciding what to do.

This model of practical reasoning can be used both descriptively and normatively. Psychological research (to which I shall refer later) casts doubt on its accuracy as a description of human decision-making. Normatively, many might want to say that if anyone should use good arguments about the consequences of their decisions, judges should.[21] However, at this stage in the analysis, I take no stand on this normative issue. My only concern is to consider whether the overkill argument, as typically used by judges, is a good one in terms of this model of practical reasoning. This seems an appropriate question to ask because adoption of the model is at least consistent with, and is perhaps even presupposed by, the use of empirically testable, consequence-based arguments in practical reasoning. Consequence-based arguments appeal to

[21] The legitimacy of judicial law-making depends greatly on the soundness of the reasoning by which it is supported. The use of speculative consequence-based arguments about human behaviour in a largely rhetorical way by elected lawmakers may be thought more acceptable because their job is to give effect to their ideological values in a way and to an extent which is not true of judges. In our private lives, speculation about the likely consequences of our decisions is normally an acceptable decision-making procedure. In other words, it may be that the acceptability of speculative arguments about behavioural consequences is a function of the role of the person making the argument and the social context in which the argument is being used.

knowledge of the way the world works, and the model provides a criterion for good decision-making based on such arguments.

THE OVERKILL ARGUMENT AND GOOD PRACTICAL REASONING

(i) The Empirical Content of the Overkill Argument

Viewing the overkill argument as an exercise in practical reasoning, the objective implicit in the use of the argument is to avoid any increase in the amount of defensive behaviour as a result of the outcome of the case at hand. Courts have only two relevant strategies from which to choose—either to impose liability or not.[22] The problematic aspect of the overkill argument concerns the likely impact of uncontrollable factors on the achievement of the objective. Whether the imposition of liability will increase defensive behaviour depends partly on uncontrollable factors, including states of nature and strategic behaviour. If the court was convinced that the imposition of liability, combined with the operation of uncontrollable factors, would certainly not increase defensive behaviour, the overkill argument would obviously provide no good reason to decide in the defendant's favour. Conversely, if the court was convinced that the imposition of liability, combined with the operation of uncontrollable factors, certainly would increase defensive behaviour, then, given the objective implicit in the overkill argument, the argument would provide a sound *prima facie* reason to decide for the defendant. It is important to note that the overkill argument would provide only a *prima facie* argument against the imposition of liability. If we make the plausible assumption that, in addition to avoiding any increase in defensive behaviour, the court also desires objectives which could only be achieved by the imposition of liability, the overkill argument would only provide a conclusive argument against liability when coupled with a judgement that achieving the objective of avoiding any increase in defensive behaviour was more desirable than achieving such objectives as could be achieved by the imposition of liability, to whatever extent the court believes the imposition of liability would in fact achieve those objectives.[23] In other words, the overkill argument implies (as previously noted) an optimum balance between the scope of liability and the amount of defensive behaviour.

If the court thought that there was a risk (somewhere between 0 and 1) that the imposition of liability, coupled with the operation of uncontrollable factors, would increase defensive behaviour, it would be faced with a complex calculation. Again, making the plausible assumption that, in addition to the objective of not increasing defensive behaviour, the court also desires objectives which could only be achieved by

[22] For this reason, courts are not confronted with the problem that it may not be easy or indeed possible to identify all available strategies.

[23] Assessing the extent to which the imposition of liability would be likely to achieve the objectives sought by doing so might present problems analogous to and just as difficult as those involved in assessing the likely impact on the amount of defensive behaviour of the imposition of liability.

the imposition of liability, it would have to balance the importance of avoiding an increase in defensive behaviour, and the probability of achieving that objective, against the importance of the objectives which could be achieved by the imposition of liability, and the probability of achieving those objectives.

Analysing the overkill argument in this way reveals difficulties additional to that of predicting the likely operation of relevant uncontrollable factors. One is the need to attach values to the various conflicting objectives of the decision-maker. If a court is to assess the strength of the overkill argument, it needs to decide the relative importance of avoiding an increase in defensive behaviour on the one hand, and of achieving the desirable objectives which could be achieved by the imposition of liability on the other. This is a normative, not an empirical, issue. Another difficulty is that of measuring the achievement of desired objectives. In the case of defensive behaviour, there are two problems: the first is to establish a baseline from which to judge whether there has been an increase in such behaviour (or, in other words, to decide how much relevant defensive behaviour is occurring at the time the decision falls to be made); and the second is to establish criteria for measuring increases in defensive behaviour. In principle, these measurement issues are empirical, not normative.[24] But it seems clear they might be very difficult to resolve in a rigorous way.

The argument in this section can be summarized by saying that a proper assessment of the soundness of the overkill argument would require the resolution of three empirical issues: assessment of the likely operation of relevant uncontrollable factors; measurement of the amount of relevant defensive behaviour occurring at the time the decision for or against liability falls to be made; and specification of criteria for measuring increases in defensive behaviour.

(ii) Establishing the Empirical Content of the Overkill Argument

Recall that there are two versions of the overkill argument. The 'stronger version' says that a decision in favour of the plaintiff *will* provoke defensive behaviour, and the 'weaker version' asserts the existence of a *risk* that a decision in favour of the plaintiff will provoke defensive behaviour—although courts typically do not attempt to quantify the risk of defensive behaviour even in rough terms. Both versions imply a judgement of the probability that a specified event—the strategy of imposing liability—will produce a specified outcome—an increase in defensive behaviour. As noted earlier, the distinction between unique and repetitive events is important to an assessment of the probability of uncontrollable factors. Whether the relevant event is unique or repetitive depends partly on how it is defined. If defined as 'the imposition or non-imposition of liability in the case at hand' it is clearly unique. But if we define it as laying down, or not laying down, a rule which would support the imposition of liability in the case at hand, it may be a repetitive event if courts in more than one jurisdiction have been faced with the decision whether or not to lay down the rule in

[24] Remember that I am assuming an agreed definition of defensive behaviour.

question. If the event were defined as (for instance) 'expanding the scope of the liability of surgeons', it is even more likely to be repetitive. However, the more widely the event is defined, the higher the value which must be placed on avoidance of an increase in defensive behaviour if achievement of that outcome is to be judged more desirable than the achievement of outcomes which would require the imposition of liability. For instance, it would be harder (other things being equal) to justify using the overkill argument as a reason for never expanding the scope of the liability of surgeons than to justify its use as a reason for not expanding the liability of surgeons by deciding a particular claim against a surgeon in favour of the plaintiff. Although it is not always made clear, the event which courts who use the overkill argument seem most often to have in mind is the laying down of a rule which would justify the imposition of liability in the case at hand.

In this light, we can state the empirical thrust of the stronger version of the overkill argument in the following terms:

> Laying down the rule which would support the imposition of liability on the defendant in this case will provoke increased defensive behaviour on the part of the defendant and others similarly placed.

Note that this strong form of the argument is not problematic merely because it *is* strong. Events can produce outcomes with such regularity that, despite any logical qualms we might have about the validity of inductive reasoning,[25] for all practical purposes it is rational to treat the outcome as certain to follow from any individual occurrence of the event. The rising of the sun is a good example. But the less often a particular event has, to our knowledge, produced a particular outcome, the less justified we are, as a matter of practical reasoning, in treating the outcome as certain to follow from any occurrence of the event. Moreover, if, to our knowledge, a particular event has occurred, even if only once, without producing the outcome in question, we would not be justified in treating that outcome as certain to follow from any particular occurrence of the event. The validity of the strong form of the overkill argument depends on how frequently and regularly the laying down of the rule in question has provoked defensive behaviour. In order to justify a statement that laying down the rule will certainly provoke defensive behaviour, it would have to be shown that the laying down of such a rule in the past had always provoked defensive behaviour. Alternatively, if there were instances of the laying down of the rule which had not provoked defensive behaviour, it would have to be shown that such instances were explicable by reference to some factor absent from all situations in which the laying down of the rule had provoked defensive behaviour, and that the factor in question was absent from the situation in which the court's decision would take effect.

A major problem in validating the strong form of the overkill argument (in particular) resides in the distinction between association and causation. Even if it could be shown that every instance of the laying down of the rule in question had been

[25] A helpful discussion of the philosophical 'problem' of induction is the article 'Induction' by Max Black in P. Edwards (ed.), *The Encyclopedia of Philosophy* (Macmillan, New York, 1967).

followed by an increase in defensive behaviour, it would not follow that the laying down of the rule was a cause of the increase in defensive behaviour. In theory, in order to justify the conclusion that the laying down of the rule was a cause of the increase, it would be necessary to hold all other possibly contributing factors constant while varying that factor. In practice, it would be almost impossible to do this in relation to the impact of legal rules on human behaviour.

Of course, it does not follow from the practical impossibility of establishing the validity (or invalidity) of the overkill argument in a rigorous experimental way that we might not find support for it by using less rigorous anthropological or sociological techniques (such as well-designed questionnaires and surveys). However, such techniques, being less rigorous, are less likely to establish the validity (or non-validity) of the strong form of the overkill argument. On the other hand, such techniques might provide empirical support for the weaker form of the argument which asserts that there is a risk that the imposition of liability in the case at hand will provoke an increase in defensive behaviour. In relation to medical malpractice litigation, for instance, there is a certain amount of empirical evidence to support the conclusion that the imposition of liability on doctors in respect of the way they treat their patients generates a risk of defensive behaviour on the part of doctors resulting from the threat and fear of being sued.[26] From the present point of view, however, such evidence suffers from at least two serious failings. For one thing, all it seems to establish is that, faced with the risk of incurring legal liability, doctors may act defensively. It does not establish, in relation to any particular legal rule, that the laying down of that rule has generated an increase in defensive behaviour. Indeed, such evidence as we have about the effects of particular changes in the law which have expanded the scope of the liability of doctors is that either they have had little or no effect on the behaviour of those to whose conduct the new rule was directed, or they have generated compliance (as opposed to over-compliance or defensive behaviour).[27] We might postulate a link between particular expansions in the scope of liability and defensive behaviour by saying that all expansions of liability increase the threat and fear of being sued; and from this conclusion argue that any increase in the threat and fear of being sued will provoke an increase in defensive behaviour. However, there is no evidence of such a link between particular expansions in the scope of liability and increases in the likelihood of being sued. On the other hand, for instance, there was a very substantial increase in medical negligence litigation in Britain in the 1980s and 1990s but without any significant increase in the scope of the liability of doctors.[28] Indeed, over that period, the legal rules governing the scope of medical liability remained practically unchanged. The empirical evidence, then, does not support even

[26] Dewees, Duff and Trebilcock, n. 14 above, 104–6. See also P. M. Danzon, *Medical Malpractice: Theory, Evidence and Public Policy* (Harvard University Press, Cambridge, Mass., 1985), 146–9.

[27] Dewees, Duff and Trebilcock, n. 14 above, 107–8.

[28] It might be argued that the House of Lords effectively jettisoned the *Bolam* test in *Bolitho* v. *City and Hackney Health Authority* [1998] AC 232 in favour of a test more likely to justify the imposition of liability on doctors. Even if this is correct, it does not invalidate the argument in the text because the noted increase in medical malpractice litigation predated the decision in *Bolitho*.

the weaker version of the overkill argument in the form in which it is typically deployed (that is, as a reason for not imposing liability in the case at hand).

The second serious failing of the existing empirical evidence is that it does not enable us to assess the magnitude of the risk of defensive behaviour or to measure levels of defensive behaviour. This is a problem because, although the validity of the weaker form of the overkill argument does not depend on precise quantification of the probability of an increase in defensive behaviour or of its likely magnitude, its strength does depend on making rough assessments of both of these factors. If there were only a small risk of a small increase in defensive behaviour, the overkill argument would be much less potent than if there were a large risk of a large increase in defensive behaviour, given that courts who deploy the overkill argument also desire objectives which could only be achieved by the imposition of liability. No matter how highly the objective of avoidance of an increase in defensive behaviour is valued, the strength of the overkill argument still depends on the ability to make some assessment of the probability and likely size of any such increase. As far as I can see, such empirical evidence as we have does not give us that ability.

My conclusion, then, is that the little empirical evidence we have about the relationship between 'defensive medicine' and the scope of legal liability provides no significant support for the overkill argument in that context, in either its weaker or its stronger form. In fact, the evidence does not enable us to make any statement one way or the other about the propensity of any particular obligation-imposing legal rule to provoke defensive medicine. We simply do not know enough to make such statements. Moreover, there is no reason to think that the shortcomings of the empirical evidence about the prevalence of defensive medicine are not shared by existing empirical evidence about defensive behaviour in other contexts. It seems fair to say that, because of lack of reliable information about the effects of legal rules on individual conduct, judges have no good grounds for treating either the stronger or the weaker version of the overkill argument as valid in terms of what we know about the behavioural consequences of legal rules. We cannot say, of course, that the overkill argument, at least in its weaker form, is invalid. Rather, we simply do not know whether it is valid or not.[29] In other words, the decision whether to impose liability or not falls to be made under conditions of uncertainty about the likely behavioural effects of the decision because the information we have on this issue does not enable us to assess the probability that the imposition of liability (in any particular case) will provoke an increase in defensive behaviour. Any such judgment of probability will necessarily be speculative and intuitive.

This conclusion brings us to the following question: if use of the overkill argument cannot be justified by reference to what we know about the behavioural effects of legal rules, can it be defended at all?

[29] As a result, judges deciding the same case can assess the strength of the overkill argument differently without fear of being proved wrong. An illuminating example is *Spring* v. *Guardian Assurance Plc* [1995] 2 AC 296, discussed by Robertson, n. 7 above, 145–55.

EXPLAINING AND JUSTIFYING SINGLE-FACTOR CONSEQUENCE-BASED ARGUMENTS IN CONDITIONS OF UNCERTAINTY

The question just posed is of very great importance not only in the context of judicial reasoning, but much more generally, because many of the most important decisions about what to do in life fall to be made in conditions of uncertainty about the likely impact of relevant uncontrollable factors. How, it might be asked, can it be rational for a person to make a decision about what to do on the basis of the likely consequences of the various strategies open to them, in circumstances where they are uncertain about what the consequences of their conduct will be? This question is acutely pertinent to the overkill argument because, as we have seen, we have no reliable evidence either for or against the validity of the argument, or which would enable us to quantify, even roughly, the probability that any particular legal ruling will provoke defensive behaviour.

Psychologists have been investigating human decision-making in conditions of uncertainty for many years,[30] and have identified a number of techniques (called 'heuristics') commonly used to make decisions in such conditions. Three well-established heuristics which may be involved in thinking about the probability of future events are availability, representativeness, and anchoring and adjustment. Availability refers to assessment of the probability of an event according to the ease with which the decision-maker can recall occurrences of the event in question or can imagine the event.[31] For instance, a person may put a high estimate on the risk of their child being abducted or murdered as a result of such incidents receiving a lot of publicity and so being easy to recall. Causal thinking is important in the process of imagining events: the more and the stronger the reasons a person is given or can construct for the occurrence of a particular event as a result of particular circumstances, the higher the probability they are likely to attribute to the occurrence of that event as a result of those circumstances (we might call this the 'plausibility heuristic').[32] Representativeness refers to a mental process which involves something like stereotyping.[33] For instance, someone may judge the probability that a person described to them falls into a particular category, such as lawyer, not by reference to

[30] For a good summary of research in the period 1983–91 see J.W. Payne, J.R. Bettman, and E.J. Johnson, 'Behavioural Decision Research: A Constructive Processing Perspective' (1992) 43 *Annual Review of Psychology* 87.

[31] A. Tversky and D. Kahneman, 'Availability: A Heuristic for Judging Frequency and Probability' (1972) 5 *Cognitive Psychology* 207; A.S. Levi and J.B. Pryor, 'Use of the Availability Heuristic in Probability Estimates of Future Events: The Effects of Imagining Outcomes versus Imagining Reasons' (1987) 40 *Organizational Behaviour and Human Decision Processes* 219.

[32] A. Tversky and D. Kahneman, 'Extensional Versus Intuitive Reasoning: The Conjunction Fallacy in Probability Judgment' (1983) 90 *Psychological Review* 293, 308; 'The Simulation Heuristic' in D. Kahneman, P. Slovic, and A. Tversky (eds.), *Judgment under Uncertainty: Heuristics and Biases* (Cambridge University Press, Cambridge, 1982), chap. 14.

[33] D. Kahneman and A. Tversky, 'On the Psychology of Prediction' (1973) 80 *Psychological Review* 237.

the proportion of lawyers in the population but according to how well the description of the person fits their image of lawyers. Anchoring and adjustment is a process in which some value (which might be the probability of an event) is estimated by adjustment of a previously given or estimated value rather than independently. In one experiment, for example, people gave preference to the asking price for a piece of real estate over other relevant information in estimating its value.[34]

Research has shown that use of decision-making techniques such as these can result in estimates of probability which diverge from probability values arrived at by statistically valid techniques; and, for this reason, they are sometimes referred to as 'biases' in decision-making. However, it is also recognized that such heuristics are used in making judgements of the probability of future events in circumstances where, because of lack of information, statistically-based assessments of probability are unavailable or unreliable. In such circumstances, instead of treating such heuristics as biases, would it be possible to treat them as alternatives to statistical techniques? Putting the matter more crudely, can heuristics, such as representativeness and availability, explain how people (such as judges using empirically testable consequence-based arguments) guess probabilities in circumstances where there is no alternative to guessing?

At the descriptive level, this is an impossible question to answer (except by guessing) because, as far as I am aware, psychological research provides no evidence on which an answer could be based. By reference to the availability and anchoring-and-adjustment heuristics, for instance, we might hypothesize that a judge who has recently heard anecdotal claims by doctors that they have engaged in defensive medicine may be led to put a high estimate on the probability of defensive behaviour in response to the case before the court, even in the absence of any statistically valid support for such a judgement. We might also hypothesize that judges who use the overkill argument are good at thinking of reasons why potential defendants might react defensively to obligation-imposing legal rules, and so are likely to put a high estimate on the probability of such behaviour.[35] But there is no 'objective' evidence for such hypotheses.

There are various other decision-making criteria which, it has been suggested, people use to deal with uncertainty about future outcomes. For example, it is argued that in conditions of uncertainty, people who are optimistic by nature tend to estimate the probability of desired outcomes more highly than people who are pessimistic by nature;[36] and that people who favour a particular strategy on moral grounds, based on concepts such as fairness, rights, or duties, tend to favour the strategy regardless of the statistical probability that it will produce the desired out-

[34] G.R. Northcraft and M.A. Neale, 'Experts, Amateurs and Real Estate: An Anchoring and Adjustment Perspective on Property Pricing Decisions' (1987) 39 *Organizational Behaviour and Human Decision Processes* 84.

[35] An 'empathy heuristic'?

[36] J Baron, *Judgment Misguided: Intuition and Error in Public Decision Making* (Oxford University Press, New York, 1998), 11–13.

come.[37] We might hypothesize, therefore, that judges who use the overkill argument tend to be pessimistic about the rationality of those to whom obligation-imposing legal rules are directed; or that they use the overkill argument, despite the lack of evidence to support it, to bolster the outcome which they favour on grounds unrelated to expected consequences.[38] Put crudely, we might hypothesize that the probability of a defensive reaction to a decision for the plaintiff will seem higher to a judge who is inclined to deny liability for reasons unrelated to expected consequences than to one who favours the imposition of liability for such reasons.[39] Again, however, in the absence of evidence to support such hypotheses, it would be unsafe to accept any of them as a good explanation of consequence-based judicial reasoning in conditions of uncertainty.

At a normative level, the question is: what criteria of acceptability should we apply to single-factor, empirically testable consequence-based arguments which rest on judges' intuitive guesses about the probability that people will react in certain ways to obligation-imposing legal rules addressed to them? To the extent that reliable evidence relevant to the validity of a consequence-based argument is available, it might seem reasonable to expect courts to take steps to apprise themselves of it. On the other hand, acquiring knowledge of such evidence is a costly exercise, and English courts have traditionally been unwilling to engage in lengthy empirical inquiries about the likely consequences of their decisions. However, if a court allows sound and relevant evidence about likely behavioural consequences to be adduced, it should be unacceptable for the court then to support its decision with uninformed judgements of the probability of such consequences.

[37] Ibid. 103–8. For an illuminating discussion of the failure of the US Supreme Court to use sound empirical evidence about the behaviour of juries see J.A. Tanford, 'The Limits of Scientific Jurisprudence: The Supreme Court and Psychology' (1990) 66 *Indiana LR* 53.

[38] This hypothesis perhaps finds some support in the fact that the overkill argument (as a result of its having been used by appeal courts) has acquired a sort of authority, independent of its empirical validity, as a policy factor weighing against the imposition of tort liability in a variety of circumstances. The position seems to have been reached where merely stating the overkill argument is considered sufficient to establish its validity: e.g. *Phelps* v. *Hillingdon BC* [1999] 1 All ER 421, 442 *per* Stuart-Smith LJ, J. Monahan and L. Walker, 'Empirical Questions Without Empirical Answers' [1991] *Wisconsin LR* 569 recommend that 'unsupported empirical assertions, if otherwise plausible . . . be treated like precedential authority' (593). The authors offer no criterion of 'plausibility'. For a suggestion see P.E. Meehl, 'Law and the Fireside Inductions (with Postscript): Some Reflections of a Clinical Psychologist' in M.L. Levine (ed.), *Law and Psychology* (Dartmouth, Aldershot, 1995) 27–8.

[39] 'courts . . . ought to think very carefully before resorting to public policy considerations which will defeat a claim that ex hypothesi is a perfectly good cause of action. It has been said that public policy should be invoked only in clear cases in which the potential harm to the public is incontestable, [and] that whether the anticipated harm to the public will be likely to occur must be determined on tangible grounds instead of on mere generalities . . . Even if one should put the matter in a more neutral way, I would say that public policy ought not to be invoked if the arguments are evenly balanced: in such a situation the ordinary rule of law, once established, should prevail': Lord Lowry in *Spring* v. *Guardian Assurance Plc* [1995] 2 AC 296, 326. In this passage, which addresses the argument that the imposition of liability for a negligent employment reference might provoke defensive behaviour on the part of employers asked to give references, his Lordship contrasts consequence-based arguments ('public policy') and non-consequence-based considerations ('a perfectly good cause of action'), and acknowledges the existence and importance of the probability issue.

A stronger position would be that consequence-based arguments should be used by courts in support of imposing or not imposing liability (as the case may be) only if, and to the extent that, they are supported by statistically valid evidence. However, given the pervasiveness of speculative consequence-based reasoning in all walks of life, we would need a very strong argument to justify requiring judges to eschew such reasoning entirely. A different, and more realistic, approach would be that judges should openly acknowledge that consequence-based arguments, made in conditions of uncertainty about likely consequences, must inevitably be based on decision-making heuristics and criteria which do not depend on knowledge of likely consequences. Just as judges have increasingly, in the last fifty years, become willing to acknowledge openly that they make law as well as apply it, so also it would be desirable for them to acknowledge openly that consequence-based arguments made in conditions of uncertainty are inevitably based on considerations unrelated to likely consequences. It is a good thing for judges to acknowledge explicitly that obligation-imposing legal rules are designed to affect, and may have effects on, the behaviour of those to whom they are directed; but it is not a good thing for judges to support decisions for or against the creation of an obligation-imposing rule (or, indeed, any other type of rule) by arguments about the likely consequences of the rule which are unsupported by evidence.[40]

Of course, such an open acknowledgment of the impact of ignorance on the validity of consequence-based arguments is only the beginning of wisdom. It must be supplemented by criteria of good decision-making in conditions of uncertainty. If we do not know what the consequences of various available strategies will be, we need criteria for the choice of strategy which do not assume such knowledge. In the legal context, the task of developing such criteria is of great importance given pervasive ignorance about the behavioural consequences of legal rules. One possible approach would be to ask whether some or all of the various decision-making heuristics identified by psychologists might not themselves provide acceptable decision-making criteria in the face of uncertainty about consequences. Such an approach would have the virtue of rescuing consequence-based reasoning in conditions of uncertainty from a blanket charge of 'irrationality'. On a completely different tack, we could concentrate on developing decision-making criteria which address the intrinsic value of competing strategies rather than their expected consequences. In fact, much judicial reasoning pursues precisely this project, as do the many varieties of non-consequentialist ethical theory. Either approach is bound to generate much controversy. What does seem clear, however, is that ignorance about the likely behavioural consequences of

[40] In *Perrett* v. *Collins* [1998] 2 Lloyd's Rep. 255 Buxton LJ said of the overkill argument (and certain other consequence-based arguments against liability), as used in relation to alleged negligence of an aircraft safety inspector: 'the Court should be very cautious before reaching or acting on any conclusions that are not argued before it in the way in which technical issues are usually approached, with the assistance of expert evidence' (276–7). An important question which I cannot pursue here is whether open acknowledgment that much consequence-based legal reasoning lacks empirical support would result in cases being decided differently. For instance, would courts be more willing to impose liability on doctors if they openly acknowledged the empirical weakness of the overkill argument?

legal rules raises serious questions about how the use of consequence-based 'policy' arguments in conditions of uncertainty can be justified.

CONCLUSION

Single-factor, empirically testable consequence-based arguments (such as the overkill argument) are a common feature of judicial reasoning. Many such arguments imply estimates of the probability of future events in conditions of uncertainty—that is, in the absence of evidence which would enable such probabilities to be quantified, even roughly. To the extent that this is the case, the validity (or invalidity) of such arguments cannot depend on knowledge of likely consequences. When evidence is available to support single-factor consequence-based arguments, courts should use it or give reasons why it should be ignored (such as the expense of adducing it). When evidence is available to support a single-factor, consequence-based argument but is not used, or when supporting evidence is unavailable, courts should openly acknowledge that the argument does not rest on knowledge of likely consequences, and should attempt to articulate its underpinnings.

If the basic thrust of this conclusion is correct, it has implications for consequence-based reasoning more generally. To the extent that a decision-maker is ignorant of the likely consequences of the decision to be made, consequence-based reasoning (in any context) cannot be rationally supported by appeal to knowledge of likely consequences. One of the touted attractions of consequence-based reasoning over reasoning which is not based on expected consequences is that the former offers an objective criterion of decision-making which the latter cannot. Even if it be agreed that reasoning which is not based on expected consequences cannot be objective in any important sense,[41] I would argue that the promise of objectivity cannot be made good by consequence-based decision-making criteria to the extent that we are ignorant about the likely consequences of our conduct. But this is a large claim which cannot be defended here.

[41] For a powerful statement to the contrary see M. Smith, *The Moral Problem* (Blackwell, Oxford, 1994).

Perspectives on Causation

Jane Stapleton*

1. ABSTRACT

In this essay I offer a new understanding of the nature of causation and of the nature of legal disputes about causation in particular. Contrary to traditional rhetoric, most of these disputes centre not on a dispute of fact but on competing perspectives on agreed facts. Of the various factors that can affect a person's choice of perspective in the context of private and criminal law, notions of individual responsibility are central. Legal analysis, particularly in judgments, should confront this phenomenon explicitly. The essay ends by proposing an analytical approach that would facilitate this.

2. TWO LEVELS OF ENQUIRY

The term 'causation' is used to convey the results of two types of enquiry. The 'first-level' enquiry concerns 'how things came about'. This is a genuine question of fact in the sense that there exists a single correct answer to it. Take the following example: two hunters carelessly shoot into a wood, both bullets hitting a beater who dies, the medical evidence being clear that either shot would have been sufficient to kill.

To describe what happened in full we would need to include:

- A list of all the factors necessary for it to have occurred (but-for factors)—including, for example, the presence of the victim at the relevant spot in the wood, gravity, the decisions of the great-grand-mothers of the victim to have children and so on; plus
- A list of any factor present which, though not a but-for factor, would have been one had another factor/set of factors not been present (the so-called 'NESS'[1] factors)—including, for example, Hunter No. 1 shooting into the wood.

* I am most grateful to Peter Cane, Nils Jansen, Nigel Simmonds, and Helen Steward for helpful discussions. Particularly warm thanks go to Helen Beebee and Tony Honoré who generously gave extensive and constructive criticism on drafts of this essay.

[1] This test, that to be 'causally relevant' a factor must be a necessary element in a set of conditions jointly sufficient to produce the observed transition, was originally put forward by H.L.A. Hart and A.M. Honoré in *Causation in the Law* (Oxford University Press, Oxford, 1959). It has become known by the acronym coined by Richard Wright in his later version: 'Causation, Responsibility, Risk, Probability, Naked Statistics and Proof: Pruning the Bramble Bush by Clarifying the Concepts' (1988) 73 *Iowa Law Review* 1001. Honoré has described this version as 'only marginally different from ours': Tony Honoré, 'Necessary and Sufficient Conditions in Tort Law' in David Owen (ed.), *Philosophical Foundations of Tort Law* (Oxford University Press, Oxford, 1995) 363 (hereafter 'Honoré 1995') at 366 (see also 364).

The content of these lists is objective and does not depend on the perspective taken. They are independent of time frame and normative influences. If it were always true that by 'causation' we simply meant this first-level understanding and explanation of how things came about, it would be true to say that 'causation is a question of fact'.

We might be interested in this first level of enquiry for a number of reasons. The interest of scientists in knowing the full story of how things happened is obvious enough.[2] But some understanding of this 'full set' of relevant factors is also an implicit prerequisite to answering a distinct 'second-level' enquiry the answer to which is also often couched in causal language.

This is an enquiry that asks: what 'made a difference' in bringing about a specified transition between states. *The answer to this 'what made a difference' enquiry depends on the perspective through which the objective phenomenon is judged.* A crude analogy is how, viewed through a camera, which features stand out from the background depends on the focus setting we choose. In other words, in asking what 'made a difference' in bringing about a transition there is no one correct 'factual' answer because our judgement of what 'made a difference' changes according to the perspective from which we choose to ask the question in relation to the objective phenomenon. In light of this we can see why this second-level question of 'what made a difference', often labelled as a type of causation question, cannot be treated as a question of objective fact.[3]

We can also see that any answer to the second-level question of 'what made a difference' will treat some of the factors listed in the answer to the first enquiry (about how things came about) as forming merely the 'background' to factors selected as making a difference. This will be so even though it is true for most of these background factors that the transition would not have occurred without its presence.

We might be interested in this second level of enquiry for a number of reasons. The scientist might be interested in it in order to advise on how, in future, such transitions might be prevented or promoted.[4] For example, an agricultural scientist might investigate how it was that a crop fell over before the time for harvest. If she were to characterize fully how this came about she would cite all factors in the above two lists, including gravity. But in asking the more focused question of what had 'made a difference' (relative to the desired situation where the crop did not fall over) she would choose an analytical approach which, at the very least, would treat gravity as irrelevant.[5]

[2] Importantly, the fact that the beater's death was 'over-determined' does not detract from the scientist's understanding of the real-world transition to death because at this level of enquiry the scientist is not concerned to attribute moral responsibility or otherwise rank the explanatory potency of factors.

[3] Similarly there is no merit in the descriptive assertion that causal issues in past case law were merely 'factual' on which see the discussion in H.L.A. Hart and A.M. Honoré in *Causation in the Law* (2nd edn., Oxford University Press, Oxford, 1985) p. xxxiv and ff. It is another matter to promote, as this essay later does, the normative argument that legal analysis should be constructed so that this was achieved.

[4] Of course, it is not the case that every second-level enquiry is motivated by a concern to control some phenomenon in the future.

[5] Note that sound scientific method requires the scientist to record the parameters of her study in detail, including all assumptions and the (rationale for the) choice of comparator class. On the importance of choice of comparator class, see section 5 below.

A doctor investigating the factors producing a rare childhood leukæmia would similarly adopt an approach that enabled her to ignore the but-for factor of the child's parents' decision to have a child.

The form of most legal rules requires that the lawyer be interested in this second level of enquiry. Take private law and criminal law. Here it is typically a necessary but not sufficient precondition of legal liability that the defendant's conduct was a 'cause' of the transition about which the plaintiff or the State complains. More generally, the law typically[6] requires as a central (though not the only) prerequisite of liability that the defendant was individually responsible,[7] that his conduct is judged to have 'made a difference' in responsibility terms. As we will see, this 'did the defendant make a difference' issue has in the past sometimes found accommodation in the law under the conceptual label of 'causation' and sometimes elsewhere such as under the 'duty' idea and the unhappily-named[8] 'remoteness' concept.

3. THE NATURE OF LEGAL DISPUTES FRAMED AS DISPUTES ABOUT CAUSATION

Legal disputes that are framed as disputes about causation sometimes turn on the answer to the first-level enquiry of 'how things came about'. For example a liability dispute might turn on establishing that a particular pharmaceutical had the effect of blinding its users. The dispute being on a question of toxicological fact, it is addressed by scientific evidence.

But sometimes legal disputes that are framed as disputes about causation concern cases where the facts are agreed: here the dispute is really about the answer to the second-level enquiry of 'what made a difference' among those agreed facts. Such cases are intriguing to the legal theorist and of more pressing concern to appellate courts.[9] Take the following four classic examples regarded as problematic by moral philosophers and lawyers:

- Case 1 (see above): two hunters carelessly shoot into a wood, both bullets hitting a beater who dies, the medical evidence being clear that either shot would have been sufficient to kill.
- Case 2 (the desert traveller problem): Enemy No. 1 poisons V's water barrel. Later an unassociated Enemy No. 2 empties the barrel and V later dies of thirst.

[6] This essay does not address other types of legal rules, for example vicarious and other strict liabilities and those that require one party to insure another in relation to an outcome. See n. 17 below.

[7] By which, in this essay, I mean fault-based responsibility for behaviour (as in the concepts of negligence, recklessness, and intentional wrongful behaviour): see nn. 6 and 17. For individual responsibility to be argued, it is a necessary (see section 4) but not sufficient (see section 5) requirement that the defendant's behaviour be made to appear abnormal, and stand out from a background. Compare the notion of Hart and Honoré that a cause is an 'intervention' on the 'set stage': Hart and Honoré, n. 3 above, 35 and 74, on which see nn. 14 and 41 below.

[8] See section 9.

[9] It is rare for leave to appeal to be granted on a question of fact. Appellate cases 'on causation' typically involve cases of agreed facts.

- Case 3: a person, who voluntarily watered her elderly neighbour's orchids when the latter went away on holiday, omits to do so when the neighbour takes a holiday and the orchids die.
- Case 4: one person carelessly breaks another's leg but on the latter's way to hospital in an ambulance that vehicle is struck by lightning and the person is killed.

It is striking that we do not have difficulty understanding these situations in the sense of 'how things came about' because the facts are known. Indeed, if it was always true that by 'causation' we simply meant this first-level understanding of how things came about, then lawyers and philosophers would be wrong to describe the 'problem' in these four cases as a problem of causation. Indeed, the problem an ordinary citizen might see here is, if the parties agree on the facts, how can one argue before the court that the defendant was a cause and the other argue that he was not? This difficulty is overcome once it is appreciated that, despite the framing of the dispute in causal terms, the real dispute is about whether what the defendant had done was 'important', had 'made a difference' in responsibility terms.

Whether a defendant 'made a difference' is a matter of perspective. For example, from one perspective the conduct of Hunter No.1 can be seen as sufficient to kill the beater (who was alive the second before the bullet of that hunter hit him and dead the next) and therefore Hunter No.1 appears to have made a difference in responsibility terms in relation to the death. From another perspective that conduct can appear not to have made a difference at all to the death because the conduct of Hunter No.2 would have killed the beater anyway.

To sum up: those legal disputes framed as disputes about causation which are of most importance to legal theorists and appellate courts are disputes where the facts are agreed. Here the real nature of the dispute is about whether the defendant 'made a difference' in responsibility terms in relation to the outcome, and a necessary preliminary to judging whether a factor made a difference is a choice of perspective. From the fact that the dispute here is not about facts but about the choice of perspective from which to view these objective facts, we can understand why there is a need for the disputants explicitly to defend their choice of perspective.

4. MAKING A DIFFERENCE: THE CHOICE OF PERSPECTIVE

In this section I expand my central argument: that even where all the facts are agreed, there are choices in relation to the perspective from which to judge them in terms of whether a factor made a difference.

Take the hunters' case. Imagine for the moment, not a legal dispute about individual responsibility for the death, but a public policy debate among economists about the costs of accidents. The economist will not focus on the allocation of individual responsibility for past outcomes (they are 'sunk costs') but on the future allocation of wealth, or, as he might put it, 'allocative efficiency'. He wants to arrange social relations in a way that will optimize wealth, and he has an analytical approach that he believes can determine how to do this and what to take into account when analysing transitions.

This is the point to emphasize: that, in an allocative context,[10] it is the nature of what the person wants to allocate and the rules he regards as appropriately governing that distribution which will pinpoint for him the factors which 'make a difference' in a transition, and therefore the perspective he takes of the agreed facts.

Clearly, for this economist, gravity will be of no interest, even though it is part of the full story of how hunting accidents occur. In terms of his goal of the optimum allocation of the costs of hunting accidents, it cannot be a factor that makes a difference to that public policy question.

On the other hand, if the rules that he believes govern his allocative goal—let's say these are the 'cheapest cost avoider rules'—determine that the beater's presence is the factor which is the cheapest cost avoider (in the sense that removing beaters from woods would be a cost-effective move), this pinpoints the presence of the beater as something which 'made a difference' and therefore determines the perspective the economist takes on the facts. The economist's public policy advice, then, would be to ban the use of humans as beaters. If we forced the economist to couch that advice in causal language he would say that the presence of beaters in woods was a 'cause' of their deaths and of the associated costs.

Now staying with the hunters' case, let us imagine, not a public policy debate concerned with the allocation of wealth at the macro level, but a legal dispute about the allocation of individual responsibility for the death of a specific beater. The argument here is exactly the same: that it is the nature of what the person wants to allocate and the particular principles he regards as appropriately governing that distribution which will pinpoint for him the factors which make a relevant difference in cases of agreed facts. It is these principles which give him his perspective on the facts and will influence the causal usage he adopts as well as any 'causal tests' he might urge on a court.

In other words, in criminal and private law proceedings where the facts are agreed, such as the hunters' case, our views about individual responsibility determine which of the but-for/NESS factors relevant to the first enquiry (of how things came about) we think made a relevant difference and therefore which perspective we adopt. Though we agree that we are addressing the question of allocation of responsibility, we might each have different attitudes to individual responsibility, and therefore we might not agree about who had made a relevant difference. We might then go on to express this disagreement in different causal usage and urge different 'causal tests' on the court in order to facilitate the allocation of individual responsibility each of us has embraced.

For example, in the hunters' case there is no dispute about the facts. It is a problem of individual responsibility and how to manipulate a prerequisite of legal liability (couched in causal terminology) in such a way as to emphasize the pattern of

[10] There are, of course, other motives for 'what made a difference' enquiries: see n. 14 below.

responsibility desired.[11] In court the dispute is between those whose principles of individual responsibility regard neither hunter as responsible for the death and those whose (different) principles of individual responsibility regard each hunter as responsible (unless some ground for a defence or excuse is present). The first group can try to achieve exculpation of the hunters by urging the court to adopt a perspective, the but-for 'test of causation', which views the beater's prospects in the light of the other hunter's behaviour and delivers the result that the hunter's conduct did not make a difference. In contrast, those who have determined that individual responsibility should be imposed on both hunters (so long as other prerequisites are satisfied) can urge the court to adopt a perspective, enunciated as the so-called 'NESS test', which focuses on the impact the hunter's behaviour would have had on the victim's prospects in the absence of any impact of the abnormal behaviour of the other hunter (namely, sufficiency to kill): from this perspective the hunter's conduct clearly did make a difference.[12]

The point to note is that whether the individual hunter made a difference is not an objective fact: our answer to the question depends on the background against which we choose to ask it, the perspective we choose to take. That choice is not dictated by any natural law but by our views about individual responsibility, which are merely masked by the perspective we assert and the causal language we might use to express it.

There may well be good reasons for us to adopt one view on responsibility rather than another. The point to emphasize is that, whatever the dispute about the strength or weaknesses of these arguments about individual responsibility (and of any parallel policy arguments: see section 9), it is these arguments and their relative strengths that constitute the nature of the dispute in such cases, not a factual dispute about how things happened. Statements that a particular 'test of causation' 'captures the essence of the doctrine of causation',[13] as Richard Wright asserts about the NESS perspective, masks the true nature of the dispute here.

5. MAKING A DIFFERENCE: ABNORMALITY AND CHOICE OF COMPARATOR CLASS

Before the plaintiff can construct a case for individual responsibility, which, as we have seen, is typically one of the prerequisites of legal liability, she must at least make

[11] As noted throughout this essay, even if a plaintiff convinced the court that the defendant was *individually responsible* for the outcome this is not sufficient to establish that he should be legally *liable*: see section 9.

[12] Another device is the 'substantive factor test': a mere slogan behind which courts, seeking to impose responsibility (and also liability) for over-determined outcomes, sometimes shelter.

[13] Wright, n. 1 above, 1019. Indeed, no test can do this, given the multiple roles which causal 'packaging' serves: sometimes delivering scientific understanding about 'how things happened'; sometimes expressing the judgment about what had made a difference and thereby serving, in private and criminal law, as one of the prerequisites to the allocation of individual responsibility.

the defendant's conduct appear to be abnormal in some relevant way[14] even where that conduct constitutes a but-for relation to the outcome complained about. For example, in the context of civil or criminal responsibility it is hard to see how the decision of Lee Harvey Oswald's great-grandmother to have children was a factor that made a relevant difference in the assassination of President Kennedy in Dallas in 1963 because it does not even appear (and it is hard to see how it could be made to appear) to be abnormal in responsibility terms.

Establishing that the defendant's conduct was abnormal is a necessary prelude to the plaintiff establishing that the defendant made a difference in responsibility terms, though, as we will see in section 6, a defendant may concede that his conduct was abnormal but still argue that it did not make a difference in responsibility terms in relation to the outcome. [15] But in this section it is worth noting that in some legal disputes the defendant even disputes that his conduct should be seen as abnormal at all.

There are two ways in which disagreement on this 'abnormality' issue can arise. The first is straightforward. Take Case 3, the watering of orchids case. Our attitude to the elderly neighbour's claim that her neighbour, say D, was individually responsible for the death of the orchids would, no doubt, be crucially influenced by the pattern of past waterings by D. Had this occurred only once twenty years ago and never since then, even though the elderly person had gone on many holidays each year since that time, the attitude to the issue of responsibility would be significantly different from that in the case where D had over the previous twenty years watered the plants each and every time the elderly neighbour took her numerous holidays. But let us assume the facts are agreed: D watered them on each of the two holidays the elderly neighbour took over the past year. The issue of abnormality might at first seem to be an objective statistical one: is it normal behaviour for someone, who has watered plants in this way twice over the past year, to omit to do so the next time the neighbour takes a holiday? Of course, we do not have, nor will we ever collect, the

[14] While this appearance of abnormality is an essential prerequisite in the context of the allocation of individual responsibility, it is important to note that it is not necessarily essential in other types of 'what made a difference' enquiries. It is arguable, for example, that the beater's presence was not abnormal or an 'intervention', and yet the economist might pinpoint it as a factor which made a relevant difference in his enquiry into allocative efficiency. A clearer example is the following: say yesterday a medical scientist discovered that a necessary precondition to a child developing a particular type of leukæmia is that the mother had eaten pistachio nuts in the second trimester of her pregnancy. In the context of discussing and explaining the process by which disease befell today's sufferers (i.e. not in a context of the allocation of individual responsibility) we would, with this knowledge, now appreciate that the woman's conduct had 'made a difference'. Ordinary people might well express this in terms of the conduct being a 'cause' of the leukæmia. This is so even though it is hard to see how the conduct is abnormal or an 'intervention': contrast Tony Honoré, 'Medical Non-Disclosure, Causation and Risk: *Chappel* v. *Hart*' (1999) 7 *Torts Law Journal* 1 at 5, ' a cause is an intervention in the existing or expected course of events'.

[15] Moreover, if a person's behaviour was not relevant to the first-level enquiry of how the outcome came about—because it was neither a but-for nor NESS factor in relation to it—it will not be judged to have made a difference even if it is judged abnormal. For example, if a person is on the point of dying of a fatal and irreversible dose of poison the failure of another to go to his aid (even if this is itself perceived as a highly abnormal omission in the circumstances) is not part of the story of how the death came about and therefore cannot in any context be regarded as having 'made a difference' to the transition to death.

necessary data on this. All each of us can do is guess. But we might guess differently. Our guesses are influenced by the necessarily subjective experiences of life that each of us has had. Those who have mixed with the socially altruistic and reliable may guess one way, those who have mixed with fickle misanthropes may guess another way.

But there is a second, far more important, way the disagreement about abnormality can arise in case law. When we know that we are being asked the abnormality question in the context of a process of attribution of individual responsibility, our different notions of such responsibility will influence our 'guesses' in different ways. Indeed, because the answer to the abnormality question can vary according to the comparator group we choose, when the defendant says that his conduct was not abnormal it is less a genuine guess about what patterns of behaviour are actually like, and more an invitation to the court to look at this question in a way which will show that behaviour to be normal. In sum: the defendant's overall argument that he is not individually responsible may lead him to dispute that his conduct was abnormal at all. He will, therefore, urge on the court a perspective on the facts in relation to which his conduct appears normal. In contrast, as we have seen, the success of the plaintiff's construction of a responsibility argument depends on her choosing an appropriate comparator class relative to which the defendant's conduct does look abnormal. Here are some examples of this phenomenon.

First, where a newborn baby dies of starvation the conduct of the parents in failing ever to feed it is, as a matter of physical fact, identical to the behaviour of persons who have never met the child. From that perspective, that of the comparator class of citizens in general, it appears 'normal'. But according to our cultural consensus the primary responsibility to feed a child rests on its parents—a consensus reflected in practice. If, then, the State (in a criminal prosecution of the parents) or the child's estate (in a civil claim for damages) frames the case from the perspective which emphasizes parental status, the omission of the parents no longer looks normal. Looked at in the context of the narrow comparator class of parental behaviour, the parents' omission comes into focus as abnormal.[16]

For a second example, imagine a law is enacted which, starting on Tuesday, reverses the permitted direction of flow of a particular one-way street from east to west. Q is the first person to drive on that street on Tuesday but, having forgotten the new rule, Q drives eastwards along the street. He collides with the second car to be driven along that street that day, a car conforming to the new rule. The collision results in the death of the other driver (and the road is closed until the date of trial). From the perspective of objective physical fact, Q's behaviour is no different from that of the past behaviour of all other previous drivers. When the state prosecutes and the victim's estate sues Q, they will argue that Q was responsible for the death. To construct this argument they must urge the court to adopt a perspective from which, at the least, Q's behaviour appears abnormal. For Q's behaviour to emerge as abnor-

[16] What is more, we have social agreement on the issue of individual responsibility here, and this would also pinpoint the behaviour as having made a difference in responsibility terms.

mal they must use as the comparator class a hypothetical group of people driving on the road after Tuesday whose behaviour reflects the assumption that people normally (remember to) obey the law.

For a third example, let us look at how mental states, which are central to (though not exhaustive of) our notions of individual responsibility, can influence our choice of comparator class so that a factor appears abnormal. Say, for example, that X has hidden a detonator under a public footpath outside a police station. Many pedestrians walk across the footpath before one, D, innocently steps exactly on the spot necessary to trigger the detonator and its attached explosives. Many police are killed. The general view, no doubt, would be that D was not individually responsible for the deaths.[17] One technique D can use to present this argument to a court (if he was prosecuted or sued in relation to the deaths) is to urge that it adopt a perspective in which D's conduct is seen not to have been abnormal at all, and therefore not to have made a difference.[18] Formulating the comparator class as 'pedestrians walking across the pavement' ensures that D does not appear to be a factor that made a difference: D's conduct is not abnormal behaviour from this perspective; nor is an explosion within the normal consequences of such behaviour.

But let us change the non-physical facts slightly in a way that will change our attitude to the individual responsibility of the pedestrian. Say D* was not innocent but suspected a detonator and explosives were hidden somewhere under the pavement of the relevant street and walks along it in the hope and with the intention of triggering an explosion and killing people. D* happens to step on the relevant spot and triggers a lethal explosion. A likely view now would be that D* was individually responsible for the deaths. A legal finding in line with this responsibility view can be facilitated by feeding this mental element into the formulation of D*'s conduct ('a pedestrian walking across a pavement intending to detonate explosives under the pavement') and comparing it with a comparator class in which we now emphasize the mental innocence of the class: '*innocent* pedestrians walking across the pavement'. This ensures that D*'s conduct, physically identical to that of D, comes into focus as an abnormal factor that made a difference. In other words, it is because intention is so significant in responsibility terms, that we are led to see D*'s conduct as having made a difference and to construct the comparator class in such a way as to emphasize this element.

In practice the law allows the choice of comparator class to be manipulated by plaintiffs to a significant degree to ensure the defendant's conduct appears to be abnormal. This is most striking in omission cases where the plaintiff must also be particularly careful to construct her case in a way which establishes that she has been damaged. Let me explain. In legal rules where damage is the gist of the action the plaintiff must show that she has suffered 'damage', a notion which can only operate

[17] At least in any of the senses of individual responsibility reflected in criminal and private law (as I have defined it: see n. 7 above). I leave aside the question of outcome responsibility and the basis of strict liabilities, on which see Honoré, 'Responsibility and Luck' (1988) 104 *Law Quarterly Review* 530.

[18] Another technique is discussed in the following section: to concede that it may be abnormal conduct but to argue that it did not make a difference in terms of responsibility.

against a construction of what her prospects (or, as I have called them elsewhere, her 'normal expectancies'[19]) in life would otherwise have been. Clearly there is a large degree of guesswork required here, and this inevitably introduces the potential for subjectivity to creep in.

But more importantly, there is room for normativity also to affect the issue. In cases where the complaint is that D omitted to do X, the damage requirement forces the plaintiff to define the comparator class against which the defendant's conduct and plaintiff's prospects are assessed in such a way that it can be said that normally members of that class would do X. Say an asbestos manufacturer, D, omitted to install exhaust fans and employees suffered injury that the exhaust fans would have prevented. However, all other manufacturers in the asbestos industry had also failed to use the fans. If the comparator class of employers which is selected is the narrow class of asbestos manufacturers, D's conduct will not appear abnormal and P's normal expectancies would include that injury. It would then be hard for the plaintiff to explain how D's conduct had damaged the plaintiff's prospects and therefore how it had made a difference.

However, the plaintiff overcomes these difficulties if the comparator class is chosen to be, say, the wide class of citizens in general *and* it is judged that such a class would have used the fans had they been in the position of the manufacturer. Courts in industrial injury cases routinely accept this comparator class and reject the defence argument that the appropriate comparator class is that of like manufacturers ('industry practice').[20] This phenomenon highlights both the guesswork and therefore subjectivity involved in judgments about abnormality (and the sister concepts of 'prospects' and 'damage') in such cases and, more importantly, how they can be influenced by normative attitudes to individual responsibility via the manipulation of comparator classes. After all, the plaintiff's case turns on an assertion about what ordinary reasonable citizens would have done if they had been in the position of the asbestos manufacturer, something on which no data can exist. All we can do is guess. In such cases, the abnormality judgment will be irreducibly subjective as well as, given that there is a choice of plausible comparator classes, inevitably influenced by normative views about what the defendant *should* have done.[21]

[19] On this inter-relationship see J. Stapleton, 'The Normal Expectancies Measure in Tort Damages' (1997) 113 *Law Quarterly Review* 257.

[20] Another important example is where an employee is injured in circumstances where the injury would have been prevented had he worn a safety device which the defendant-employer concedes should have been provided. Where the evidence is that the relevant employee never chose to wear the device on the days it happened to be supplied, the defendant is free to argue that his own omission-to-supply did not make a difference because, but for the careless failure to provide the device, the employee would still have been injured because the employee would not have worn it. But the inventive plaintiff would urge the court to accept that a reasonable employer would not only have supplied the device but insisted on its use. Against a comparator class of reasonable employers defined in *this* way, the defendant's omission comes into focus as abnormal. Contrast *McWilliams* v. *Sir William Arrol & Co. Ltd.* [1962] 1 WLR 295 and *Bux* v. *Slough Metals Ltd.* [1974] 1 All ER 262.

[21] As well as being vulnerable to the criticism that the process can illegitimately lay down pace-setting standards of behaviour. See Stapleton, n. 19 above, 257, at 281. The same dynamic affects the recognition of duties of affirmative action and the approach to breach of duty.

6. THE PACKAGING OF THE 'MAKING A DIFFERENCE' ISSUE: AS CAUSATION; AS REMOTENESS; ETC.

We have seen that, before a plaintiff can construct an argument that the defendant was individually responsible for an outcome, she must at least be able to portray the defendant's conduct as abnormal. But as we have seen in section 5, in most real-world disputes it is not difficult for plaintiffs to construct a plausible argument that the defendant's conduct was abnormal.

Yet this will not be sufficient because the defendant might concede the abnormality of his conduct and still argue that it did not make a difference in relation to the outcome about which complaint is made. For example, in the hunters' litigation there would be no dispute that the conduct of each hunter should be seen as abnormal.[22] Rather, the dispute is about the perspective to take when asking whether that abnormal conduct of one hunter had made a difference in terms of responsibility for the death, given the beater would have died anyway. The desert traveller problem is of the same type (see Appendix). So too is the lightning case, where the dispute is unlikely to centre on whether carelessly breaking another's leg is abnormal but whether, in terms of individual responsibility for the victim's death, it made a relevant difference.[23]

At this point we can re-introduce the language of causation. In the previous two sections, where I discussed how our notions of individual responsibility could influence judgements about whether a factor made a difference (section 4) or was abnormal (section 5), I purposely avoided using causal language. At the outset I explained that causal terminology can be and is used to convey the results of both the factual

[22] The agreed 'fact' that they acted 'unreasonably' reflects this abnormality consensus. On the reasonableness standard being itself implicitly generated by comparing conduct with a comparator class (here presumably of other hunters): see Stapleton, n. 19 above, at 268.

[23] Here are some other examples. First, imagine that at the time she decided to have a child Lee Harvey Oswald's great-grandmother had been a nun. Using the comparator class of nuns such conduct will appear abnormal, a point she might be happy enough to concede. But were a prosecution or civil suit to be brought against her in relation to Kennedy's death she would, no doubt, succeed in her argument that her 'abnormal' conduct did not make a difference in responsibility terms in relation to the death: she had not acted carelessly or with the intention of facilitating murder etc. Secondly, consider the situation described in n. 14 above: the discovery that a necessary precondition to a childhood leukæmia is that the mother had eaten pistachio nuts in the second trimester of her pregnancy. If we used the comparator class of the behaviour of mothers once this discovery had been made and disseminated, the behaviour of mother in the past might well look abnormal (though why we would be interested in such a bizarre comparison is hard to see). Even so, *in the context of the allocation of individual responsibility* we would accept the argument of the past mothers that their behaviour, though a but-for relation to the leukæmia, had not made a relevant difference. A third example is this. Imagine a crowd of pedestrians watching a building burn down. Say we know as statistical facts that most ordinary citizens do not run into burning buildings to attempt to rescue those trapped, but most priests do. D, a priest, is present but does nothing to rescue those trapped. Judged against the class of ordinary citizens his conduct is normal. Compared to the class of priests it is abnormal. If sued in relation to the injuries suffered by those trapped (and assuming any attempt at rescue would have prevented these injuries), D might concede that his behaviour was abnormal and yet argue that, for responsibility reasons, it should not be seen as having made a relevant difference.

first-level enquiry of 'how things came about'; and the second-level enquiry about what made a difference in bringing about the relevant transition.

It is now important to note that the results of both types of enquiry may alternatively be delivered in other ways.[24] In particular, at the second level of whether a factor made a difference the parties can choose to express their dispute either in causal or in non-causal terms. For example, in the lightning case the underlying dispute is one of individual responsibility: should the careless D be responsible for the death? The basic argument of the plaintiff is that, in responsibility terms, D made a difference, whereas D argues that, although his conduct may appear abnormal, it is not a factor that made a difference in responsibility terms in relation to the death. However, within the current structure of legal reasoning this response of D, that D 'did not make a difference', may be couched in alternative ways in his defence to the statement of claim: that D was not a cause of the death; or that, even if D was a cause of the death, the death was 'too remote' a consequence of the careless act for it to be fair to hold D responsible for it.

Understanding these points allows us to understand why in many cases the current analytical legal categories of causation and remoteness appear interchangeable with one judge using causal language and another using remoteness to express the same underlying reasoning and outcome. This point also allows me to set out (in sections 7 and 8) the associated disagreement between legal theorists as to what causation in law does or should cover.

7. CAUSAL MINIMALISTS *V.* HART AND HONORÉ

Our two levels of enquiry may find accommodation in legal analysis in different configurations. For example, some (the causal minimalists) prefer the legal category known as causation to consist of no more than the first-level enquiry of what happened. Under this analytical configuration, a factor that satisfied a but-for relation to the outcome would qualify as a 'cause' and there would be 'no further causal question remaining for the courts to discuss'.[25] Great-grandmother Oswald would be a cause of Kennedy's death and her exculpation from legal liability would be worked out using another analytical concept such as remoteness of damage, in the terms of which the reasons why she is to be viewed as not making a difference in responsibility terms would be presented.

One advantage of this way of accommodating the two types of enquiry is that, under it, the legal category known as causation only concerns itself with issues of fact. An associated advantage of this configuration is that, under it, the enquiry relating to

[24] e.g. the scientist setting out the exhaustive first-level lists of factors which explain how something happened does not need to use causal language. Indeed, the first order task neither requires nor is illuminated by 'causal theories', let alone theories about responsibility. It does not require us to distinguish between or rank factors that contributed to the occurrence of the transition.

[25] Hart and Honoré, n. 1 above, 3.

whether a factor made a difference is conducted in terms of analytical categories in which normative arguments concerning individual responsibility are traditionally more acceptable, and in which judges are more accustomed to addressing them explicitly in their resolution of the dispute. As we have seen, the answer to the question of whether a but-for/NESS factor made a difference turns on such arguments.

For clarity in legal reasoning and consistency in determinations, these competing responsibility arguments should be exposed and the resulting choice of perspective defended. To allow the issue of whether a factor made a difference to be dealt with in terms of the analytical category of causation runs the large risk that such crucial normative arguments about individual responsibility will be suppressed under the slogan that causation is a question of fact: a slogan inappropriately imported from those situations where causal language is used to express the results of the first-level factual enquiry of how things came about into situations where causal language is being used to express the results of the second-order enquiry of what made a difference, to which there is no one correct 'factual' answer. The real nature of the dispute is masked and the judge is tempted merely to assert an outcome rather than address the normative responsibility dispute. In this light, the conceptual configuration reflected in the approach of the causal minimalists is attractive.

An alternative configuration is implicitly suggested by the insights of Hart and Honoré, though those authors did not explicitly extend their work directly to prescribing a particular analytical approach for judges. Hart and Honoré examined the way ordinary people used causal language and metaphors and found meaningful general patterns in this phenomenon.[26] They argued that the same patterns of meaningful usage could be observed in the case law: a result they expressed as 'it is the plain man's notions of causation . . . with which the law is concerned'.[27]

Hart and Honoré attacked the approach of the causal minimalists on two grounds. First, they attacked it for being at odds with this ordinary usage. Certainly, the approach of the causal minimalists generates a class of causes that is wildly over-inclusive by this common usage standard, because it includes as causes of a murder, for instance, the decision to have children by every blood-line ancestor of the murderer. It is unlikely[28] anyone would ever *say* great-grandmother Oswald was a cause of Kennedy's death, and it might be thought bizarre if a court concerned with individual responsibility were to do so.

Secondly, they attacked the claim of the causal minimalists to the effect that, apart from the what-happened enquiry, causal usage was 'a mere disguise for arbitrary

[26] Specifically: Hart and Honoré distinguished the question whether D was a 'causally relevant condition' (for which they preferred the NESS test to that of but-for: see Honoré 1995 at 364) from questions whether D was also a 'cause' of the consequence. They argued, *inter alia*, that general patterns of usage in relation to the latter were associated with whether the causally relevant condition was or was not accompanied by the intervention of later voluntary human conduct or conjunction of abnormal events: Honoré, n. 1 above, at 369.

[27] Hart and Honoré, n. 1 above, 1.

[28] Though, even here, not impossible: a person might say she was a cause but that she 'wasn't important' in a responsibility sense. One of the points of this essay is that any such variation in causal usage is irrelevant because there is a consensus that she did not make a difference in responsibility terms.

decision or judicial policy' and that all other issues should, therefore, be subsumed into the one normative question whether liability *ought* to be imposed (to be addressed under analytical categories other than the legal category of causation).[29] Again Hart and Honoré hit a nerve here. To the ordinary lawyer, just as much as to the ordinary citizen, the reason we do not call Mrs Oswald a cause is neither arbitrary nor an issue of expediency or policy. Moreover, it would seem odd to adopt an approach under which we would say that great-grandmother Oswald was a cause of Kennedy's death but that the reason she would not be held liable was merely because a court had decided that liability was not 'required by the "scope", "the purpose", or the "policy" of'[30] the legal rule.

Our discussion of the two types of enquiry gives us an insight into why Hart and Honoré's attack has such resonance. They had noticed that sometimes we use causal language to convey our judgements about what appears to have made a difference, something the law also is interested in and which courts have in the past also used causal language to convey. An approach to the legal category of causation that prevents causal language being used to express such judgements will seem artificial and not express 'the plain man's notions of causation'. Moreover, our consideration of the two types of enquiry has revealed that sometimes the disagreement about what made a difference does not hinge on issues of policy[31] but on our different notions of individual responsibility.

Despite the landmark insights of their work, the approach of Hart and Honoré's is limited in two significant respects. First, while their identification of abnormality as a factor lying behind causal usage was correct in the context of the allocation of individual responsibility,[32] they did not sufficiently emphasize the relativity of the notion of abnormality, and in particular the influences which might affect our associated choice of perspective on the facts. Moreover, they focused on areas of uniform usage, when for law the most troublesome cases are where the parties assert different causal usages. Let me say a little more about these two points.

8. LIMITATIONS OF HART AND HONORÉ

Uniform Usage

Hart and Honoré detected the theme of abnormality in causal usage, in particular that human conduct or events which are judged abnormal are often regarded as 'breaking the chain of causation' from a particular but-for 'intervention' to a consequence.[33] They were right to debunk the idea that the uniformity of causal language

[29] Hart and Honoré, n. 1 above, 3–4. [30] Ibid.

[31] On the interplay of individual responsibility arguments and policy arguments, see section 9 below.

[32] It does not hold in all the contexts in which ordinary people use causal language: see the pistachio/leukæmia example in n. 14 above.

[33] See n. 26 above. In my view, it is quite plausible that particular visions of individual responsibility might regard the voluntary conduct of others and freakish natural events as relevant. But my argument is

here was somehow either an arbitrary product of expediency or a 'policy' consensus. But our discussion of the two types of enquiry suggests that, even in cases where there seems to be uniform causal usage, as in the great-grandmother Oswald case, the uniformity does not derive from some objective notion of 'causal connection' but from a consensus view about individual responsibility which leads to a particular perspective on the facts being taken, under which the factor in question does not appear to have made a difference in relation to that death. In other words, whatever variations might exist between our sets of principles of individual responsibility, they have this in common: they do not pinpoint the conduct of Mrs Oswald as having made a difference.[34] Without even enunciating what these various sets of rules might be, this at least suggests the following common moral principle: that merely being a but-for/NESS factor in relation to an outcome is never sufficient reason for the imposition of the sort of individual responsibility which private law and criminal law impose.

Non-uniform Usage

Since Hart and Honoré focused on general patterns of causal usage their insights are of limited use in the context of legal disputes which, though framed as disputes about causation, arise from facts which are agreed. This is because they do not address the two most troubling features of such situations. First, their work does not clearly explain how it is that judges might have available to them more than one way of delivering the judgment that D was not individually responsible for the consequence. Take the lightning case for example. There is, no doubt, a wide consensus that D should not be adjudged individually responsible for the death even though his blow (which broke the victim's leg) bears a but-for relation to the death. Adopting a perspective on the facts that shows D not to have made a difference will reflect this view of individual responsibility. But as we have seen, judgments about whether a factor made a difference can be expressed in causal language or in some other conceptual vehicle, such as the unhappily named[35] 'remoteness' category.

Thus one way the judge can express this judgment that D was not individually responsible for the death by lightning is to adopt the sort of causal usage that Hart and Honoré identified as underlying the notion of *novus actus interveniens*: namely, that D's blow was not a cause of the death of the victim because the lightning was a freakish natural event which 'severed' the chain of causation. Alternatively, a judge holding an identical view on the issue of individual responsibility, and therefore on the perspective to adopt to the facts, might prefer the causal minimalists' configuration and

that it is the relationship of such phenomena to our notions of responsibility which is the fundamental relationship: that these phenomena are associated with patterns of causal usage is secondary, an artifact of the process by which causal usage in contexts of the attribution of responsibility is determined by notions of responsibility.

[34] And this would be so even if the facts allowed her conduct to be portrayed as abnormal: as in n. 23 above.

[35] See section 9.

confine the legal category known as causation to no more than the first-level enquiry of what happened. As the blow was a but-for part of the history of what happened, this judge would hold that the blow was a cause of the death (i.e. even though the freakish factor of the lightning had also intervened). He would go on, however, to hold that D was not individually responsible because the consequence of death was so abnormal a consequence of a blow that it was 'too remote'. Since Hart and Honoré's purpose was to decipher general themes of usage, they did not emphasize this (perhaps) minority usage under which even a freakish intervening event would not 'sever causation'. Their limited purpose, however, left un-illuminated the phenomenon of appellate judgments in which, while agreeing on the outcome in responsibility terms, judges make such diametrically opposed holdings on the question whether D was a cause of the outcome. This is a particularly disturbing phenomenon for the ordinary citizen.

There is a second, far more central, difficulty in real legal disputes to which Hart and Honoré's work, with its focus on general themes of usage, did not speak. This is where, unlike the previous lightning case, there is no consensus about individual responsibility and the dispute about responsibility is presented to courts in terms of a dispute about causation. Take the following variation on the previous case: a person, D, grazes another's leg, but when the victim arrives at the hospital emergency room he is given a massive overdose of painkillers by mistake and dies from the overdose. Given the current structure of legal reasoning, when the victim's estate sues D it would couch its claim in terms, *inter alia*, that D was a cause of the death and that that consequence was not too remote a consequence of his blow. The defendant might respond that D was not a cause of the death because the overdose was so abnormal as to constitute a *novus actus*; or alternatively, and equivalently as we have just seen, that even if D was a cause of the death the consequence of death was so abnormal a consequence of a blow that it was 'too remote'.

The disagreement here cannot be resolved by reference to the 'short-cut' of 'ordinary notions of causal connection'.[36] The very words of the pleadings expose the absence of an agreed causal usage in the circumstances. Moreover, this disagreement in causal usage merely masks the real nature of the dispute: whether D should be regarded as individually responsible for the later negligent medical treatment.[37] The

[36] Hart and Honoré, n. 1 above, 6. Nor did Hart and Honoré explicitly claim they could: 'the study of the dominant trends of usage, is not to provide a code for the use of that language: still less is it to construct rules from which legal decisions on causal questions can be deduced' (3). Later writings of Professor Honoré can, however, give the contrary impression: see e.g. Tony Honoré, 'Medical Non-Disclosure, Causation and Risk: *Chappel* v. *Hart*' (1999) 7 *Torts Law Journal* 1.

[37] Similarly, the orchid case, Case 3, might be framed as a dispute about causation: whether or not the neighbour was a cause of the death of the orchids. But this masks the real nature of the dispute, which is whether she should be held individually responsible for the death; whether her conduct 'made a relevant difference' in responsibility terms. Thus even if the plaintiff could present the neighbour's omission as 'abnormal' conduct (by an appropriate choice of comparator class), the dispute between the parties would still be whether this made a difference in responsibility terms. The neighbour would, no doubt, argue the libertarian vision of individual responsibility: that she should be free to change her mind, even if her neighbour was relying on her etc. (just as she might argue she had no responsibility to rescue a stranger even where most other citizens would do so, see n. 49 below).

causal usages are different yet each is plausible because there is no obvious uniform consensus about the responsibility issue as there is with Mrs Oswald. In short: while Hart and Honoré noted the relativity of the concepts of 'intervention' and 'abnormality',[38] they did not emphasize the importance of choice: that by choosing different perspectives on agreed facts we can change what is seen as an 'abnormal event' or 'intervention'. More importantly, they did not address the phenomenon that a person's attitude to individual responsibility has a critical feedback effect both on this choice of perspective (and, therefore, on what is seen to be abnormal) and on the question whether (even if it is conceded that the behaviour is abnormal) it made a relevant difference. But where legal disputes are framed as 'causation' disputes even though the facts are agreed, the very nature of the dispute involves such a disagreement about individual responsibility.[39]

9. THE NEEDS OF LEGAL ANALYSIS

Where does this leave courts and practitioners?

The law must decide not only what happened but also whether the defendant was individually responsible. In a legal dispute where the facts are agreed, such as the four cases mentioned at the outset, the dispute is about individual responsibility even though it might be presented to the court in the language of a dispute about causation. For the sake of enhancing the clarity and consistency of legal decision-making, we need an analytical approach that unmasks the nature and precise content of such responsibility disputes. We should therefore locate these disputes in analytical categories where judges feel obliged both to confront these responsibility issues and to provide explicit reasons for adopting one view of the dispute rather than another.

As we have seen, the legal category of causation has proven to be an inadequate category for this purpose. The category is infected with misleading slogans about causation being a 'pragmatic' matter or, even more bizarrely in legal disputes where the facts are agreed, that causation is a 'question of fact'.[40] These slogans offer the court the opportunity to evade open discussion of the responsibility dispute. It is not difficult (though it is invidious) to cite examples of judgments in such cases of agreed facts which have turned on causal assertions which the judge has attempted to defend by

[38] Hart and Honoré, n. 3 above, 33–41.

[39] As well as involving an associated dispute about conflicting policy arguments for and against the imposition of legal liability: see section 9.

[40] Of course, people often also disagree about other elements of a legal rule, such as whether a particular defendant's conduct was 'reasonable'. But the special problem with legal disputes couched in terms of causation is that, unlike disputes about reasonableness, there tends to be an expectation that such disputes can be examined using the same objective techniques and answered in the same objective terminology as disputes about how physical transitions came about: that just as a scientist is involved in discovering the 'correct' answer to the question whether certain moisture changes killed flowers, when answering the question whether the neighbour 'caused' the death of the orchids in Case 3, the law is also involved in a process of finding an objective, 'correct' answer.

labelling them 'pragmatic' or 'common-sense', to the consternation of ordinary citizens caught up in the legal process.

The preferable way forward is to reserve causation in law for the results of the factual issue of what happened, even though this might require 'causation in law' to depart from 'the plain man's notions of causation'.[41] Thus if the defendant's conduct bore a but-for or NESS relation to the outcome complained of, it would qualify as a 'cause' in law. The responsibility dispute would then be dealt with in terms such as remoteness or duty in which judges are more accustomed to dealing explicitly with arguments about responsibility.[42] Of course, even here there will be a parallel project to ensure that empty slogans or mere assertions do not suppress the nature of the dispute.

In fact, many courts already embrace this suggested configuration of analysis in disputes that might otherwise have been framed as disputes about causation. In particular, the judicial focus on the duty concept in the modern era owes much to the judicial perception that it is preferable to deal with omission cases as ones raising the issue of whether a duty of affirmative action should be recognized rather than as disputes about causation, an approach which has significantly illuminated this area of decision-making.

The Terminological Awkwardness of 'Remoteness'

It is worth noting that while judges have become much more open in their analysis of the duty context, allowing considerable progress in the project to unpack and evaluate the arguments which influence them,[43] the same cannot be said for analysis proceeding under the remoteness label.[44] Indeed, the very term, 'remoteness', hampers

[41] The approach I have proposed is functionally very close to that of the causal minimalists and admittedly suffers from this drawback of that approach. In practice, however, the only disputes on agreed facts that get to court framed as disputes of causation are ones where such 'common sense' notions do not provide a determinate answer. (No one would sue or prosecute great-grandmother Oswald.) Here even Hart and Honoré accept that the court's determination will be 'powerfully and properly influenced by judicial conceptions of policy or justice': Hart and Honoré, n. 1 above, 5. Hart and Honoré claimed that patterns and principles of causal usage in past case law reflect the ordinary person's notions of causation. (This claim can mislead: the general pattern of usage they deduced from the allocative context of case law, that 'a cause is an intervention', does not square with common usage in non-allocative contexts such as the pistachio/leukæmia example in n. 14 above.) But even if the claim were sound, it does not provide an argument that this coincidence of usage should continue. My argument is that (1) current analytical approaches fail to expose the crucial fact that 'causal disputes' (in cases of agreed facts) are really disputes about responsibility and (2) this phenomenon supports the adoption of a meaning for causation in law which, though over-inclusive by 'common sense' standards, should provide an improvement in clarity and consistency of reasoning, goals which do not typically restrain day-to-day causal usage.

[42] Both those touching on whether to see the defendant's *conduct* as abnormal at all and those which touch on the consequences issue.

[43] Some of these results are tabulated in J. Stapleton, 'Duty of Care Factors: A Selection from the Judicial Menus' in P. Cane and J. Stapleton (eds.), *The Law of Obligations: Essays in Honour of John Fleming* (Oxford University Press, Oxford, 1998) 59.

[44] Under one vision of individual responsibility a person might, in certain circumstances, be properly regarded as individually responsible for a consequence even though he could not foresee it: *Re Polemis* [1921] 3 KB 560. In *Overseas Tankship (UK) Ltd.* v. *Morts Dock and Engineering Co. (The 'Wagon Mound'*

appreciation of what has in the past and could in the future be dealt with here because, like its unhappy cousin 'proximity', it misleadingly suggests temporal or spatial concerns. The awkwardness of the term can easily be illustrated. If in today's world a crane-operator carelessly lets a plank crash into the hold of a ship, and this results in a freakish explosion that destroys the ship, the current legal orthodoxy concerning individual responsibility for consequences[45] would guide the court not to impose liability. Given the context is physical loss from misfeasance by the defendant himself, this result could not be couched in 'no duty' terms[46] and the form of the example also precludes the result being explained in terms of there being 'no breach'. Currently the only formulation left for the court to use is that of the third analytical category: that the defendant crane-operator is not liable because the damage is 'too remote', an odd usage given how direct, immediate, and physically close the explosion was to the crane-operator's act.

The awkwardness of describing this third consequence-focused category in 'remoteness' terms will be even more exposed if the suggested configuration of legal reasoning is adopted. This is because cases of over-determination such as the hunters' case would now be addressed in this category.[47] Again, it is odd to think of expressing the individual defendant-hunter's argument that he was not responsible for the death of the beater in terms of the death being 'too remote'. Moreover this tag masks a significant difference in nature between the crane-operator's responsibility argument about consequences and that of the hunter. The argument of the former focuses on the freakish/unforeseeable nature of the consequence, while the responsibility argument of the hunter focuses on another characteristic of the consequence: that it would have happened anyway. So while it is true that adoption of the suggested configuration might highlight the awkwardness of the 'remoteness' terminology here, this would be no bad thing. Its abandonment would assist the goal of exposing the nature and diversity of the underlying dispute about responsibility.

Examples of the Suggested Configuration

For a simple example of how the suggested configuration would work, take the hunters' case again. Both hunters would be held to have been a cause of the death

No. 1)[1961] AC 388 the Privy Council replaced this with a new orthodoxy: that a person should not be regarded as individually responsible for a consequence he could not have foreseen. Subsequent case law showed that this change did little to confine a court's option to impose liability, cutting it off only in relation to those rare claims where the consequence was so freakish that it could not plausibly be presented as foreseeable. The notion of foreseeability (including the width of the class of consequence that must be foreseeable) has proven highly malleable in the hands of courts. Indeed, the label 'foreseeability' has offered courts a device that can be used to mask the substance of the reasoning which had guided the direction of that manipulation.

[45] See n. 44 above.

[46] For the courts have accepted, and for good systemic reasons, that where physical loss results from the affirmative act of the defendant a duty will be owed (specific immunities situations apart): *Mobil Oil Hong Kong Ltd.* v. *Hong Kong United Dockyards Ltd.* [1991] 1 Lloyd's Rep. 309.

[47] For, again, the defendant will not be able to dispute that a duty was owed and breached.

because both are part of how the death came about. The responsibility debate, hitherto suppressed beneath the debate between advocates of the but-for and NESS theories *of causation*, would now be addressed in the consequence-based category (at present described as the 'remoteness of damage' category). In this analytical location, those who have in the past advocated NESS on the basis that it enabled both hunters to be found individually responsible should be called upon to provide a normative justification for that allocation of responsibility which did not rely merely on some assertion that the NESS test imposition 'captures the essence of the doctrine of causation'. Similarly, those who in the past advocated that the but-for test should be applied to the hunters would need to provide a normative justification.

For a second example, take cases in which the defendant's omission to control a third party bears a but-for relation to the harm committed by that party. Here the court should concede that the omission qualified as a 'cause in law' and then proceed to handle the dispute in other terms: whether a *duty* (of affirmative action) should be owed; or whether a *breach* was committed; or whether, even if the defendant should be seen as in breach of a duty that is owed, he should be regarded as individually responsible for the particular *consequence*. These are all concepts that allow a detailed examination of factors which courts have in the past identified as relevant to individual responsibility in such failure-to-control cases. These include the nature of the defendant–victim relationship, the defendant–third party relationship, the foreseeability and/or likelihood of the third party conduct, the degree to which the defendant's conduct facilitated the latter,[48] and so on.

Policy Arguments

As a final point, we should note the interplay of individual responsibility arguments and other (call them 'policy') reasons for and against legal liability.[49] Earlier it was noted that to be found legally guilty or liable for an outcome, it is traditionally assumed that a necessary, but not sufficient, condition is that you must be individually responsible for the outcome. In other words, private law and criminal law are, among other things, concerned with the allocation of individual responsibility. To be seen as individually responsible, it is necessary, though not sufficient, that you be seen as having made a difference in some relevant way; and to be seen to have made such a difference in responsibility terms your conduct must at least be seen to have been abnormal. We have seen that notions of individual responsibility influence how plaintiffs frame their claims that D's conduct was abnormal and made a difference,

[48] A prisoner might have a certain propensity to bash other prisoners, but when a warder supplies him with alcohol that likelihood increases without becoming inevitable.

[49] A party often couches his defence in both ways. Thus a person defending his failure to rescue a stranger may argue both: that in principle he has no individual responsibility to be 'his brother's keeper', that as he had made no commitment to the victim he has a 'right' to choose his own course of action, etc.; and that in policy terms society would not run as efficiently and harmoniously if duties of affirmative action were owed to complete strangers. Often a legally recognized precept may be enunciated in either way: for example, the well-known maxim that a defendant 'must take his victim as he finds him'.

and how defendants frame opposing arguments that their conduct was not abnormal and that, even if it was, it had not made a relevant difference in responsibility terms. One, but not the only, way such claims can be couched is in causal language.

But individual responsibility is not the only precondition of legal liability. Other powerful arguments can weigh in favour of and against a finding of liability even in a case where there is no dispute that D *was* individually responsible.[50] Such broad systemic policy concerns explain, for example, the immunity from tort liability enjoyed by judges, advocates, and so on. They also play a large role, for example, in preliminary proceedings in the tort of negligence where the dispute is whether, assuming the allegations of fact against the defendant can be proved, the defendant should be held to have owed a duty to the plaintiff.[51]

Such arguments can also support the case for the imposition of liability. For example, to hold neither hunter liable seems to many commentators to be objectionable, in that it would mean that the victim of two shots would be worse off, in terms of legal redress, than the victim of one. This might bring the law into disrepute, and so imposition of liability can be supported on the basis of this sound argument from policy.

In cases where the parties agree about what happened, framing the dispute in terms of causation not only may suppress the nature of the underlying dispute about individual responsibility but is even more likely to suppress accompanying underlying disputes about policy arguments. Framing the dispute in other terms should improve analytical clarity at both levels because, as with explicit responsibility-based arguments, courts are more accustomed to dealing with policy arguments in these other conceptual terms. For example, if in future courts were to analyse in non-causal terms the dispute in simultaneous over-determination cases such as the hunters' case, this should not only facilitate the enunciation of the two conflicting visions of individual responsibility that underlie it, but also force a clearer enunciation of the parallel policy arguments for and against the imposition of legal liability.[52]

10. CONCLUSION

Understanding the nature of causation and legal disputes about causation in the way I have suggested turns tradition on its head. The traditional lawyer's view is that usually you cannot be responsible for an outcome without being causally connected

[50] Such policy arguments can also form part of the reason for causal usage and disagreements about their weight can be reflected in difference of causal usage.

[51] Elsewhere I have argued that the duty concept is well designed for the examination of systemic policy factors: see J. Stapleton, 'Duty of Care: Peripheral Parties and Alternative Opportunities for Deterrence' (1995) 111 *LQR* 301 and n. 43 above, 59.

[52] The content of the conflicting visions of individual responsibility often proves hard to enunciate (hence the superficial attraction of packaging them as mere causal assertions). Courts are more comfortable with the evaluation of policy disputes. It is, therefore, of particular importance that the latter are exposed openly to the court.

to it, and that this causal connection has to be established before you can construct a case for responsibility. In contrast, I argue that in legal disputes where the facts are agreed, it is notions of individual responsibility that determine the perspective a party adopts when looking at those facts to identify what had made a difference in bringing about the relevant outcome. In such cases, notions of individual responsibility can affect whether we call something a 'cause'. Thus where such disputes are framed as disputes about causation, this merely masks the true nature of the dispute: a dispute which involves competing visions of individual responsibility.

Finally, I have argued that the way forward for judges and practitioners in cases of agreed facts is to reserve the category of causation in law for issues of fact (the first-level enquiry about how things came about) and to deal with responsibility-based disputes, such as that raised by the two hunters case, in terms of concepts which will facilitate clear analysis of the substance of the dispute. The project of unpacking such debates about individual responsibility (and any parallel policy disputes), currently masked by causal slogans, will provide legal theorists with rich and exciting material.

APPENDIX: THE DESERT TRAVELLER CASE

Enemy No. 1 poisons V's water barrel. Later, an unassociated Enemy No. 2 empties the barrel. Later still V dies of thirst.

In the context of a legal dispute about individual responsibility arising from these facts, it is unlikely that there would be any disagreement that the behaviour of both enemies can be seen as abnormal. Yet these facts generate a notorious disagreement among lawyers and philosophers. Though this has typically been framed as a dispute about causation, it is in fact a dispute about individual responsibility for an outcome: whether on these agreed facts the behaviour of the enemies should be seen as having 'made a difference' in responsibility terms in relation to the traveller's death. It is the particular view of individual responsibility that sets the corresponding choice of perspective from which the facts are to be assessed.

For example, on one vision of individual responsibility, neither enemy should be said to be responsible for the death, given the conduct of the other enemy. In the past, this attitude to responsibility was expressed in terms of the but-for perspective on the facts, or 'the but-for test of causation'. As we have seen, each enemy fails to satisfy this test because the relevant hypothetical used to assess the traveller's prospects includes the abnormal conduct of the other enemy. Those prospects are judged from the perspective of hindsight.

According to a second and different vision of responsibility, both enemies should be held responsible for the death. Given the current framework of legal reasoning, an advocate of this allocation of responsibility might package it for the court under the guise of the NESS 'test of causation' applied to a suitably widely specified outcome, for example 'death by lack of a supply of fresh water'.[53] Because that test assesses the impact of the behaviour of one enemy on the prospects of the victim from a perspective which ignores the abnormal behaviour of the other, the behaviour of the first enemy can be made to appear to have 'made a difference'.[54] Here the victim's prospects are judged from the perspective of a hypothetical, fictitious set of circumstances.

Yet a third vision of responsibility might judge that only Enemy No. 1 should be held individually responsible. In terms of the current structure of legal reasoning, this view of responsibility[55] might be presented to the court in the form of a 'test of causation'[56] which focuses on the question whether the defendant's conduct 'doomed' the victim, destroying his prospects as judged from the perspective of how they stood at the time of that defendant's conduct.[57] In other words, the conduct of Enemy No. 1 can be made to appear to have made a difference if we adopt the perspective of asking: did Enemy No. 1 change the victim's prospects such that the victim was, as a result of that conduct, henceforward doomed to suffer the outcome of which he complains, that outcome being defined at a suitable level of generality such as 'death due to lack of fresh water'.[58]

[53] The desired pattern of responsibility would be even more firmly secured if it could be assumed that the poison was pungent because the death could be more closely specified as 'death by dehydration', see n. 62 below and accompanying text.

[54] Contrast Wright, n. 1 above, 1024 who asserts that, under NESS, there is only one actually sufficient set (the one including Enemy No. 2's conduct), and this set pre-empts the potential causal effect of an alternative hypothetically sufficient set (i.e. the one including Enemy No. 1's conduct). This is only true if we make certain other factual assumptions: see n. 60 below.

[55] This argument does not have reciprocal force for Enemy No. 2. Many people would regard the responsibility of Enemy No. 2 as depending on unstated facts: for example whether or not his act cut short the traveller's life expectancies as they stood after No. 1 acted: see nn. 62–3 below and accompanying text.

[56] A comparable result is alternatively achieved if the *damage* of which complaint may legitimately be made is widened to include the loss of the chance of avoiding the overt outcome (in which case responsibility can attach even before the outcome occurs), though the consequences of the later doctrinal move are very much wider: see J. Stapleton, 'The Gist of Negligence: Part 2' (1988) 104 *Law Quarterly Review* 389.

[57] The idea that individual responsibility may be triggered by culpable behaviour that merely dooms a person to some fate provides a way of rationalizing the different legal outcomes in *Jobling* v. *Associated Dairies* [1982] AC 794 and *Baker* v. *Willoughby* [1970] AC 467. Let us say that in contexts outside the law it is true that dooming by culpable conduct attracts individual responsibility. Let us also imagine that there is, nevertheless, a good reason why the law refuses to impose *liability* in such cases where a later factor, which is present in the story, would have produced the outcome by itself. That reason may itself be outweighed, however, where the subsequent factor is behaviour which the law regards as wrongful. As we have seen, there is a good policy reason for liability here: unless liability is imposed, the victim of one piece of wrongdoing would be worse off than the victim of two; and the law would be seen to be allowing wrongdoers to shelter behind each other's wrongs. These results bring the law into disrepute and the policy of their avoidance may be thought to justify adoption of devices to allow imposition of legal liability for merely dooming a person in such cases. In a parallel way, the idea that individual responsibility may be triggered by merely dooming a person plus this policy reason help to rationalize legal liability in cases of multiple sufficient *simultaneous* factors such as the two hunters case.

[58] The coherence of a perspective based on merely dooming a person depends on a sufficient correspondence between the actual outcome and the specification of the fate to which the defendant doomed the victim. If D1 infects V with a terminal disease but V is then shot by D2, few if any would accept that D1 was individually responsible 'for the death'.

A fourth vision of responsibility might judge that only Enemy No. 2 should be held individually responsible.[59] To deliver this view of responsibility[60] a party might urge the court to adopt the fiction that the conduct of No. 2 introduced 'a condition, lack of water, that in the circumstances, including the absence of an alternative water supply, is sufficient to bring about and does bring about (the traveller's) death by dehydration'.[61] Here the court is being urged to judge the impact of the last-to-act enemy on the traveller's prospects from the perspective of a different hypothetical set of circumstances that ignores the abnormal behaviour of the earlier enemy.

At this point it is worth emphasizing that one of the central difficulties with discussions of the traveller problem is that, as usually stated, it omits factual details which would probably be crucial to many people's allocation of individual responsibility. One such detail is whether the poison was so pungent the traveller would never have drunk it. If so, some might say that Enemy No. 1 doomed him to death by dehydration and No. 2 made no difference to the traveller's prospects howsoever viewed.[62] Even if the poison was odourless, a person's allocation of responsibility might well depend on another detail: whether the poison would have killed instantaneously,[63] or was so slow-acting[64] that it would have killed later than the time the traveller died of dehydration.

Nevertheless, this short discussion of the traveller problem confirms that a variety of views on individual responsibility of the parties is possible, and that for each a separate 'causal' test can be chosen to yield an appropriately shaped answer to the question whether either or both of the enemies had 'made a difference' in responsibility terms. The argument in this essay has attacked the masking of this dispute about responsibility in terms of a dispute about the correct 'causal' test to apply.

[59] Surprisingly this is the view of eminent advocates of the NESS test: '[it is] clear that the emptying of the can caused the traveller's death and that the poisoning of the water did not': Wright, n. 1 above, 1024. See also Honoré, n. 1 above, 378.

[60] Some people would regard the responsibility of Enemy No. 1 as depending on unstated facts: for example whether or not the poison was pungent. The rationalization of Wright (of the view that only Enemy No. 2 was a cause of the death) is flawed by its implicit reliance on the factual assumption that the poison was not pungent (and that therefore the plan of No. 1 was death by poisoning, which plan was pre-empted by No. 2): n. 1 above, 1024. See nn. 56–57 and accompanying text

[61] See Honoré, n. 1 above, 378. In fact what Enemy No. 2 had actually done was introduce a condition of lack of *poisoned* water.

[62] If the poison had been pungent, the traveller's estate cannot show that the traveller had future opportunities of which Enemy No. 2 deprived him: contrast Honoré, n. 1 above, 378 and 380.

[63] If this was the case, some might regard No. 1 as responsible, a result which could be delivered via a loss of a chance formulation of damage (see n. 56 above). Others might regard No. 1 as not responsible, a result which could be delivered by specifying his plan as death by poisoning and focusing on the precise mechanism of death by lack of fresh water, namely death by dehydration (the poisoning mechanism being 'pre-empted' by No. 2). Some might regard No. 2 as not responsible: this could be delivered by a perspective on the traveller's prospects as they stood when No. 2 acted (he improved them). Some might regard No. 2 as responsible: this could be delivered by a perspective on the traveller's prospects as they stood at the outset (i.e. in the absence of the conduct of No. 1).

[64] Here most would regard No. 2 as responsible because, from whichever perspective we assess them, the traveller's prospects were damaged by No. 2. As euthanasia attests, it is possible for a person's conduct to be a (first level) factor in how the death of another came about, even where the operation of some prior factor meant that the person had been doomed to die. On the responsibility of No. 1, see preceding n.

Can Negligence be Culpable?

A.P. Simester

Reasonableness is in the lifeblood of law. Our legal system does not, indeed cannot, specify with precision what is to be done in every variety of circumstance. Instead, its rules are often stated in terms of what is reasonable, or of what a reasonable man would do. Jurors are enjoined to find the accused guilty of a negligence-based offence only if his conduct has fallen below the standard to be expected of a reasonable man: that standard is left to them with no further definition. In contract law, objective tests for the formation and interpretation of contracts are elucidated by reference to reasonable understandings: '[t]he judicial task is not to discover the actual intentions of each party; it is to decide what each was reasonably entitled to conclude from the attitude of the other'.[1] Actions in estoppel are concerned to protect reliance upon reasonable, rather than unreasonable, expectations that the defendant has in some way fostered. Similarly, principles of causation normally exclude the defendant's responsibility for harmful consequences unless such harms are reasonably foreseeable.

Very often, in contexts like these, reasonableness operates as part of a balancing between competing legal interests. As such, especially in private law, it helps to determine whether the plaintiff's interests should take priority over those of the defendant—to determine who should pay when something goes wrong. Sometimes, however, the reasonable man functions not just as a partial component of the relative merits in a case, but as the core ingredient. When it does so, it operates as an indicator of culpability.

Most obviously, this occurs in the criminal law. At least in serious offences, the very judgment against a defendant—the criminal conviction—carries an implication of culpability. The conviction is a public, condemnatory labelling of the defendant: a finding that she is 'guilty' of wrongful, blameworthy, and prohibited action. Indeed, its public aspect is part of what defines the criminal law. The criminal law has a communicative function and social significance that the civil law lacks, a significance to be seen in such contexts as the application for a visa, or for admission to practise as a lawyer. One who makes such an application may be required to disclose his previous convictions, but will not be asked for details of recent contractual disputes. The tabloid newspaper may trumpet on the front page that some figure of public note is a 'Criminal', but is less likely to dub her a 'Tortfeasor'.

Criminal law is the clearest case, in that a negligence-based conviction necessarily involves the public imputation of culpability. Nonetheless, the same claim can sometimes be made for tortious negligence. Not always. The decision that D should compensate P for loss suffered need not be explicable in terms of culpability. Culpability

[1] *McCutcheon* v. *David MacBrayne Ltd.* [1964] 1 WLR 125, 128 (Lord Reid). Cf. *Smith* v. *Hughes* (1871) LR 6 QB 597, 607 (Blackburn J); *The Hannah Blumenthal* [1983] 1 AC 854.

is not integral to the private law verdict: it is not at the heart of tort. Rather than attributing blame and sanction, tort law is concerned with moving money. Underpinning tort claims is a need for the plaintiff to show reason why, on balance, the defendant should compensate the plaintiff—why the defendant should carry the loss. That reason need not be culpability-based. Indeed, there is a variety of motives for imposing liability. Compensation may be merited because the defendant has held himself out as competent in a specialist activity and, thereby, voluntarily set himself a standard of behaviour which, should he fall short of that standard, grounds the imposition of liability without the need independently to establish culpability. Imagine, for example, that David establishes a practice as a specialist surgeon. Even though he may have commenced practice only recently, his inexperience is no excuse if he makes a mistake that a typical, competent practitioner would not make. David may not deserve blame when he does so, should his be an understandable error for an inexperienced surgeon to make. But in this type of case, the law properly makes no concession to inexperience, and holds David liable in negligence. Similarly, supplementary considerations underwrite a tortious remedy in cases such as *Rylands* v. *Fletcher*: the ruling that the defendant should, in effect, insure the plaintiff against losses in such cases can be justified by reference to the defendant's voluntary creation of a potential hazard, rather than by any finding that the defendant was wrong so to do. Product liability may appear to be strict, yet can be rationalized in terms of economic insurance and the assumption of risk; reasons that do not justify a criminal conviction.

However, not all tort cases can be explained by factors extraneous to culpability. Suppose that D, who does not pretend to be a surgeon, finds himself alone with an injured victim with no hope of assistance, and must perform an operation to save the victim's life.[2] In this sort of case, considerations of moral culpability *do* inform the standard that tort law demands. Or conjecture an example where D is walking along the pavement. He does not notice where he is walking, with the result that he trips and crashes into another pedestrian, who goes crashing to the ground and is injured. In these types of cases, what ground is there for transferring assets from D to P? It cannot be said that D has held himself out, or taken up some specialist or dangerous activity.[3] In these, classic, cases of negligence, tort law does not intervene to redistribute wealth simply because D has caused harm to P. Blameless accidents do not

[2] Cf. R.W.M. Dias (ed.), *Clerk and Lindsell on Torts* (16th edn., Sweet & Maxwell, London, 1989) 10–76; *Restatement of the Law of Torts* (1965–9) 2d (hereafter *Restatement*) §289 comment j.

[3] Neither is it, as Kelley suggests, that D has failed to adhere to a community or industry convention: 'Who Decides? Community Safety Conventions at the Heart of Tort Liability' (1990) 38 *Cl. St. LR* 315. Kelley argues that individuals in a community co-ordinate their activities with each other according to established patterns of behaviour, in order to avoid undue interference into each others' lives. Reliance upon conformity to those patterns is necessary for the community to be able to function effectively. Legal fault is therefore found whenever D breaches a co-ordinating norm of behaviour, which is intended to protect those who rely upon it. But established community standards of behaviour, while important, do not by themselves determine legal fault in negligence. Absent an assumption of risk, the defendant who acts contrary to convention is generally not liable if he does so without blame: e.g., in an emergency or under necessity (*Cordas* v. *Peerless Transportation Co.*, 27 NYS 2d 198 (1941); *Restatement* §§296, 289 comment j), or involuntarily (*Billy Higgs & Sons Ltd.* v. *Baddeley* [1950] NZLR 605; *Waugh* v. *James K Allen*

attract liability. Rather, in these cases, it is blame itself that provides the underlying motive for reallocation; and which rationalizes the finding, in legal terms, that D has fallen below the minimum standard of care and must compensate P.

In certain contexts, then, substantive law depends upon the proposition that a defendant's negligent conduct is something for which she may legitimately be blamed. The proposition itself is largely uncontroversial, both in legal circles[4] and beyond. Most persons think, or perhaps assume, that negligence is blameworthy—that it is a standard of fault, and not a standard of strict liability.[5] Yet does negligence really disclose culpability? Consider the standard legal test for negligence, enduringly summarized by Baron Alderson:

> Negligence is the omission to do something which a reasonable man, guided upon those considerations which ordinarily regulate the conduct of human affairs, would do, or doing something which a prudent and reasonable man would not do.[6]

Baron Alderson's test reflects upon a defendant only indirectly. In negligence, whether criminal or civil, the law seemingly is concerned neither with what the defendant did nor with why she did it. Instead, it complains about what she did not do. *Prima facie*, rather than examine the motives, intentions, attitudes, etc., lying behind the defendant's own actions, the law focuses on one negative facet of her outward conduct: whether that conduct differs from the behaviour expected of a 'prudent and reasonable man'.

If negligence is truly a measure of culpability, there would seem to be a problem about this approach. Let us suppose, for argument's sake, that the reasonable man standard identifies what the defendant ought, in the circumstances, to do; that if the reasonable man would Φ, the defendant's failure to Φ is undesirable and a matter for regret. Even so, it does not follow from the proposition that an action is undesirable

Ltd. [1964] 2 Lloyd's Rep. 1), or if he is an infant (n. 15 below), or profoundly insane (*Beals* v. *Hayward* [1960] NZLR 131, 138; *Buckley* v. *Smith Transport* [1946] 4 DLR 721; *Canada (Attorney-General)* v. *Connolly* (1990) 64 DLR (4th) 84; *Hanbury* v. *Hanbury* (1892) 8 TLR 559, 560; *Slattery* v. *Haley* (1923) 3 DLR 156, 160), or reasonably mistaken (cf. *Latimer* v. *AEC Ltd.* [1953] AC 643, 656; *Roe* v. *Minister of Health* [1954] 2 QB 66, 84; *Woolridge* v. *Sumner* [1963] 2 QB 43; *The Bywell Castle* (1879) 4 PD 219), or subject to a paralysing fear (*Holland* v. *Tenn RR*, 8 So 524, 527 (1890)). Moreover, sometimes conventional practices are themselves found to be unreasonable: it is standard law that customary practice is relevant but not determinative evidence of negligence. So, for instance, in *Helling* v. *Carey*, 83 Wash. 2d 514, 519 P 2d 481 (1974) an ophthalmologist was held to be negligent for failing to test a patient aged under 40 for glaucoma, notwithstanding that it was an industry-wide practice not to do so. It also counts against Kelley's claim that it is uncontroversially a mistake for, and a misdirection to instruct, the jury to put themselves in the shoes of the defendant (*Arland* v. *Taylor* [1955] 3 DLR 358; *Eyers* v. *Gillis & Warren Ltd.* [1940] 4 DLR 747; *Restatement* §283 comment c; J.G. Fleming, *The Law of Torts* (7th edn., Law Book Co., Sydney, 1987) 97 n. 10): there would seem to be no basis for treating such a move as erroneous (rather than neutral) were the jury meant only to determine the content of local social rules.

[4] Subject to some notable exceptions: n. 10 below.

[5] *Per* H.L.A. Hart, 'Negligence, *Mens Rea* and Criminal Responsibility' in *Punishment and Responsibility* (Oxford University Press, Oxford, 1968) 136, 136: ' "I didn't *mean* to do it: I just didn't think." "But you should have thought." . . . most people would think that, in ordinary circumstances, such a rejection of "I didn't think" as an excuse is quite justified.'

[6] *Blyth* v. *The Company of Proprietors of the Birmingham Waterworks* (1856) 11 Ex. 781, 784; 156 ER 1047, 1049. Cf. *Hazell* v. *British Transport Commission* [1958] 1 WLR 169, 171.

that the actor should be blamed for it. Imagine that Pam, a doctor, injects Alex with a painkiller that produces an allergic reaction and causes his death. Pam's killing Alex is undesirable, a matter for regret, but not (on these facts) a matter for blame. All things considered, Alex should not receive the injection. But if his allergy was unknown, and unknowable, Pam is not culpable for injecting him. Expressed in terms of criminal law doctrine, there is the *actus reus* of a homicide, but no *mens rea.*

BLAME AND INADVERTENCE

Judgements of blame are not moral judgements of action *per se.* Neither are they judgements of persons. Rather, blame combines person with action. It is necessary, but not sufficient, that the defendant's action is undesirable. When we blame, we disapprove not of the action *simpliciter*, but of the defendant *for doing* that action.[7] The difficulty for negligence lies in justifying that link between behaviour and defendant. Given that negligence is assessed by reference to the conduct of a hypothetical figure rather than to the defendant, on what footing can we apply our judgement of that behaviour to her? How does the standard of care in negligence tell us anything about the defendant herself? As criminal lawyers might say, the reasonable man standard identifies an *actus reus*, and apparently suppresses any distinction between that and *mens rea.*

Among recent writings, the dominant theory of criminal culpability is expressed in terms of choice. Where the defendant has brought about some undesirable outcome, it is said that she is culpable for doing so if she acted intentionally or advertently, i.e. if she knowingly *chose* to bring about or risk that outcome. In effect, the link between harmful behaviour and the defendant herself is constituted because the defendant has chosen to act for bad reasons. She has aligned herself with the harm. Moral considerations, on this view, may be understood as reasons for or against action which operate *ex ante* through modifying the defendant's evaluation both of her prospective conduct, and of the defendant herself were she to behave in that way.[8] Blame is the *ex post* judgement that follows when her preference is wrong.

The 'choice' analysis presupposes advertence. It offers no moral tools with which to blame an inadvertent wrongdoer. Thus it cannot apply to negligence, which ignores the defendant's cognitive state. Indeed, those who subscribe to this account characteristically suggest that negligence is not culpable at all. If choice is the exclusive ground of blame, the attachment of moral wrongness to unforeseen actions is unwarranted because, when the defendant is unaware of a prospective harm, the moral reasons for or against causing that harm cannot affect the defendant's *ex ante* assessment of her actions. Suppose that Diana walks into a room and flicks on the light switch. We do not expect her to pause before doing so and consider whether the

[7] Cf. J.C.B. Glover, *Responsibility* (Humanities Press, New York, 1970) 64; T. Nagel, 'Moral Luck' in *Mortal Questions* (Cambridge University Press, Cambridge, 1979) 24.

[8] See, e.g., J.L. Mackie, *Ethics: Inventing Right and Wrong* (Penguin, Harmondsworth, 1977) 208–11.

switch may be miswired. It makes sense in such cases that a person will not dwell on apparently irrelevant considerations. Failing to select between unknown options is therefore not something for which one can be blamed:

> in so far as I am ignorant of what I am doing or bringing about, the actions which are for this reason unintentional can be seen not as belonging to me as a conscious agent, but to have been foisted upon or obtruded into my course of action by the facts or circumstances of which I was unaware.[9]

This is a powerful objection, which in various forms has swayed a number of writers.[10] One cannot blame a defendant for negligently 'choosing' to do a morally bad act, since inadvertent options are not themselves 'chosen'. Indeed, unlike intentional wrongdoers, an inadvertent defendant may be horrified when she realizes what she has done. The defendant's fault, if any, lies in her failure to realize a particular consideration is relevant, not in her choice to disregard it.

It seems right to decouple the culpability of advertent and inadvertent actions.[11] In a sense, the complaint in negligence is not about D's choice to do wrong, but rather about her *failure to choose* to do what was right. Yet it is a *non sequitur* to conclude that inadvertence cannot be culpable. Choice is a sufficient but unnecessary foundation of culpability. This is because moral considerations should prompt more than just choices between prospective actions. Suppose that killing James is an unjustified action. Then, with the choice theorists, we can say that D should choose neither to kill nor to risk killing him. But, I think, more than this follows: D should also *take care* lest she kill James. The fact that an action is harmful or to be avoided generates two types of moral reason: a reason not to do that action, and a reason to take care lest that action be done. It is simply untrue that one ought to avoid killing another only if one notices the risk of doing so. Homicide does not become acceptable merely because it is done inadvertently. Perhaps negligent defendants are not so culpable as persons who choose to kill or risk killing; we cannot infer that they would have behaved as they did had they foreseen the risk. Either way, mere inadvertence does not imply blamelessness for V's death.[12] Implicit in the moral duty to act for good reasons is a duty to consider such reasons.

[9] Ibid. 210.

[10] e.g. M.S. Moore, 'Choice, Character, and Excuse' (1990) 7 *Social Philosophy and Policy* 28 (though see now his *Placing Blame: A Theory of Criminal Law* (Clarendon Press, Oxford, 1997) chap. 9; J. Hall, 'Negligent Behaviour Should be Excluded from Criminal Liability' (1963) 63 *Col.LR* 632; J.W.C. Turner, 'The Mental Element of Crimes at Common Law' in L. Radzinowicz and J.W.C. Turner (eds.), *The Modern Approach to Criminal Law* (1948) 195.

[11] Contrast J. Hampton, 'Mens Rea' (1990) 7 *Social Philosophy and Policy* 1, 27, who seeks to explain negligence in terms of prior choice by suggesting that culpable negligence is due to a faulty character that D 'knew better than to develop in this way'. This, surely, is implausible. One does not usually develop one's character deliberately. Moreover, to ground culpability for later negligence, D's failure to rectify her character would have to be chosen in the knowledge that the very negligence she later exhibits is the sort of consequence that might ensue.

[12] Compare E. D'Arcy, *Human Acts* (Oxford University Press, Oxford, 1963) 114: '[t]o the plea "I'm so sorry, I just did not think", the answer will often be, not "Oh I see; then you are not to blame", but "That's no excuse; you *should* have thought; a person in such a position has a *duty* to think".'

That having been said, it does not follow that negligent inadvertence *is* blameworthy. So far, in denying the exclusivity of the choice thesis, all that has been achieved is the preservation of moral space to show that inadvertent behaviour can be culpable. We still need to establish how an ascription of culpability can be sustained.

In particular, it is not enough to rely on the (true) proposition that reasons not to inflict harm exist independently of the defendant's own practical reasoning and choices. There is no direct link between reasons and fault. All things considered, Pam has an overriding reason not to inject Alex with the painkiller that will cause his death. But she is blameless when she acts without considering that reason. Omniscience is not required. We are therefore thrown back to the original question: if, all things considered, there is reason not to Φ, when does D's Φing warrant an adverse moral inference about D? The choice theory accounts for one set of cases. Our challenge is to find an alternative basis for blame, one which offers a non-arbitrary distinction between those reasons D should consider (even if she does not) and reasons that D may neglect without censure.

Impliedly, legal doctrine takes the reasonable man to perform precisely that function. But does it? *Prima facie*, it is open to the defendant to claim that if the law employs an 'objective' third-person standard to assess her behaviour, it cannot, without more, use the news that her behaviour is unreasonable to infer that she is culpable. The defendant may answer:

> perhaps the man on the Clapham omnibus would not act as I did. But I am not like that hypothetical 'person'. Why, therefore, do I deserve blame for not doing what someone else would do? Baron Alderson's standard tells us about a reasonable man, or perhaps about Baron Alderson. But how is it a comment on *me*?

Sometimes, moreover, it seems right for the defendant to reply in this way. Suppose that D is lying in the sand at a beach, and does not notice when someone else's child falls over in the water and begins to drown. A normal person would have seen the child. Is D negligent? Not if she is blind.[13] To blame, convict, or impose liability on a blind person for failing to see would be wrong and unfair. The case of blindness illustrates the fallacy of thinking that the reasonable man supplies an 'objective' test without reference to the defendant's peculiar characteristics—and perhaps the fallacy of personalizing the reasonable man himself. Rather, the negligence standard is partly objective, or imposed, and partly subjective or personalized. In terms of conventional doctrine, if the defendant is blind, or one-legged,[14] or a young child,[15] so too is the

[13] Compare, in tort law, *Bernard* v. *Russell*, 164 A 2d 577 (1960); *Keith* v. *Worcester St R.R.*, 82 NE 680 (1907); *Balcom* v. *City of Independence*, 160 NW 305 (1921). See G.B. Weisiger, 'Negligence of the Physically Infirm' (1946) 24 *NCLR* 187; D.R. Lowry, 'The Blind and the Law of Tort' (1972) 20 *Chittys LJ* 253.

[14] Cf. *St Louis I.M. & S. Ry* v. *Maddry*, 21 SW 472, 474 (1893).

[15] O.S. Gray, 'The Standard of Care for Children Revisited' (1980) 45 *Mo. LR* 597; H. Shulman, 'The Standard of Care Required of Children' (1928) 37 *Yale LJ* 618. See e.g. *Charbonneau* v. *MacRury*, 153 A 457 (1931); *McHale* v. *Watson* (1966) 115 CLR 199; *Yorkton Agricultural Assoc.* v. *Morley* (1967) 66 DLR (2d) 37. Compare *DPP* v. *Camplin* [1978] AC 705, 718 (provocation).

reasonable man. The blind defendant is expected to behave like a reasonable blind person, not as if sighted.

The problem calls for an unpicking of the reasonable man; for a shift of focus, away from the law's fictitious creation and toward the defendant. If the test of negligent conduct is to ground a valid attribution of blame, it ought to set an objective standard in respect of those shortcomings of a defendant for which she may be held morally culpable—while not penalizing subjective characteristics such as blindness. So understood, the 'reasonable man' is really the defendant, subject only to attribution of those faculties where an objective standard is warranted. The accounting of her behaviour as negligent implicitly must reflect some shortcoming of the defendant herself in respect of that behaviour; a shortcoming for which the law is justified in saying, the fact that you are unlike our reasonable man is no answer.

TOWARD A REASONABLE DEFENDANT

The ambition of this essay is limited. It seeks only to sketch how culpability in negligence might be underpinned, and its approach will be detailed just in outline. Very generally, a finding of negligence depends upon the conclusion that the defendant has failed to act for adequate reasons—reasons that would be regarded as adequate by a reasonable man, and for which a reasonable man would act. It seems to me that the most promising road to understanding this failure is by examining that which is missing, i.e. action for (adequate) reasons. Here the ground is more familiar. The gist of action for reasons is intentional action, or behaviour motivated by the desires and beliefs of the actor. Conventionally, action occurs for reasons when combinations of (a) desire for some result, and (b) belief that her behaviour may help to produce that result, supply the reasons for which (c) a person behaves as she does.[16] Expressed in these terms, the essence of negligence is that the defendant fails to behave for the reasons that would motivate a reasonable person. If that is right, we may better understand how a defendant might fail to match the behaviour of a reasonable person by examining how and why she fails to be like a reasonable person in her desires, beliefs, and their motivational upshot.

The model of action for reasons offers three main cases where it is unreasonable to act as does the defendant. We might reject either (a) the defendant's desire, or (b) the defendant's belief, or both, as being unreasonable. Here the defendant's own reason for action is, in itself, defective. Alternatively, where the defendant's reasons are ostensibly valid, they may be defeated[17] by other factors which make it, on balance,

[16] Cf. D. Davidson, 'Actions, Reasons, and Causes' in his *Actions and Events* (Oxford University Press, Oxford, 1980) 3, 5. Davidson uses the term 'pro-attitude' in lieu of desire, or want; terms which otherwise must be construed liberally. For an account that avoids Davidson's commitment to see motivating reasons as causes see, e.g., A.P. Simester, 'Paradigm Intention' (1992) 11 *Law and Phil.* 235 and 'Agency' (1996) 15 *Law and Phil.* 159.

[17] That is, outweighed or excluded. See the discussion below, 105. I disregard cancelling conditions (cf. J. Raz, *Practical Reason and Norms* (2nd edn., Princeton University Press, Princeton, NJ, 1990) 27), which I take to deny the status of ostensible reason.

unreasonable (c) to act as does the defendant. A reasonable person, being a rational moral agent, can be expected to recognize reasons for behaving in various ways, to evaluate possible behaviour in the light of those reasons, and to behave according to that evaluation. The negligent defendant will have failed to do one or more of those things.

From here we must wade into detail and make specific arguments, even if only in outline. There is, I think, no other way. What counts in a judgment of blame is not that the defendant failed to act for good reasons, but why. At a very general level, one may adopt an account along the lines proposed by Hart, that D is culpable whenever she had the capacity and a fair opportunity to avoid causing harm.[18] That type of account is interesting and revealing; ultimately, however, it elucidates by paraphrase, without removing the need for detailed analysis of when one has a fair opportunity to avoid the harm. The same is true of an excuse-based analysis, i.e. that D is culpable for acting contrary to the balance of reasons if she does so without excuse.[19] Indeed, analysis of culpability in terms of excuses begs questions not only of detail but also of logic. While it is surely true that the grounds of exculpation should be intertwined with those of culpability, it does not follow from denial of an excuse that the ascription of culpability is justified. What is needed is a positive account, one that shows which of the defendant's shortcomings are *in*excusable.

(A) DESIRES

It is convenient to begin with desires, although they present no problem distinctive to negligence. Wanting to do the things one should not is at the heart of advertent wrongdoing. By contrast, the primary issue in negligence is the defendant's failure to foresee harm—a failure of belief. The present discussion is therefore abbreviated in the knowledge that other, including choice-based, accounts of culpability must cover much the same ground.

First, the paradigm cases. It would seem that the desires that may be expected of a reasonable defendant, and the weight of those desires,[20] are and should be primarily objective. Account may be taken, so far as relevant, of the defendant's innocuous

[18] N. 5 above, 152. A further problem with Hart's account is considered below, 103–4.

[19] Cf. Raz, n. 17 above, 186–7: 'Other things being equal, [the reasons for an action] are sufficient grounds for taking the action, and barring reasonable ignorance or other excuses, grounds for finding fault with the actor's conduct, if he fails to take the action.' See also R.D. Milo, *Immorality* (Princeton University Press, Princeton, 1984) 224.

[20] There is generally more than one reason for or against particular actions. In order to evaluate an action, therefore, one's desires must also have *weight*. Characteristically, in negligence, the relative weighting will reflect what is sometimes termed 'the gravity of the injury'. Cf. R.F.V. Heuston and R.A. Buckley, *Salmond & Heuston on the Law of Torts* (19th edn., Sweet & Maxwell, London, 1987) 252; also *Paris* v. *Stepney BC* [1951] AC 367, 381, where the House of Lords rejected Asquith LJ's remark in the Court of Appeal [1950] 1 KB 320, 324 that '[a] greater risk of injury is not the same thing as a risk of greater injury; the first alone is relevant to liability'.

desires which are additional to those a reasonable person would necessarily possess.[21] But the question whether behaviour is reasonable should not otherwise be influenced by the values[22] and desires of the particular defendant.[23] It is vital to the authority of a legal system that this be so. A key characteristic of law is that it coerces people from doing what they want, by imposing a standard of acceptable behaviour and demanding that they conform to that standard. If the desires that the law would have us act upon were displaced, in each case, by those of the particular defendant then the law would have no standard to impose.[24] Whatever one takes to be the purposes of law, their achievement requires the co-ordination of individuals' behaviour through the external imposition of values: by ordering ('do not') rather than asking ('unless you want to'). Individuals cannot be permitted to conduct themselves above or outside the compass of the law merely because they have different moral values. Both a criminal legal system which aims to prevent wrongs and a tort system that provides a means of private redress for wrongs must be able to determine wrongful behaviour by a standard independent of the defendant.

That is an authoritarian justification: *ceteris paribus*,[25] it is desirable that a defendant's behaviour conform to law. Characteristically, however, the law exercises authority for more particular reasons, and those reasons lend moral weight to the standards it imposes. The reasons may be intrinsic (e.g., not to murder) or instrumental. Suppose that a parking offence is created, not for its own sake but as an element of some more general transportation strategy. In such case the law acts as a conduit to the strategic objective. Individuals, correspondingly, have reason not to offend that relies not only on the desirability of showing respect for law, but also on the desirability of that further objective.

In terms of culpability, an objective standard of desires can also be justified outside the legal system. Indeed, the very idea of blame presupposes a standard external to the defendant.[26] The moral duty to avoid doing an action is derived from the fact that the action is harmful or wrong, not from the defendant's acceptance that it is. It follows that a defendant's having and acting upon morally aberrant values and desires is an aspect of her character for which we may blame her *ipso facto*. To say that a defendant is motivated by bad reasons is not merely to say that what she does is a bad thing; it is to express disapproval of her, for being a person who acts for such reasons: to say that she is bad.

[21] e.g. to play football. My innocuous desire to play a serious game of rugby justifies in part my bringing the ball-carrier crashing to the ground.

[22] Desires and values are not the same thing: our actions are motivated by desires, but their judgement depends upon the values to which those desires give volitional utterance. Whether one's desires are reasonable, therefore, depends whether those desires accord with admirable, or at least acceptable, values.

[23] Subject in extreme cases to an exception on the grounds of incapacity, which cannot be pursued here.

[24] 'To permit one who knows but does not accede to the community valuation of interests to have an individual standard would at once destroy the law': W.A. Seavey, 'Negligence—Subjective or Objective?' (1927) 41 *Harv. LR* 1, 11.

[25] Many complex issues are packed into this proviso, even against the background of liberal-democratic regimes such as this essay assumes. I cannot explore them here.

[26] I pass over the question whether our moral judgements have any authority over those whose values differ from our own: it is a general problem for legal and moral systems, unspecific to negligence.

Divergence

Core cases are all very well, but others lie at a distance from the paradigm so far considered. Logically, it is possible for the values of a legal system and those of general morality to conflict, even explicitly. In *Toledo, &c. Railway Co.* v. *Pindar*,[27] for instance, the plaintiff Pindar was held contributorily negligent for saving some horses rather than a sum of money when both were threatened by fire, on the ground that the former were much less valuable than the latter and that the suffering of the horses was of no legal account. While the decision may reflect considerations specific to tort, it is hard to see how that approach could be defended in contexts where culpability provides the rationale for judgement; especially in criminal law. If the defendant's behaviour is morally acceptable it cannot be the subject of blame and, therefore, should not be subject to criminal condemnation or punishment.

To a large extent, the analysis offered here is content independent. It does not seek to identify *which* acts defendants are required (i.e. under a duty) to avoid. This is because, generally speaking, the moral constraints upon law are exculpatory not inculpatory. Let there be no judgement without blame. But there may be blame without legal judgment. My failure to rescue a stranger may be reprehensible, lawful, and properly so.[28] Similarly, in the evaluation of reasonableness, not all considerations will be straightforwardly moral in character. It may be noble to prefer the interests of others yet, for reasons of convenience or self-interest, acceptable not to. Thus, in *Marshall* v. *Gotham Co. Ltd.*,[29] where measures required to minimize the risk of a mine roof falling were complex, expensive, and partial rather than comprehensive, the House of Lords ruled that the defendants were not negligent in continuing to mine without such precautions. It can be in the interests of a community that individuals be free to act selfishly; in turn, the defendant may benefit from considerations such as the effect on the community if everyone were prevented from behaving as did she.[30]

On the other hand, the justified content of law may depend on values over which there is genuine disagreement. This presents no particular difficulties for the analysis of negligence. When we criticize particular rules,[31] as many of us do, we implicitly argue that the reasons for which the defendant is required to act should in some way

[27] *Toledo, Peoria & Warsaw R. Co.* v. *Pindar*, 53 Ill. 447, 5 Am. R 57 (1870); cf. *van Schaick* v. *Hudson River R. Co.*, 43 NY 527 (1871). See H.T. Terry, 'Negligence' (1915) 29 *Harv. LR* 40, 45.

[28] See, e.g., A.P. Simester, 'Why Omissions are Special' (1995) 1 *Legal Theory* 311.

[29] [1954] AC 360. See also *Overseas Tankship (UK)* v. *The Miller Steamship Co.* [1967] 1 AC 617, 642; *Cooper* v. *Dallas*, 18 SW 565, 566 (1892).

[30] Cf. *SA Ambulance* v. *Wahlheim* (1948) 77 CLR 215, in which a driver with defective hearing was excused for failing to hear an ambulance siren. The view has been taken that one knowing of such a defect should not drive at all: *Roberts* v. *Ring*, 173 NW 437 (1919), although in that case the driver also had defective sight. It is also arguable that a non-culpability rationale warrants liability in such cases: D may go ahead, but should underwrite the costs of doing so.

[31] Or note, perhaps with satisfaction, that times have changed: J. Wilson reminds us that a ' "reasonable" man in Calvin's Geneva would have testified to the fact that the sight of female ankles was shocking.'—*Reason and Morals* (Cambridge University Press, Cambridge, 1961) 35.

be modified. A committed anti-vivisectionist might argue that a reasonable person should want to prevent vivisection sufficiently strongly that he would consider it acceptable to bomb an animal testing laboratory; a devoted spouse, when denying that euthanasia is immoral, impliedly contends that the desire to preserve life should not always be overriding. Others will dissent. The disagreement simply manifests how difficult it can be to concur whether an outcome is morally desirable.

Such cases are troubling for negligence only because, earlier in this essay, I grounded negligence in a duty to take care. An agent might be said to have discharged her duty to 'take care' when, after careful deliberation, she decides that doing or risking some *actus* is morally permissible in circumstances where both law and society would regard it as *reus*. Indeed, such a person may even be 'conscientious', a person who cares a great deal about her actions and about the values those actions reflect. Note, however, that this type of case is not one of negligence *simpliciter* but of recklessness or intention. To be sure, the agent may be less blameworthy, *ceteris paribus*, than one who believes what she does to be wrong.[32] But, for the reasons given earlier, disagreement cannot by itself license disobedience.

Less graphic than the outright rejection of legal values, and perhaps more significant, is the regional variation to be found in modern society. What is sensible in the restaurants of Mayfair may be folly on the streets of Soho. There is nothing culpable about diversity, and the law can and ought to accommodate these differences. If D's values are reasonable in the context within which she acts and not already contradicted or outweighed by reasons the law has created, then behaviour according to those values should also be counted reasonable when judged in negligence. In such cases, the defendant can legitimately deny wrongdoing and claim that she acted for permissible reasons. At the same time, if variation *per se* does not inculpate neither does it exculpate. The practices and values of a community, or industry, are always open to review, and conventions may be wrong even when widespread.[33]

(B) BELIEFS

The most important factor in any explanation of negligence is defective beliefs. In the troubling cases, the defendant cares about the harm she causes, and would not have chosen to cause it. Unfortunately, she did not see the risk. What goes wrong when beliefs are faulty? Either the belief that the defendant acts upon is unreasonably acquired, or there is some further belief, relevant to her behaviour, that unreasonably is not considered. Expressed in this way, it is the *process* by which the defendant accumulates and considers beliefs that has failed. Correspondingly, in negligence

[32] A typically difficult case might be where the defendant subscribes to a value that calls impermissible something we count as permissible (for instance, meat-eating) and only derivatively counts as permissible something we forbid (for instance, using force to release battery hens). This consideration may well mitigate, though it presents no problem specific to negligence.

[33] Cf. *Helling* v. *Carey*, 83 Wash. 2d 514, 519 P 2d 481 (1974).

defendants are not always attributed with an identical, standard set of beliefs. What need to be reviewed are not the defendant's beliefs, themselves, but some of the abilities involved in accumulating and considering those beliefs.[34] It is upon assuming such abilities that one can enquire whether there is anything the actor should have known, realized, or considered and did not.

Processing beliefs is a complex psychological phenomenon that can be modelled here in only fairly simple terms. The failures which might prevent a negligent defendant from accumulating or considering a particular belief seem broadly to be threefold in type:

(i) To pay attention to available information.[35] In particular, to perceive that which one's physical senses register, and to recall that which one remembers;
(ii) To remember that which one perceives or infers; and
(iii) To apply intelligence to that which one perceives and recalls.

In respect of each, the question for analysis is to what extent are we entitled to demand an objective standard of the defendant. It should be emphasized, however, that the division of faculties made here, and the analysis that follows, is meant to be suggestive rather than precise. To go further would exceed the aims of this essay. But some such organization is necessary if, as will be argued, negligence requires an objective standard in respect only of certain aspects of the defendant's reasoning.

A preliminary point. Standardized models of reasoning are attributed in negligence only for the sake of their output. Their value to us lies in establishing a set of reasonable beliefs about possible consequences which can and should be taken into account when deciding what to do. Culpability, however, demands that the particular defendant ought to be measured not only against what she should have believed, but also against what she did believe. In other words, the pool of information for evaluating action is the *union* of that information which she should reasonably have possessed, and that which she did in fact possess.[36] A defendant who realizes something will explode if dropped is blameworthy unless she acts accordingly, whether or not an ordinary person would have known the facts. In this the law concurs: '[t]he defendant is credited with such perception of the surrounding circumstances and such knowledge of other pertinent matters as a reasonable man with the actor's own superior knowledge, if any, would possess'.[37]

[34] Hence the defendant's unreasonable failure to hold a given belief might be due to an unreasonable, antecedent failure. For example, it is not *ipso facto* negligent to miswire an electrical plug if I am certain that the blue (positive) wire is the earth. My negligence lies earlier, in misreading a manual containing wiring instructions. Had I correctly read a reputable but erroneous instruction manual, it might well be reasonable to labour under a misapprehension. In that case we should not treat the miswiring as negligent.

[35] The term 'information' is used here in a broad sense to encompass beliefs and raw perceptions, as well as that which is available to be perceived (e.g. by looking).

[36] Subject to any inconsistency; we do not enquire simply what it would have been reasonable to believe, but also whether the defendant's own beliefs were reasonable. In principle, it is possible to conduct oneself non-negligently because of a reasonable belief, even an erroneous one, which other defendants in the same position need not hold.

[37] Fleming, n. 3 above, 98. See also *Restatement* §289; *Clarke* v. *Holmes* (1862) 7 H & N 937; *Argyll* v. *Beueselinck* [1972] 2 Lloyd's Rep. 172.

Attention

Sometimes a defendant fails to think about the significance of her behaviour. If D is lying on the beach and does not think to check on her children who are playing in the water, we may conclude she is to blame when they swim too far out and are drowned. It is not that D has culpably misunderstood some aspect of her conduct or environment. Rather it is that she has (culpably) failed to pay any sort of attention.[38] The example shows one role of attention—as a prompt, effectively making connections between perceptions, memories, beliefs, and desires. Although the process normally occurs non-reflectively, its upshot, if the relevant concerns are important enough, is to prompt reflective evaluation and advertence to the potential concern. We might say that 'if D had shown the care and concern for others that she should reasonably possess, she would have thought of the danger'. In doing so we blame D. We are not merely criticizing what happened, that she failed to notice the danger. We are criticizing her. Paying attention is necessarily the first step in discharging the duty that underpins liability and blame for negligence—the duty to take care lest harm occur. D's failure in the example to think about the situation is blameworthy because it reflects upon her; it reflects an insufficient concern to comply with that duty and to avoid the harm. And this is a shortcoming in D, one for which we may disapprove of her and which adversely informs our assessment of her moral worth.

On the other hand, failure to notice something is generally not deliberate, and it may be thought that the non-reflective nature of attention generates an objection to the view taken here, that inattention can be culpable. A non-reflective process, the objection runs, can be thought of as something that merely happens to D, a mental event in respect of which D is passive. As such, the attribution of moral responsibility to D for the occurrence (or non-occurrence) of that mental event is inappropriate. We are morally responsible for what we do, but not for what happens to us.

It is the last proposition that is problematic. I have argued elsewhere that moral responsibility depends not on the act–event distinction, but on voluntariness.[39] Indeed, that is why liability for mere events or states of affairs may sometimes be justified. Thus the important question for moral responsibility is not whether D chose not to attend, but whether D can avoid her failure. And normally she can.

In most cases, the defendant can rectify the source of her inattendance. Where a person is careless, she can seek to improve her character, to become the sort of person who cares more, and correspondingly alter or condition her cares and concerns, including those which prompt attention. Alternatively, an agent's failure to attend may be traceable to particular factors, such as her impulsiveness, preoccupation, or distraction. In such instances the appropriateness of the explanation ought to be

[38] Contrast this case with one where the children are strangers. The comparison illustrates a point which is only touched upon in this essay: even in law, reasons affecting judgements of culpability (the 'standard' of care) necessarily overlap with those determining the range of one's obligations (the 'duty' of care).

[39] A.P. Simester, 'On the So-called Requirement for Voluntary Action' (1998) 1 *Buffalo Crim. LR* 403, 407–12.

examined. For example, I might be so excited by the offer of an ice-cream that I forget to complete a task undertaken earlier. Now it is not to be assumed that, to be counted reasonable, the defendant must be bereft of emotions. But one may be blameworthy for failing to control one's emotions, or for failing to learn how to do so: 'we need to take care not to be blinded or distracted by anger, greed, lust, ambition, etc. . . . [W]e hold people responsible not only for exercising such capacities of self-control; we hold them responsible for acquiring them, so that lack of such capacities does not excuse.'[40] This holds true even if we are unaware of a weakness. Our duty to take care, which requires us to exercise self-control, obligates us also to acquire the capacity to do so; in effect, we may be expected to ascertain our faults and to remedy or at least compensate for them.

Additionally, even if one is unable to rectify the causes of one's inattention, one may still be expected to compensate. Just as someone who knows of her blindness is expected to take the care that a blind person should, so too with non-physical limitations: if, for example, D should know she is likely to forget something, we may expect her to allow for that by taking additional precautions. Similarly, a person who does not care about some risk can still make herself pay attention, and choose to consider whether that risk exists.

More directly, a person may also be culpable for these shortcomings, *simpliciter*. That one fails to care enough about something, or is distracted by anger, is something for which one may normally be blamed without more. Even if someone cannot alter her character, we may fairly blame her for being one who cares insufficiently, or at least for behaving as if so.[41] And to the extent that inattention is due to such dispositional traits, it may be blamed too. Conversely, where these conclusions cannot be drawn, we should exculpate. Inattention caused by extraneous factors, e.g. when a patient is injected with morphine to suppress pain, warrants no reproof.

One objection to the argument made here is that it seemingly takes no account of the time frame over which activity occurs, and therefore risks proposing a standard of attention which is impossibly strict. The law's reasonable man, it is said, is hypothetically consistent, and maintains the standard of care without even momentary variation. In the context of attention, this suggests a defendant is expected *continuously* to pay vigilant attention to his environment. Yet ordinarily a person's attention may wander, especially during prolonged and concentrated periods of activity such as long-distance driving. In these cases, to expect unwavering concentration appears to

[40] Milo, n. 19 above, 87, 88. Cf. G. Watson, 'Skepticism About Weakness of Will' (1977) 86 *The Philosophical Review* 316, 331–2.

[41] Subject to the sort of exceptional case contemplated by H.G. Frankfurt, 'Identification and Externality' in his *The Importance of What we Care About* (Cambridge University Press, Cambridge, 1988) 58, 64: 'surely it is possible for a person to recognize that a certain passion is unequivocally attributable to him, even when he regrets this fact and wishes that the passion did not occur in him or move him at all. Perhaps after long struggle and disillusion with himself, a person may become resigned to being someone of whom he himself does not altogether approve'. Even here, we may expect the defendant to take precautions that compensate for her inattention; where she does not do so, we may reasonably dismiss the suggestion that her failure to care is external to her, a value that she resists.

impose a standard of strict liability rather than of culpability. My thoughts on this issue are tentative, but it seems to me that the law's position is not so inflexible. The law requires only invariably *reasonable*, imperfect attention (hence, for instance, the possibility that a defendant might understandably be distracted[42]). Reasonable fluctuations are not excluded. Moreover, there is no reason why the standard should not accommodate circumstances. After spending thirty hours on duty during an emergency, a doctor may be excused a mistake that would be culpable had she been fresh. By contrast, the driver who can no longer maintain reasonable concentration should stop and rest.

Perception and Recall

Two key aspects of paying attention are perception and recall. They repay some further consideration here, by illustrating how the law's standard of care in negligence can be given substance within the approach taken by this essay. In general, the expectation of reasonable perception explains most questions raised in negligence by non-standard physical abilities. The naturally clumsy person,[43] for instance, if she has reason to perceive her clumsiness, can be expected to take extra care that her behaviour does not have unintended consequences. So also the driver who suddenly collapses might be excused blame for losing control of her vehicle,[44] unless she has done so before.[45] An objective standard of perception of physical sensations in practice creates a duty of self-knowledge on the part of the actor.

By contrast, a defendant cannot be blamed for a failure of perception due to malfunction of the senses:[46] one can be negligent for not looking, and for not perceiving, but not for failing to see. Thus the blind ought to be excused from having to perceive everything that one would normally be expected to notice. Instead, they are to be expected to recognize that they are blind and behave as would be sensible for a blind person. It also follows from the characterization of perception as a standard *function* that there are no grounds for expecting one to perceive and hence know about things that one's sensory processes have never had the chance to register.[47] It cannot be

[42] *West Ky. Tel. Co.* v. *Pharis* 25 Ky. LR 1838 (1904); n. 52 below.

[43] To the extent that this reflects a 'physical' defect (i.e. of motor control over one's limbs) rather than inattention. See F. James and J.J. Dickinson, 'Accident Proneness and Accident Law' (1950) 63 *Harv. LR* 769.

[44] Cf. *Robinson* v. *Glover* [1952] NZLR 669; *Waugh* v. *Allan* [1964] SC 102.

[45] Cf. *Gordon* v. *Wallace* (1973) 42 DLR 3d 342; *Boomer* v. *Penn* (1965) 52 DLR (2d) 673.

[46] Unless her sensory failure is itself blameworthy, as when it is due to self-induced intoxication. See, e.g., the facts of *Lipman* [1970] 1 QB 152 and *Majewski* [1977] AC 443.

[47] Conversely, one may be culpable on the basis of greater than normal experience. Fleming's remark, though a claim about the law, seems morally apt: 'an employer, therefore, with greater than average experience of a particular risk may have to respond with more than average precautions; while a father who permits his child to go to school despite symptoms which a competent doctor would diagnose as scarlet fever, will be judged by whether he is a layman or a medic', n. 3 above, 99. Cf. *Stokes* v. *GKN* [1968] 1 WLR 1776; *Restatement* §289 illustration 12. Analogously, an expert rally driver should exercise his superior skill to protect a passenger: *McComiskey* v. *McDermott* [1974] IR 75.

culpably negligent to be ignorant of something one has no reasonable opportunity to perceive, as is implicit in *Davis* v. *Concord and Montreal Ry.*:

> If a person of average prudence, put exactly in the place he was, possessed of the same knowledge and *means of knowledge* of the danger and the means of avoiding it, would or might have done as [the actor] did, he was without fault.[48]

The same view is reflected in *Geier* v. *Kujawa*, where a German girl was excused for failing to use a seat belt whilst in a car in part on the ground that she had not seen one before.[49] Similarly, one explanation of the allowance generally made in law for young children is that adults are assumed to have accumulated perceptions justifying a maturity that children, with limited experiences, cannot develop.

(Even so, uninformed action may be negligent. *Geier* v. *Kujawa* is consistent with *The Lady Gwendolen*, where brewers who ran a shipping service in order to transport stout were held liable for their failure to meet the standard of care required of shipowners. Their claim that they were shipowners only incidentally was robustly dismissed: '[t]he law must apply a standard which is not relaxed to cater for their factual ignorance of all activities outside brewing: having become owners of ships, they must behave as reasonable shipowners'.[50] In this the law coheres with moral expectations. The fault of the brewers lay not *per se* in their ignorance of what to do, but in their becoming shipowners without finding out.)

Ignorance of risk is often a matter of imperfect rather than non-existent attention. When D is lying on the beach and sees her children playing in the water, it may be that she feels they are safe only because she has failed to recall that there is a dangerous undertow nearby. Had she thought more carefully—attentively—about the matter, she would have remembered the undertow. Subject to exceptions for blameless incapacity,[51] such cases may be adjudged culpable by analogy with other varieties of inattention, suggesting that an objective standard may justifiably be demanded of defendants. If D has a memory of something apparently relevant to her actions, she ought normally to recall that item. Given, for example, that D knows the 'give way' rules of the road, she may be expected to bear them in mind while driving. This is not to saddle the defendant with infallible recall. We do, and should, allow for forgetfulness due to some distraction: even though I might know something which ordinarily one would think of when acting, I may understandably not recall it when distracted, for instance, by concern for the welfare of my terminally ill sister.[52]

[48] (1895) 44 A 388, 391 (my italics).

[49] [1970] 1 Lloyd's Rep. 364. Cf. *Linnehan* v. *Sampson* (1878) 126 Mass. 506; Terry, n. 27 above, 49; contrast, however, *Restatement* §290.

[50] [1965] P 294, 305.

[51] I have in mind cases such as temporary clinical amnesia.

[52] *West Ky. Tel. Co.* v. *Pharis*, 25 Ky. LR 1838 (1904). See also *Pigg* v. *Bloom*, 177 NW 2d 441, 446; *Wand* v. *Shelbina*, 420 SW 2d 348, 350; *Restatement* §289 comment k.

Memory

In law, it seems that the defendant is negligent if she forgets something which normally one would not.[53] My own view is that this conclusion is justified. One might suspect, however, that in requiring a standard memory the law diverges from morality. Seavey, in particular, suggests that it is inapt to criticize another for having a poor memory:

> Memory seems to be a purely mechanical process existing independently of the will. . . . Not only do we forget much that we will to remember, but we remember many things we would like to forget. Thus the mental processes connected with memory approximate the purely physical processes. In view of this it would seem that liability should not be based upon a standardized memory.[54]

We do not attribute negligence when the defendant's shortcoming is, say, poor sight; why should we do so when it is poor memory? One reason is that there are steps one can take to remember something. Indeed, it is for this reason that we tend to regard 'I forgot' as only a mitigating excuse—often we reject such a plea, provided the defendant has the general capacity to remember and is not suffering, say, from Alzheimer's disease,[55] because we think it betokens mental sloth. One can usually take measures to improve a weak memory.[56] Alternatively, where one realizes the significance of an item of information, one may be expected to make a concentrated effort to remember it, or to take additional measures to remind oneself.[57]

Additionally, even if memory is mechanical in the way Seavey envisages, nonetheless we can expect to have a better memory for things more important to us;[58] things in which we are more interested. (If I forget my appointment for a haircut, that is less a cause for surprise, and for an adverse inference about my cares and concerns, than if I forget to attend my own wedding.[59]) Our recollection of the things we should

[53] *Froom* v. *Butcher* [1976] QB 286, 295; *Reynolds* v. *Los Angeles Gas & Elec. Co.*, 122 P 962 (1912); *City of Charlottesville* v. *Jones*, 97 SE 316 (1918) (note that these are all tort cases). Although not expressed in such terms, the decisions can be distinguished on the footing that the forgetfulness may have been temporary (and thus a failure of recall rather than memory).

[54] Seavey, n. 24 above, 20.

[55] With this proviso I have in mind instances where the defendant *cannot* remember, and the biochemical ability to write long-term memories into the brain by rearranging neurons is lost; in other words, where there is (demonstrably) an involuntary incapacity. Cf. the note by Taubenfeld *et al.*, 'A Molecular Correlate of Memory and Amnesia in the Hippocampus' (1999) 2 *Nature Neuroscience* 309.

[56] For an example of a programme designed to do so, see C.L. McEvoy and J.R. Moon, 'Assessment and Treatment of Everyday Memory Problems in the Elderly' in M.M. Gruneberg, P.E. Morris and R.N. Sykes (eds.), *Practical Aspects of Memory: Current Research and Issues* (John Wiley, Chichester, 1988) ii, 155.

[57] See, e.g., the measures discussed in D.J. Herrman and M. Palmisano, 'The Facilitation of Memory Performance' in M.M. Gruneberg and P.E. Morris (eds.), *Aspects of Memory* (2nd edn, 1992) i, 147.

[58] Cf. *Restatement* §289 illustration 4; *Basset* v. *Fish* 75 NY 303 (1878).

[59] *Per* R.A. Duff, *Intention, Agency and Criminal Liability* (Blackwell, Oxford, 1990) 163, for the bridegroom to forget his wedding 'itself manifests an utter lack of concern for his bride and their marriage. Had he cared at all for her, he *could* not have forgotten their wedding. The fact that he forgot it shows that he did not care; and that lack of concern, as manifested in his conduct, is the fault for which she rightly condemns him.'

remember is improved, simply, when we care more about those things.[60] Failure of memory is thus analogous to inattention: it may be culpable in virtue of reflecting our failure to care sufficiently.

At a pragmatic level, the law has supplementary evidential reasons to treat cases of abnormal memory lapse as negligence. A claim that 'I forgot' is all too easy for the defendant to make,[61] and is also very difficult to distinguish from a failure to pay attention. Even were Seavey correct, to admit memory lapse as a defence would make a false claim thereof both tempting and powerful. Further, in the majority of cases the inadvertence which accompanies negligence is likely to follow, at least in part, from the fact that something has been forgotten. The defendant's liberty to show this in her own defence would therefore drastically and unwantedly alter the nature of negligence, particularly in the civil law.

Intelligence

Tort law demands a reasonable level of intelligence of the defendant. 'It is not enough that the defendant did the best he knew how.'[62] The position is less clear in criminal law.[63] Consider, for example, the facts of *Elliot* v. *C*,[64] where C, a 14-year-old girl in a remedial class at school,[65] set fire to a shed by igniting white spirit. On a charge of arson it was found, *inter alia*:

> That the [defendant] had given no thought at the time that she started the fire to the possibility of there being a risk that the shed and contents would be destroyed by her actions [and] in the circumstances this risk would not have been obvious to her or appreciated by her if she had given thought to the matter.[66]

What should the law do about such cases?[67] The evidential difficulties associated with establishing low intelligence do not seem to be prohibitive, as perhaps they are for

[60] J.A. Meacham and J. Singer, 'Incentive Effects in Prospective Memory' (1977) 97 *Journal of Psychology* 191. And by paying them more attention: A.D. Baddeley *et al.*, 'Attention and Retrieval from Long-Term Memory' (1984) 113 *Journal of Experimental Psychology: General* 518; B.B. Murdock, 'Effects of a Subsidiary Task on Short-Term Memory' (1965) 56 *British Journal of Psychology* 413. *Per* A.D. Baddeley (*Human Memory: Theory and Practice* (Lawrence Erlbaum Associates, Hove, 1990) 148), '[i]t is almost certainly the case that motivation will influence the subject's willingness to attend to the material to be learnt'.

[61] Compare automatism: ' "blackout", to use one of the titles, is one of the first refuges of a guilty conscience': *Cooper* v. *McKenna, ex parte Cooper* [1960] Qd. R 406, 419.

[62] *Vaughan* v. *Menlove* (1837) 3 Bing. NC 468, 471 (where, arguably, the case was one of deliberate risk-taking or recklessness). See also *Restatement* §289 comment g.

[63] Contrast *Creighton* (1993) 105 DLR (4th) 632; *Hudson* [1966] 1 QB 448; and *Hardie* [1985] 1 WLR 64 with *Elliott* v. *C* [1983] 1 WLR 939; *R. Stephen* (1984) 79 Cr. App. R 334; *Ward* [1956] 1 QB 351; and *Stone and Dobinson* [1977] QB 354.

[64] [1983] 1 WLR 939.

[65] At first instance (ibid. 942), '[t]he justices were of opinion that the defendant was of very low intelligence for her age of 14 years'.

[66] Ibid. 945.

[67] What the Divisional Court *did* was, following *Caldwell* [1982] AC 341 and *Lawrence* [1982] AC 510, to convict her of *reckless* destruction of property. (Leave to appeal was refused by the House of Lords: [1983] 1 WLR 939, 951n.) The judgment is perhaps the nadir of modern English criminal law.

claims of memory lapse. We do have means with which to assess intelligence, and at first instance in *Elliott* v. *C* the justices made findings of this very type. Further, sub-intelligence is in important ways a different type of mental shortcoming from the others considered already. Intelligence neither reflects one's character or values, nor is it within one's control.

There is a distinction between the mistake which is understandably made by a stupid person (A), and the mistake which is stupidly made by one not stupid (B). We may criticize B's stupidity in making that mistake, because B could and should have done better than she did. Her failure reasonably to exercise her intelligence manifests a culpable failure to be sufficiently careful. By contrast, A's mistake does not reflect upon her moral worth. It may be deplored but not criticized. Like physical limitations such as blindness, stupidity is a condition that cannot much be altered by someone who suffers from it. Moreover, a person of low intelligence is likely to be poorly placed to take precautions against the harmful consequences of her own stupidity. Neither can low intelligence be attributed to the defendant's failure to care sufficiently—to a defective aspect of her character for which, like desires, we may blame her *simpliciter*.

It seems, therefore, that arguments such as those in favour of requiring a standard memory do not apply to the intellect. Similarly, low intelligence is distinguishable from cases of unreasonable inattention, which might normally have been avoided were the defendant a more caring and concerned person. So there is good reason, at least in the criminal law, not to expect reasonable intelligence of the defendant but, rather, to expect *that she reasonably use the intelligence she has*.[68] Correspondingly, when finding fault with low intelligence, the reasonable man of tort does not articulate judgements of blame.[69]

Hart's Capacity Conditions

The analysis of intelligence presents a useful opportunity to re-examine Hart's 'capacity and fair opportunity' account of culpability. In the context of criminal negligence, Hart proposes the following conditions of liability:[70]

(i) Did the accused fail to take those precautions which any reasonable man with normal capacities would in the circumstances have taken?
(ii) Could the accused, given his mental and physical capacities, have taken those precautions?

[68] This view suggests that those with above-average intelligence must meet a higher standard of care. Perhaps there are reasons to limit what may be asked of persons with superior abilities. But if they exist, such reasons do not seem to deny moral culpability.

[69] Tort law's expectation of a reasonable intelligence may be justified, if at all, only by supplementary considerations which lie outside the scope of this essay: perhaps by a 'social engagement' rationale, whereby those who want the advantages of being treated as responsible, autonomous participants in human society must accept the obligation to meet an objective standard even when they cannot meet that standard; or by a more general need for private law to balance conflicting interests like liberty and security when regulating social intercourse. See, e.g., A.M. Honoré, 'Responsibility and Luck: The Moral Basis of Strict Liability' (1989) 104 *LQR* 530.

[70] N. 5 above, 154.

Satisfaction of condition (i) is taken by Hart to establish, objectively, a fair opportunity to avoid the relevant harm, while condition (ii) reflects the subjective requirement of capacity. To illustrate, suppose that in *Elliott* v. *C* the defendant C was incapable of recognizing the conflagration that might follow her actions. Condition (ii) shows, straightforwardly, that she ought not to be convicted, since her incapacity preempts the attribution of blame.

Taken by itself, this result seems correct. Indeed, the same test would appropriately preclude blame for a failure of perception due to blindness, or for a failure of memory due to clinical amnesia. However, these cases are plausible only because they turn exclusively on the application of condition (ii). The problem with using Hart's analysis more generally is that it joins two conditions which serve different purposes. Condition (ii), the subjective enquiry into a defendant's general capacities, is a condition of moral responsibility, not of culpability. As such, it excludes blame and cannot ground it. Rightly, a failure to satisfy condition (ii) exempts the defendant in *Elliott* v. *C*. But the converse is not true. It does not follow, if C has subjective capacity, that she *is* blameworthy.

The positive task, to establish when culpability is warranted, falls to condition (i). Yet *that* condition—the 'fair opportunity' criterion—is objective. On Hart's condition (i), the defendant would be expected to have reasonable intelligence, not to use reasonably the intelligence that she has: culpability is assessed by comparison to a hypothetical figure. With the greatest of respect to Hart, for the reasons given earlier in this essay it is difficult to see how that objective test can establish culpability. Its application looks only at the existence, on the facts, of an opportunity to avoid harm; not at *why* the defendant missed that chance.

The difficulty is not resolved by applying Hart's conditions in combination. To see this, an example may help. Suppose that in *Elliott* v. *C* the risk was not obvious to C but that she was just capable of comprehending it, had she thought very hard about the matter for some hours; while a person of reasonable intelligence would have recognized the risk straightforwardly. On Hart's test, C would be culpable for burning down the shed. But it does *not* follow that C is culpable; unless it was *reasonable*, and not merely *possible*, for one of *her* limited intelligence and experience to comprehend the risk. In the absence of arguments like those made specifically in this essay about attention and memory, the fact that a hypothetical 'normal' person would have avoided the harm says nothing about whether the defendant had a fair opportunity to do so. To hold otherwise is to fall victim to the fallacy of personalizing the reasonable man.

(C) WHAT IS TO BE DONE? THE BALANCE OF REASONS

Assessing negligence requires the identification of ostensible reasons for or against her behaviour which the defendant ought to have taken into account; we have discussed this process under conditions (a) and (b). But implicit in condition (c) is that it is also essential to establish, given those reasons, how the defendant should actually behave. Reasons must be evaluated. They must be weighed and measured against each other. Indeed, a defendant who acts inadvertently and for the wrong reasons may yet avoid the charge of negligence if, in fact, her behaviour turns out to be supported by reasons she did not recognize. Luck is no less intrinsic to negligence than it is to the rest of the law.

An evaluation of reasons requires a process of rational deliberation, a transition from the recognition of ostensible reasons to judgement that one either may or should not behave as did the defendant. The main problem for this transition arises when ostensible reasons conflict, so that it is necessary to resolve which of those reasons should be acted upon by eliminating defeated (i.e. outweighed or excluded) ostensible reasons from consideration. For much the same rationale that governs desires and values, it seem appropriate here to demand an objective standard of the defendant. The justification is both institutional—that the law is warranted by its role, as a system for guiding behaviour through proscriptions, in not permitting the defendant to supplant its own evaluation of her behaviour—and intrinsic: preferring defeated reasons is a fault for which, without more, one is culpable. This view is reinforced by appeal to the nature of reasons. The existence of an ostensible reason provides a ground, subject to attribution requirements, for blaming a defendant who does not act as that reason requires.[71] But the existence of a defeated reason provides no such ground.[72] The defeated reasons drop out of the judgement, leaving only the undefeated, now conclusive, reasons for action to supply grounds for blame.

In the context of blaming, an evaluation of reasons must be rational, practical, and not absolute. It may be reasonable not to consider all the reasons relevant to one's behaviour, even deliberately. Most graphically, the circumstances may generate a reason for acting urgently. In *Cordas* v. *Peerless Transportation Co.*, for example, the actor was confronted with the immediate prospect that he 'would suffer the loss of his brains'[73]—a future that pre-empted further consideration as well as supplying an ostensible reason to act. The limitation on considering reasons is, however, more general than cases of emergency. Trivial matters do not demand the same attention or careful consideration as affairs of greater moment. Yet, even when the consequences are at their most serious, reasonable conduct is not conduct that is right, all things considered.[74] It is conduct guided by reasonable reasons; by reasons for which a reasonable person might act. No defendant is omniscient. Indeed, one may even be vindicated when acting unreasonably, e.g. on a hunch that turns out to be right. The policeman who arrests on such a hunch is right,[75] but unjustified. Conversely, even

[71] Cf. Raz, n. 17 above, 186–7; subject to qualification in the text above, at n. 19.

[72] Though the defeated reason may still be cause for regret: B.A.O. Williams, 'Ethical Consistency' in J. Raz (ed.), *Practical Reasoning* (Princeton University Press, Princeton, NJ, 1978) 91.

[73] 27 NYS 2d 198, 199 (1941). The agent, a taxi driver, had taken an uninvited fare who 'immediately advised him "to stand not upon the order of his going but go at once," and added finality to his command by an appropriate gesture with a pistol addressed to his sacroiliac'.

[74] For discussion of related distinctions, see J. Bennett, *The Act Itself* (Oxford University Press, Oxford, 1995) chap. 3.

[75] Cf. G. Williams, 'Offences and Defences' (1982) 2 *LS* 233, 244–7.

reasonable men make mistakes. We can ask no more than that a person is reasonable. And hope that she is right.

CONCLUSION

Let exploration return to doctrine. The analysis in this essay suggests that it is possible, after all, to defend some judgements of negligence in terms of a defendant's blameworthiness. Sometimes the defendant's failure to meet an objective standard does reflect adversely on him: on those occasions, we are right to extend to him our moral judgement of his actions. Conversely, if it is to comprise a standard of culpability, the reasonable man test ought to be subjective to the extent that the defendant's shortcomings do not disclose fault. In particular, apart from physical limitations a defendant should be exempted blame for the harms caused by shortcomings of intelligence.

It should be no surprise that the reasonable man sets a mixed standard, part personal and part imposed. Without external standards of comparison, judgement is impossible. Without reference to the defendant, judgement cannot lead to blame. The device of the reasonable man is, in a sense, one means by which the law seeks to reconcile the impersonal with the humane. In a wider sense, reconciliation is at the core of reasonableness. To be reasonable is, in a sense, inhuman. For reasonableness is not so much a state as an approach, a tool that articulates the shared understandings, principles, and expectations of a society; a framework for discussion, argument, disagreement, and even agreement—not only over issues of culpability, but also about such questions as our obligations in society and our values as human beings. It provides not answers, but an opportunity to get near them. As such, the reasonable man is no more than a conduit for shared human judgements. Yet that is no small thing. Ultimately, we are irredeemably human. So we cannot always know what is right. Sometimes, all we can do is form judgements, and aspire that they be reasonable.

Towards a Theory of Contract

Stephen A. Smith*

A complete theory of contract law should answer two questions. The first is an analytic question about the nature of contractual obligation. What sorts of events give rise to a contractual obligation and what is the content of the obligations thus created? In particular, how are those events and obligations similar or dissimilar to the events and obligations that are the focus of tort law, unjust enrichment law, or equity? Where, in other words, should contract be situated on the map of private law? The second question is a normative or justificatory question: how, if at all, can contract law be justified? What is the moral basis, if any, for enforcing contractual obligations? Do rights, utility, or something else—or nothing else—underpin contract law? The analytic and normative questions are related. The justification for contractual obligation turns in part on what sort of a thing a contractual obligation is. And—though the point is more complex and controversial—our understanding of the nature of contractual obligations is determined in part by our views on what sorts of obligations are, or at least might conceivably be, legitimately enforced.

This essay presents the beginnings of a theory of contract; the beginnings, that is, of answers to the analytic and normative questions about contract law. The answer that will be given to the analytic question is the traditional or orthodox answer that contracts are promises or something closely akin to promises. The answer to the normative question is more complex: contractual obligations enforce individual rights—promissory rights—but we cannot explain promissory rights without acknowledging the good that promising helps to bring about, which is the good of special relationships. The main theme of the discussion of the normative question—and the main theme of this essay—is, however, easily summarized: contract is like property. To understand better how contract can be justified we should turn not to tort or unjust enrichment theory but to property theory.

In order to understand why contract is like property, and why this similarity supports the view that contracts are essentially promises, we need to know what was thought to be wrong with the traditional account of the promissory theory, and what alternatives were proposed to that account. We begin, then, with a brief tour of modern contract theory. For convenience sake the discussion is organized around different answers to the analytic question, but, as will be evident, the normative question is never far away.

* I would like to thank Mark Gergen, Didier Frechette, Tony Honoré, Jeremy Horder, Andrew Simester, John Finnis, Anne de Moore, Nicholas McBride and Timothy Endicott for comments on earlier versions, and the Social Sciences and Humanities Research Council of Canada for financial assistance in preparing this essay.

THREE ANSWERS TO THE ANALYTIC QUESTION

Contractual Obligations as Self-Imposed Obligations ('Promissory Theories')

The traditional and orthodox view is that the distinguishing feature of contractual obligations is that they are self-imposed: contractual obligations are obligations that individuals place upon themselves. The idea that contracts are promises is the best-known example of such a view. A promissory obligation, on the orthodox understanding,[1] is a self-imposed obligation: a promise is created by communicating an intention to undertake an obligation to do the promised thing. This explains why, on the orthodox view, contractual obligations are distinct from obligations in tort. If I have promised to sell you my car I have an obligation to sell you my car because I promised to do so. But my obligation to drive my car carefully so as not to harm you (and others) exists whether or not I want to be under such an obligation. Tort obligations are imposed by law, contractual obligations, on this view, are imposed by the parties.

The phrase 'self-imposed obligation theories' is a mouthful, so I shall refer hereafter to such theories as 'promissory theories'. But it should be kept in mind throughout that not all theories in this category regard contracts as promises strictly speaking. There are other types of self-imposed obligations apart from promises, some of which—notably agreements—have been suggested as alternatives to the idea of contracts as promises. For the purposes of this essay, the distinctions between different sorts of self-imposed obligations are not important. The alleged virtues and vices of promissory theories that are discussed in this essay are equally virtues and vices—or not as the case may be—if contracts are agreements or some other variant of self-imposed obligation.

The main attractions of promissory theories of contract are well-known. The basic and fundamental requirement of offer and acceptance, the significance of intention and freedom of contract, the defences of duress and undue influence, and the primary remedies of expectation damages and specific performance, all have an evident connection with the idea that contractual obligations are self-imposed. To be sure, when we look more closely at these and the other doctrines making up the common law of contract, significant questions arise for defenders of promissory theories. Consideration, estoppel, the objective test of formation, mistake, frustration, and implied terms generally, to name just a few of the more obvious candidates, all present challenges of varying degrees of difficulty for promissory theories. I shall not, however, discuss in this essay criticisms based on these or other ways in which it is alleged promissory theories fail to fit the facts—the rules and legal decisions—that make up contract law. Even were space not a consideration, objections of this sort, though not insignificant, are unlikely at the end of the day to be fatal to promissory

[1] See e.g. J. Raz, 'Voluntary Obligations and Normative Powers' in Supplementary vol XLVI, *Proceedings of the Aristotelian Society* (1972). For a contrary view, see, in the same volume, N. MacCormick, 'Voluntary Obligations and Normative Powers'.

theories. Certain problematic doctrines—for example consideration—are equally problematical for nearly all plausible theories of contract. Other doctrines—for example mistake, frustration, implied terms, and mitigation—are arguably explicable on the basis of more sophisticated notions of intention, responsibility, and, more generally, of the nature of promises. Yet others—the objective test in formation and unilateral contracts are two possibilities—may require that we redraw the boundaries of contract law, pushing some of what we had thought was contract into tort or another category. Some scholars will argue that what is left after such moves is not worth calling a theory of contract, or at least not worth calling a promissory theory, but it seems unlikely that any blow will be decisive in this battle.

In any event, the main reason for not focusing on 'fit' objections to promissory theories is that the most influential and sophisticated critics of promissory theories have not themselves focused upon such objections. Their objection is an essentially moral objection (this is where the analytic and normative questions meet). The objection is that it would be illegitimate for the state to enforce promises *qua* promises and thus that something else besides the enforcement of promises must be going on. What I will call the 'moral' objection to promissory theories of contract has been articulated in slightly different forms by, amongst others, Fuller and Purdue (hereafter 'Fuller'),[2] Atiyah,[3] Raz,[4] and Benson.[5] The basic idea, however, is not in dispute. Enforcing promises *qua* promises is enforcing a duty to benefit others, and thus is inconsistent with J.S. Mill's harm principle (or, to adopt more Kantian language, inconsistent with the distinction between misfeasance and non-feasance[6]). Enforcing a promise,

[2] L. Fuller and W. Purdue, 'The Reliance Interest in Contract Damages' (1936) 46 *Yale LJ* 53, parts I and II.

[3] P. Atiyah, *The Rise and Fall of Freedom of Contract* (1979) 1–7.

[4] J. Raz, 'Promises in Morality and Law' (1982) 95 *Harvard L Rev.* 916.

[5] P. Benson, 'Contract' in D. Patterson (ed.), *A Companion to the Philosophy of Law and Legal Theory* (1996).

[6] Fuller's article (n. 2 above) is easily the most influential publication, in the modern era, for the view that enforcing promises *qua* promises is not a proper role for the law . But Fuller himself nowhere makes this claim as explicitly as I have done above. Fuller's article focuses on contract damages and his criticism of enforcing promises can only be implied from his argument that expectation damages are a 'queer kind of compensation', in that they compensate the plaintiff by giving him something he never had. Furthermore, in later work Fuller made clear that he believed it was legitimate in certain circumstances to enforce promises *qua* promises: L. Fuller, 'Consideration and Form' (1941) 41 *Columbia L Rev.* 799. Atiyah, whose work in this area has been nearly as influential as Fuller's, makes his antipathy to enforcing promises clearer though he is still not unequivocal. Representative is the following from the introduction to *The Rise and Fall of Freedom of Contract* (n. 3 above) 4:

> The protection of mere expectations cannot (it is suggested) rank equally with the protection of restitution interests (arising from benefit-based liability) or reliance interests (arising from reliance-based liability). A person whose expectations are disappointed, but who suffers no pecuniary or other loss from the failure to perform a promise, has surely a relatively weak claim for complaint or redress.

The clearest articulations of the moral objection to promissory theories are found in more philosophical accounts, such as (in contemporary work) those of Raz or Benson. For example, in reviewing Atiyah's *Promise, Morals and The Law* (n. 20 below) Raz writes (n. 4 above) 937: '[i]t follows from the harm principle that enforcing voluntary obligations is not itself a proper goal for contract law. To enforce voluntary obligations is to enforce morality through the legal imposition of duties on individuals. In this respect it does not differ from the legal proscription of pornography.'

on this view, is like enforcing a duty to be charitable. When a promise is broken, the promisee is often harmed as a result of having detrimentally relied on the promise. But in enforcing a promise *qua promise*, that harm is irrelevant. A promissory obligation exists regardless of whether the promisee has relied—and often the promisee will not have relied (or will have relied to an extent less than the value of the promise). Thus, the objection goes, the content of that obligation may be, and often is, a pure or partial obligation to benefit another. Enforcing such an obligation, like enforcing charity, is not a proper function of the law (or at least not a proper function of private law)—and this is so whether one regards the law from a utilitarian or rights-based perspective.[7] Enforcing promises is enforcing morality as such. Advocates of this objection do not recommend that people should break promises without compunction. We should keep our promises—just as we should give to charity. But keeping promises, like giving to charity, is a virtue, not an obligation (or if it is an 'obligation' it is a 'supererogatory' obligation of the sort that is not appropriate for legal enforcement). Private law should get involved only when one individual has or is about to harm another.

At this point the following question may be asked: why should it count against a description of the law—an answer to the analytic question—that the description portrays the law as doing something illegitimate? Why assume the law is morally justified? This is a question—a rather large question—of general jurisprudence and as such cannot properly be addressed in this essay. Two observations must suffice. The first is that the moral objection can be reformulated as an issue of consistency with other parts of the law. Whether or not it is legitimate for the law to enforce obligations to benefit others, legal obligations of this sort are unusual, at least when enforced on a regular basis. There are clear instances where the law does to a greater or lesser degree enforce obligations to benefit others, but such obligations are, and are clearly recognized to be, exceptions to the general rule that we are under no *legal duties* to benefit our neighbours. There is no general or even limited duty to rescue at common law. The question, then, is why should contract law be different (keeping in mind that contractual obligations are frequently owed to complete strangers). Stated thus, the 'moral' objection is also an 'inconsistency' objection, namely that promissory theories of contract are inadequate, since they suppose that contractual obligations are inconsistent with the widely and firmly held legal principle that individuals are not liable for failures to benefit others.

[7] J.S. Mill, the originator of the 'harm principle', was of course a utilitarian, but the principle can easily be, and often has been, expressed in Kantian language (see e.g. Benson, n. 5 above). In Kantian language, the relevant distinction is between misfeasance, which the law may regulate, and non-feasance, which the law may not regulate. On this view, breaking a promise *qua* promise is non-feasance, rather than misfeasance, because it does not involve infringing another's rights to his or her property or bodily integrity. Thus keeping promises is merely an ethical duty or virtue rather than a legal duty. This is not to deny that there are respectable arguments for the enforcement of morality as such in particular, limited ways: see e.g. R. George, *Making Men Moral* (1993). It is difficult to think, however, of any plausible defence of a general duty to benefit others of the sort that, assuming the harm-principle objection is correct, would be needed to support the enforcement of promises *qua* promises.

At this point the question may be rephrased from 'why assume the law is moral' to 'why assume the law is coherent'? This brings us to the second observation. No assumption can be made when doing contract theory that the law is in fact moral or coherent. Nevertheless, in so far as an interpretation reveals the law to be moral and coherent, that interpretation will help us to understand the law better. We do contract theory, and legal theory generally, in order better to understand law. Better understanding is achieved in so far as law can be shown to reveal an intelligible order: that is what understanding is, it is trying to make intelligible order out of apparent disorder. And intelligible order, in the case of law, is one that, if not actually coherent and morally justified, is at least of the sort that might be regarded by participants in the practice as coherent and morally justified.[8] Making sense of the law means, *inter alia*, making sense of the way that law is understood from the inside, by participants—and law is understood from the inside as coherent and justified. The law may not turn out to be explicable in this way—it may in fact be a chaotic collection of unjustified decisions and rules—but the search for intelligible order is and always has been the criterion of success for those proposing theories of law. The precise type and strength of the link required between morality (and coherence) and a theory of law is the main issue that distinguishes rival schools of general jurisprudence. For our purposes it is enough to acknowledge—as nearly all contemporary legal theorists, natural lawyer and positivist alike, do acknowledge—that a completely value-free description of law is either an impossibility or of little interest to scholars.

Promissory theories of contract remain popular amongst contract lawyers, but surprisingly few attempts have been made to rebut the moral objection to such theories. Some scholars, such as Neil MacCormick,[9] have in effect argued that the objection has no force because promises are essentially 'induced reliance' obligations rather than the self-imposed obligations they are traditionally understood to be. For reasons that will become clear in the next section of this essay, I think this move misunderstands promises, but even if I am wrong it should be clear that the 'promissory theory' that MacCormick defends bears little resemblance to the promissory theory described above. (Rather, it resembles the induced reliance theories described in the next section, and as such will be assessed, *qua* theory of contract, in that section.) The best-known attempt to address the moral objection directly is found in Charles Fried's *Contract as Promise*.[10] Fried does not mention the 'harm principle' by name, but he is clearly addressing it when he asks whether enforcing promises is, as he puts it, consistent with the 'basic liberal distinction between the good and the right'.[11] It may be good that one keeps one's promises (just as it is good to give to charity), but why, Fried asks, is there a duty to do so, why does the promisee have a *right* to performance? How is it possible 'that by my words I should make wrong what before was

[8] See J. Raz, 'Authority, Law and Morality' (1985) 68 *The Monist* 3. For a stronger view of the link between understanding and justifying law, see R. Dworkin, *Law's Empire* (1986).

[9] MacCormick, n. 1 above; see also T. Scanlon, 'Promises and Practices' (1990) 19 *Philosophy & Public Affairs* 199.

[10] C. Fried, *Contract as Promise* (1981) chap. 2.

[11] Ibid. 7–8.

morally indifferent?'[12] Fried provides the following summary of his answer to the moral objection:

> There exists a convention that defines the practice of promising and its entailments. This convention provides a way that a person may create expectations in others. By virtue of the basic Kantian principles of trust and respect, it is wrong to invoke that convention in order to make a promise, then to break it.[13]

Fried's answer contains three propositions. The first is that there is, just as a matter of fact, a convention of promising, and that this convention defines how promising is understood. The second proposition is that one of the things that promising is conventionally understood to do is to create expectations in others. The third proposition, which, though not explicit in the above summary, is clearly implied, is that *because* of the expectations created by promising, it is wrong (meaning here a breach of a legally enforceable duty) to break a promise.

The first two propositions—that promising has a conventional meaning and that part of this meaning is that making a promise creates certain expectations—are relatively uncontroversial, at least in the general terms in which they are advanced. But they clearly are insufficient to support a legal duty to keep a promise. There are many ways of creating expectations that do not support legal duties to fulfil those expectations, and this is true regardless of whether the expectations arise from the conventional meanings of words and actions. There is a convention in western societies that a dinner guest will bring a small gift for the host. But it has never been suggested that a guest who fails to do so should be legally liable. If the expectations created by promising create moral duties it must be because there is something special about those expectations. Understood in its normal sense of 'expected to happen', the only sort of 'expectation' that promising creates is an expectation that the promisor will do what he or she promised. Not all promises create such an expectation—consider an alcoholic's promise to stay sober—but even ignoring this qualification, it seems clear that Fried is not referring to expectations of this sort. The only significance of the statistical likelihood that a promisor will do as promised is that the promisee (and others) may rely upon those expectations. Whether or not there exists a general obligation not to let people down in whom you have induced assumptions about how you will act (something Fried denies[14]), such an obligation is not an obligation to keep a promise. As Fried himself stresses,[15] promissory obligations are different from induced-reliance obligations because they bind regardless of whether the promisee has relied (and, we may add, they also differ in that expectations can be induced other than by making promises). An obligation to ensure the reliability of induced assumptions is a reliance-based obligation, not a promise-based obligation.

Which 'expectations', then, is Fried referring to in the quoted passage? It appears that by 'expectations' Fried means beliefs about the moral effects of making a promise. In particular, what is relevant about a promise for Fried is that it creates the

[12] C. Fried, *Contract as Promise* (1981) chap. 9. [13] Ibid. 17. [14] Ibid. 10–11.
[15] Ibid.

belief that the person making the promise is under a moral obligation to keep the promise. Fried writes: '[a]n individual is morally bound to keep his promises because he has intentionally invoked a convention whose function it is to give grounds—moral grounds—for another to expect the promised performance'.[16] In this key sentence Fried refers rather mysteriously to the 'function' of promising as that of giving moral grounds to expect performance, but by 'function' he must mean simply that this is how the convention of promising is understood, that is, when a promise is made it is understood (by convention) to create a duty to perform. Fried cannot mean that the convention of promising does in fact create such a duty because, apart from making both the first part of the sentence and Fried's other references to expectations ('beliefs') redundant, Fried earlier argues explicitly that the convention of promising does not have this effect. Having explained why the convention of promising arose, exists, and is useful, Fried concludes, rightly, that 'this by itself does not show that I am morally obligated to perform my promise'.[17]

Thus interpreted, Fried's argument is that because a promisor has, by intentionally invoking a convention, created a belief that the promisor is under a moral obligation to do the promised thing, the promisor is in fact under such an obligation. In short: there is a duty to keep promises because we believe there is a duty to keep promises. Fried himself notes that his argument has a 'bootstrap quality' to it: '[t]o have force in a *particular case* promises must be assumed to have force generally. Once that general assumption is made, the effects we intentionally produce by a particular promise may be morally attributed to us.'[18] But why? Fried does not tell us. The remainder of Fried's argument is found in just three sentences:

> To renege [on a promise] is to abuse a confidence the promisor was free to invite or not, and which he intentionally did invite. To abuse that confidence is like (but only *like*) lying: the abuse of a shared social institution that is intended to invoke the bonds of trust. In both speech and promising there is an invitation to the other to trust, to make himself vulnerable; the liar and the promise-breaker then abuse that trust.[19]

If we leave aside any possible concerns for induced reliance, in so far as Fried is making a substantive argument here it is the same argument we just saw, namely that a promisor is under an obligation to keep a promise because others believe he is under such an obligation. But the fact that other people believe I have an obligation to keep my promises cannot in itself be a justification for me actually having such an obligation. Or at least it cannot be a justification without eliminating entirely the distinction between positive and critical morality (something Fried surely did not intend to do).

This is not to deny that others' beliefs about my moral obligations may be relevant in determining how morally I ought to act. One way such beliefs are relevant is that they are often tied to beliefs about how, as a matter of fact, I am likely to act. If you believe there is moral duty to keep promises then you will probably expect me to keep

[16] Ibid. 16. [17] Ibid. 14. [18] Ibid. 12 (emphasis in original).
[19] Ibid. 16 (emphasis in original).

my promises. I should take this and other facts about what you believe into account when deciding whether to make and keep my promises. But for reasons that should be clear by now, any duty founded on the link between promising and expectations about what a promisor will in fact do is a reliance-based duty, a duty not to let others down who detrimentally rely upon a promise.

Breaking a promise may of course disappoint not only a promisee's material expectations about how a promisor will act, but also disappoint the promisee's moral expectations. By this it is meant that a disappointed promisee may be upset and indignant for the same reason that we get upset and indignant at people who act recklessly without actually harming anyone. Victims of breach may well feel morally indignant that their trust in another has, as Fried puts it, been 'abused' (though it is worth pointing out that only intentional breaches could have this effect). But surely moral outrage and indignation, however genuine, are not in themselves good reasons for imposing a legally enforceable duty. The mere fact that individuals feel their rights have been abused is not, and has never been thought to be, a sufficient reason for legal redress: what matters is whether individuals' rights have in fact been abused.

A second way in which others' moral beliefs may be relevant to how I should act arises because particular actions or omissions can acquire symbolic meanings. In western societies it is a convention that you should take off your hat when entering a church. There is also a convention that you should shake hands when introduced to a stranger. In explaining these and similar conventions there is often little more that can be said than that the relevant actions are regarded as appropriate or not by the society in question. You ought to take your hat off when entering church because failing to do so is seen as a mark of disrespect, and it is a mark of disrespect because people think it is a mark of disrespect. By analogy, it may be argued that breaking a promise is understood as a particular type of insult, as one way of failing to respect another—in the same way that failing to shake hands is an insult. Fried's frequent references in *Contract as Promise* to the importance of conventions in understanding promising suggests that this is indeed how he understands the wrong of promise-breaking. But, again, the mere fact that an action is understood, by convention, as wrong does not mean that it should attract legal liability—just as a majority's view that homosexuality is wrong should not make homosexuality illegal. There is no legal duty to shake hands when you have been introduced to someone, nor is there a legal duty to take your hat off when you enter a church. That an action is understood, by convention, as wrong does not preclude the state from asking whether proscribing that action is consistent with the harm principle. The law's refusal to enforce morality as such does not change when that morality is grounded in conventional views. Legally speaking, breaking a convention is and should be relevant only when doing so harms another individual, for example by infringing property rights. This observation is essentially the same one that was made in the previous paragraph: the law does not and should not concern itself with mere feelings of moral outrage: actual harm is required.

To conclude: Fried's response to the moral objection to promissory theories of contract is unpersuasive. Stripped to its essentials, his argument is that promises create obligations to perform because they are conventionally understood to create such obligations. This argument does not just have a bootstrap 'quality' to it, it is a pure bootstrap argument.

Reliance Theories

The main response to the moral objection to promissory theories has been not to try to rebut the objection but instead to try to develop non-promissory theories that are not vulnerable to the objection. We shall consider two such alternative theories. The first I shall call the reliance theory of contract. No comprehensive or canonical account of this theory exists. The best-known modern[20] accounts of reliance theories are found in the work of Fuller,[21] Atiyah,[22] and Gilmore,[23] but none of these writers attempts to develop the theory in anything like the philosophical rigour or comprehensiveness with which Fried develops a promissory theory.[24] The main features of the theory are, however, familiar enough and relatively uncontroversial. According to a reliance theory, a contractual obligation is essentially an obligation not to let someone down whom you have induced to rely upon you. It is, in other words, an obligation to ensure the reliability of induced assumptions.[25] It follows that a breach of contract, properly understood, occurs when, in certain circumstances, one person has induced another person to rely upon him or her and that other person does so to his or her detriment. The qualification 'in certain circumstances' indicates that not every act of inducing reliance supports a legal duty not to let the relying person down. The person inducing the reliance must be viewed, in a difficult to define sense, as legally responsible for the harm caused by the induced reliance.

Promissory obligations, as they are conventionally understood,[26] and induced reliance obligations overlap, but they are not identical. A common way of inducing someone to rely upon you is to make a promise, but it is not the only way. If, knowing that you need to cross a river and that you trust me, I tell you there is a safe bridge

[20] For a useful survey of modern reliance theories, see R. Barnett, 'The Death of Reliance' (1996) 46 *Journal of Legal Education* 518. For references to earlier work in this vein, see P. Atiyah, *Promises, Morals and Law* (1981) chap. 1, and Atiyah, n. 3 above, 775–7.

[21] Fuller, n. 2 above: as noted earlier, Fuller himself never extended his ideas on reliance as far as some others have done.

[22] See Atiyah, n. 3 above, n. 20 above; 'Contract, Promises and the Law of Obligations' in P. Atiyah, *Essays on Contract* (1986).

[23] G. Gilmore, *The Death of Contract* (1974).

[24] Significantly, each of the above scholars resisted monotheistic accounts of the law, and thus none of them suggested, even implicitly, that an induced-reliance theory could explain as much of contract law as the theory described above purports to explain. But since it is this theory—and not particular scholars—that is our interest we will ignore such matters of exegesis.

[25] This phrase comes from M. Spence, 'Australian Estoppel and the Protection of Reliance' (1997) 1 *Journal of Contract Law* 1.

[26] The best philosophical explanation of the conventional view is found in Raz, n. 1 above. For a contrary view see MacCormick, n. 1 above, and Scanlon, n. 9 above.

around the next bend, I have not made a promise, but I have induced you to rely upon me. Nor does all promising induce reliance. I may promise to do something, but add at the same time that you should not, for one reason or another, rely on me performing that promise. A promisee may also simply, and rightly, refuse to believe that a promisor will keep a promise (e.g. an alcoholic's promise to stay sober). Moreover, even where a promise does induce reliance, the reason the promisor is under an obligation to perform, according to this view, is not because of the promise, but because reliance was induced. Thus, in so far as the reliance theory provides a reason for giving legal effect to promises, promises are not given effect *qua* promises but *qua* reliance-inducing acts.

The claim that contractual obligations are reliance based is often associated with the idea of contract being absorbed into tort law.[27] Though useful in highlighting that reliance-based obligations are, like tort obligations, externally imposed rather than self-imposed, the contract-as-tort picture should not be pushed too far. Damage to property or person, whether through detrimental reliance or otherwise, is of course a crucial element of the cause of action in tort. So too, the idea that inducing reliance gives rise to a contractual obligation only in certain circumstances is similar to the requirement, in the tort of misrepresentation, that the parties have a 'special relationship' or that the defendant 'assumed responsibility'. The little work that has been done on the question of when inducing reliance ought to trigger an induced reliance obligation suggests, rightly it seems, that the same sorts of considerations used to define a 'special relationship' or an 'assumption of responsibility' are relevant.[28] Nevertheless, there does not exist a general tort of letting someone down whom you have induced to rely upon you. An induced-reliance obligation is more akin to, if not identical with, the classical conception of promissory estoppel—albeit without the restriction, at least in England, that estoppel may be raised only as a defence. In both cases, liability is incurred for making a statement that was intended to, and did, induce detrimental reliance in the recipient. It follows that, like estoppel, an action for 'induced reliance' lies in the shadowy area between tort and contract, as they are classically understood. It lies in between the obligation to keep a promise and the obligation to tell the truth.

Whatever its legal classification, a reliance account of contract is not vulnerable to the harm principle objection, or at least not vulnerable in the same way that promissory theories are vulnerable. An induced-reliance obligation is triggered by detrimental reliance: for there to be liability someone needs to be made worse off. Thus harm in the uncontroversial sense of detrimental reliance exists if an induced-reliance obligation is breached. There is a moral objection to induced-reliance theories, but it is different from the moral objection to promissory theories. The objection is simply that, absent a promise, the fact of inducing reliance is, regardless of whether the relying party is made worse off as a result, an insufficient ground for a legal duty. Unless I

[27] See e.g. G. Gardner, 'An Inquiry into the Principles of the Law of Contracts' (1932) XLVI *Harvard LR* 12.

[28] On which see Spence, n. 25 above.

make a promise I am and ought to be free to change my mind. You may choose to rely upon my statements, but that is your choice. As Fried puts it, 'why should my liberty be constrained by the harm you would suffer from the disappointment of the expectations you choose to entertain about my choices?'[29] In other words, there is no moral ground between contract and tort, as they are classically understood: there is an obligation to keep promises and an obligation to tell the truth and nothing in between. (And estoppel, on this view, must, if defensible, be understood as an essentially promissory obligation.) There is no easy response to this objection, although it has to be said that the question has attracted little attention from legal or moral theorists. Scholars have spent considerable effort examining the variety of rules that allegedly lie in the ground between tort and contract (e.g. estoppel, good faith, unconscionability, abuse of right), but little attention has been paid to the theoretical foundations of such rules. It is not difficult to think of examples in which the fact of inducing reliance seems, intuitively, sufficient to support an obligation but the stronger the example, the more plausible the counter-argument that the relevant reliance-inducing statement was actually a promise.[30]

Whatever the force of the moral objection to induced reliance theories of contract, there exists another, more straightforward objection to such theories. It is that reliance theories cannot account for certain central features of contract law. The standard 'fit' objection to reliance theories is that contractual liability neither requires nor is measured by the extent of the promisee's reliance.[31] Expectation damages—the value of the promised performance—not reliance damages is the norm in contract law. As Fuller argued at length, the 'expectation' interest is in many cases a good proxy or substitute for the 'reliance' interest[32]—but, as Fuller also acknowledged, the two measures clearly are not identical.[33] And, though the point did not seem germane to Fuller, the 'expectation as proxy for reliance' theory cannot work without doing serious violence to judicial language and reasoning—to the way that judges reason, and to the way they understand what they are doing. Fuller's explanation is thus external to the practice of law.[34] For the same reasons that a plausible theory of law

[29] Fried, n. 10 above, 10.

[30] Consider an example put forward by MacCormick, n. 1 above: a person walking along the cliff edge of a bay spots a swimmer in trouble below. He lowers a rope-ladder, which the swimmer swims towards, thereby eliminating the only other possibility of saving himself by swimming to a beach in the next bay. The person lowering the rope, having induced the swimmer detrimentally to rely upon him, is now under a duty, McCormick suggests, not to lift up the rope.

[31] For an early statement of this objection, see G. Cohen, 'The Basis of Contract' (1933) 46 *Harvard LR* 553.

[32] '[E]ven if our interest were confined to protecting promisees against an out-of-pocket loss, it would still be possible to justify the rule granting the value of the expectancy, both as a cure for, and as a prophylaxis against, losses of this sort': Fuller, n. 2 above, 60–1. Atiyah added the point that in practice the law often awards reliance damages despite purporting to be awarding expectation damages: Atiyah, n. 20 above, 41.

[33] Fuller, n. 2 above, 64.

[34] It is beyond the scope of this essay to defend the priority of internal accounts of law except to note that making a human practice intelligible means, *inter alia*, taking seriously the way that participants in the practice understand what they are doing. See E. Weinrib, *The Idea of Private Law* (1995) chaps. 1 and 2.

will make intelligible law's claims to be justified and coherent,[35] a plausible theory will make intelligible law's claims that the reasoning and concepts it employs are meaningful. Fuller's attempt to explain away expectation damages renders that reasoning and those concepts unintelligible. The legal explanation of contractual damages is, on Fuller's account, a sham.

A second, more significant, inconsistency between the reliance theory and the actual law of contract concerns the most basic requirement for a valid contract: the requirement of offer and acceptance. According to the logic of the reliance account, the crucial question in establishing contractual liability ought to be whether reliance has in fact been induced. But the question the law asks is whether there has been an offer and an acceptance, that is, whether the parties agreed to undertake certain obligations. The test for agreement is admittedly an objective one, but it is still a test for agreement—not for reliance. Promises often induce reliance but, as noted earlier, not all do so, and, as significantly, there are ways of inducing reliance apart from making promises. As with expectation damages, an attempt could be made to explain offer and acceptance as a proxy for what the law is really concerned about, namely induced reliance. Such an account would presumably point to the evidentiary advantages of assuming that promises, and only promises, always lead to the sort of reliance that the law should worry about. The rules on offer and acceptance would need to be squeezed hard, but, even assuming for the sake of argument that such an explanation could be developed, this explanation, like Fuller's explanation of expectation damages, is entirely external to the legal explanation of the rules on offer and acceptance. From the legal perspective the rules of offer and acceptance are about what they appear to be about, namely establishing the existence of an agreement. In sum, the difficulty with the induced-reliance theory is that the central features of contract law are unconcerned with reliance.

Transfer Theories

For the reasons described above, relatively few critics of promissory theories have been persuaded to support reliance theories. In recent years some of these critics have begun to develop a second alternative to promissory theories. The origins of what I shall call the 'transfer theory' of contract can be traced back to at least Hegel and Kant,[36] but unlike promissory and reliance theories its central tenets are not yet part of the common knowledge of contract lawyers. And even more than the reliance theory, the transfer theory has yet to be developed by its advocates in anything like a comprehensive way.[37]

[35] See text accompanying n. 8 above.

[36] On the historical origins of the transfer theory, see Benson, n. 5 above, 42.

[37] The most complete exposition of a transfer theory is probably found in R. Barnett, 'A Consent Theory of Contract' (1986) 86 *Columbia LR* 269. Shorter, but particularly sophisticated explanations of transfer theories are found in Benson, n. 5 above, and P. Benson, 'The Idea of a Public Basis of Justification for Contract' (1995) 33 *Osgoode Hall LJ* 273.

The idea underlying the transfer theory of contract is nevertheless reasonably clear: contracts are transfers of already existing rights.[38] A contracting party is regarded as having possessed, prior to the contract, various rights, one of which is the right to the performance of some act. When that person makes a contract, the relevant performance-right is transferred to the other party. The other party now owns this right and may legitimately enforce it. Failure to perform is thus akin to theft (if intentional) or conversion (if accidental). The breaching party is attempting to take back what he or she has freely given away.

As Benson observes, a transfer theory analogizes a contract to the 'widely recognized and simple model of completed gifts and exchanges'.[39] In a simple gift or simultaneous exchange of property, one person transfers property to another, which property is then owned—immediately—by the transferee. Contracts are similarly about the transfer of 'rights', the only difference—an important one—being that what is transferred are not rights to physical property, but rights to the performance of some act: '[w]e have to analyse the transfer that constitutes a contract as a transfer of non-physical, but actual, possession'.[40]

It should be evident that the transfer theory is not vulnerable to the harm-principle objection. If the victim of a breach owns the right to performance, then failing to perform is a harmful wrong, akin either to theft or conversion depending on the relevant mental state. Breach is viewed, 'not merely as failing to confer a benefit to the promisee in virtue of their contract, but as interfering with what already belongs to the promisee in virtue of their contract'.[41] It is also clear that this theory is not vulnerable to at least the first of the 'fit' objections that were made against the induced-reliance theory. If the plaintiff owns the defendant's performance, then expectation damages and specific performance are appropriate remedies. If you steal or break my property, it is right that you should compensate me for the full value of the property.

Whether a transfer theory fits as well with other features of contract law, such as offer and acceptance, is not clear, but it is difficult to speculate in this regard—partly because little has been written on these issues, but also because the abstract nature of the theory means it is hard to be certain how it applies in concrete cases. But regardless of how well it may fit the law, the transfer theory is in any event vulnerable to a more general, and hence more serious, objection. The objection, a conceptual one, is that the right which, according to the transfer theory, is transferred in a contract does not exist prior to the contract. That right must be created before it can be transferred.

This objection to the transfer theory is not that it is impossible to conceive of rights to performance being transferred. Although the law places certain limits on the transfer of contractual rights of a personal nature (which suggests that the analogy to ordinary property rights breaks down at certain points), the assignment of contractual rights is long established in the law. Indeed, what the law calls assignment of contractual rights is indistinguishable from how a transfer theory regards all contracts,

[38] Barnett, n. 37 above, 297: 'contract law concerns enforceable obligations arising from the valid *transfer* of entitlements that are *already vested* in someone' (emphasis in original).

[39] Benson, n. 37 above, 319.

[40] Ibid. 319.

[41] Benson, n. 5 above, 42.

namely as the transfer of already existing rights to performance of some act. The problem, rather, is that to transfer, or assign, a right or a piece of property, the transferor must already own that right or piece of property. The rights that contracting parties are, according to the transfer theory, meant to be transferring are rights they do not own. To be sure, if I agree in a contract to hand over the keys to my house to Jane next Friday I did, prior to making the contract, have the right to hand over my keys to Jane next Friday. One of my rights of ownership is the right to alienate that right. More generally, I have the right, subject only to not infringing other people's rights, to do what I like with my keys next Friday. But this is not the right that I have supposedly transferred in my contract. According to the transfer theory, Jane's right is not a right to do whatever she wants with my keys next Friday but rather a right to the performance of my promise. These are different conceptions of the word 'right'. The 'right' to decide what I am going to do next Friday is in Hohfeld's language a privilege or a liberty.[42] What Jane has obtained is a claim-right, a right to the performance of a particular act. This claim-right is not something that I own. I cannot, prior to making my promise, be under a duty to myself to give Jane my keys next Friday, and even if I could in theory be under such a duty I was not actually under that duty since I plainly was at liberty to do whatever I wanted with my keys prior to making the contract. This objection to the transfer theory cannot be avoided by saying that the right I have transferred to Jane is my liberty-right to do whatever I want with my keys next Friday. If that were the right transferred then Jane could require me to hand over my keys to Bill next Friday. The only right Jane has *vis-à-vis* my keys and me is the specific right that I give her my keys next Friday. Moreover, my obligation to perform takes effect immediately: there is nothing further that Jane need to do.

The conclusion to be drawn from the above discussion is that the common sense intuition that a contract is different from a mere assignment of rights is correct. If a promisee owns the rights to the promisor's performance it must be because the contract has created and not merely transferred those rights.

A FRESH START: CONTRACT AND PROPERTY

For many contract scholars the search for a unifying theory of contract is a pointless exercise, a will-o'-the-wisp. Our brief tour of modern contract theories appears to support this conclusion. The orthodox view that contracts are promises appears to be inconsistent with the principle—fundamental both in law and in morality—that the state should not enforce obligations to benefit others. The most popular alternative view, that contractual obligations are obligations not to let others down whom you have induced to rely upon you, appears inconsistent with certain central features of contract law. A second alternative view, which regards contracts as transfers of exist-

[42] W.N. Hohfeld, 'Fundamental Legal Conceptions' (1913) 23 *Yale LJ* 16, 29–44.

ing rights, appears wrongly to suppose that contractual rights can exist prior to a contract.

Should we then abandon the search for a theory of contract? In the remainder of this essay, I will suggest that, notwithstanding the present state of contract theory, the search should not be abandoned, and I will begin—though only begin—to sketch what such a theory looks like. In general shape, the theory is a promissory theory of contract: a theory that regards contractual obligations as essentially self-imposed obligations.

Our survey of modern theories has highlighted three requirements that any plausible theory of contract must satisfy. First, in order to avoid the harm-principle objection it must be shown that breaching a contract infringes one of the promisee's *rights*. Secondly, in order to avoid the objection to transfer theories it must be shown that the promisee's right is *created* by the contract. Finally, in order to avoid the objections to reliance theories it must be shown that the content of the promisee's right is a right to the *performance* of an undertaking. We can summarize these requirements by saying that a plausible theory must explain how a contract creates, at the very moment of its completion, a present right to the performance of a future act. This right is owned by its beneficiary and becomes a part of the beneficiary's present wealth, similar to the beneficiary's rights to her car, house, or other property. Described in the language of promising, a plausible theory must explain how promises create rights to the performance of a promise.

This of course brings us back to where we started, to the original objection to promissory theories. The idea underlying the harm principle objection to promissory theories is that it makes no sense to suppose, as promissory theories must suppose, that contractual rights are *created* by the contract. How could it be that simply by uttering certain words, for example 'I agree to deliver this pen to you tomorrow ', I create a right—the right to have this pen delivered to you tomorrow—where none existed before? Promissory theories of contract appear to involve a magical sleight of hand, whereby something is created out of nothing. The critics of promissory theories thus believe, or perhaps just assume, that contract law, like tort law, must be about protecting already existing rights—hence the reliance and transfer theories.

The first step in resurrecting promissory theories is to understand why at the level of principle this assumption is mistaken; why, that is, there is nothing unusual *in principle* about the idea that certain actions could create rights—including contractual rights—where none existed before. (I leave to one side for the moment the different question whether *promises* may create rights.) If this possibility seems unusual it is only because contract lawyers and contract scholars are used to thinking about contract law as part of the law of obligations, alongside tort and unjust enrichment. The rules making up tort law and unjust enrichment law are indeed concerned with the protection rather than the creation of rights. This is not to deny that many (perhaps all) of the rights recognized in tort law or unjust enrichment law are only recognized in law by the rules of tort law or unjust enrichment law. In a sense, such rights are, *qua legal* rights, 'created' by these legal doctrines. But it is not supposed that the individuals subject to the rules themselves create the rights that tort law and unjust enrichment law protect. In so far as it makes sense to speak of such rights being created, it is the courts and legislatures that create the rights, not ordinary citizens. It follows that, if contract law is thought to allow individuals to create rights where none existed before, then contract does indeed fit uneasily with what are thought to be contract's closest neighbours, namely tort and unjust enrichment.

If, however, we look beyond tort law and unjust enrichment law it should be evident that there is nothing unusual about legal rules that provide for the creation, and not merely the protection, of rights. It is not unusual because this is one of the things that property law does. One of the fundamental functions of property law is to determine in what circumstances an individual has created a property right to a particular thing and—part of the same question—what is the nature of the right thus created. Because the stock of 'things' on our planet are now nearly all already owned, property law in practice concerns itself primarily with issues about the nature of the rights thus created, about the meaning of ownership. But there are—and logically must be, if our property-owning regime is legitimate—rules dealing with what individuals must do in order to create (as opposed to receive from another) a property right. Unlike our bodies, things do not come into the world attached to people. Nor are the things that make up the earth part of a mythical communal pie that was at some point in time cut up and distributed to the inhabitants of the earth. First ownership of things happens by individuals doing particular acts. In law, individuals come to own previously unowned land by virtue of doing acts showing that they are the 'first possessors' (with all that entails) of the relevant land. Similarly, the rules dealing with treasure trove, adverse possession, wild animals, accession (adding to things of others), and alteration (mixing with things of others)[43] show how, by doing certain acts, individuals may create new property rights to things or to land. Of more significance in modern times, the regime of intellectual property provides for the creation of rights to ideational entities. It follows that if property rights are legitimate, it must be because certain property-right creating acts have been explicitly or implicitly recognized as legitimate ways of creating property rights.

It is of course no simple matter to explain how individuals may by certain acts legitimately create property rights in things (broadly defined). Far more effort has been expended attempting to justify property than contract and it is fair to say this effort has produced little consensus on the explanation. But—and the observation is an important one—the response of property theorists to the difficulties inherent in trying to explain and justify property rights has never been to analogize property to those areas of the law concerned with the protection of rights, such as tort law or unjust enrichment law. It is rightly recognized that no matter how our concepts of property are manipulated, property cannot be explained without an explanation of how it is possible to create rights where none existed before. Of course many scholars have denied that the rules that do and have governed the creation of property rights are

[43] See e.g. B. Rudden and F.M. Lawson, *The Law of Property* (2nd edn., 1982) 74–5.

legitimate. The relevant question, however, is not whether any particular legal system's property right-creating rules are legitimate, but whether any rules providing for the creation of property rights could be legitimate. Fewer critics have denied this possibility, and in particular none of the critics of promissory theories of contract has made this objection. Moreover, even those critics who deny that any process of property-right creation could be legitimate do not deny that this is what must be shown for property rights to be justified.

Our first conclusion, then, is that from a legal perspective we should not think it strange that contract law might contain rules providing for the creation, rather than the protection (or transfer), of rights. Property law has this role; thus contract may have a similar role. It further follows that, if, as I have suggested, contract law is fundamentally about the creation of rights, then contract should be viewed as closer to property law than to tort law or unjust enrichment law. Contract and property are similar, in that each provides rules specifying both what acts are required in order to create a particular sort of right and what is the content of the right thus created. The difference between contract and property lies in the nature of the acts and the nature of the rights thus created. In property, the relevant acts are, broadly speaking, acts indicating an intention to take control or possession of some thing. In contract, the relevant acts are acts indicating an intention to undertake an obligation. In each case, the relevant acts create ownership over some thing, broadly defined. In property, the thing typically is land or a material object. In contract, the 'thing' is the performance of an act. On the right-creation view of contract, a contract creates what is in effect a property right in the promisee, albeit a property right in the performance of an act. It also follows that not all that common lawyers normally regard as contract law is properly considered contract law. In particular, and broadly consistent with the approach of civil law systems, the rules regarding breach of contract and its consequences are not strictly part of the law of contract—just as the rules on theft and negligent damage to property are not considered part of the law of property. Those parts of contract *are* part of tort law, of the law of wrongs. Contract law, on the view considered here, is concerned solely with the creation and definition of rights—not with their protection.

To suggest that a parallel may be drawn between contract and property does not of course show that contract is actually similar to property, much less that this similarity in any way legitimates contract law. For that, a substantive argument is needed why the particular acts that make up a contract ought to be regarded, like the acts constituting adverse possession or taking possession of treasure trove, as sufficient to create new rights, and more specifically as sufficient to create rights to the performance of a future act. In developing that substantive argument, however, the comparison with property may again be useful. If contractual rights are similar to property rights then the structure of the justification for contract rights is likely to be similar to the structure of the justification for property rights. The content of the substantive justification is unlikely to be the same—the right to property and the right to the performance of a contract are too dissimilar—but the *structure* of the argument may be similar. Our second conclusion, then, is that contract theorists would do well to read property theory (and vice versa, although that is not my concern here).

Property, Contract, and Promises

To determine whether the acts that make up a contract are analogous to the acts that create property rights we need first to characterize the nature of those acts. What sorts of acts make up a contract? The obvious suggestion to begin with is that promises, or something closely akin to promises (e.g. agreements) are what make up contracts. As noted earlier, there is a natural affinity between the central doctrines of contract law and the idea of contracts as promises. The main objection to promissory theories is not that they fail to fit the law (though this objection certainly is made), but that they are inconsistent with the harm principle. If it is possible for promises to create rights, that objection can be overcome.

What justification, then, can be given for why making a promise should, at least in some circumstances, be understood, like the acts that create property rights, as creating new rights, and in particular rights to the performance of a future act? As suggested above, it may be helpful to look to property theory—or at least to some aspects of property theory—when answering this question. Not all property theory is relevant, since much of it focuses solely on whether property rights, however created or obtained, are or could be legitimate, and is silent on issues regarding the original creation of property rights. Such work typically explains why property rights are or are not a good thing generally and what shape such rights ought to have, rather than how and why particular people are granted such rights in the first place. Theorizing of this sort often has implications for when individuals ought to be regarded as having obtained, other than by transfer, title to particular things, but those implications need to be spelled out to assist us in thinking about right-creation in contract law.

If we look to work that purports to explain how property rights might be obtained other than by transfer, we find, very broadly speaking, two sorts of accounts. The first, which I shall call static explanations, suppose that, just because of their status as people (or a sub-category of people), all (or some) people should be regarded as having property rights to particular things. For example: 'all individuals have a right to ownership of a portion of the earth's surface'. Whatever the intrinsic merits of such arguments, it seems clear that they are not what we are looking for, which is an explanation of how and why particular acts validly create new property rights. To explain that we need to turn to the second type of explanation of how property rights are created *de novo*, which I shall call dynamic explanations. Such accounts attempt to explain how and why doing particular acts gives the persons doing those acts valid title to some previously unowned thing. The treasure is mine, because I found it. Locke's labour theory of property, whereby an individual acquires property through mixing his labour with land or material, is the best-known example of this second type of explanation.[44] Whatever one thinks of Locke's particular version of a dynamic

[44] J. Locke, *Two Treatises of Government* (ed. P. Laslett, 1988 [1690]) 285–302.

explanation for property, it seems clear that something along these lines is necessary if we are to explain the right-creating property rules we actually have—and if we are to use that explanation in trying to understand contract.

Dynamic theories can themselves be divided broadly into two categories. A desert-based (or what might also be called an entitlement-based) theory explains the significance of property-creating acts on the basis that, having done certain acts, an individual deserves or merits a property right. It is *fair* that the individual be considered the owner of the property. Again, Locke's theory of property is sometimes understood in this way: having devoted time and effort labouring on some thing it is only fair that I now be given property rights in that thing.[45] It seems clear that a desert-based procedural theory will not illuminate contract law. The things that a promisee needs to do in order to create a contract are not the sorts of things which could show that the promisee merits or deserves contractual rights, at least if merit and desert are understood in their normal sense. Extensive contractual rights can be obtained through doing nothing more than saying 'I agree'. Not insignificantly, desert-based theories encounter similar difficulties explaining property law.[46] One problem with such accounts (though not the only one), is that extensive property rights, like extensive contractual rights, can be created through acts involving minimal time, effort, or any other meritorious characteristic. The apparent exception of acquiring ownership through lengthy adverse possession confirms the rule, since the acts required to obtain adverse possession, though significant, are in no sense meritorious.

The other form of dynamic explanation for property rights, which I shall call an intention-based explanation, regards the significance of property-creating acts as flowing, at least in part, from the fact that they manifest particular intentions of the property-creating actor. More specifically, what is usually thought to be significant about property-creating acts on this view is that they manifest an intention to create a new normative relationship between the individual and the thing in question.[47] That relationship, broadly speaking, is one of control over some thing *vis-à-vis* the rest of the world, and thus the relevant acts, again broadly speaking, are acts that communicate such a manifested intention to the rest of the world. Different explanations can be and have been given for why manifest intentions should matter in this way. For example, both Hegel's idea that only through owning property can individuals express their true freedom and the economists' idea that granting property rights stimulates productive labour are consistent with the importance of intentional actions in creating property rights.

There is an evident link between intention-based theories of property and promissory theories of contract. A promise, on the conventional understanding, is formed by communicating an intention to undertake an obligation. Both property-creating and contract-creating acts are, on the intention-based view, about the intentional

[45] Ibid. 291. [46] See e.g. J. Waldron, *The Right to Private Property* (1988) chap. 6.

[47] See e.g. I. Kant, *The Philosophy of Law* (trans. W. Hastie, 1887) 81–4; G.W.F. Hegel, *Philosophy of Right* (trans. T.M. Knox, 1965) ss. 41–71; C. Rose, 'Possession as the Origin of Property' in her *Property and Persuasion* (1994) and, generally, S. Munzer, *A Theory of Property* (1990) 67–75.

creation of new norms. Each is constituted by power-conferring rules. In the case of property, the normative relation is with the rest of the world, and thus the relevant communicative act is directed at the rest of the world. In the case of contract, the normative relation is with a particular person and thus the relevant communicative act must be directed at that person.

It seems useful, then, for contract theorists to look more closely at intention-based theories of property. Broadly speaking, any plausible intention-based theory of property must have two parts. The first, the teleological part, explains why allowing individuals to create property rights is a good thing generally. The second, the deontological part, explains why property rights have to be in the form of rights, why they are property *rights* (and not merely ordinary reasons to act one way or another). Neither part of the theory stands alone—the right has to be explained in light of the good, and vice versa—but the distinction is useful for expository purposes. The teleological part of a property theory typically goes something along the following lines: allowing individuals to create property rights is a good thing because necessary in some way for individuals to achieve good lives, for example because of the importance of expressing our individuality or having control over a private space to act or creating social wealth. The deontological part of the story explains why, in order that creating property rights actually achieve its role in helping to realize the specified good, those property rights must be *rights*. 'Rights' are understood here, broadly speaking, as rights to exclusive use and possession of a thing, and in particular the right to preclude others from using that thing, even if they need it more than the owner does.

It seems reasonable to suppose that there is a link between intention-based accounts of property rights and the best explanation of contract rights. Any plausible explanation of property must turn in some way on the fact that property rights allow individuals to create an area in which they can act free from the claims of others, while any plausible explanation of contract must turn in some way on the fact that contracts have precisely the opposite effect. Property is a barrier to the rest of the world, contract a means of joining that world. But rather than pursue the comparison with property further, it is time now to focus directly on contract by considering what sort of dynamic intention-based explanation might be given for promissory obligations and hence for contract law. Any such explanation must explain both why promising is in general a good thing and why the good thing that promising is entails that promises create rights to performance.

One common way of filling in the content of the first part of the story, of explaining why promising is a good thing generally, is on utilitarian or other instrumental grounds.[48] Promising, on this view, is valuable not in itself but as a tool that helps us to achieve things we could not achieve without the institution of promising. Promises help us to become happier, richer, have more of our preferences satisfied or in some other way better off. As Fried and others have pointed out, there is a problem with

[48] See e.g. J. Bentham, *The Theory of Legislation* (ed. C.K. Ogden, 1931) 109–23 and 148–98.

utilitarian and other instrumental theories of promising.[49] The problem is not that the practice of promising has no instrumental benefits: clearly it does. Rather, the problem is that a purely instrumental account seems unable to satisfy the second, deontological requirement for a plausible account of promising, namely explaining why promissory rights are *rights*. Promissory rights, like other rights, operate as exclusionary reasons for action.[50] When we reason correctly, the effect of a promise is to exclude or pre-empt the normal 'balance of reasons' factors that we would take into consideration when deciding whether to do a particular act. Promisors should do what they have promised because they have promised, regardless of whether in a particular case more good could be achieved by breaking a promise (exceptional circumstances aside). This is a problem for instrumental accounts because there are always cases where, on a strict instrumental calculus, it will be more valuable to break the promise than to perform it. This is true even when the value of maintaining the practice of promising generally is taken into account. Moreover, even if we could come up with instrumental reasons why, in practice if not in theory, promises should always be treated as exclusionary reasons for action, such an account is inconsistent with how promising (and contracting) is understood from the internal perspective, by the participants in the practice.[51] Promissory rights are not understood as instrumental markers, as rules of thumb: the fact that one has made a promise is regarded as a true exclusionary reason for doing the thing promised. Like reliance theories of contract, instrumental theories of promising (and of contract for that matter) are inconsistent with how the practice being explained is understood from the inside.

The above critique is far too brief to convince committed advocates of instrumental theories of promising. Its function was primarily to remind readers of the standard objections to such accounts and, more importantly, to set the scene for consideration of an alternative, non-instrumental explanation of promising. A, if not the, primary virtue of the alternative explanation is precisely that it is not vulnerable to similar objections. According to what I shall call the 'relationship' theory of promising,[52] promising is intrinsically and not merely instrumentally valuable. It is valuable in and of itself apart from any consequences that it may help to bring about. The reason promising is intrinsically valuable is that promises and promissory duties both create and are constitutive of a valuable relationship between promisors and promisees. Promises bring promisors and promisees closer together, into a special relationship. They do this because a promisor, having made a promise, is obliged to treat the promisee differently from everyone else. The promisee's interests are not weighed

[49] Fried, n. 10 above, 15–16; D. Lyons, 'Utility and Rights' in J.R. Pennock, and J.W. Chapman (eds.), *NOMOS XXIV: Ethics, Economics and the Law* (1982); but compare R.M. Hare, 'Utility and Rights: Comment on David Lyons' Essay' in the same volume.

[50] J. Raz, 'Promises and Obligations' in P.M.S. Hacker and J. Raz (eds.), *Law, Morality and Society* (1977).

[51] N. 34 above.

[52] What follows draws heavily on the work of Raz, nn. 50 and 1 above, but note that Raz would not agree with the conclusions I draw, having stated explicitly that enforcing promises is inconsistent with the harm principle: Raz, n. 4 above.

alongside the interests of everyone else, as they would be in ordinary moral reasoning. Rather, as the recipient of the promise, the promisee's interests are treated in a special way; they are different from, and superior to, the interests of all others (save in exceptional circumstances). If I have promised to give Dave $100 next Friday, then next Friday I should give Dave $100 even if I subsequently learn that the reasons which motivated me to make the promise (say a desire to be charitable) would now be served better by giving the money to Jane. Having made a promise to Dave I must now treat Dave as special, as different from anyone else whom I might, absent my promise, have good reason to give the money to. This feature of promises was first described by Raz:

> (PO) principles [which Raz believes correctly explain promising] present promises as creating a relation between the promisor and promisee—which is taken out of the general competition of conflicting reasons. It creates a special bond, binding the promisor to be, in the matter of the promise, partial to the promisee. It obliges the promisor to regard the claim of the promisee as not just one of the many claims that every person has for his respect and help but as having pre-emptory force.[53]

Thus promises create special relationships. Crucially, promises are intrinsically rather than instrumentally important in creating such relationships. Making a promise is not merely a tool for achieving a closer relationship (though it may also be that), it is an intrinsic part of the relationship. Take away the promise and the relationship is not the same. The value of the relationship and the value of the promise are inseparable. The final step in the argument is to acknowledge that special relationships are themselves intrinsically valuable. In the sense just defined, they are part of what it means to have a good life. Again, this connection was explained by Raz: '[t]he moral presuppositions of this conception of promising are the desirability of special bonds between people and the desirability of special relations that are voluntarily shaped and developed by the choice of participants'.[54]

The relationship explanation of promissory rights is not vulnerable, as are instrumental explanations, to the objection that it cannot explain why promissory rights are *rights*. The explanation is not vulnerable because the role of promising in creating special relationships is inseparable from the nature of promissory rights as promissory rights. Promises have the value that they have only when they are treated as creating rights, as creating exclusionary reasons for action. On a utilitarian calculus, it is acceptable in principle to break a promise if doing so will create more utility. Promising may have greater utility if it is understood that sometimes promises can be broken. Similar reasoning does not apply to the relationship explanation of promising because once it is understood that promises may be broken, then by definition promises lose their intrinsic worth. Were it understood that promises could be sometimes broken, then they would never—and not just in a particular case—create the sorts of relationships that make them valuable. It is precisely because promises create exclusionary reasons for action that they have intrinsic value—hence to deny that

[53] Raz, n. 50 above, 227–8. [54] Raz, n. 4 above, 928.

they create such reasons would eliminate this intrinsic value. For the same reason, the relationship explanation does not support the view that promises should sometimes be broken where doing so will allow the promisor to create 'more' valuable relationships than would arise if the promise was performed. Once the possibility of this sort of breach is acknowledged promises will never create valuable relationships. Thus on the relationship explanation of promising, both halves of the explanation—the teleological part and the deontological part—are integrated in a way that is not possible under an instrumental explanation.

Are promissory rights thus created rights whose infringement constitutes a harm? There is no reason to suppose otherwise. If property rights are genuine rights then so too are promissory rights. There is nothing in the story of the creation of promissory rights that is different in a significant way from similar stories told about property rights. To be sure, not all rights are of similar weight.[55] This may help to explain why not all promises are enforced. And just as property rights cannot be created in certain sorts of things it is undoubtedly the case that, consistent with the rules on unenforceable contracts, promissory rights cannot be created in respect of certain sorts of acts. But these and other considerations serve only to limit the scope of the promise principle; they do not alter its basic justification. The relationship explanation for why promises create rights is just that: an explanation of how promises create rights. No other argument is needed.

To summarize: contract law is like property law in that it is fundamentally about the creation, rather than the protection, of rights. Both contract and property specify ways in which rights can be created where none existed before and delineate the scope of those rights. Furthermore, each justifies those rights because of the role they play in helping us to lead good lives. Contract law allows people to create rights to performance. This is valuable because of the intrinsic value of such obligations in creating special relationships and thus in achieving valuable lives.

[55] As Raz notes, '[d]uties [which are grounded in rights] are special in the role they assume in practical reasoning. . . . They have pre-emptive force. . . . [but] it is not part of the very notion of a right that rights have great weight or importance. Some rights may be absolute, others may have little importance': J. Raz, *The Morality of Freedom* (1986) 186.

Inducing Breach of Contract

Roderick Bagshaw

INTRODUCTION

It is a tort for a stranger to a contract to induce a breach of it. Most English tort lawyers would accept this as an accurate statement of the common law before proceeding to quarrel over the meaning of 'induce', or its legal synonym 'procure', and the necessary mental element. Some might query whether inducing breach of contract is properly described as *a* tort rather than *part of* a tort.[1] Equally some would feel unable to accept the statement without adding with the same breath the opinion that the majority of the Court of Queen's Bench in *Lumley* v. *Gye*[2] made a grave mistake in committing English law to such a proposition. This essay seeks to respond to that opinion by providing a defence for *Lumley* v. *Gye*, and thereafter it investigates the sources of the query and quarrels.

LUMLEY V. *GYE*

It is not the purpose of this essay to defend everything that was said in *Lumley* v. *Gye*, but rather to defend the existence of the tort that is commonly associated with the decision. Nonetheless, since the facts of the case amount to a paradigm example of the tort of inducing breach of contract being committed it may be worth briefly recounting them. The claimant in *Lumley* v. *Gye*, the lessee and manager of a theatre where opera was performed had a contract with the singer, Johanna Wagner. The claimant sued the defendant, a rival promoter of opera, for maliciously enticing and procuring Johanna Wagner both to refuse to perform her contract and to depart from employment as a dramatic artiste. The defendant demurred, arguing that the action for enticing servants was strictly limited to cases where there was a master–servant relationship between the claimant and the person enticed away. A majority in the Court of Queen's Bench rejected the defendant's argument. Crompton J cautiously stated that he saw 'no reason for confining the [tort] to services or engagements under contracts for services of any particular description',[3] whilst Erle J was prepared to accept the broader principle that procurement of the violation of a right is a cause of action.[4] It took later cases to confirm that the tort is not limited to contracts relating to services[5] and that it is a tort to induce or procure a breach of any variety of

[1] Perhaps a *species* of the *genus* interfering with trade by unlawful means. T. Weir, *Economic Torts* (Oxford University Press, Oxford, 1997) 28: 'I believe that the tort of inducing breach of contract has now been absorbed into the general tort of causing harm by unlawful means.'

[2] (1853) 2 E & B 216, 118 ER 749.

[3] Ibid. 227.

[4] Ibid. 232.

[5] e.g. *Bowen* v. *Hall* (1881) 6 QBD 333.

contract. Nonetheless, *Lumley* v. *Gye* is regularly identified as 'the origin' of this tort[6] and some books even refer to the tort as 'the principle in *Lumley* v. *Gye*'.[7]

SHOULD CONTRACTS BE PROTECTED BY TORT LAW AGAINST STRANGERS?

Common Objections

The tort of inducing a breach of contract protects contracts against strangers. It is sometimes argued that the tort is therefore improper because a party to a broken contract should have a remedy only against the other party.[8] There are obvious reasons why a party might *want* a remedy against a stranger who induced the breach *in addition* to any remedy against the other party. For instance, the other party might be insolvent, or the breach might have caused forms of loss too remote to be recovered in contract,[9] or suing the other party might be incompatible with a desire to preserve good relations with him or her.[10] But those who want actions confined to between the contracting parties suggest that these reasons are insufficient. Their assumption seems to be that in entering a contract each party 'has to take' the risk that the other party may default and that the remedies provided by the law of contract may be less than ideal. But it is not clear what reasoning, if any, supports the assertion that a party 'has to take' such a risk. No doubt a person familiar with commercial life will be *aware* of such a risk, but it is difficult to see how such a person, when making a contract, *expresses any willingness* or otherwise takes upon himself or herself the risk that strangers will interfere with his or her economic well-being without redress.

Others have objected to the tort on the basis that it allows contracting parties to *create* obligations for strangers. But closer consideration reveals that although the

[6] e.g. W.V.H. Rogers (ed.), *Winfield and Jolowicz on Tort* (15th edn., Sweet & Maxwell, London, 1998) 621.

[7] e.g. R.F.V. Heuston and R.A. Buckley (eds.), *Salmond and Heuston on the Law of Torts* (21st edn., 1996) 348.

[8] e.g. D. Howarth, *Textbook on Tort* (Butterworths, London, 1995) 484: '*Lumley* v. *Gye* was wrongly decided and so were all cases that subsequently have approved of it and extended it, since . . . there is no reason to give the plaintiff remedies beyond its contractual remedies'.

[9] Tony Weir doubts in 'The Staggering March of Negligence' in P. Cane and B.J. Stapleton (eds.), *The Law of Obligations, Essays in Celebration of John Fleming* (Clarendon Press, Oxford, 1998) 126, whether the remoteness rule associated with *Hadley v Baxendale* (1854) 9 Ex. 341 would apply to a deliberate breach of contract inspired by a bribe, thus challenging the view that the tort action for inducing such a deliberate breach might afford a more generous remoteness rule. David Howarth argues in his *Textbook on Tort*, n. 8 above, 475, that the remoteness rule would only be more restrictive in contract than in tort if the claimant had neglected to tell the other party to the contract of the special losses that he or she might suffer if there was a breach, but even this stern position cannot accommodate the possibility of special losses caused by risks which were unknown at the time of formation of the contract but reasonably foreseeable at the time that the breach of it was procured.

[10] In situations such as that dealt with in *South Wales Miners' Federation* v. *Glamorgan Coal Co.* [1905] AC 239 the suggestion that the claimant should sue the other party to the contract rather than the 'procurer' is a suggestion that an employer should sue his or her employees for their temporary absence after they return to work.

premise is true this is not a fatal objection. There are many circumstances in which a person can create obligations for others without the consent of those others. Thus if I catch a rabbit on a common, or register a patent, or issue a share certificate, I create obligations for strangers. At its simplest they may be obliged to respect my new property, and it will be a tort for them to interfere with it without my consent. There seems at least a glimmer of an analogy between being the first to catch the rabbit and the first to sign the soprano to an exclusive service contract. It may be worth noting here, however, that generally the obligations which I can create and impose on a stranger without his or her consent are negative in form.

Borrowing Justifications from Private Property

To establish a secure foundation for the tort associated with *Lumley* v. *Gye* it is not sufficient merely to demonstrate the weakness of the objections most commonly raised against the protection of contracts against strangers. It is necessary to establish what it is which makes a party's interest under a contract a 'thing' which should be protected by tort law against the world. This is, of course, a different exercise from seeking to explain why contracts should be enforced against the parties to them and why the contractual remedies should take the form that they do. Because the quest is for a justification for supposing that a contract creates for each party to it a 'thing' which deserves protection against the world, it seems a valid strategy to consider whether any of the justifications for recognizing private property rights can be transferred to this use.[11] The purpose of such a transfer is not to establish that contracts *are* property, still less that contracts relating to land *are* interests *in land*. The purpose of the transfer is merely to borrow well-tested arguments for protecting interests against the world.

Three arguments that are often used to justify the institution of private property may be suitable:[12] first the argument that the private property institution extends the range of choices open to human beings and thus increases their freedom; secondly the argument that the institution makes possible the existence of a market for scarce commodities which will ensure that they are allocated so as to maximize social wealth; thirdly, the argument that the private property institution provides a suitable reward (and hence an incentive) for productive endeavour. The next five sections will consider how far these borrowings can be used to justify the recognition of an interest which could justify the existence of the tort of inducing breach of contract.

[11] The link between tort protection of contracts and property has been noted and used by many commentators. See, e.g., C.E. Carpenter, 'Interference with Contract Relations' (1928) 41 *Harvard LR* 728, 733; R.A. Epstein, 'Inducement of Breach of Contract as a Problem of Ostensible Ownership' (1987) 16 *Journal of Legal Studies* 1; F.S. McChesney, 'Tortious Interference with Contract Versus "Efficient" Breach: Theory and Empirical Evidence' (1999) 28 *Journal of Legal Studies* 131.

[12] The arguments borrowed are identified, refined, and discussed in J.W. Harris, *Property and Justice* (Clarendon Press, Oxford, 1997).

Increasing Freedom

There seems to be little doubt that legally enforceable contracts extend the choices open to human beings and thus increase their freedoms.[13] Contracts permit human beings to engage confidently in a wider range of activities than would be possible without contracts. But the crucial question is whether legal protection of contracts *against third parties* adds anything to this value. On this, it seems that the protection of contracts against third parties increases the security of contracts, and by thus making it easier for a party to rely on his or her contract assists the institution in extending the range of choices.

The Risk of Exploitation

But before accepting this as a justification for tort law's protection of contracts against strangers we should consider whether such protection for one party unacceptably restricts the liberty of the other party to the contract. Particularly when dealing with employment contracts it might be thought that protection of the employer's contractual rights provides an unacceptable opportunity for oppression. The suggestion is that, by making liable a stranger who induces a breach (particularly if the tort extends to 'harbouring', as Crompton J in *Lumley* v. *Gye* was sure that it did[14]) the law makes it harder for a servant or employee to leave an unsatisfactory contract, and thus contains echoes of slavery.

One answer to this concern may be that the servant or employee is only held to a contract that he or she voluntarily entered. Even if the servant or employee had little practical alternative but to enter a contract with terms which granted the employer a degree of power equivalent to that held by the master of a slave, the problem would seem to be with the initial validity of such a contract rather than with its protection by tort law against third party interference.[15] There would be a basic incoherence in maintaining that the contract is sufficiently fair to be enforced against the servant by the master but that the law should nonetheless facilitate the attempts of strangers to persuade the servant to breach the same contract by limiting the scope of tort protection. But whilst it would be incoherent to limit the scope of the tort in order to facilitate breach, such a limit might nonetheless be legitimate to reflect the position of the stranger. Thus, we might argue that, although the servant has bound himself or herself to the contract through what contract law is content to treat as consent, the stranger has never indicated any willingness to tolerate the existence of such exploitative 'properties' in the world and should be free to campaign against them. This could

[13] The argument is not that *all* contracts increase freedom, but that the legal mechanism of contract in general does so. Equally, the argument is not committed to the ideology often referred to as 'freedom of contract'.

[14] 2 E & B 216, 224–5.

[15] Some contracts are illegal because of the extent to which they restrict personal liberty *Horwood* v. *Millar's Timber and Trading Co.* [1917] 3 KB 305) or stifle the employee's capacity to work (*A Schroeder Music Publishing Co. Ltd.* v. *Macaulay* [1974] 1 WLR 1308).

be used to explain cases such as *Brimelow* v. *Casson*[16] which hold that a stranger who regards himself or herself as driven by a moral duty to induce a breach of a contract may have a defence of justification even when the contract was *prima facie* enforceable between the parties to it.

Market Instrumentalism

The relationship between the dimension of contracts protected against strangers and the capacity of the market to maximize social wealth is complex. It is important not to confuse the additional value which comes from treating contracts as creating an interest which is analogous to private property (which is what this essay is focusing on in this section), with the general value of contracts as a means of organizing exchange.[17] The institution of private property makes certain commodities available for trade and exchange, and thus maximizes social wealth. Many contracts can also be traded and exchanged.[18] This feature of such contracts makes available 'new commodities' which can be allocated through other contracts so as to maximize social wealth. Thus as a matter of general contract law I can sell a contractual right to demand a certain sum of money, a construction contract, the contractual right to attend a sporting event, or the benefit of a contract with a management company to make available a film-star's services. If contracts were not protected against interference by third parties such contracts would be a far less secure 'thing' to trade in, and the market would be less certain of allocating such 'new commodities' so as to maximize social wealth.

Efficient Breach

One objection to this, however, is that it fails to take account of the need not to discourage 'efficient breach'. An efficient breach of contract is one which will be conducive to the maximization of social wealth. 'Breaching is more efficient than performing where the costs of performing exceed the benefits to all parties. The costs of performing exceed the benefits when a contingency materializes that makes the resources needed for performance more valuable in an alternative use.'[19] Given this, it is worth noting at the outset that in many situations where a breach of contract is induced the inducer makes no claim that the resources needed for performance could be more valuably allocated. Thus trade unions or protest groups that pursue their ends through interference with contracts will rarely be motivated by a desire to see the resources needed for performance allocated in the most efficient way.

The situation where the tort of inducing breach of contract might most obviously come into conflict with an 'efficient breach' is where the inducer seeks to get the performance diverted to himself or herself. Thus in *Lumley* v. *Gye* the inducer, Gye,

16 [1924] 1 Ch. 302.

17 Even here the role of contract is complex. See e.g. H. Collins, *The Law of Contract* (3rd edn., Butterworths, London, 1997) chap. 1.

18 Not all contractual rights can be assigned. For exceptions, see e.g. J. Beatson, *Anson's Law of Contract* (27th edn., Oxford University Press, Oxford, 1998) 458–60.

19 R. Cooter and T. Ulen, *Law and Economics* (2nd edn., Addison Wesley, Reading, Mass., 1997) 215.

sought the benefit of the soprano's services, consequently depriving Lumley of the exclusive arrangement that he had bargained for. It is often argued that in such a situation it would be an 'efficient breach' for the soprano to break her contract with Lumley and sing for Gye instead if Gye could make more from her performance than Lumley.[20] Clearly if the law wants to encourage this allegedly efficient outcome it should not deter Gye from inducing the breach.

But would breaches of contract by parties who thought that they were in the same position as Johanna Wagner necessarily be efficient? There are problems in assuming that one party, such as the soprano, can easily discover what profits the two impressarios might be able to obtain from her performance, and further problems with dealing with losses incurred by a party such as Lumley as a result of thinking that he or she was going to get the performance in the period before the existence of Gye's capacity to increase social wealth to a greater extent was discovered. Having a tort which allows Lumley to claim compensatory damages from Gye, including losses which might not be available in an action for breach of contract against Johanna Wagner, would help to ensure that these matters were considered by Gye in deciding whether a breach would be efficient. Moreover, the market instrumentalist justification of private property suggests that it may be more efficient to treat entitlements as generally inviolable even against the person who claims that re-allocation of the property to him or her would be 'more efficient' and then to allow further negotiations to re-allocate efficiently. Thus it might be more efficient to treat the contract as creating an interest analogous to an item of private property that Gye must seek to acquire from Lumley.[21] The fact that there is no discernible groundswell of legal opinion in favour of 'efficient theft' may lean against facilitating allegedly efficient breach of contract by limiting the scope of tort protection. If non-performance of the contract between Lumley and Wagner really would be efficient in this situation then Gye should be capable of persuading Lumley, if Lumley is economically rational, to trade his contractual rights. Thus the message of the tort seems to be that once Gye is aware that allocation of the performance to him would involve Wagner breaking a contract with Lumley then it is wrongful to encourage Wagner to breach instead of seeking to persuade Lumley to trade his contractual rights.

Rewards for Productive Endeavour

There is a value in encouraging productive endeavour through rewards. Productive endeavour is that which tends to increase social wealth. By definition it should be productive for two free, rational, and fully-informed human-beings to negotiate an exchange between themselves. As such we could argue that they deserve to be rewarded with the grant of an interest which can be protected against strangers. As

[20] This assumes that it would cost the same amount in expenses incurred for the soprano to sing for Gye instead of Lumley.

[21] For a recent argument that the likely bargaining costs support such a position as a first-best economically-efficient solution see, F.S. McChesney, 'Tortious Interference with Contract Versus "Efficient" Breach: Theory and Empirical Evidence' (1999) 28 *Journal of Legal Studies* 131.

J.W. Harris has shown, however, whilst justice may support the claim that they should be rewarded, the nature of the reward may be merely a matter of convention.[22] But it is not difficult to think of examples of situations where a party would argue that an appropriate reward would be for him or her to have his or her contract protected against strangers because of the amount of effort and resources he or she had invested in it. Obvious examples might be recording companies and football clubs which insist that strangers should be prevented from 'poaching' emerging artistes or young footballers under contract after so much has been invested by companies and clubs in building their careers.

HOW TO DESCRIBE THE INTEREST PROTECTED BY THE TORT OF INDUCING BREACH OF CONTRACT

If some or all of the three borrowed arguments have been convincingly transferred then a secure foundation has been established for holding that a contract creates an interest which tort law might have justification in protecting against third parties. It is not suggested that the law of torts should provide absolute protection for this interest. The next section will introduce some of the countervailing interests of potential defendants which will have to be weighed in deciding what degree of protection, if any, the law of torts should provide. But before moving on to this it might be worth briefly considering how the interest created by a contract and potentially protectable by tort law against strangers should be described. Some description of the form of the protectable interest may be valuable because any tort that protects it may have features which reflect the boundaries and contours of the protectable interest as well as features which reflect compromises to take account of the countervailing interests of potential defendants.

A first step towards a description is the recognition that what we are seeking is a description of the interest that a party to a contract can claim a provisional entitlement to against *the rest of the world.* The emphasized portion is crucial in unlocking the problem, since a party's entitlement against *the rest of the world* (which the tort of inducing breach of contract will protect to some extent) is not necessarily the same as a party's rights against the other party to the contract.

It could be argued that the interest which a party to a contract has a provisional entitlement to against the rest of the world includes *at least* the other party's willingness to perform. In addition it might be argued that a party has a provisional entitlement to the other party's existing capacity to perform. Thus absolute protection by the law of torts would make it a tort to do anything which interfered with either the party's willingness or existing capacity to perform. The description '*existing* capacity to perform' is intended to exclude the idea that the creation of a contract between the two parties might create a right indirectly enforceable through tort law to demand

[22] Harris, n. 12 above, 208–9.

that strangers provide positive assistance in fulfilling contracts. But the line between act and omission is as difficult to draw here as elsewhere in the law.

A provisional description for the protectable interest does not solve the problem of what degree of protection it is appropriate for tort law to accord to it, and this is the problem that the next section addresses.

WHAT PROTECTION DOES THE INTEREST DESERVE FROM THE LAW OF TORTS?

The Interests of Potential Defendants

Protection of the contractual interest against strangers will restrict the freedom of those strangers. Thus the appropriate scope of any protection that the law of torts provides cannot be determined merely by assessing the nature or significance of the interest protected. The effect of the proposed restrictions on the interests of those who could be defendants in tort actions must also be taken into account. Evaluation of a particular liability rule requires reflection on how these interests are balanced or accommodated.

Two general points are worth making before moving on to consider the quarrels over the accommodation of interests. First, the task of defining an acceptable balance in this area was made more difficult by the apparent extension of the tort of inducing breach of contract to all varieties of contracts. So long as the tort only protected the interests of masters in contracts of service then the interests of potential claimants were easier to treat as having a single degree of value and the severity of any proposed restriction on the freedom of potential defendants was easier to judge.

Secondly, the appropriate accommodation of the interests of potential claimants and potential defendants may depend on assumptions about the distribution of particular interests within society. Thus, for example, the intensive restrictions placed by the law of torts on freedom to behave in ways which might physically injure the body are easier to justify because it can be assumed that all those restricted will equally be beneficiaries of the restrictions.[23] Similar notions of equal distribution seem to underpin the adoption by the tort of private nuisance of a standard of liability based on interference beyond what is tolerated in a specific locality as ordinary 'give and take'.[24] Generalizations about the distribution of the interest protected by the tort of procuring breach of contract are far more difficult to make. Again, the extension of the tort's protection beyond contracts of service has complicated matters. Before 1853 it might have been possible to identify the section of society likely to have an interest in preventing servants from being lured away. Further, it might have been possible to establish that it was the same section of society which was likely to feel the restriction on liberty that such an actionable wrong entailed. Indeed it may be signif-

[23] There is some over-simplification here, given the existence of non-human legal persons.

[24] Though the equality is undermined to some extent by the fact that claimants in private nuisance apparently require an interest in land, whilst mere occupiers of land can be potential defendants.

icant that in *Lumley* v. *Gye* itself both claimant and defendant were impresarios. After the extension of the tort to all forms of contract, however, it is harder to generalize about who may benefit and who may feel restricted by the tort. One controversial recent case presented facts close to the inverse of *Lumley* v. *Gye*, with session musicians suing a defendant who had allegedly procured a breach by their employer.[25]

It is still possible to maintain that those who benefit from the tort are the same section of society who may be restricted by it so far as the tort operates between broadly equal competitors for the same performance. Where two opera impresarios compete on broadly equal terms for the exclusive services of the same soprano they will not know who will benefit and who will be restricted by the tort in advance, and may be able to agree that whoever wins the signature should be free to enjoy the soprano's performance without further competition thereafter. From this perspective there is good sense in a law of torts that distinguishes between what is wrongful once a contract has been signed and what is wrongful in competition before a contract is signed.

The more problematic aspect of the tort, then, is its capacity to restrict certain forms of non-competitive behaviour. Thus the tort protects contracts against the organization of certain forms of industrial action by trade unions and, similarly, has the capacity to stifle certain forms of direct action by protest groups. Here the scope of the tort is more obviously political, rather than merely representing an efficient compromise between broadly equal competitors, and statutory intervention has reflected this.[26]

Introduction to the Quarrels

The difficulty in establishing that a single liability rule reflects a fair balance across the range of situations now potentially covered by the tort may help explain the persistence of quarrels over the scope and content of the liability rules. The query raised at the outset was whether the tort of inducing breach of contract is part of some wider genus-tort, perhaps part of the tort of unlawful interference with trade. The property analogy and the analysis in the previous sub-section have both suggested that there are possible reasons for protecting a party's interest created by a contract differently from other less specific economic expectations. Broadly, to summarize, it has been suggested that there are possible reasons for the law of torts to provide one set of rules to govern what can be done in competing for a contract, and another set to govern what respect must be shown to the interest created when one of the competitors has successfully obtained a contract. Thus a possible foundation for a tort of inducing breach of contract *separate* from a wider tort of unlawful interference with trade has been laid.

The next task then is to investigate in more detail what should be the conditions for liability under this separate tort. Identifying these conditions will involve

[25] *Millar* v. *Bassey* [1994] Entertainment and Media Law Reports 44.

[26] Trade Union and Labour Relations (Consolidation) Act 1992, Parts II and V.

determining the appropriate degree of tort protection for the interest created by a contract and will also establish the borderline between the separate inducing tort and the more general interference with trade tort. Such an investigation requires the exploration of at least four related quarrels. The first concerns the identification of the essence of the tort of inducing or procuring breach of contract. Here the dispute is largely between those who think that the essence is a particular state of mind and those who think that the tort also requires a particular form of prohibited behaviour on the part of the defendant, perhaps the use of 'unlawful means'. A second quarrel reflects uncertainty about the necessary state of mind for commission of the tort. All participants in the first quarrel are agreed that a particular state of mind is a vital constituent part of the tort, but for those who hold the first view on the first quarrel definition of the necessary state of mind is equivalent to definition of the scope of the tort. A third quarrel arises between those who hold the second view on the first quarrel. Here the controversy is about the definition of the prohibited form of behaviour. One central issue within this quarrel is whether preventing performance of a contract, and thereby bringing about its breach, is part of the tort of procuring breach of contract or part of the general interference with trade tort. A fourth quarrel centres on whether a breach of contract is a necessary condition, or whether non-performance of primary contractual obligations or even disappointment of general business expectations can be sufficient.

These quarrels are not merely about doctrinal elegance or tidy classification, but are related to anxiety over the appropriate level of protection. Whilst a high level of protection might be acceptable as a compromise between broadly equal competitors such a tort might *also* catch other categories of strangers. For instance, if it was accepted that any act making a breach more likely could suffice for the tort, and the necessary state of mind was generously interpreted by the judiciary, the consequence would be a substantial restriction on the freedom of strangers who might never expect to benefit from the same restriction of others. An appropriate level of protection must also reflect the practicalities of proof.

The existence of such quarrels reflects that there are different options for determining an appropriate level of protection. Thus the risk of an unacceptable restriction on freedom can be dealt with by adopting a narrow mental element (second quarrel) or by defining 'procuring' narrowly and/or insisting that the use of unlawful means by the defendant is a necessary element (first and third quarrels). The next sections will compare these options.

The Quarrels over the Necessary Mental Element

Much of the discussion so far has assumed that the essence of the tort of inducing breach of contract is the special interest that a contract creates. In *Allen* v. *Flood*[27] the House of Lords rejected the possibility of a tort where wrongfulness turned wholly on

[27] [1898] AC 1.

the defendant's state of mind, and this may be taken as settling the first quarrel in favour of those who argue that some form of prohibited behaviour is also necessary to constitute the inducing tort. There is far more life, however, in the second quarrel over what mental element must accompany the prohibited behaviour to give rise to liability.

Part of the uncertainty over the mental element has flowed from a failure to distinguish between the defendant's state of mind towards the contract, the breach, the claimant, and the damage. Difficulties have also arisen, however, from uncertainties over the definition of intention, and a failure to appreciate the difference between what must be proved and how it should be proved.

An orthodox view of the necessary mental element is that 'A must have knowledge of the contract between B and C and act with the intention of bringing about a breach of it'.[28] It seems, however, that the reference to 'intention' in this proposition is not a reference to the concept of intention as used by careful moral philosophers. Such philosophers regard a person as intending everything which is part of that person's reason for acting in a particular way. Thus a person intends those things which he or she seeks to achieve through a chosen action, either as an end or as a means to an end.[29] But such philosophers deny that a person intends all the side-effects of his or her action, even if the person knows that these side-effects are inevitable and even if the person welcomes them. The man who chooses to walk to the newsagent to buy a newspaper ordinarily does not intend to wear down the soles of his shoes.[30]

There are two indications that the commentators and judges who describe inducing breach of contract as a tort which requires an intention to cause a breach of contract are not using the word 'intention' to refer to this pure philosophical concept. First, it would be difficult to find such pure philosophical intention to induce a breach in many cases which are regarded as paradigm examples of the tort. Thus an impresario seeking to persuade a soprano to sing at his theatre, in the knowledge that this would put her in breach of her 'exclusive' contract with another impresario, would probably describe that breach as a known and inevitable side-effect of success rather than a chosen means or end. Indeed the case law suggests that a person can certainly be liable although he or she did not know that a breach of contract would be a necessary consequence of his or her action, and even if he or she hoped that the terms of the contract would allow a termination without any breach.[31] John Fleming has boldly claimed that for the purposes of the tort '[i]ndifference is equated with intent'.[32] Secondly, the prominence given to the question whether the defendant knew of the contract suggests a focus other than the moral philosophers' concept of intention. Since it is hard to see how bringing about a breach could be part of the defendant's reason for action unless the defendant had knowledge of the contract. It

[28] Rogers (ed.), n. 6 above, 627.

[29] See e.g. J. Finnis, 'Intention in Tort Law' in D.G. Owen (ed.), *Philosophical Foundations of Tort Law* (Clarendon Press, Oxford, 1995) chap. 10.

[30] Ibid., 235–7.

[31] *Emerald Construction Co. Ltd.* v. *Lowthian* [1966] 1 WLR 691.

[32] J.G. Fleming, *The Law of Torts* (9th edn., LBC Information Services, Sydney, 1998) 762.

is possible that knowledge could be a matter to be proved as a foundation for an inference of pure intention. There is no indication in the case law, however, that this is the role that knowledge plays. Thus it seems that the required mental state for the tort of procuring breach of contract is a sufficient degree of knowledge of the likelihood that conduct may bring about a breach of contract, and a choice to persist with that conduct despite the knowledge.

Some commentators have sought to curtail the scope of the tort that this dilute form of intention to bring about a breach would otherwise entail by arguing for a further requirement that the defendant must be shown to have intended to harm the claimant.[33] Some support for such a requirement can be found in an obiter dictum of Lord Devlin.[34] Again, however, there are difficulties in finding such intention in the paradigm cases. Moreover the authorities are firm in support of the view that a defendant still commits the tort even if he or she thinks that the breach procured will improve the claimant's position in the long term.[35] It seems that even if a separate intention to harm the claimant is required it is once again only intention in a dilute form. Lord Wedderburn of Charlton describes the dilute form of intention required in the following terms: 'intention imports no desire to injure but it is sufficient that there is deliberate conduct by a defendant who appreciates, or is sufficiently reckless in regard to, the probable consequences on the plaintiff'.[36]

There are three main objections to the adoption of the mental element of dilute intention. First, a tort with no constraining condition other than this dilute mental element would catch many people who were not former competitors trying to continue competition after the contract was signed. This has encouraged attempts to define the prohibited behaviour necessary for the tort so that it excludes, for instance, advising, 'inconsistent dealing', and, possibly, preventing performance. Secondly, the dilute mental element arguably leads to too wide a liability where a defendant procures breach of one set of contracts, for instance between an employer and his or her employees, in the knowledge that this may lead to breach of other contracts, for instance between the employer and his or her customers. This sort of situation has been particularly influential in inspiring the suggestion that there should only be liability to victims of indirect interference whom the defendant was 'aiming at' or 'targeting'.

Thirdly, the dilute intention to bring about a breach cannot be the appropriate mental element if liability extends to cases where the alleged interference falls short of bringing about a breach. But provided that liability extends no further than interference which brings about the non-performance of primary obligations then only a minor adjustment to the mental element may be needed.

[33] T. Weir, n. 1 above, argues (at 14) that 'intention to harm' the claimant must be found, and (at 43) that 'you have to be targeted in order to sue'.

[34] *Rookes* v. *Barnard* [1964] AC 1129, 1212, 'there must be . . . the intention to cause the breach and to injure the plaintiff thereby'.

[35] *South Wales Miners' Federation* v. *Glamorgan Coal Co.* [1905] AC 239.

[36] *Clerk and Lindsell on Torts* (17th edn., Sweet & Maxwell, London, 1995) para. 23–12.

Would it be appropriate to urge the courts to reconsider their dilute sense of intention and to advocate the adoption of the philosophers' concept in its place? Whilst the narrower mental element would clearly reduce the risk of the tort undesirably interfering with the interests of defendants three problems with such a suggestion are worth noting. Most importantly, a narrow mental element might be thought to offer insufficient protection to an interest in some ways akin to a property interest. Thus there could be many cases where the defendant had clearly shown no respect for the claimant's contractual interest, but where the breach was merely a side-effect of seeking a gain. Such a narrow mental element would risk not covering those cases where the tort is most easily justified, cases of competitors continuing after the contract has been signed. Secondly, adoption of the moral philosophers' concept requires an individuation of ends. Whether bringing about a breach of contract was part of a defendant's intention in the moral philosophers' sense would often depend on how narrowly or broadly the ends of the defendant were defined. Thirdly, there would be severe practical problems in proving a defendant's intention in the moral philosophers' sense. Proof of a defendant's state of mind almost inevitably involves inference, and it is far easier to specify the facts that could safely found an inference of knowledge and willingness than to specify the facts that could safely found an inference of moral philosophers' intention.

The Quarrel over the Prohibited Behaviour

If the mental element is as dilute as the discussion above suggests then this will increase the pressure to define narrowly the forms of prohibited behaviour that can lead to liability. The following three sections will consider whether advice, inconsistent dealing, and prevention of performance are forms of behaviour which should be excluded from the scope of the tort of inducing breach of contract.

Persuasion and Advice

Some commentators state that a distinction should be drawn between persuading a party to break a contract and advising a party to do so, with only the former being actionable.[37] Others, however, have cast doubt on the utility of the distinction.[38] It is too easy for a person who is seeking to bring about a breach to disguise persuasion as advice. Undoubtedly, even if the need for such a line is accepted it will still be a difficult one to draw.[39] One attempt makes the distinction depend on whether the defendant created a reason for breaking the contract or merely pointed out a reason which already existed. A second attempt appears to undermine the dilute mental element by distinguishing between those who give advice which they intended to

[37] Buckley and Heuston (eds.), n. 7 above, 352: 'the better view is that merely to give advice or information is not inducement'.

[38] *Camden Nominees* v. *Forcey* [1940] Ch. 352, 366.

[39] See e.g. J.D. Heydon, *Economic Torts* (2nd edn., Sweet & Maxwell, London, 1978) 30–1.

persuade a party to breach a contract and those who give advice for some other purpose, nonetheless knowing that a breach is likely to result.

Can the property analogy assist in determining whether it is necessary to draw this difficult distinction? Directing a party's attention to a reason for not performing of which the party was previously unaware does damage the 'property' created by a contract, since it may well make the party less willing to perform. Thus if advice is given with the knowledge that it is likely to make a party unwilling to perform his or her contract then it is arguable that this should be actionable unless justified. This establishes, as expected, that the pressure to limit the scope of the tort does not reflect the scope of the protectable interest.

The pressure may, however, reflect the fact that many of those who might advise a party to break a contract would not be rival competitors for the performance. It would be unfortunate if providers of independent advice were caught by a broad tort, since this would neglect the special value of encouraging widespread knowledge for individual autonomy and the efficiency of the market. If independent advice is not excluded from the tort through a limited definition of the prohibited behaviour then the defence of justification will be crucial in preventing non-competitive advisors from being held liable.[40] A restricted definition of the prohibited behaviour would thus have the advantage of removing the need for advisors to justify their advice, but the disadvantage of requiring a distinction, most probably, between independent advice and a rival competitor's pseudo-advice. Given the rarity of the problem in the case law it might be thought acceptable to leave independent advisors with the onus of justifying their actions.

Inconsistent Dealing

This sub-heading covers two clusters of problematic situations. First there are those cases where the defendant has dealt with property in a way that is inconsistent with contracts affecting that property. Here the difficulty is to co-ordinate the tort with rules that exist to facilitate secure dealing with property. To avoid the tort applying inconsistently to different categories of contracts Professor Treitel has suggested that such co-ordination can be achieved by making use of the flexibility inherent in the defence of justification.[41]

The second cluster of situations often described as involving inconsistent dealing covers cases where the party had already broken the contract before he or she started to deal with the defendant, or at least manifested an intention and willingness to do so without any persuasion by the defendant. The argument for the defendant's behaviour being tortious in such a case is that the behaviour makes it easier for the party to sustain the breach or to go through with it. Moreover, if such behaviour was not tortious then difficult questions about implied inducements would arise: there is a thin line between an inducer communicating that he or she is willing to deal if the party

[40] It is important to note that what must be justified is not the breach of contract but the action which made that breach more likely.

[41] G.H. Treitel, *The Law of Contract* (9th edn., Sweet & Maxwell, London, 1995) 564–5.

becomes free of prior engagements and encouraging the breaking of such engagements. Thus it appears that the choice is between limiting the definition of the necessary prohibited behaviour with the consequent need to draw a difficult distinction, or leaving the defendant with the opportunity to argue that his or her behaviour did not *cause* the breach (or its continuance). On balance the causation approach seems preferable to introducing a difficult distinction into the definition of the prohibited behaviour.

Preventing Performance

Most commentators agree that it should be *a* tort actionable by the impresario if a stranger ties the soprano up and thus prevents her from fulfilling her contract.[42] The main dispute concerns whether the tort that I have committed if I have prevented performance is the same tort that I would have committed if I had persuaded the party to break his or her contract. If it is the same tort then, given that only a dilute mental element is apparently necessary, the scope of the tort will be broad and the resulting restriction on the freedom of potential defendants will be significant. A person would risk committing the tort if he or she willingly did anything which he or she knew could lead to performance of a contract being prevented. There are three strategies for avoiding this.

Supporters of the first strategy argue that preventing performance of a contract can be tortious, but that preventing performance is a separate tort from procuring breach and is subject to special conditions. Many would argue that to commit a tort by preventing performance the defendant must both use 'unlawful means' to prevent the performance and have a narrower state of mind, perhaps that he or she was 'aiming at' the claimant. Thus preventing performance is separate from procuring breach of contract but absorbed into the genus-tort of interference with trade by unlawful means. First strategists are prepared to concede that the tort of procuring breach is distinct because it does not require these special conditions: A breach of contract can be procured by whispering an offer in a soprano's ear, not in itself an unlawful act, and thus 'unlawful means' is not a necessary condition. Further, the case law supports the application of the dilute mental element for the procuring breach tort.

Tony Weir did much to popularize the distinction between persuading a party to break a contract and preventing performance.[43] But whilst he still insists that special conditions are necessary before there can be liability for preventing performance, he is now unwilling to make concessions as to the requirements of the procuring breach of contract tort. He believes that whispering encouragement to commit a deliberate breach of contract into a soprano's ear is 'unlawful means' and that the whisperer will only commit a tort if he or she was 'aiming at' the claimant.[44] Thus Weir is the standard-bearer of the second strategy which treats procuring breach and preventing performance as part of the same tort, but seeks to impose stringent conditions

[42] Buckley and Heuston (eds.), n. 7 above, 351.
[43] T. Weir, *A Casebook on Tort* (8th edn., Sweet & Maxwell, London, 1996) 609.
[44] Weir, n. 1 above, Lecture 2.

throughout the uniform tort.[45] This strategy clearly suggests that the conclusions reached above on the quarrel over the mental element necessary for the procuring tort are erroneous.

The third strategy, like the first, involves two torts, but the distinction under this strategy is between direct and indirect interference. Supporters of the third strategy argue that directly preventing performance is equivalent to inducing a breach by persuasion.[46] They insist that although most of those who directly prevent performance as a matter of fact use unlawful means, as a matter of law this form of the tort can be committed by using otherwise lawful means. Heydon offers as an example *Esso Petroleum Co. Ltd.* v. *Kingswood Motors (Addlestone) Ltd.*,[47] where the defendant took over a petrol-selling company, prevented it from fulfilling its agreement with its petrol supplier, and was held liable for interfering with the supply contract.

From the perspective of the protectable interest the distinction between procuring breach and preventing performance echoes the division between the party's willingness to perform and the party's capacity to perform. Should these aspects of the protectable interest receive different levels of protection?

So far as a party's capacity to perform is contingent on third parties refraining from certain behaviour which could prevent performance a case can be made for *only* restricting behaviour that is otherwise unlawful. From the point of view of the claimant this reduced protection might be explained by an equivalent of the *nemo dat* principle. It could be argued that whilst a party to a contract can make promises that he or she is not presently able to fulfil without the co-operation of others, and can create legal obligations on himself or herself to the other party in the same terms, that other party cannot claim a provisional entitlement against the rest of the world to more than 'the party's willingness to perform and the party's capacity to perform *in the absence of interference by unlawful acts*'. But this equivalent of the *nemo dat* principle tends towards treating the 'property' protected by the law of torts as a 'property' that is *transferred* rather than *created* at the time that the contract is made. If we take seriously the idea that contracts *create* protectable interests, in some ways analogous to private property, then this suggests then the scope of the protectable interest does not itself require a confinement of the tort which protects this interest so that it does not cover preventing performance. It could be argued that potential defendants can reasonably be expected to modify their behaviour so as to avoid knowingly and willingly damaging the created 'property' by positive acts without justification. If the analogy with property does not require the limitation of liability to cases where unlawful means are used to prevent performance, then still less does it require a reconceptualization of the tort of procuring breach of contract as an instance of interfering with trade by unlawful means. Indeed one objection to the second strategy is that it does not take seriously the idea that there is some special protectable interest created by a contract. The second strategy offers the same level of tort protection to

[45] For an assessment of Weir's current views see R. Bagshaw, 'Can the Economic Torts be Unified?' (1998) 18 *OJLS* 729.

[46] Heydon, n. 39 above, 29, 31.

[47] [1974] 1 QB 142.

interests under existing contracts and other economic interests, such as the prospect of future contracts.

Supporters of liability dependent on the use of unlawful means often argue that the boundary between lawful and unlawful means is far clearer than the distinction between positive acts and omissions or between justifiable and unjustifiable positive acts. This argument cannot be discounted, but it must be noted that clarity is purchased at the expense of arbitrariness. If unlawful means is made a necessary condition then the level of protection against the prevention of performance will be parasitic on notions of wrongfulness developed elsewhere in the law. Such a parasitic standard raises the question why behaviour which the law stigmatizes as unlawful in order to protect the position of one person should be capable of founding a tort claim by another person, whose position was not intended to be protected by the definition of the behaviour as unlawful, merely because of the concurrent existence of an intention to harm that second person. An example may make this difficult point clearer: say that X breaks a contract with Y, knowing that this breach will cause Y to disappoint Z, and X does so with the intention of bringing about the disappointment of Z. In such a case there is the requisite mental element and what is arguably unlawful means, the breach of contract. But breach of a contract between X and Y is not defined as unlawful in order to preserve the position of Z. So why should Z be able to establish a tort claim parasitic on what was wrongful between X and Y? In case it is objected that the intuitive force of the example, if any, is a consequence of using a breach of contract as the unlawful means it is worth pointing out that a parallel argument could be made if X was an impresario who committed false imprisonment on a soprano, Y, in order to bring about the disappointment of another impresario, Z. Why should Z be able to base a parasitic claim on a tort that exists to protect Y's liberty?

Not only is the requirement of unlawful means arbitrary, but it also risks obscuring the importance of the distinction required by the nature of the protectable interest between positive acts and omissions. In the controversial case of *Millar* v. *Bassey*[48] the claimants alleged that Shirley Bassey was responsible for the losses they had suffered when she broke her contract with Dreampace, a producer of records, and Dreampace consequently broke its contracts with them. On the alleged facts Shirley Bassey's breach of contract certainly seemed to have prevented performance of the contracts between Dreampace and the claimants. But the focus on whether the breach of contract was 'unlawful means' led to the difficult question whether it should be classed as a positive act being overlooked. If the breach of the contract between Shirley Bassey and Dreampace was held not to be a positive act harming the claimants' interest in Dreampace's capacity to perform, then the claim should have been struck out regardless of whether a breach of contract is unlawful means and regardless of Shirley Bassey's state of mind towards the claimants.

So should a distinction between procuring a breach of contract and preventing performance by positive acts be rejected? The argument above has suggested that the

[48] [1994] Entertainment and Media Law Reports 44.

distinction is not required by the nature of the protectable interest, and indeed that drawing the distinction tends to undervalue the protectable interest. There is no obvious reason for treating a former competitor who seeks to destroy the value of a contract by preventing performance as interfering with a less important interest than a former competitor who seeks to obtain the performance for himself or herself. The distinction should also be rejected because of the problems that would be caused by the additional conditions proposed for liability on the preventing performance side of the line. Thus whilst the restriction of liability for preventing performance to situations where unlawful means have been used might be supported as a conveniently clear, if arbitrary, limitation in the interests of liberty the need for such a limitation is more obvious in cases where the claimant's general economic interests are at stake than when the claimant is known to be a party to a contract. Further, the focus on unlawful means risks distracting attention from the important positive act/omission distinction. Lastly, any proposal to restrict liability for preventing performance using a narrower mental element is open to the same objections as were mentioned above when considering the appropriate mental element for the procuring tort.

Should the third strategy also be rejected? Tony Weir criticizes the distinction that third strategists urge between direct and indirect interference as 'inappropriate, dangerous and incomprehensible'.[49] In more moderate terms the objection to the third strategy is that it requires a difficult distinction to be drawn between 'direct' and 'indirect' without any real explanation of the moral significance of such a line. Indeed it might be added that most of the possible examples of actionable direct interference without unlawful means seem to turn on the difficulty of applying the procuring tort to a non-human legal person. It is difficult to know where to locate a company's 'willingness to perform'.

But we should not allow forceful rhetoric to persuade us to overlook the possible merits of a 'direct'/'indirect' distinction. The most obvious way of drawing it is to ask whether the interference occurred through the acts or omissions of some human agent interposed between the defendant and the contract. Thus if I whisper in the soprano's ear or tie her to a chair then my interference will be direct, but if I persuade her taxi driver not to drive her to the theatre or blackmail someone else into tying her to a chair then my interference will be indirect. If this version of the distinction is accepted then the reason for imposing, or at least considering imposing, different standards of liability in the indirect form is clear: We require special reasons for making me responsible for the consequences of the behaviour of another. Thus, even if the argument above is accepted, and the interest created by a contract is recognized as one more appropriately protected by a single tort rather than by two, we may still want to require additional conditions in cases of indirect interference.

[49] Weir, n. 43 above, 609.

The Fourth Quarrel: Is Breach Necessary?

The analysis developed above seeks to explain why persuading a party to break a contract and preventing performance need not be separate torts with separate conditions of liability. This section deals with the question whether breach of contract should be a condition of liability. It has been suggested, for instance, that inducing non-performance of primary contractual obligations should be sufficient.[50] This issue has particular importance because many forms of prevention of performance may result in frustration or the invocation of a *force majeure* clause rather than a breach of contract. Does the property analogy shed any light on this controversy?

A starting point here is to ask whether the provisions which the parties make between themselves to govern a failure to perform primary obligations should define the 'property' which deserves protection against strangers. It seems implausible that when a party accepts that the other party's non-performance brought about by unprotected industrial action is to be excused by *force majeure* he or she equally accepts that the unprotected industrial action by strangers should be non-tortious. And this impression is confirmed if we treat the 'property' which the tort protects against strangers as 'the other party's existing capacity to perform'. Agreeing to a *force majeure* clause does not alter 'the other party's existing capacity to perform', so that 'interest' can still be protected against positive acts by strangers.

The question whether the tort can be extended to other degrees of interference with contract is more difficult. It is a question which can be rephrased as asking how far the interest created by the contract should be treated as having a protected dimension of, say, 'expected profitability'. Some of the arguments borrowed from private property could be deployed to support such an interest, but there is a strong case for saying that such an interest is too indeterminate and should therefore only be protected by the general tort of interference with trade by unlawful means.

If there is a single tort which covers both inducing a breach of contract and direct interference with a contract which prevents performance of primary obligations one remaining problem is the name of such a tort. The difficulty stems from the fact that directly preventing performance is not ideally described as inducing or procuring breach. The most obvious alternative to this unideal solution, however, would be to recognize two torts with the word 'interference' in their names, direct interference with contractual rights and interference with trade by unlawful means.

Protection of Non-contractual Interests

The property analogy may also illuminate other controversies such as whether it should be a tort to induce breach of statutory duties or of family obligations. In each case we can ask whether such obligations should be recognized as having a dimension which should be protected against *the rest of the world.* This is unlikely to be the case

[50] *Torquay Hotel Co. Ltd.* v. *Cousins* [1969] 2 Ch. 106.

with statutory duties generally, though there may be some situations where statutory terms carry out a function equivalent to contracts.[51]

CONCLUSION

This essay has sought to defend *Lumley* v. *Gye* and the existence of a tort of inducing or procuring breach of contract both by demolishing some of the arguments used against the tort and by borrowing justifications for private property as reasons for treating contracts as creating a special interest protectable against strangers. The essay has also attempted to establish that many of the proposed restrictions on the scope of the tort have been motivated by concern over the extent to which it may restrain freedom rather than reflecting the scope of the protectable interest. Some of the strategies for responding to this concern for freedom have been criticized for ignoring or neglecting the special protectable interest altogether or introducing confusing complexity into the tort, though an argument for maintaining the distinction between direct and indirect forms of interference has been offered. If the arguments put forward in this essay are convincing then the orthodox judicial view of the scope of the tort of inducing or procuring breach of contract can be portrayed as reflecting rational concerns rather than being the unfortunate end product of a succession of errors.

[51] See e.g. *Associated British Ports* v. *Transport and General Workers Union* [1989] 1 WLR 939.

Objectivity, Subjectivity, and Incomplete Agreements

Timothy A.O. Endicott*

What is a court's role in adjudicating contract disputes? I will approach that question in two sections that deal with objectivity and incompleteness in agreements. I will assume that the central purpose of the law of contract is to enable people to enter into certain sorts of legally binding agreements. That assumption leads to the puzzles which I will address.

It might seem that the court's role in resolving a contract dispute is just to hold the parties to the resolution that they intended. The court should ask, 'what outcome to a dispute like this did the parties intend?' Where the parties had no intention, or had different intentions, the court's task is either to find that there is no contract (if the issue is fundamental) or to imagine some counterfactual intention (if the issue is subsidiary to a set of shared intentions that is substantially complete).

That view fails, partly because the law uses objective tests for the existence and content of a contract. I will try to explain the use of objective tests by claiming that questions of the existence and content of an agreement are objective questions (section 1). The content of an agreement is not the content of the parties' intentions. The content of an agreement is determined by the meaning of the conduct by which the parties agreed. Objective tests are not a departure from the law's central purpose of enforcing agreements. A court adjudicating a contract dispute, therefore, faces a central task of answering this objective question: 'what commitments did each party give the other reason to think that they were assenting to?'

This objective view of agreement might seem to support a different view of contract adjudication: that the task of the court is just to enforce the terms of the agreement. Those terms being determined by objective tests, it does not matter if the parties had no intention, or conflicting intentions, as to how such a dispute should be resolved. So the court only needs to identify the terms of the agreement using an objective test, and enforce those terms.

That view of the role of courts is too limited. I will argue that the terms of agreements, understood on the objective view of agreement, are typically incomplete in significant respects (section 2). The conclusion is a view of the role of courts in which they must commonly give an outcome that was not intended by the parties, and that is not determined by their agreement. Courts must do so if they are to give effect to the intentions of the parties, and to their agreements.

* Balliol College, Oxford. I have benefited from discussions with Brian Langille, Arthur Ripstein, J.C. Smith, and Stephen Waddams, and with the contributors to this volume.

The court's role in deciding disputes over the existence and the content of contracts is not entirely interpretive; courts ordinarily have authority to elaborate incomplete agreements. The extent of that authority depends on the doctrine of the law that the courts administer. But that authority is not limited to the authority (i) to give effect to the intentions of either party, or (ii) to impose the outcome that the parties agreed to, or (iii) to interpret the contract. In any conceivable form of the law of contract, courts have authority (iv) to elaborate incomplete agreements. They have that authority even if the doctrine of the law denies that they have authority to do anything other than to give effect to the intentions of the parties.

THE OBJECTIVITY OF AGREEMENTS

Why does the law use objective tests, if contractual obligation is voluntary? Two contrasting answers have been popular:

1. The law uses objective tests for evidentiary reasons and reasons of policy. Objective tests help courts to know what the parties intended, and they promote certainty and avoid fraud. Contracts are agreements, and agreements are subjective, so the law departs from the parties' agreement to the extent that it uses objective tests. But there can be good extrinsic reasons for the law to depart partially from the requirement of agreement. The law does so (i) because we do not have any more reliable way of finding out what the parties intended than an objective test, and (ii) to pursue important policy goals. On this view, objective tests need special justification, because contractual obligation is essentially voluntary obligation.
2. Contractual obligation is not generally justified by agreement, but on some other (objective) ground such as the reasonable reliance of the parties, or the benefit that each gains from the transaction. On this view, objective tests are justified because contractual obligation is not essentially voluntary obligation.

G.H.Treitel has defended the first view; Patrick Atiyah has defended the second. They share the view that questions of the existence and content of an agreement are subjective questions. Treitel contrasts 'actual agreement' with 'the objective appearance of agreement',[1] and Atiyah implies the same distinction by talking of 'real subjective agreement',[2] and by distinguishing between asking 'whether the parties have really agreed in their innermost minds', and asking 'whether their conduct and language are such as would lead reasonable people to assume that they have agreed'.[3]

I will defend a third answer to the question why the law uses objective tests—an answer that shares Treitel's view that contracts are, generally, enforceable agreements:

[1] Treitel, *The Law of Contract* (9th edn., 1995) 1.
[2] *An Introduction to the Law of Contract* (5th edn., 1995) 82.
[3] Ibid. at 9.

3. Whether someone has entered into an agreement (and, if so, on what terms) is an objective question of what that person has done. To the extent that contracts are agreements, the only subjective questions in identifying contracts are questions of whether the conduct that ostensibly forms an agreement is the intentional conduct *of* each party. On this view, objective tests in contract law are justified because contractual obligations are typically voluntary obligations, and the existence and content of such voluntary obligations are determined by objective tests.

On this objective view of agreement, the use of objective tests is neither a qualification nor an obstacle to the orthodox view of contracts as agreements. Some instances in which contract theorists have claimed that the law uses subjective tests can be better explained as instances of the operation of objective tests. And some doctrines of English contract law commonly thought of as instances of the objective approach need other (genuinely extrinsic) justification on grounds of policy.

I will illustrate the objective view of agreement by discussing some cases of mistake in reaching an agreement. I will illustrate a potential objection to the objective view of agreement by discussing ambiguous agreements. Then I will try to say what *is* subjective about agreements.[4]

Mistakes in Communication

In *Riverlate Properties Ltd.* v. *Paul,* the lessors made a mistake in drafting a lease document. The lessors intended to make the lessee pay half of the costs of structural repairs. In the lease document, however, they wrote that she would pay half of the costs identified under clause '6(b), (c) and (d)', rather than '6(a), (b) and (c)'. Clause 6(a) concerned structural repair. The lessors claimed a right to rescind, subject to the lessee's option to accept rectification. The Court of Appeal held that the lessors had no such right, because the lessee did not know of the mistake, and 'was not guilty of anything approaching sharp practice'[5] in relation to the mistake.

On the subjective view of agreement, there was no agreement as on whether the lessee had to contribute to the costs of structural repairs. The lessors intended that she should, the lessee herself intended that she should not. Their intentions did not agree. In Atiyah's view, *Riverlate* shows that contract law is not centrally concerned with agreement. Atiyah has cited *Riverlate* as support for the view that contractual obligations are not generally justified by the agreement of the parties: he considers it an example of cases in which 'lawyers have treated a case as contractual even though genuine assent is missing'.[6] In Treitel's view, we need a special explanation of why the

[4] The objective view of agreement is controversial, but it is not novel. Anne De Moor gives a clear statement of the objective view of contract interpretation in 'Intention in the Law of Contract—Elusive or Illusory?' (1990) 106 *LQR* 632; but De Moor contends that the existence (as opposed to the content) of a contract is determined by the intention of the parties, and I do not make that distinction. For particularly strong statements of the objective view see David Goddard, 'The Myth of Subjectivity' (1987) 7 *Legal Studies* 263; Brian Langille and Arthur Ripstein, 'Strictly Speaking—It Went Without Saying' (1997) 2 *Legal Theory* 63. I discuss Langille and Ripstein's views below.

[5] [1975] 1 Ch. 133, 145.

[6] *The Rise and Fall of Freedom of Contract* (1979), 745.

lease is enforced in spite of the lack of agreement. We can find an explanation in the uncertainty that would result if a lease could be upset by an intention that the lessee did not know of.[7] We can find a further explanation in a policy of avoiding the danger of fraud by parties in the position of the lessors. The objective test is like a common law Statute of Frauds.[8]

On the objective view of agreement, the lessors agreed to a lease in which the lessee had no obligation to contribute to the cost of structural repairs. They did so by giving the lessee reason to believe that they were so committing themselves. Russell LJ suggests that the lessors would only be relieved from the consequences of their mistake if the lessee had known of it, or had been guilty of sharp practice. But what if the lessee had merely had reason to know that the lessors had made a mistake? That would be enough (on the objective view) to support the conclusion that the lessors had not agreed to a lease in which the lessee did not have to contribute to the costs of structural repairs. Stephen Waddams has argued that in such a case the promisor should not be held to the mistaken terms, and that Russell LJ's approach was:

> unduly rigid in its apparent failure to recognise the extension of relief to a case where the defendant ought to have knowledge of the mistake but cannot be shown to have had actual knowledge.[9]

I think that Waddams' proposal comports with the objective approach. The result in *Riverlate* was right, but it can be better explained by the objective view of agreement. The lessors agreed to a lease in which there was no requirement that the lessee should contribute to the cost of structural repairs. The lessors intended to enter into a different agreement, but they actually agreed to the lease as it was written, because they gave the lessee reason to take them to be committing themselves to the lease as it was written. The agreement of the parties (and not just their legal rights and duties) is determined by that objective test.

I do not mean that objectivity is part of the meaning of the word 'agreement'. The notion that two people who have the same intention are in agreement is not false. The word 'agreement' is equivocal: it just means some view or project or understanding (or I do not know what else) that the parties have in common. There are two senses of 'agree' and 'agreement' in particular. In the *active* sense, to agree is to do something, and an agreement is something that you and I might *make*, or *enter into*, or *reach* (and something we might fulfil, or repudiate). In the *stative* sense, to agree is to be a certain way, and agreement is a state we could discover that we *are in*. If we both hate gherkins, we agree in the stative sense even if we have never heard of each other.

[7] Cf. Treitel, n. 1 above, at 1: '[t]his objective principle is based on the needs of commercial convenience. Considerable uncertainty would result if A, after inducing B reasonably to believe that he (A) had agreed to certain terms, could then escape liability merely by showing that he had no "real intention" to enter into that agreement'.

[8] Cf. *Tamplin* v. *James* (1880) 15 Ch.D 215, 221 (CA): the buyers thought that a property sold at auction included more land than it did. James LJ said, '[i]t would open the door to fraud if such a defence was to be allowed'.

[9] 'Contracts—Mistake—Rectification with Optional Rescission' (1975) 53 *Can. Bar Rev.* 339 at 340.

My claims that agreements are identified by objective tests should be understood as claims both (i) that agreements in the active sense are identified in that way, and (ii) that the stative sense of agreement (which *is* a subjective matter) is not generally relevant to contract law.

Agreements are objective in this way for the same reason that promises are. Both agreements and promises are objective because communication is.[10] Speaking is (among other things) a way of communicating intentions, but the meaning of an utterance is not determined by the speaker's intentions. It is not simply determined by the meaning of the words a speaker uses, either. It is determined by the reasons that a speaker gives (by using the words that he or she uses) for another person to believe that the speaker has one intention or another.

The House of Lords has made this point in *Mannai Investment*, a recent case on the effect of a patent mistake in a notice to determine a lease. The tenant had written 'January 12' in the notice—but the tenant had power to determine the lease only on its anniversary, which was 13 January. The tenant's intention was irrelevant, as the notice was to be construed objectively. But the House of Lords held that the notice was effective to determine the lease on 13 January. Lord Hoffmann said:

> It is of course true that the law is not concerned with the speaker's subjective intentions. But the notion that the law's concern is therefore with the 'meaning of his words' conceals an important ambiguity. The ambiguity lies in a failure to distinguish between the meanings of words and the question of what would be understood as the meaning of a person who uses words.[11]

Understood against the background of the lease, Lord Hoffmann held that the meaning the notice conveyed was that the lease should determine on 13 January. Lord Clyde held that that was 'the evident intention' of the notice,[12] and that is a good phrase for the effect of the communications that make a contract: their effect is not to bind their maker to act on his or her intention; their effect is to bind their maker to act on the intention that he or she has made evident.

Lord Hoffmann introduced his reasoning in *Mannai* by saying, 'I propose to begin by examining the way we interpret utterances in everyday life'.[13] That must be the right place to start, if the point of a notice under a lease is to communicate an intention to the landlord. And Lord Hoffmann's elegant speech gives a persuasive account both of the effect of communications in ordinary life, and of the way in

[10] And note that the notion of a promise and the notion of communication lack the ambiguity between subjectivity and objectivity that is part of the notion of agreement.

[11] *Mannai Investment Co. Ltd.* v. *Eagle Star Assurance Co. Ltd.* [1997] 3 All ER 352, 376. Lord Hoffmann drew an analogy with the interpretation of commercial contracts (at 380). And the House of Lords has adopted a similar approach to the interpretation of statutes, holding that even the ordinary meaning of a statutory provision is to be ascertained in light of the purposes of the statute: *Attorney-General* v. *Prince Ernest Augustus of Hanover* [1957] AC 436. In *Arbuthnott* v. *Fagan* [1996] LRLR 135, Steyn LJ drew on the *Hanover* case to support the proposition that, in the interpretation of a contract, '[t]he meaning of words cannot be ascertained divorced from their context.' In *Mannai Investment*, Lord Steyn wrote a separate speech concurring with Lord Hoffmann's approach to the interpretation of the notice.

[12] [1997] 3 All ER 352, 383.

[13] Ibid. 375.

which both contractual communications and notices under a contract ought to be interpreted.

Suppose that you tell a 5-year-old that you are planning a trip to the farm tomorrow. If you decide not to make the trip, is she justified in saying that you have broken a promise? Does the answer depend on *whether you intended to be bound*? Or on *whether you intended her to take you as binding yourself*? Or on *whether she took you to be binding yourself*? I do not think it depends on any of those facts about the subjects involved. It depends on whether saying what you said, in the context, is a way of binding yourself. It depends on whether that sort of expression of intention counts as promising—which depends on the conventions that make up the English language, and on the practice of promising, and potentially on a host of conventions and shared understandings (about trips, and farms, and about *this* trip on *this* occasion, and so on). Those practices and other facts typically provide ways of voluntarily binding yourself; they typically do not make obligation depend on intention, and perhaps they could not do so. That is the paradox of promising: the practice of promising gives a facility for people to give effect to their will only because it gives them a way of committing themselves to something that may go against their will.

Suppose that we agree that I will pay you a stated price for goods of 'satisfactory quality'. Whether you carry out your promise depends on whether the goods you deliver are satisfactory—not on whether you think the goods are satisfactory, and not on whether I think the goods are satisfactory, and not on whether they conform to the standard of satisfaction (if any!) that either of us had in mind when we agreed. And we agreed, even if you and I had different standards in mind at the time. Your obligation is to deliver satisfactory goods, and 'what is satisfactory?' is not a question about you. The content of your promise is not determined by what you (or I) had in mind as satisfactory.

On this view of agreement, tests that some writers have treated as subjective are not actually departures from the objective approach. Ewan McKendrick says that the subjective approach plays a residual role in contract law where the offeree knows that the offeror is suffering from a mistake as to terms, or where the offeree is at fault in failing to notice such a mistake.[14] I will argue that the law's response to both situations can be better explained as taking the objective approach.

Offeree's Knowledge

The first situation is that in *Hartog* v. *Colin and Shields*.[15] The defendant offered to sell Argentine hare skins at prices quoted 'per pound', which was a blunder for 'per piece' (there are about three Argentine hare skins to the pound). The plaintiffs failed in their action to enforce a contract at the low prices stated in the offer. This case is different from *Riverlate*, because the court found that the plaintiff 'did in fact know' that a mistake had occurred.[16]

Treitel and Atiyah agree with McKendrick that *Hartog* departs from the objective approach: Atiyah says that in a case like *Hartog*, 'the law abandons the objective inter-

[14] *Contract Law* (2nd edn. 1994), 17–19. [15] [1939] 3 All ER 566. [16] At 568.

pretation of the first party's intentions'.[17] But, with respect, this view reflects an unsatisfactory view of the nature of an objective test. When the court looks at what B knew about A's intentions, it is not applying a subjective test, because it is not asking what A intended. The law is looking at what B had in mind, but:

(i) in looking at B's knowledge, the law is looking at what B had reason to believe (B knows nothing that B has no reason to believe), and
(ii) the law is looking at B's knowledge for the purpose of interpreting the communication A made to B.

Hartog does not depart from the objective approach, because a reasonable person who knew that A had made a blunder in communicating a term would not treat A as having agreed to price hare skins per pound.

Note that, in *Hartog*, the court not only found that the buyer knew of the mistake, but also held that, because of the practice in the trade and a course of dealing in which the parties stated prices 'per pound', the plaintiff 'could not reasonably have supposed' that the seller intended to offer a price per piece.[18] On the objective approach, there is, in that case, no agreement at a price per piece, even if the plaintiff had no actual knowledge of the mistake. If the buyer had reason to know that the seller meant to sell per piece, then the seller has not agreed to sell per pound, and that fact does not change if a silly buyer honestly believes that the seller meant 'per pound'. If the rule that knowledge of a fundamental mistake prevents an offeree from enforcing the mistakenly communicated promise were a subjective test, then it ought to make a difference if an offeree who ought to have known was genuinely oblivious. This is a further reason to conclude that *Hartog* does not depart from the objective approach: the knowledge of the buyer does not matter because it is his or her knowledge, but because such knowledge reflects a reason that the buyer has to treat the seller as meaning 'per pound'.[19]

Contrast mistakes that do not entitle a party to avoid a contract, such as mistakes as to the value of goods: knowledge (or a reason to know) of that sort of mistake does not give the offeree reason to treat the seller as meaning something different. Commercial life being what it is, a reasonable buyer might well take advantage of a seller who offers goods below the market rate, even if the buyer knows that the seller is undervaluing them.

It might seem that a buyer ought to be able to jump at a mistake in communication just as a buyer can jump at an undervaluation. No doubt, reasonable consumers often snatch at purchases when they can see perfectly well that a store clerk must have

[17] Atiyah, n. 2 above, at 84; cf. Treitel, n. 1 above, at 1: 'there will be no contract if (in spite of the objective appearance of agreement) B *actually knows* that A in fact has *no* intention to contract with him, or to contract on the terms alleged'.

[18] [1939] 3 All ER 566, 568.

[19] Was there a contract for the prices stated per piece? The court did not say. I propose that it ought to depend on whether the buyer's acceptance of the mistaken offer counts as an indication of assent to a contract at the prices per piece. If not, then I suggest that the seller has agreed to sell per piece, and the buyer has agreed to buy per pound; see discussion of *Raffles* v. *Wichelhaus*, in discussion of ambiguous agreements, below.

put the wrong price tag on goods. They probably even manage to feel aggrieved if the store refuses to sell at the mistaken price. And there may be good reasons for a scheme of regulation of contracts that holds the store to an obviously mistaken price. But if the law does so it will not be enforcing the store's agreement.

In *Riverlate*, the offeree had neither knowledge of the communication mistake nor reason to know; in *Hartog*, the offeree had both. I propose that the crucial distinction is that in *Hartog* the other party had reason to know of the mistake, and in *Riverlate* she did not. It is hard to say whether that feature is decisive in English law, because it is hard to find cases in which the court finds that an offeree had reason to spot the mistake, but not actual knowledge of it. In *Centrovincial Estates plc* v. *Merchant Investors Assurance Co. Ltd.*,[20] the defendants had been paying £68,320 *per annum* in rent; the plaintiffs wrote to propose a new rent of '£65,000', which the defendants accepted on the day they received the letter. The plaintiffs immediately telephoned to say that they had meant to propose £126,000, but the defendants insisted that they had a contract at £65,000. The plaintiffs failed in their application for a declaration that there was no contract, and McKendrick cites the decision as 'a good example of the application of the objective test'.[21] But if the basis of the decision is that the defendants can enforce the mistaken figure unless they had actual knowledge of the mistake, then I submit that, on the objective view of agreement, the decision does not enforce an agreement.

Centrovincial was decided on a summons for summary judgment, and Slade LJ said that there was not yet any proof that 'the defendants either knew *or ought reasonably to have known* of the plaintiffs' error'.[22] On those terms, the *ratio* does conform to the objective approach—except that we might ask why the facts assumed on the motion for summary judgment did not support the conclusion that the defendants had reason to know of the plaintiffs' error. In the context of the previous rent (and in circumstances in which it was even plausible for the plaintiffs to propose to double the rent), it seems that the defendants had reason to expect the rent to rise. So perhaps they had reason to know of the plaintiffs' mistake.

The case is unclear because it does not say whether the mere fact that the other party has offered surprisingly favourable terms can be a reason for the offeree to know of a mistake. I propose that Slade LJ's approach does not seek to enforce the agreement of the parties, if the court is never prepared to hold that a person in the position of the plaintiff in *Centrovincial* has reason to know of the mistake simply on the ground of the low figure in the letter from the landlord. What if the landlord had had in mind a rent of £126,000, but misplaced a decimal point, and written '£1260.00'? Then, on the objective approach, the landlord should not be treated as having agreed to a rent of £1,260, because in the context the figure itself would give the tenant reason to spot the mistake.

[20] [1983] Com. LR 158. [21] N. 14 above, 16. [22] At 158, emphasis added.

Offeree's Fault

McKendrick's second instance of a residual subjective test may be doubted for a similar reason. Just as a reasonable person who knows of a blunder would treat it as a blunder, a reasonable person would notice a mistake in a context in which they would be at fault if they did not. McKendrick's example is *Scriven Bros.* v. *Hindley*, but that is a peculiar case. It is true that Lawrence J applied a subjective test: he said that the jury's findings that the plaintiff intended to sell tow and the defendant intended to buy hemp 'shew that the parties were never *ad idem* as to the subject-matter of the proposed sale; there was therefore, in fact, no contract of bargain and sale'.[23] That holding seems to mean that any mistake by a buyer as to the nature of goods (e.g. the mistake made by a buyer who saw tow and thought it was hemp) would negative his or her consent to the sale. So in Lawrence J's view the law takes a subjective approach to identifying contracts *of bargain and sale*. But the reasoning in *Scriven* suggests that a mistaken buyer is *ordinarily estopped* from asserting his actual intention, so that there is a 'contract by estoppel'. The idea of such a contract seems to be that the parties have not agreed, but the mistaken party is estopped from pointing out the lack of agreement.[24] On the facts in *Scriven*, there was held to be no contract by estoppel, because the plaintiffs caused the defendant's mistake by their negligence. Someone had marked the hemp and tow with the same markings, to swindle the bank that financed the shipment. In those circumstances 'it was peculiarly the duty of the auctioneer to make it clear . . . which lots were hemp and which were tow'.[25]

No doubt the outcome in *Scriven* was right, but it could have been explained better (and more simply). To hold that the parties had not reached an agreement for the sale of tow, the court did not need to ask what the buyer intended; a reasonable auctioneer who had induced the customer to believe that the lot was hemp would not take the customer to be bidding for tow. The duty that the court identified gave the auctioneer reason not to take the buyer to be bidding for tow, and bidding for a lot of tow in that context does not count as agreeing to buy tow. So on an objective test, there was no agreement for the sale of tow.

Ambiguous Agreements

Suppose you agree to bring me a painter for my boat. If I have in mind a rope and you have in mind a person who paints boats, then it seems that we have no agreement at all. And, you might say, that shows that the objective view of agreement is wrong: we cannot reach the conclusion that you and I have not agreed by applying an objective test, because to all appearances we did agree.

I think that the objective approach can explain our lack of agreement. An ambiguity in what you say you will do is a reason not to take you to be committing

[23] [1913] 3 KB 564, 568.

[24] For an argument against the view that objective tests are a form of estoppel see De Moor, n. 4 above, 641.

[25] [1913] 3 KB 564, 569.

yourself to resolve the ambiguity in one particular way (and there is not necessarily any reason to take the other party to be undertaking a disjunctive obligation: you did not agree to bring me 'a rope or a person who paints, one or the other', you agreed to bring me a painter). So a reasonable person to whom an ambiguous promise is made would take the promisor to have undertaken an ambiguous commitment—a commitment to do something, which the promisor may be interpreting one way or the other. Such a promisee will not take the promisor to have undertaken either to bring a rope *or* to bring a person who paints.

We might say that we have agreed that you will bring me *something* for my boat, but our agreement is fundamentally incomplete. We do not actually have to identify the intentions of the parties to come to that sensible conclusion. I think this view is supported by the fact that mere multiple meaning in the language of an agreement does not determine that the agreement is ambiguous: if the context of our agreement gives reason for us to treat each other as talking about a rope (if, for example, you know that I have just painted the boat, and I've told you that I need to tie the boat to the dock), then you have obviously agreed to bring me a rope—and if you brought me a person who paints, even if by some mental lapse you really had that in mind when you promised to bring a 'painter', then you have not done what you agreed to do.

The problem is harder, though, if there is no reason for each party to know of the ambiguity of their language. Waddams suggests that a plaintiff in a case like *Hartog* has no reasonable expectation of delivery at a price that he or she ought to have known was a mistake. But, he says:

> The difficulty arises where neither party has reason to know the other's meaning, as occurred in the well-known case of *Raffles* v. *Wichelhaus*. In such a case where the parties are at cross-purposes and neither has reason to know the other's meaning there will be held to be no contract. This may result in the defeat of the plaintiff's reasonable expectation, but it is not an expectation for which the defendant can be held responsible for the latter had no reason to anticipate it. The defendant has simply not promised what the plaintiff understood, any more than has the sender of a message that is altered en route.[26]

Perhaps this difficulty is a serious objection to the objective view of agreement: on that view, A actually does promise what B reasonably understands A to promise. But if Waddams is right, when A's promise is ambiguous, A has not promised what B reasonably understood A to promise.

I do not think that even this difficulty is fatal. It is a popular view that there was no agreement in *Raffles* v. *Wichelhaus*.[27] The seller was to ship 125 bales of cotton on the *Peerless* from Bombay—but there was one *Peerless* from Bombay in October and another in December. The buyer refused the shipment, which came on the December *Peerless*, and the seller failed in an action for the price. Langille and Ripstein say that 'because they were talking about different ships, they did not agree'.[28] Waddams treats *Raffles* as a case of 'non-promise'.[29]

[26] Stephen M. Waddams, *The Law of Contracts* (3rd edn., 1993), para. 87.
[27] (1864) 159 ER 375.
[28] Langille and Ripstein, n. 4 above, 79.
[29] Waddams, n. 26 above, para. 87.

But the parties did agree to the sale of 125 bales of cotton from Bombay on the *Peerless*. Their agreement was certainly incomplete. If the court was right to let the buyer off, however, that is not merely because the agreement was incomplete, but because the court had no reasoned basis on which to complete the agreement by choosing one *Peerless*, and because of the importance of the incompleteness. In the following two variations on *Raffles*, I think we should say that there was an enforceable agreement:

(i) if there had been reason for the court to choose one *Peerless* as the one to which reasonable parties would have been referring (say both parties had reason to know that the October *Peerless* was a passenger vessel);
(ii) if the two ships had left Bombay on the same day, and the difference in the parties' understanding had made no difference to the value of the transaction to both sides.

In those scenarios the parties ought to have had a contract—even though they intended to contract for delivery on different *Peerlesses*.

What if the seller had the December *Peerless* in mind when the agreement was made (as was in fact the case), but for some reason tried to perform by delivering the cotton on the October *Peerless*? If there was no agreement, the buyer ought to be able to reject such a delivery, on the ground that there was no contract. But I submit that in such a case, the buyer should be bound to accept delivery for exactly the same reason as in any ordinary contract: he had agreed to it.

Instead of saying that there was no agreement, it seems better to say this: that the parties agreed to the sale of cotton to be delivered on the *Peerless*, that the agreement was incomplete because of the ambiguity, and that the seller would not be in breach if he did not deliver on the October *Peerless*, but would be in breach if he did not deliver on the December *Peerless* either; the buyer would not be in breach if he refused delivery on the December *Peerless*, but would be in breach if he refused delivery on the October *Peerless*. To do otherwise would be to say that the buyer could refuse to accept delivery on the October *Peerless*—the ship he had intended—because of the difference in understanding.[30] There may be good reasons for the law to reject such a contract, in which the obligations of the parties are not mutual, in favour of saying either that there was no contract, or that there was a contract for delivery on a single *Peerless*. But those reasons would be reasons not to hold the parties to what they had agreed to.[31]

[30] Cf. a related point that Waddams makes about rectification as an alternative to rescission in mistake cases: 'the plaintiff should not by his own mistake entitle himself to avoid even the transaction he intended' (1975) 53 *Can. Bar Rev.* 339 at 342. My point is that an ambiguity should not entitle a party to avoid even the transaction he intended.

[31] One reason might be just to keep things simple and manageable; such non-mutual obligations would create potential remedial paradoxes in cases such as *Hartog*.

The Subjectivity of Agreements

All questions concerning what counts as entering into an agreement are objective questions. But no one enters into an agreement without intentionally doing what counts as entering into an agreement. If Wayne Gretzky reasonably thinks he is giving an autograph, and in fact he signs a form of contract, he has not agreed to anything. He has not even agreed if it is reasonable for the other party to think that he has agreed—if, e.g., a third party fixed things so that Wayne had good reason to think that he was signing an autograph, and the other party had good reason to think that Wayne was signing a contract. Such a person may have reason to think that Wayne is committing himself, but it is not a reason that Wayne has given, and it is not a reason for which he is responsible. Whether A intended to do what counts as agreeing is a subjective question about A, and not an objective question about what A did. Whether two parties have agreed is a subjective question just in so far as it turns on whether they intended to act in a way that counts as agreeing.

If a court is to hold people to their agreements, then, it must identify their intention in order to decide whether they agreed. But the court need not find an intention to be bound to do X before it can hold that the party entered into an agreement which binds him or her to do X. The relevant intention is not the intention to do what the party said he or she would do, either (in *Hartog*, the seller said he would sell at 10¼d. per pound). The relevant intention is the intention to act in a way that, understood in the context, counts as agreeing.

I should emphasize that, if we take the objective view of agreements, we should also conclude that there may be very good reasons for the law not to hold parties to some agreements. There may be reasons, in some areas of the law, to let people out of an agreement on the ground of a mistake in communication that the other party had no reason to realize was a mistake. And we can imagine a situation in which there was an agreement (on the objective view) that neither party intended to enter into—and then it would be quite reasonable for the law to decline to enforce the agreement. Conversely, there may be good reasons to find contracts where there was no agreement (e.g., reasons to hold people to obviously mistaken communications).

My argument is not that contract law should always and only enforce agreements. But, to the extent that it does so, the law must use objective tests for the existence and terms of contracts. And, in fact, English law is very firmly committed to those tests. The parties cannot even give evidence of their intentions—not because of any special exclusion, but because it is not even arguably relevant to any question of the parties' rights and obligations.[32] In *Mannai Investment*, Lord Hoffmann said that the court's task in construing a contract is 'to ascertain what would objectively have been understood to be [the parties'] intention'.[33] And in his 'general remarks about the prin-

[32] At least, in commercial contracts. See *Prenn* v. *Simmonds* [1971] 1 WLR 1381, *per* Lord Wilberforce at 1385; *Reardon Smith Line* v. *Hansen-Tangen* [1976] 1 WLR 989, *per* Lord Wilberforce at 996.

[33] *Mannai Investment Co. Ltd.* v. *Eagle Star Life Assurance Co. Ltd.* [1997] 3 All ER 352 at 380.

ciples by which contractual documents are nowadays construed' in the *Investors Compensation Scheme* case, he put this principle first:

Interpretation is the ascertainment of the meaning which the document would convey to a reasonable person having all the background knowledge which would reasonably have been available to the parties in the situation in which they were at the time of the contract.[34]

INCOMPLETE AGREEMENTS

It is tempting to think that, if the objective view of agreement is correct, and if contract law enforces (some) agreements, then all questions of the existence and the content of a contract can be answered by applying the objective test of what a reasonable person would make of the conduct of the parties. Then it seems that the role of a court is (not to impose on the parties those obligations they *intended* to undertake but) to hold the parties to just those obligations that they *agreed* to undertake.

I agree that the role of contract interpretation is typically to apply the objective test of what a reasonable person would make of the conduct of the parties in its context. But I will argue that in disputes over rights under a contract there is commonly more than one good answer to that interpretive question. Reasonable people commonly differ over the question of what to make of the conduct of the parties.

This view of contract leads to the conclusion that there are commonly significant indeterminacies as to the content (and concerning the existence) of contracts. The parties may deliberately leave potential questions of their rights and duties unanswered; and, even if they do not do so, significant indeterminacies are frequently unavoidable (they are unavoidable in, for example, most contracts for the sale and supply of goods and services).

Brian Langille and Arthur Ripstein argue that some traditional approaches to frustration doctrine are based on the subjective view of agreement—the view on which 'the private contents of the parties' minds is thought to be determinative of agreement'.[35] They point out that such a view leads to the conclusion that courts deciding disputes over claims of frustration need to impose a fair or reasonable or just outcome on parties who did not intend that outcome. Langille and Ripstein neatly sum up a popular view, which they seem to share: that judges should not do that.

The problem with doing what is fair or reasonable and just to contracting parties independent of their intentions is that it seems to run contrary to the spirit of contract law. Contracts enable parties to make their own arrangements.[36]

In a footnote, they add that 'the power to make private arrangements that contract law confers should be taken seriously'.[37] I take them to imply that, because contract law enables parties to run their own affairs, the law should not impose obligations on the parties that they did not agree to undertake. I will argue that this view would be

[34] *Investors Compensation Scheme Ltd.* v. *West Bromwich Building Society* [1998] 1 ELR 896, 912.
[35] Langille and Ripstein, n. 4 above, 64. [36] Ibid. 68. [37] Ibid. 68 n. 10.

unjustified: there is no inconsistency between enabling people to make their own arrangements and imposing obligations on them that they did not voluntarily undertake; in fact, it is necessary to do so in order to facilitate private ordering.

I agree with Langille and Ripstein that questions about what two parties have agreed to are objective questions.[38] I see nothing in that view, however, to support their conclusion: that on the objective view of agreement, 'agreements themselves turn out to be highly determinate'.[39] In their view, 'the world contains enough detail, both natural and conventional, to resolve issues the parties to a contract had not anticipated'.[40] That means that cases in which the agreement does not determine the parties' rights and duties are rare and extraordinary, like *Raffles* v. *Wichelhaus*–in fact, there is no agreement in such cases.

It is difficult to generalize convincingly about the degree to which the terms of contracts are determinate. I agree that an agreement *can* divide risks that the parties did not think about—that is an implication of the objective view of agreement. But I will argue that agreements generally do not divide all such risks. It is common for an agreement not to answer questions of allocation of risk, because the agreement allocates risks in the way that reasonable persons in the positions of the parties would treat it as allocating risks. And on a vast range of questions of risk allocation under commercial transactions (even transactions as simple as a sale of goods), reasonable people might disagree. It is an important function of courts to answer such questions when they are disputed, even if the parties' agreement does not give the court reason to choose one answer over another. If that is the case, there are attractions in a view that Langille and Ripstein find 'entirely bankrupt': that 'courts appropriately respond to the lack of explicit agreement by resorting to some external standard of justice beyond the agreement of the parties'.[41]

Do the courts have to resort to some external standard of justice beyond the agreement of the parties? Yes, always, if they are to decide that the agreement of the parties ought to be enforced. But do they resort to such a standard in deciding whether there is an agreement, and what rights and duties to ascribe to the parties to an agreement? On the objective test, one aspect of justice is built into the identification of an agreement and its content, because a reasonable person will not take an unjust view of the intentions of the other party. Perhaps that is what Langille and Ripstein mean when they reject the view that courts should enforce 'some *external*' standard '*beyond* the agreement'. But I want to say that there is a role for justice in the determination of obligations under a contract that is distinct from (external to) the agreement of the parties.[42]

[38] But Langille and Ripstein suggest that questions of what a person *intended* are also objective questions. They have an objective theory not only for what a statement means, but for what a speaker *means by* a statement. They conclude that 'what a party means really is fixed by what others reasonably take him or her to mean'. See ibid. 80–1. I think they should have said that 'the meaning of what a party says really is fixed by what others reasonably take him or her to mean'.

[39] Ibid. 64. [40] Ibid. [41] Ibid. 80.

[42] Of course, there are many situations in which the law imposes contractual obligations even if the parties did not agree to them (e.g. mandatory terms in car insurance contracts), and does not enforce

Consider a contract for the sale of goods with no price term. Under the Sale of Goods Act 1979, section 8(2), 'the buyer must pay a reasonable price'. The courts had done the same, at least in some cases, at common law before the Act was passed. The Uniform Commercial Code does the same (and does so, unlike English law, even if the parties have provided that the price is to be agreed—section 2–305). In deciding the price of goods under such a legal provision, the court is no longer asking what the parties agreed to. The court is setting a price, and the parties did not agree to a price.

There is reason to think that that sort of judicial action is not extraordinary, but is part of a general function that they appropriately fulfil in answering questions left unanswered by the objective test of agreement. If that is right, then courts deciding disputes over mistakes (or frustration) may often appeal to values other than those that the parties agreed to pursue. I also want to say something further: that such an external standard of justice itself cannot be expected to resolve all the disputed points that a court may be called on to resolve. It is a crucially important part of a scheme of contract law that courts should answer questions of the parties' rights and duties that are answered neither by their agreement, nor by the considerations of justice and public policy that courts rightly appeal to.

That judicial role is not at all inconsistent with the notion that the central purpose of contract law is to enable parties to enter into their own voluntary obligations. If we think about some simple examples of incomplete agreements, we will see that it is necessary for courts to elaborate such agreements. It may seem to be a necessary evil: incomplete agreements pose a dilemma for courts that want to enforce agreements, but do not want to impose any obligations that the parties did not agree to undertake. But I will argue that the elaboration of incomplete agreements is not necessarily an evil: courts that are determined to take seriously the parties' power to make their own arrangements need to impose obligations that the parties did not agree to undertake.

I will call an agreement 'incomplete' if there are questions about what counts as performance that are not answered by an objective interpretation of the communications by which agreement was reached. The effect of the agreement is indeterminate in cases that turn on those questions. Note that I am using the term 'incomplete' broadly: it is more commonly used for an agreement that leaves *so much* open that the court ought to treat it as unenforceable. Most agreements are incomplete in my broad sense. Vagueness is a paradigmatic source of incompleteness, and it is a feature of most agreements.

obligations they did agree to (prohibitions on trading with the enemy are the neatest example). In those situations courts must apply a standard of justice independent of the parties' intentions. But those cases can be rationalized as exceptions by a theory that claims that courts should ordinarily impose just those obligations the parties agreed to undertake. I want to say that imposing obligations that the parties did not agree to is a *standard* function of courts, and that it is consistent with the notion that the purpose of contract law is to facilitate voluntary arrangements.

Vague Agreements

A agrees to sell B a shipment of citrus pulp pellets, to be delivered in good condition.[43] Suppose that there are one billion pellets in the shipment. Imagine a series of one billion hypothetical cases. Seller A_0 delivers the pellets, and all are in good condition. Seller A_1 delivers the pellets, and one pellet has gone off (and in A_2's shipment 2 pellets have gone off, and so on . . .). Seller $A_{1,000,000,000}$ delivers the pellets, and every one of them has gone off. Sellers A_0 and A_1 and A_2 have performed; seller $A_{1,000,000,000}$ has not performed. In the series from A_0 to $A_{1,000,000,000}$, which seller was the last to perform?

I propose that there was no last seller who did what he or she agreed to do, because the agreement was vague.[44] The shipment is in good condition if the pellets are all in good condition; it is not in good condition if they are all bad. Any two adjacent sellers in the series are in the same legal position, though, because each pair of adjacent sellers has done what amounts to the same thing. Suppose, however, that a court has to decide a dispute in each case over whether the seller performed. A_0 obviously wins, and $A_{1,000,000,000}$ obviously loses. But somewhere in between, a court faced with all 1,000,000,000 cases will have to draw a line between the last winner, who has performed, and the first loser, who is in breach (call the last winner 'A_i' and the first loser 'A_{i+1}').

There is nothing in the agreement that can help the court to decide which seller is the last to have performed. In fact, there is nothing in justice, fairness or reasonableness either: wherever the court draws the line, nothing will distinguish the last winner from the first loser in a way that justifies the view that one performed the agreement, and the other did not. The difference between what A_i has done and what A_{i+1} has done is immaterial. Justice and fairness and reasonableness (and the meaning of 'good condition' in the context) might justify holding that both performed, or that neither performed, but will not justify the view that A_i performed and A_{i+1} did not perform.[45]

A court deciding such a series of one billion cases will need to answer questions that are not answered by the parties' agreement. And this feature of litigation is a very general feature of any regime of contract law, because vagueness cannot be eliminated from contracts. It is easy to see why, if we consider the usefulness of terms as to good condition or satisfactory or merchantable quality (whether they are express, or implied at common law, or imposed by statute or by trade association standard terms). The seller *could* warrant that no more than *i* citrus pulp pellets should be bad,

[43] Cf. *The Hansa Nord* [1976] QB 44.

[44] Could we say that *only A_0 has performed*; and all the others are liable for damages that vary with the degree to which the shipment was not good? No, because a shipment of 999,999,999 good pellets and one bad pellet *is* in good condition: the seller has not agreed to deliver a perfect shipment, but a good shipment. So (whether the term is a warranty, or a condition, or intermediate) there is no breach unless there is *material* wastage, and 'material' is vague.

[45] For a discussion of the importance of such 'sorites' arguments in understanding the nature of law, see T.A.O. Endicott, 'Vagueness and Legal Theory' (1997) 3 *Legal Theory* 37.

but the gain in precision and predictability might not be especially useful to the parties, and it might be much more useful to agree to a vague requirement of good condition, than to work out precisely how much wastage is acceptable to each party—and to reach agreement on the point. Vague terms such as 'good condition' are useful to parties to a contract partly because they save each party the trouble of working out precisely what is wanted, and partly because they enable both parties to go ahead with an agreement, even when they do not agree on precisely what is to be delivered and paid for.

Moreover, *general* standards are useful in the practice of any seller who makes repeat sales (and they are necessary in any legislation that sets out to regulate the quality or condition of goods). As soon as the same term is used to regulate the sale of a variety of goods, precision becomes simply impossible: then there is no way to replace a vague requirement of satisfactory quality with similar but precise standards. So vague terms are so useful that no good scheme of contract law would refuse to enforce them, and no sensible contracting parties would follow a general strategy of avoiding them (although we could certainly imagine some vague terms that could be made more precise to the advantage of both parties).

Vague *doctrines* and rules of law are similarly ineliminable from contract law. Contract law provides any number of illustrations, even if there is no general doctrine of unconscionability. Consider the Unfair Contract Terms Act and the EC Directive on unfair terms in consumer contracts, and the vagueness of the techniques that the courts applied to exclusion clauses before those legislative steps were taken (such as the doctrine of fundamental breach). Consider the role of reasonableness in mitigation, and the doctrine of remoteness in assessing damages. Consider the requirement of materiality in the law of misrepresentation, and the requirement that a frustrating event be fundamental. Consider Ormrod LJ's test in *The Hansa Nord* (that the consequences of a breach of an innominate term should go to the root of a contract if the breach is to justify rescission). Such doctrines are unavoidably vague because (like a term as to quality in a Sale of Goods Act) they must apply generally to a variety of transactions.

Just as it is sometimes better for parties to agree to precise terms rather than vague terms, there may be respects in which some doctrines would be improved if they were made more precise; and it may be wise in some circumstances for parties to a contract to avoid the effect of a vague doctrine (that is sometimes a good reason, e.g., for parties to use a *force majeure* or hardship clause to settle what would be left unsettled by the vagueness of the frustration doctrine[46]). But none of this means that contract doctrine would be improved if its vaguenesses were eliminated. It would not be good to eliminate vagueness from contract doctrine even if it were possible—and I am not sure the notion even makes sense. Contract law could not do the things that it typically aims to do, without vague doctrines.

[46] See E. McKendrick, 'Frustration and Force Majeure—Their Relationship and a Comparative Assessment', in E. McKendrick (ed.), *Force Majeure and Frustration of Contract* (1991).

Finally, not only are contract terms often vague, and specific contract doctrines characteristically vague, but there is no precise answer to the objective question of what counts as agreeing. If you agree when you intentionally speak or act in a way that a reasonable person would treat as expressing an intention to be bound, then the requirement of agreement itself is vague. So vague terms are unavoidable in contracts, and vague doctrines are unavoidable in contract law, and the general requirement of agreement is vague. With a little ingenuity, we could imagine series similar to the citrus pulp pellet series for any vague term, and for any vague doctrine, and for agreement itself. If you accept these claims, this is the result: the scenario of the one billion citrus pulp pellet cases shows that a court called on to resolve disputes may need to answer questions of the parties' rights and duties that are not resolved by their agreement, or by justice (which does not distinguish between A_i and A_{i+1}), or by public policy, or by anything else.

But that, it may seem, does not necessarily pose any threat to a view such as Langille and Ripstein's view that agreements are 'highly determinate'. It all depends on *how* vague agreements and the doctrines of the law are. If there is only a trivial number of cases in which the agreement does not answer the question whether a party has performed, then it is plausible to say that the courts' function only exceptionally includes doing something other than what the parties intended. But if there is a great number of cases in which the application of the agreement is indeterminate, then the court must frequently do so.

Of course, there is no precise answer to the question, '*how vague* is a contract for the sale of citrus pulp pellets in good condition?'[47] There are certainly clear cases of good condition and bad condition (cases in which no reasonable person would deny that the shipment is, or is not, good). They do not start and stop at any precise point, though. Good condition is 'higher-order vague': the borderline cases cannot be precisely divided from the clear cases. In fact, I do not expect that there are any clear borderline cases (cases in which no reasonable person would deny that the application of the agreement is indeterminate).

We are in no position, then, to say in how many of the one billion cases the application of the term 'good condition' is indeterminate. We can say this, though: however many there are, there is nothing exceptional or extraordinary about them. Citrus pulp pellets decay, and there is nothing bizarre about a shipment of citrus pellets with any degree of decomposition. And since litigation is somewhat more likely in cases where it makes sense for the parties to disagree, there is nothing bizarre about a dispute over the application of a vague term to which there is no answer. Yet the court has to give an answer. Its readiness to do so cannot depend on its ability to find good reason for the particular answer that it gives (in the agreement of the parties, or anywhere else).

[47] Mind you, the notion that there is only a trivial handful of cases in which the application of the term 'good condition' is indeterminate is unattractive. If a shipment of citrus pellets is in good condition, it will still be in good condition if another handful goes off.

When a court resolves such an indeterminacy, it will be determining the rights and duties of the parties in a way that they did not agree to. They could have agreed that at least (1,000,000,000 – i) pellets had to be in good condition, but they did not. They agreed that the shipment had to be in good condition. There is more than one reasonable answer to the question, 'how many pellets can go off before the shipment is no longer in good condition?' And the seller has agreed to provide a shipment that a reasonable person would take to be in good condition, so there is more than one good answer to the question, 'what has the seller agreed to do?' How could a court have authority to impose *its* answer to that question, if the defining purpose of contract law is to enable people to make *their own* arrangements?

I propose that a court faced with the one billion citrus pulp pellet cases would have legitimate authority to find that A_i performed and A_{i+1} did not perform. That authority, though, is not an instance of its authority to hold the parties to do what they agreed to do. A_i entered into an agreement on the same terms as A_{i+1}, and A_i and A_{i+1} made materially equivalent deliveries. I think that the court's authority to treat A_i and A_{i+1} differently arises from the value to contracting parties of a regime in which disputed questions get answered, whether there is a reason for a particular answer or not. It does not run contrary to the purpose of enabling people to make their own arrangements, if courts resolve disputes about rights under a contract that are not resolved by the agreement of the parties.[48] In fact, the purpose of enabling people to make their own arrangements requires that courts do so in contract litigation.[49]

But that is not to say that it is right for a court to complete all incomplete agreements. If it is right for them to do so in some cases but not in all, what is the limit of the proper authority of courts in elaborating incomplete agreements? We might want to say that they should not do so if the agreement is *very* incomplete. But we can say more than that.

I have argued that the court may have authority to resolve a dispute even where the loser can say, 'I did not agree that a case like this should have this outcome' or even 'you are imposing on me an obligation [to deliver a shipment with no more than i pellets in bad condition] that I neither intended nor agreed to undertake'. But the court has overstepped its authority (or, at least, if the court has authority it does not arise from the value of enabling people to make binding agreements) if the loser can say, '[t]hat decision is not part of a practice that enables people like me to enter into (and avoid) the obligations that they choose to enter into (and avoid)'.

Even if the purpose of enforcing agreements is to promote people's autonomy, that purpose does not require that they should only be subject to obligations they agreed to undertake. It requires (i) providing them with useful facilities for making

[48] It will not typically run contrary to the intentions of the parties, either: it would be a bizarre transaction in which either party intended that a court should decide no questions except those answered by the agreement.

[49] For a related argument that indeterminacy in the law does not necessarily represent a deficit in the rule of law (and discussion of the circumstances in which indeterminacy in the law *does* represent such a deficit) see T.A.O. Endicott, 'The Impossibility of the Rule of Law' (1999) 19 *Oxford Journal of Legal Studies* 1.

and carrying out the agreements they want to make and (ii) not imposing any obligations on them that thwart their autonomy. And a court faced with the one billion citrus pulp pellet cases would not thwart the autonomy of any of the parties, unless it held a seller to have performed when the shipment was clearly not good, or held a seller not to have performed when the shipment was clearly good. It is actually a necessary feature of any useful facility for enforcing agreements that it should resolve unanswered questions. Imposing obligations that the parties did not agree to is not necessarily contrary to freedom of contract. In fact, it is a necessary feature of a regime that promotes freedom of contract.

If I show you my car and you agree to buy it, I do not know whether I have the right to take out the toy gecko in the rear window, or the floor mats, or the spare tyre, or the warning triangle, before I deliver it to you. We did not say anything about any of them. It would be impossible to buy and sell cars if you could not do so without reaching agreement on all such issues. If we end up in a dispute, a court will have legitimate authority to decide each issue either way. Except perhaps as regards my toy gecko? Perhaps the court's decision would be illegitimate if it said that I had sold the gecko to you with the car, but I am not sure. The court's legitimate authority is, itself, not sharply bounded.

I do not see why a court providing this useful facility to contracting parties should try to describe itself as enforcing what we had agreed to. The important point is the obvious point: that the court would be failing in its task of facilitating worthwhile agreements, if it held that there was no contract because our agreement was incomplete.

CONCLUSION

The role of courts in adjudicating contract disputes is complex. I have said nothing about their fact-finding role, or their responsibility to develop the law's principles of procedural and substantive fairness in contract formation (and the law's policies as to which agreements are enforceable), or their responsibility for fashioning remedies. I have only addressed some puzzles about their role that arise from the nature of agreements.

What must the courts do to take seriously the facility for private arrangements that contract law offers? They must do what they can to develop a useful facility for making enforceable agreements. They must, in general, use an objective test for the formation of contracts and for the identification of their terms. They must also be prepared to elaborate incomplete agreements. Here we reach a seeming paradox, because elaborating incomplete agreements means imposing an outcome that the parties did not intend. But the principle that the law should enable people to make their own arrangements simply does not require that the rights and duties that the law confers and imposes should be just those rights and duties that the parties agreed to undertake. The law may even impose strict liability. Imagine a computerized trading system in which you are bound to a contract whenever the 'sell' key on your computer is activated—even if you accidentally drop your sandwich on your keyboard. In that case, the law will *not* be enforcing an agreement, and it will be imposing an obligation on you that you did not voluntarily undertake. But, depending on the nature of the market and the needs, abilities, and so on of the traders, it may be providing a more useful technique for the making of voluntary arrangements, than it would provide if it asked whether the trader had agreed to the sale.

The role of courts in deciding disputes over contracts is not generally to give a decision that the parties intended, or even to give a decision that the parties agreed to. It is to develop and to give effect to a practice that is useful to parties in making worthwhile agreements. It is a standard part of the courts' role to give decisions that the parties neither intended that they should give, nor agreed to. That sounds crazy, because the purpose of contract law seems to require courts to do what the parties intended should be done. But it does not. It requires that the law enable them to do what they intend.

The legitimacy of imposing unintended outcomes on the parties arises (in part) from the need for resolution on points which the parties did not resolve, and which are not resolved by considerations of justice or good policy either. Giving an answer when reason does not offer support for one answer over another is a more humble function than other functions that judges perform, such as doing justice. It attracts no notice from contract theorists, because it is less exciting than the courts' function of stating and developing doctrine (for which there are often good and bad reasons). It is a function that gets left to the trier of fact. But, like doing justice and developing the law, it is an indispensable function that courts carry out in a good community.

On the Irrelevance of Motive in Criminal Law

Jeremy Horder*

> It is as firmly established in legal doctrine as any rule could be that motive is irrelevant to responsibility[1]

Most commentators on the criminal law agree that, with some odd exceptions, motive is generally irrelevant to the criminal law.[2] This general 'rule' is, however, misleadingly stated. The criminal law is a normative system, a system determining, for the most part, what we ought not to do. That fact inevitably involves the law in selective consideration of the reasons for which we acted. This is simply because whether someone ought not to have done something can turn on the reasons for which they did it.[3] Accordingly, putting aside cases of strict liability, wrongdoing is not treated as criminal if done for justifiable or wholly excusable reasons for so acting, even if the range of such reasons is legally very limited. Motives are reasons for action. So, in instances where wrongdoing is only criminal when done for unjustified or inexcusable reasons, some motives—those concerned with justifiable and excusable reasons for action—must, at least in principle, be relevant to liability. What, then, explains the strong sense that there is a rule making motives irrelevant to criminal liability?

THE SIGNIFICANCE OF MOTIVES: A SUMMARY OF THE ARGUMENT

As my opening remarks imply, in dealing with the irrelevance of motive, I shall be concerned with mitigating, rather than with aggravating, motives.[4] Why?

* I am very grateful to John Gardner, Tony Honoré, Andrew Simester, Antony Duff, Andrew Ashworth, and Stephen Gough for their comments on earlier drafts of this essay, and also for the observations on those drafts of participants in staff seminars at the Universities of Birmingham and Leicester. *I* am sure that the essay is much improved as a result, but they all might very well beg to differ.

1 Alan Norrie, *Crime, Reason and History* (Butterworths, London, 1993), 37.

2 See e.g. J.C. Smith and B. Hogan, *Criminal Law* (8th edn., Butterworths, London, 1996), 81–3.

3 See the link made between normative theory and reasons for action, in the passage from Joseph Raz's *Practical Reason and Norms* (2nd edn., Princeton University Press, Princeton, NJ, 1990), 11, cited in the text at n.13 below. The reasons for which one does something are helpfully described by John Gardner as 'explanatory' reasons, to distinguish them from the reasons that ought to influence whether one acts in a certain way or not, which he calls 'guiding' reasons: see his 'Justifications and Reasons', in A.P. Simester and A.T.H. Smith (eds.), *Harm and Culpability* (Clarendon Press, Oxford, 1996) 103. In what follows I shall be concerned almost exclusively with explanatory reasons, reasons that were in fact acted on by defendants, who now seek to rely on this as a justification or excuse for their conduct.

4 Mitigating reasons are any motivating reasons that show up admittedly criminal conduct in a light more favourable to the accused. What one might call 'shielding' motives, by way of contrast, are a narrower

Aggravating motives are not commonly found in the definitions of crimes, because legal definitions of crimes commonly seek to establish only the definitional minimum for the wrong in question.[5] It will often be possible to create different grades of the same offence, using the heinousness of motive as a criterion for gradation; but this is typically regarded as needless over-elaboration in a criminal statute, questions of heinousness being left to sentencing.[6] Let me elaborate. The existence of a crime, justifiably created, reflects a reason not to do the thing prohibited. An 'aggravating' motive for committing a crime is regarded as aggravating because it provided yet another reason not to do the thing prohibited, a reason on which the defendant culpably acted, to be added to the reasons on which the law is based. Suppose X intentionally kills Y not only to dispose of Y, but also to devastate Z. Acting in order to devastate Z is an aggravating motive, because the fact that Z will be devastated by Y's death is itself a reason *not* to kill Y, a reason that one can add to the law's normal reasons not to kill, against which X has acted. But if the reason not to kill someone (Y) intentionally on which the law is based is, *ex hypothesi*, sufficient to justify criminalization, there may be scant justification for giving a legal basis to yet further reasons not to act in that way. To do that would be to add a fifth wheel (or more) to the coach.

Unfortunately, the same argument cannot be made for excluding mitigating motives from the definition of crimes. Mitigating motives are reasons to do the thing prohibited, in spite of the prohibition. Say A intentionally kills a terminally ill relative, B, perceiving the action to be the only way of ending B's incurable pain. In such a case we can easily recognize A as having a reason to kill intentionally, a reason that conflicts with the reasons against intentional killings that are relied on and provided by the law. In consequence, we may now wish to re-examine the sufficiency or scope of the reason against intentionally killing, the reason that shapes the legal prohibition. Mitigating reasons to do the thing prohibited might shake our faith in the authority of legal definitions, such as the definition of murder. They might do this precisely because such reasons conflict with the reason(s) not to do the thing prohibited on which the authoritative definition is based, in a way that further reasons not to do the thing prohibited—aggravating motives—never do. It is the irrelevance to criminal

class of motivating reasons, such as justifying or excusing reasons, that negate, in whole or in part, the criminal character of conduct. It is the task of this essay to explain how one should distinguish mitigating from shielding reasons.

[5] The point at which the definitional minimum is reached may change over time. So, for example, the fact that non-consensual intercourse is procured *by force* is now an aggravating feature in rape, where the definitional minimum in establishing the *actus reus* is non-consensual intercourse itself. In years gone by, proof of forced non-consensual intercourse was part of the definitional minimum: see, further, Gardner and Shute, this volume. Picking out particular motives for special treatment may also involve the law in needless controversy. A topical example is the treatment of racial motive in the Crime and Disorder Act 1998: see further, F. Brennan, 'Racially Motivated Crime: The Response of the Criminal Justice System' [1999] *Criminal LR* 17, 22–3.

[6] For a sophisticated defence of the 'exclusionary rule' keeping motives out of definitions of crimes, broadly along the lines suggested in this para., see A. Duff, 'Principle and Contradiction in the Common Law: Motives and Criminal Liability', in A. Duff (ed.), *Philosophy and the Criminal Law* (Cambridge University Press, Cambridge, 1998), 175–6.

liability of certain good reasons *to commit* a criminal wrong—mitigating motives—that thus rightly invites sustained theoretical attention.

So, let me turn my attention to the privileged class of such reasons that is permitted to affect criminal liability, in whole or in part, namely the class of justifying or excusing ('shielding') reasons. Defendants who seek to justify or excuse their conduct commonly act first and seek justification or excuse afterwards, on an *ex post facto* basis.[7] In some cases this will be, for example, because, when they acted, the defendants responded more or less spontaneously to the perceived demands of an unexpected emergency (as in justificatory necessity cases), or to the dictates of passion (as in excusatory provocation cases). It is only having so acted that they turn to the law seeking, respectively, vindication or mercy. What is the significance of this? For simplicity's sake let us concentrate on what will turn out to be the theoretically more significant case of justifications, where one seeks vindication *ex post facto*. I shall argue that, if justification—vindication—*ex post facto* is to be warranted, the reasons (motives) for which defendants did the harm in question must have been reasons appropriate, at the time, for an individual to take it upon him- or herself to act on *unilaterally*, in deciding to do that harm.[8] More specifically, it must be shown that the limited range of relevant evaluative considerations confronting the defendant, and their exceptional or almost unique nature (their relative detachment from wider, more complex policy issues and implications), meant that those considerations were ethically appropriate for an individual him- or herself to act on, in doing the harm struck at by the legal prohibition. It will be my contention that the '*ex post facto*' defences are (rightly) shaped by just such considerations.[9]

By way of contrast, one will have no justification (or excuse) for doing harm or wrong, in breach of the law's *ex ante* injunction to avoid doing it, if the pros and cons at stake in one's decision could only adequately be weighed through the kind of *collective* deliberation and decision-making that goes into the formulation of such an *ex ante* injunction. What is more, this will remain true, even if one's motive was the prevention of an otherwise unavoidable and unjustified harm, in an emergency. Even in an emergency, the considerations at stake may be morally too wide-ranging and complex, or may have too many troublesome ethical implications for future or analogous

[7] There are naturally some exceptions to this, discussed in the text at n.47 below. For further examination of the issues, see P. Robinson, 'Rules of Conduct and Principles of Adjudication' (1990) 57 *University of Chicago LR* 729; Peter Alldridge, 'Rules for Courts and Rules for Citizens' (1990) 10 *OJLS* 487; Meir Dan-Cohen, 'Decision Rules and Conduct Rules: On Acoustic Separation in Criminal Law' (1984) 97 *Harvard LR* 625. An overview can be found in Gardner, n. 3 above, at 123–6.

[8] This argument will, as it happens, also apply to excuses, in that excusatory reasons must also, *inter alia*, provide a compelling explanation why a defendant acted unilaterally in wronging the victim.

[9] How individual justifications are shaped by these considerations is, however, a complex matter that varies from one justification to the next. I shall concentrate mainly on justifications that arise in emergencies, rather than on, say, consent as a justification. By so doing, though, I introduce a further layer of complexity. To be justified in acting first, in an emergency, and seeking justification *ex post facto*, it must have been the case that if one did not oneself do harm in order to avoid an unjustified harm or greater wrong, there would have been no other plausible way (say, as by seeking the assistance of the police) of preventing the latter coming about: see further, on this point, J. Horder, 'Criminal law: Between Determinism, Liberalism, and Criminal Justice' (1996) 49 *Current Legal Problems* 159, at 174–5.

cases, for an individual adequately and rightly to weigh them up, and him- or herself come to the conclusion that the demands of the law may be set aside in this instance. Even in some emergencies, in other words, there may be no moral warrant for acting first, in breach of the law, on one's individual assessment of the merits, and then seeking justification or excuse afterwards. For in many—probably most—situations, the *ex ante* commands of the law will reflect a collective attempt to provide authoritative guidance on what ought to be done, that cannot be (morally) bettered by an individual weighing up the pros and cons at stake, even if he or she—for his or her own part—believes it to be wrong to follow the law in that situation.[10]

I can seek to illustrate my main point through a contrast between two examples. In both examples, I seek to use my poverty as a justification for theft of property from someone wealthy. In the first example, I steal a computer from the wealthy person simply because, say, he or she has a large number of similar computers, and will not think the loss of this one to be in any way significant, whereas having it will give me access to important information and services I could not otherwise afford. In this instance, I am seeking vindication for my actions on the ground that, in the circumstances, a (perceived) increase in distributive justice was rightly preferred by me to the maintenance of commutative or corrective justice, as between the wealthy person and myself.[11] The problem for me, in claiming a justification on this ground, is that the question of how distributive justice stands in relation to corrective justice, in these sorts of circumstances, is a question far too complex and wide-ranging for an individual to resolve unilaterally.[12] It is a question whose resolution must be left to the collective judgement of the polity, the *ex ante* guidance provided by the law being the embodiment of the polity's collective judgement. The law, of course, grants no exception to the instruction to avoid theft, in these circumstances. This is because, when it comes to personal wealth, the polity seeks to secure distributive justice, in a principled and consistent way, through the bureaucratic systems of social security and taxation, rather than leaving it to the arbitrariness and inconsistency of individual 'self-help'. I may, of course, personally think this policy misguided or unjust. Even

[10] For the jurisprudential basis of this view, see e.g. Raz, n. 3 above, 191–4; see also his reply to critics in 'Facing Up' (1989) 62 *Southern California LR* 1153, 1160 and 1161. See also Gardner, n. 3 above, at 115–17, and the discussion in the text at and following n. 42 below. I tackle instances where one is unjustified in setting aside the law in an emergency in the text at n. 19 below.

[11] An excellent discussion of the distinction between distributive and corrective justice is to be found in J.M. Finnis, *Natural Law and Natural Rights* (Clarendon Press, Oxford, 1980), 165–86. For criticism of the original Aristotelian distinction between them, see J.W. Neyers, 'The Inconsistencies of Aristotle's Theory of Corrective Justice' (1998) XI *Canadian Journal of Law and Jurisprudence* 311. See also Stephen Perry, this volume.

[12] This point, or at least one very like it, seems implicit in Hale's comment that if necessity could justify theft, then 'men's properties would be under a strange insecurity, being laid open to other men's necessities, whereof no man can possibly judge, but the party himself': see Hale, *Pleas of the Crown*, 1, 54. Hale unfortunately blunts the effect of this good point, by muddling it with a more controversial rejection of a Natural Law principle that 'the goods of the earth can[not] reasonably be appropriated by a few to the substantial exclusion of all others': J.M. Finnis, n. 11 above, at 187. See, generally, Finnis's discussion, at 187–8, of the relationship between this principle, a regime of private property, and a system of taxation. See also Gardner and Shute, this volume.

so, I ought to have followed the *ex ante* guidance of the law, because I ought to have recognized the moral inappropriateness (due to the risk of arbitrariness and inconsistency) of my situation for unilateral resolution through self-help.

Contrast this case with the second example. In this example, the temperature in a remote region, in which I am climbing a mountain, unexpectedly plunges to sub-zero levels, and the only way to save myself from freezing to death is to break into an unoccupied cabin belonging to the wealthy person, and to take fuel and food to ensure my survival. In this example, by way of contrast, whilst distributive justice is again preferred by me to corrective justice, the circumstances are very different, and I have a case for being regarded as justified (or, at the very least, excused) in criminal law. First, the emergency situation in which I act means that my needs cannot be addressed, even in principle, through official channels. I have no option but to act unilaterally, or suffer the consequences. In itself, however, this is not enough; but, further, the emergency situation in question is exceptional and 'one-off', in that it carries with it no wide-ranging implications for other cases in which corrective justice might conceivably be 'traded off' against distributive justice, implications it would be beyond my moral competence to assess. Finally (a related point), the choice I face is simple and stark. It makes no complex moral demands of me that could only adequately be addressed through the kind of collective deliberation that goes into *ex ante* legal guidance. In what follows, I seek to show how and why the relevance of motives to criminal liability is structured by considerations such as these.

DECISION-MAKING IN EMERGENCIES: THE LIMITS OF INDIVIDUAL SOVEREIGNTY

The argument begins with Raz's distinction between normative and ascriptive theory:

> Normative theory is primarily concerned with establishing what people ought to do . . . Who ought to realise which values and how is the main problem of normative theory. Its most important concepts are ought, reasons for action, rules, duties and rights . . . The theory of ascription is concerned with the conditions in which blame or guilt can be ascribed to people . . . It is the job of normative theory to determine whose responsibility it is to realise this or that value . . . The theory of ascription deals with the ascription of blame and praise to people who fulfilled or failed to fulfil their responsibilities. It presupposes that we have a normative theory and studies the normative consequences of failure to conform to the requirements of normative theory.[13]

One of the reasons the distinction between justifications and excuses is so difficult to draw is that it does not map precisely on to the distinction between normative and ascriptive theory. Some justifications have an almost exclusively normative dimension, such as self-defence (a defence which, of course, involves a normative permission, rather than a normative demand), whereas others have an ascriptive dimension to them, like necessity (the law prohibits me from doing what I did, but I am not to be

[13] Raz, n. 3 above, 11–12.

blamed for doing it, given the necessity, and indeed it is something that—morally—ought to have been done). Some excuses, like provocation, are focused almost exclusively on ascriptive considerations, whereas others, like duress, may have at least the flavour of something normative about them (is it not, for example, in some sense something I positively ought to do when the gunman demands, on pain of death, that I commit some trivial trespass?). Unfortunately, I cannot pursue these fascinating issues further here. What I do need to do is to start by explaining why, as indicated earlier, my focus will be largely on justifications, rather than on excuses. The explanation is that when I claim a justification I claim that I acted as I *thought* I ought to have done, or was permitted to do, even if in fact I failed to do what I really ought to have done, or was permitted to do. My claim is framed in normative terms, even if (as in the case of mistake) it may be dealt with in law as an ascriptive theoretical matter.

This being so, it is relatively easy to see how some defences having almost wholly ascriptive significance, provocation being the best example, will not be a concern in this essay. For these are defences in which I did not unilaterally choose what I perceived to be the best course of action, in circumstances where the best course of action could only appropriately be determined through collective decision-making. The focus of such defences is, instead, on my very failure to act rationally, on my failure to choose my course of action in accordance with an intelligent conception of what is best. Consider provocation. Provocation raises ascriptive, as opposed to normative, issues respecting my liability. I unjustifiably wrong the victim of my provoked and angry killing (the normative issue), but the understandable nature of my loss of self-control may reduce my culpability to the point where the label 'murderer' is too grave, and 'manslaughterer' becomes more appropriate. When I am provoked to lose my self-control, and I there and then kill in consequence, I kill for a reason: the provocation. Most importantly, however, the law is centrally concerned with the fact that the loss of self-control the provocation induces propels me into action in a gust of unlooked-for passion. It is this latter fact that means that it would be wrong to regard me as rationally associating myself, at the time, with having deliberately killed in response to the provocation. I am partly responsible for my loss of self-control, and hence for what I did in consequence, but my loss of self-control distanced me, through (*ex hypothesi*) no fault of my own, from my ability to conform to the basic principle of rationality that I should act for an undefeated reason (i.e. a reason not outweighed by some countervailing reason, or set of such reasons).[14] So, however grave the provocation may have been, I will not be framing my claim to the defence

[14] See Gardner, n. 3 above, 111–12. The same analysis applies to some—but far from all—duress cases. In some duress cases I simply give in willy-nilly to an overwhelming fear for my own safety. In such cases, the way in which the threatener induces a fear of death or serious harm distorts my normal sense of the value of my own interests relative to those of others. I may then, for example, do as the threatener demands simply because he or she has demanded it, so great is the self-preservatory urge he or she is able to induce in me, leading me unjustifiably but excusably to wrong an innocent third party. Here, again, although I act intentionally, and the reasons for which I act are my reasons, my all-consuming fear prevents me from acting for reasons with which I rationally associate myself.

in stark and simple normative terms, in terms of what I thought I ought to have done, what was for the best, or such like.

So, a discussion of such cases is of marginal relevance to the present explanation of why motives are irrelevant to the criminal law. The latter explanation should be most concerned with cases in which I decide to act on a reason to do something prohibited, in spite of the prohibition, as in cases of so-called 'mercy-killing', because I think that is permitted, or for the best (a normative claim). For, in such cases, I believe I am acting rationally, for an undefeated reason. These conditions are clearly met, for example, by the defences of self-defence, of necessity, and by some instances of duress.[15] What distinguishes such cases from more general examples of cases, such as mercy-killing, in which I may also have a reason to contravene a legal prohibition? We need to start with an examination of the law's treatment of justifications for invasion of legally protected interests: cases having normative rather than ascriptive significance.

When we are justified in inflicting harm in self-defence or under conditions of necessity, the law has given us permission to act for certain reasons—to harm, or even to kill—on which we would normally be prohibited from acting. John Gardner explains the point this way:

> So far as the criminal law is concerned *all* reasons in favour of performing the criminalised action are defeated by virtue of the law's unquestionable and all-embracing authority. It means that one is left with no automatic access to any justificatory considerations, however powerful they might be apart from the law. What the law does, which nevertheless creates a role for some justificatory defences, is to provide us with *cancelling permissions* to perform, under certain specified conditions, the actions which it criminalises . . . the law's cancelling permissions do not cancel the reasons not to perform the criminalised action, but merely cancel the second-order protective reasons not to act for certain countervailing reasons. Thus justificatory arguments which the law would otherwise disallow are specifically allowed.[16]

I have cited from Gardner's essay at length, as some of the jurisprudential observations he makes will be of importance later. Let us focus, for the moment, on a narrower point about the way in which justificatory arguments work in the criminal law. Gardner's thesis illuminates most clearly the justificatory defences of self-defence and necessity. In both cases, the harm-doer (D) is permitted to act in virtue of the cancellation of the second-order protection of the reason not to do the harm. The cancellation is, of course, on highly specific terms. D must only act reasonably on the

[15] Cases where I can control my fear, but I none the less comply with the threatener's demand, as the most reasonable option in the circumstances. Such duress cases have some normative significance. English law is moving towards a position in which the application of the defence is limited to cases in which the harm done must have been less than the harm threatened, where the latter needs to be a threat of death or grievous bodily harm: see *R* v. *Gotts* [1992] 2 WLR 284 (HL). This being so, a normative dimension has been added to the defence in virtue of the need to weigh the values at stake, although the ascriptive element remains central: the need for D to fear the consequences of non-compliance. See further, J. Horder, 'Self-Defence, Necessity and Duress: Understanding the Relationship' [1998] XI *Canadian Journal of Law and Jurisprudence* 143, 161–3.

[16] See Gardner, n. 3 above, 116–17.

necessity, or out of the need for self-defence, respectively. None the less, in virtue of the cancellation of the second-order protection of the norm concerning V's interests, D's normative position has changed with regard to those interests. D is now entitled to act on a reason to invade V's interests, in a way someone not confronted with necessity or an attack on him- or herself would not be.[17]

As Gardner rightly points out, when the law grants us legal permission to act, it does so only under specified conditions. A key condition underpinning necessity and duress cases is that the wrong be done in circumstances where there was no reasonable opportunity to seek official intervention or protection, as an alternative to committing the wrong.[18] This condition has two functions. First, it serves an ascriptive function. I am not to be blamed if I acted on the necessity or under duress only when there was no realistic, law-abiding alternative. Secondly, however, the condition serves a more important normative function. It is intended to confine successful duress and necessity pleas to 'one-off' situations, such as some kinds of emergencies, wherein, because they are one-off, D's actions do not have wide-ranging policy implications for other similar or analogous situations. For where action taken in threatening or necessitous situations may have such implications, these can only rightly be addressed through collective political deliberation and legal decision-making aimed at producing *ex ante* legal guidance, on which the conduct of individuals should subsequently be based. Situations, whether they are emergencies or not, that have wide-ranging policy implications, and that hence require collective knowledge, deliberation, and expertise to guide individuals who may have to face them, are not appropriately addressed by an individual acting unilaterally, who then subsequently seeks *ex post facto* vindication in the courts.

James Griffin brings out the sense of the argument well in relation to necessity pleas.[19] A man whose only life-saving option is to cut a rope joining two climbers, one of whom has fallen from a cliff and is involuntarily dragging the other towards the edge, has a good case for saying that he acts under conditions of necessity.[20] An uncompromising consequentialist might argue, though, that a good case for a defence of necessity also exists when a doctor extracts organs from one patient to give new life to several otherwise endangered patients. In both cases, someone's vital interests are sacrificed as a means to an end, in an emergency, so why is the doctor regarded as

[17] There will still be important distinctions to be drawn between kinds of justification, but I shall not go into these in detail here, since it is not my aim to provide a theory of defences. Briefly, necessity cases involve overriding reasons on which D acts, where V's legal protection is overridden. Self-defence cases involve permissive reasons, a licence to disregard V's legal protection. In self-defence cases, unlike necessity cases, V's normative position also changes, in that in virtue of the unjust threat he poses to D, V ceases to be entitled to rely on his legal protection as a basis for resisting D's attempts to counter the threat. This does not happen in necessity cases, because in such cases V is posing no threat to D: see generally Horder, n. 15 above.

[18] See *R.* v. *Hudson and Taylor* [1971] 2 QB 202 (CA).

[19] See J. Griffin, *Value Judgment* (Oxford University Press, Oxford, 1996), 98–103.

[20] It is possible that the law provides no defence in these circumstances, but this position has been widely criticized. For further discussion of this kind of example, and of whether, if the climber who has not fallen cuts the rope, he acts in self-defence, see J.C. Smith, *Justification and Excuse in Criminal Law* (Stevens, London, 1989), 78–9; and also Horder, n. 15 above, 146–7.

clearly having no defence of necessity to a charge of murder, whereas it is regarded as controversial that the rope-cutter does not? For Griffin, the answer is this. In one-off emergencies:

> moral life is, at that point, exceedingly simple: better few dead. And the policy, Limit the Damage, is modest in two ways. It makes no great demands on knowledge: the policy is obvious. And it involves no ambitious programme of action: we respond whenever, in exceptional circumstances, our hand is forced.[21]

By way of contrast, the case of the doctor who performs a death-dealing transplant, that kills one patient in order to save the lives of several others, does not meet either of these 'modesty' conditions. Whereas the rope-cutter's action, being a 'one-off', has scarcely any wider consequential significance for what he, or others, ought to do, this is not true of the doctor's action. To begin with, the doctor's action appears to commit her to an ambitious programme of action. Is she not, in virtue of thinking this one action to be correct, obliged not only to think death-dealing transplants might well be justified, in general, but also to share her new-found expertise, and seek out other opportunities to perform such transplants? Even if the answer to this question is in the negative, her action is taken in circumstances where she cannot gauge what the implications of her conduct for herself, for doctors in similar situations, and for others in many reasonably analogous sets of circumstances, might be. Here is what Griffin says about a case like the doctor's:

> If the surgeons do it today, why not tomorrow? If this group of surgeons does it, why not others? If surgeons do it, why not, say, politicians when their moral sums come out the same? And, typically, we cannot know in the transplant case, even to a reliable degree of probability, what will most promote values. The case is far from simple . . . They [the surgeons] cannot do the calculation of total benefits against total costs . . . Anyone who aspires to a moral life based on such calculations aspires to God-like knowledge . . . The transplant case is different, I think, not just because the surgeons are deciding who is to die . . . but because, in so doing, they are pretending to know that this is the best policy.[22]

The doctor's conduct is thus unjustified because she fails to recognize the limits of an individual's ethical *nous*, when dealing with complex and far-reaching human problems, and hence accept the limits of individual sovereignty: the first of Griffin's two 'modesty' conditions. In such cases, one's duty is to accept the need for (political and legal) institutional solutions to the problems raised, and action taken unilaterally to resolve them should not be legally tolerated. The man who severs the climbers' rope, by way of contrast, can act unilaterally, because his decision and conduct are within the ethical compass of a single moral agent, and hence meet Griffin's first 'modesty' condition. The dilemma he faces is one-off, in that it has no wide-ranging

[21] Griffin, n. 19 above, 99.

[22] Ibid. at 99 and 100. For similar 'slippery slope' arguments, applied in the euthanasia context, see the New York State Task Force on Life and the Law, *When Death is Sought: Assisted Suicide and Euthanasia in the Medical Context* (1994), p. xiii, cited in G. Dworkin, R.G. Frey, and S. Bok, *Euthanasia and Physician Assisted Suicide* (Cambridge University Press, Cambridge, 1998), 47–8.

and complex implications for analogous situations, and may never be repeated (thus meeting Griffin's second 'modesty' condition). It is, uniquely, *his* dilemma. *Ex post facto* vindication of his conduct is thus ethically appropriate in a way it would not be for the doctor, who ought to be relying on the *ex ante* injunction of the law to avoid death-dealing transplants (even if, in good conscience, she thinks that it is wrong).

Both the ascriptive and the normative points just made bear on the mercy-killing case, mentioned earlier. Of relevance to the ascriptive point is the fact that it will be a rare case indeed of mercy-killing in which one can say that, objectively judged, there was no realistic alternative to killing, such as seeking further medical treatment to relieve pain, that could have been taken on the victim's behalf.[23] As far as the normative point is concerned, it should be obvious that mercy-killings are just those kinds of cases which, if not met with outright prohibition, ought to be authoritatively permitted only if the most carefully thought-out and well-defined *ex ante* guidance on the appropriate circumstances has been explicitly followed. Their legitimacy cannot be left to the guidance of individual conscience or belief, however altruistic, or (even) solely to the unconstrained professional judgement of those working in the medical profession. The ethical issues are too complex and potentially wide-ranging for that.[24] Accordingly, would-be mercy killers ought to appreciate the importance of relying on *ex ante* legal guidance (even if they think it is misguided), in their conduct, as opposed to seeking *ex post facto* vindication for what they regard as, in the circumstances, the morally justified course of action.[25]

In this regard, proponents of critical legal studies have put forward the following argument to undermine the suggestion that defences can rightly be confined to the kind of one-off emergencies that are the focus of traditional duress and necessity cases. It has been suggested that it is a commitment to an implausibly abstract individualism that explains the narrow time frame within which excuses operate. The commitment is said systematically to require the exclusion, from the sphere of legal relevance, of the broader context in which individuals commit crimes.[26] Ironically, the reverse is the case. The confinement of '*ex post facto*' excuses and justifications to the narrow time-frame of one-off emergencies is explained by the central importance of seeking to guide human conduct through *collective*—as opposed to individual—deliberation on, and resolution of, certain recurring human dilemmas (such as

[23] Whether such a step is believed by the killer to be likely to be effective or not being, of course, irrelevant, except, in some instances, as some guide to what is objectively judged to have been reasonable.

[24] Although one must clearly accept that under any plausible scenario in which euthanasia were to be legally permitted, professional medical judgement would be likely to be playing a vital role. For concerns about misdiagnosis and mistreatment in this context, see the New York State Task Force on Life and the Law, n. 22 above.

[25] The same argument ought to be deployed to explain why the 'Robin Hood' character, who thinks it right to steal from the rich to give to the poor, ought to be regarded as dishonest. 'Robin Hood's' action exemplifies and commits him to an active policy of redistribution that, even putting on one side the direct harm that it does, arrogantly presupposes a God-like ability to account adequately for all the relevant ethical considerations. For further discussion of such an example, see A. Norrie, n. 1 above, 42–5.

[26] See M. Kelman, 'Interpretive Construction in the Substantive Criminal Law' (1981) 33 *Stanford LR* 591; A. Norrie, n. 1 above, 45–7.

whether to sacrifice one to save many). In situations liable to recur (which include some emergencies) with potentially far-reaching consequences, it will be wrong for an agent to substitute his or her own conception of a just resolution of a problem for that of the polity. For his or her action will wrongly seek to tackle, unilaterally, issues appropriate solely for action guided by the broader perspective brought to bear through collective deliberation and resolution. And it has been my argument, of course, that the traditional 'time-frame' limitations placed on defences such as necessity and duress, are in fact explained by the simple absence of the expectation, in the 'one-off' circumstances in which the defendant acts, that conduct need be guided by the collective solution embodied in the *ex ante* legal prohibition.

I should underscore this point by highlighting the link between the availability of a defence and the need to rely on *ex ante* guidance, when complex and controversial policy issues are at stake, even when one is dealing with a defence such as self-defence. For, in spite of appearances, it would be a mistake to think that, if one is to have a defence such as self-defence or necessity, the circumstances in which one acted must in all instances meet Griffin's 'modesty' conditions. Defences in the criminal law are not, conceptually or morally, tied to the circumstances in which it is appropriate for someone to seek wholly *ex post facto* vindication. The picture is more complicated than that. For example, soldiers and agents of law enforcement may, much more frequently and predictably than ordinary citizens, find themselves facing the need to act in self-defence, or (perhaps more rarely) to commit wrongs under conditions of necessity. Griffin's second 'modesty' condition is not met, for example, by the circumstances in which members of a police firearms unit may be permitted to use their weapons in prevention of crime or in self-defence.[27] Those circumstances, being prone to recur, and having potentially wide-ranging implications for the relationship between civil liberties and law enforcement, may properly be subject to *ex ante* policy guidance which those using the firearms will be expected to follow. Such guidance is to be found in the non-statutory 'yellow card', issued to soldiers and police officers, that sets out when and how (if duly authorized) they may, or should, use firearms.[28] It is quite conceivable, and perhaps proper, that such guidance may endorse standards that would be regarded as too rigorous, if applied to the ordinary citizen responding to a one-off emergency, even though everyone—ordinary citizen and state official alike—may only use such force as is necessary and within the bounds of reasonableness, in the circumstances. Whatever one's views on this, however, the main point needs to be grasped. Although seeking, in one's defence, *ex post facto* vindication or mercy means having to show that the circumstances in which one acted met Griffin's

[27] Sometimes, Griffin's first 'modesty' condition will not be met either. For example, moral life is not altogether simple for the armed officer who must decide whether to shoot (a person believed to be) an armed terrorist who—at this moment, at least—is seeking to escape rather than to threaten life or limb. What the officer should do is far from obvious, even if his or her choices are limited: see *R.* v. *Clegg* [1995] 1 All ER 334.

[28] I am indebted, here, to the fascinating discussion of these issues in J. Rogers, 'Justifying the Use of Firearms by Policemen and Soldiers: a Response to the Home Office's Review of the Law on the Use of Lethal Force' (1998) 18 *Legal Studies* 486.

two 'modesty' conditions, the precise scope of defences in the criminal law is not delimited by these 'modesty' conditions. A defence may exist where either or both of the conditions have not been met.[29] In such cases, though, there will normally be a need for the defendant to have followed the *ex ante* guidance of the law (or the guidance of those charged with issuing it within the scope of their legal authority). For such guidance is, or ought to be, the embodiment of the collective effort to address and resolve difficult policy questions, whose resolution is beyond the moral compass of a single individual taking it upon him- or herself to tackle the issues in the heat of the moment. I come back to this point in a later section.

JUSTIFICATION AND EXCUSE: THE BROADER PICTURE

I have been concentrating on what one might, somewhat misleadingly, call the relatively 'context independent' defences, such as duress, self-defence, and necessity. They can be called relatively context-independent, in that their principles are formulated without the demands of particular crimes in mind: they apply across a variety of crimes. It is not uncommon, however, for terms such as 'justification' and 'excuse' to be employed in a way that is meant to be context-dependent. Examples are provided by the offences of having with one an offensive weapon in a public place 'without lawful authority or reasonable excuse', destroying or damaging property 'without lawful excuse',[30] and by blackmail. In the case of blackmail, the crime is committed when D makes, *inter alia*, an 'unwarranted' demand with menaces.[31] So the 'unwarranted' character of the demand for money or services is critical to its criminal status, and an inquiry into the status of the demand is an inquiry into the reason it was made. It would not be blackmail for me to threaten you with a writ if you do not pay me the money you owe me, but (other things being equal) it would be blackmail for me to threaten to reveal some impropriety on your part to the newspapers if you fail to give me the money that you owe me. Doubtless, there are many other such examples, where the justification, excuse, or warrant is highly context specific.[32] Do we need to

[29] So, e.g., in cases in which consent is allowed as a defence, the important fact is that the relevant ethical considerations are within the moral compass of (and are, indeed, uniquely appropriate for evaluation by) an individual. There is, for obvious reasons, no significance attached to the fact that D does not act in an emergency, or to the fact that the situation is liable to recur.

[30] See, respectively, the Prevention of Crime Act 1953, s. 1, and Criminal Damage Act 1971, s. 1(1). In the case of the latter, extensive legislative provision is made to distinguish lawful excuses from mere matters of mitigation: see s. 5(2). Such examples are discussed by Duff, in Duff (ed.), n. 6 above, 177–9. The argument that follows is meant to supplement Duff's analysis of the examples.

[31] The Theft Act 1968, s. 21(1), makes D guilty of blackmail if 'with a view to gain for himself or another or with intent to cause loss to another, he makes any unwarranted demand with menaces'. Smith and Hogan give blackmail as an example of a crime in which motive is relevant to liability: n. 2 above, 81–3.

[32] A concealed example can be found in the Theft Act 1968, s. 2, which indicates that someone is not to be regarded as dishonest if he appropriates property in the belief that the true owner will not be found. Here (if D's belief is correct) D may be justified in taking the property: the harm was done to the owner through the loss, and not D's act of appropriation.

give a different explanation for the role of justification and excuse in such cases? We do not.

In defining crimes, legislators rightly try to focus on proscribing as wrong that which we have most reason to prohibit.[33] It would make little sense to have a crime of engaging in sexual intercourse, with a 'defence' that the victim consented, because we have no reason to prohibit sexual intercourse. Accordingly, the proscribed wrong is non-consensual sexual intercourse.[34] Where serious offences against the person are concerned, that which we have most reason to prohibit is what has helpfully been termed the '*prima facie*' wrong, a wrong stated independent of whatever reasons there might be to commit it.[35] Where one has, for example, deliberately or recklessly killed, engaged in non-consensual sexual intercourse, or inflicted grievous bodily harm, something has already happened that, barring special circumstances, we have most reason to prohibit. It is, therefore, natural and proper to find justifications and excuses for such conduct located within the rules of 'supervening defences',[36] rather than integrated within the definition of the crime itself (other than through a largely superfluous reference towards the need for the defendant to have acted 'unlawfully'). For, other than the guiding reasons applicable to those context-independent defences, there will be few, if any, reasons in favour of doing as the law prohibits.

Sometimes, however, conduct will only be a *prima facie* wrong—that which we have most reason to prohibit—if done for some reasons rather than for others. In such cases, there will be no *prima facie* wrong that can be stated independent of the reasons for engaging in the conduct in question. Blackmail is an example. In other cases, often where property, and property-based, offences are concerned, it may simply be difficult to identify a clear and unambiguous *prima facie* wrong, independent of the circumstances in which conduct of the kind to be proscribed may justifiably be engaged in. Taking another person's property is, course, the classic example, although the law of theft cleverly conceals the problem, by making much of the justificatory or excusatory import of D's conduct hang on the *mens rea* question of whether he or she is to be regarded as 'dishonest'. 'Wilful' obstruction of the highway is another example, which is not an offence unless done 'without lawful authority or excuse'.[37] Where one is unlikely to be able to identify in advance all the circumstances in which to engage in the relevant conduct is not wrongful, it makes perfect sense to give the justifiability or excusability of D's conduct a prominent role in the definition of the offence, and leave the courts to sort out, as between judges and juries, who is to decide issues of justifiability or excusability in law and in fact.

For present purposes, however, there are two important points to be made about offences of this latter kind. First, when judges and juries do address their minds to the

[33] See K. Campbell, 'Offences and Defences', in I. Dennis (ed.), *Criminal Law and Justice* (Stevens, London, 1987).

[34] See further Gardner and Shute, this volume.

[35] On the use of this term in this context, see Gardner, n. 3 above, at 107–9.

[36] Andrew Simester's felicitous phrase for instances of self-defence, necessity, and so forth: see his 'Mistakes in Defence' (1992) 12 *Oxford Journal of Legal Studies* 295.

[37] Highways Act 1980, s. 137(1).

question of what justifies or lawfully excuses damaging another's property, wilfully obstructing the highway, and so forth, they will have to be mindful of many of the same considerations as shape the context-independent defences. In other words, for something to count as an instance of a justification or lawful excuse, the range of ethical considerations must be of a kind that are appropriately handled by an individual acting unilaterally. If we look, by way of example, at the treatment of theft or criminal damage, this is exactly what we find. In the law of theft, it is not dishonest for someone to appropriate property in the belief that the true owner cannot be found by taking reasonable steps.[38] In the law of criminal damage it will be a lawful excuse to show that one was only damaging another's property in order to protect further property that was in immediate need of protection. In both of these cases, the justification or lawful excuse is shaped by an implicit concern to ensure that D is acting in a one-off situation, in which the range of relevant ethical considerations can be adequately evaluated by an individual acting unilaterally.[39] The same will be found to be true of other instances of justification and excuse beyond the 'emergency' situations at issue in the context-independent defences.

There is another reason why it is important to consider crimes in which open-ended notions of justification and excuse are central to the definition. These crimes are important counter-examples to the claim that the law systematically excludes motives from definitional questions in criminal law. Norrie argues, for example, that the criminal law keeps the subversive potential of mitigating motives in check by securing its 'base categories', *actus reus* and *mens rea*, against what he calls 'moral infection'. The law, he suggests, only gives justification and excuse a subsidiary status as secondary questions, so that moral issues, such as mitigating motives, can be handled in a tightly controlled way at the secondary stage.[40] This interesting thesis unfortunately equates the 'law' with the over-rigid and prescriptive *theory* of the law found in some academic textbooks, the theory according to which one must insist that justification and excuse are treated as secondary issues. The thesis consequently overlooks the centrality of open-ended issues of justification or lawful excuse to crimes such as theft, criminal damage, wilful obstruction, and many others. I have sought to suggest that the centrality of motives to such crimes can be attributed to the absence, in these crimes, of a clear and relatively unambiguous *prima facie* wrong, of the kind one finds in the worst offences against the person. Naturally, this all makes the criminal law, as a whole, untidy and highly open-ended. There is nothing wrong with that. It is only academic over-ambition, coupled with the zeal of utilitarian law

[38] See n. 32 above.

[39] For a recent example, see *Chamberlain* v. *Lindon* [1998] 1 WLR 1252 (CA), a case of criminal damage in which D demolished V's wall, and successfully claimed lawful excuse on the ground that the wall was obstructing his right of way in circumstances where there was an immediate need to remove it. Contrast this case with *R.* v. *Hill (Valerie)* (1988) 89 Cr. App. R 74, where the damage to property was intended to intimidate the USA into removing its nuclear bases in the UK, and so the claim of lawful excuse rightly failed for the reasons under discussion.

[40] See A. Norrie, ' "Simulacra of Morality"? Beyond the Ideal/Actual Antimonies of Criminal Justice', in Duff (ed.), n. 6 above, 128.

reformers, that leads theorists to strain to find or impose order and uniformity on what is naturally a highly variegated set of laws.[41]

MOTIVES, RULES, AND PRACTICAL REASONING: THE DUTY NOT TO ACT UNILATERALLY

Central to what Gardner vividly described, in the passage cited above, as the law's 'unquestionable and all-embracing authority' is the idea that legally determined situations (as one might call them) are situations in which it is best to accept an authoritative determination of what one ought to do, rather than seeking to resolve this question through resort to one's own consideration of the applicable reasons. One is more likely, in such situations, to make good decisions and perform right actions by following the law, as the relevant authority, rather than by seeking to weigh up all the pros and cons for oneself. As Raz indicates, there are at least two kinds of reason to follow the law without simply balancing its demands against one's own assessment of what ought to be done.[42] First, when we are not in a position—factually or morally—to judge the appropriateness of the law's commands, we must either disregard the law, or follow the law and disregard our own assessment of the merits on which the law's commands are based. Practically reasonable citizens do not disregard the law (even if they think it to be in need of improvement), as the relevant authority, unless it is morally iniquitous.[43] So, compliance is, for all practical purposes, the right action. It has been my argument that when citizens face moral dilemmas outside the special circumstances of duress, necessity, and self-defence, they are likely to be in just such a position of (partial) moral ignorance, a position that requires deference to the collective effort at addressing the problem that is embodied in legal prohibition.

Secondly, however, it would be unduly limiting to regard the question of motive's relevance to criminal liability as a matter between a single individual and the state. As a citizen, one is a part of a vast political and legal effort to secure co-ordination in the interests of the common good. Such co-ordination can only be achieved if individuals defer to the judgement of the authority charged with securing it, and do not act on their own assessment of the morally relevant reasons. The point has been well expressed by John Finnis:

> [T]he reasons that justify the vast legal effort to render the law . . . relatively impervious to discretionary assessments of competing values and conveniences are reasons that also justify us in asserting that the moral obligation to conform to legal obligations is relatively weighty. These reasons relate particularly to the extent, complexity, and depth of the social interdependencies which the law . . . attempts to regulate. Such an ambitious attempt as the law's can only succeed in creating and maintaining order, and a fair order, inasmuch as individuals drastically

[41] For the most sophisticated attempt yet to follow this point through at the level of political and social theory, see N. Lacey, 'Contingency, Coherence and Conceptualism: Reflections on the Encounter between "Critique" and the Philosophy of the Criminal Law', in Duff (ed.), n. 6 above.

[42] See Raz, n. 3 above, 62–5. See also Finnis, n. 11 above, 318.

[43] Ibid. 359–61.

restrict the occasions on which they trade off their legal obligations against their individual convenience or conceptions of social good.[44]

In one-off emergencies, neither of Raz's reasons for regarding the law as excluding reliance on one's own assessment of the reasons for acting applies. For reasons indicated earlier, one is in a position in which one can grasp and adequately weigh the relevance and strength of all the relevant reasons for acting. Moreover, the very one-off character of the dilemma means that the law's efforts to co-ordinate conduct in the interests of the common good are not affected by one's conduct. The law's authority remains undiminished by permitting one to act on one's own (*ex hypothesi* reasonable) moral assessment of the situation, in such circumstances.

This second point is an important one to bear in mind when one comes to deal with some possible counter-examples to the thesis I have been developing. It follows from my argument in relation to one-off emergencies, that it is unjustified and inexcusable for individuals to seek to be guided by their moral senses, rather than by the law, when confronted by 'emergencies' with much larger ethical and political implications than can possibly be accounted for by an individual, as when someone considers euthanasia. As Griffin put it,[45] it is wrong to set oneself up as an omniscient dispenser of justice in a situation in which there is no salient, obviously reasonable policy. But suppose that X is the world's greatest expert on an incurable and painful terminal disease affecting her husband Y, as well as being a leading authority on medical ethics. X also knows Y's views about when it would be right to end his own life better than anyone else, perhaps even better than Y himself. X may quite plausibly say that the moment has come when the salient, obviously reasonable policy is to end Y's life, and there may be no gainsaying that, from the moral point of view. There may be no ethical consideration, applicable to this particular case, which X has failed to evaluate in a more complete and discriminating manner than the law itself, or any other competent authority, could have done. Even so, from the legal point of view, as Finnis implicitly claims, what matters is not simply whether X is morally justified in ending Y's life, or in assisting Y to end it. What matters is how a decision to excuse or justify X's action, on the grounds that X's action was morally justified, may affect the wide-ranging, complex, and deep social interdependencies that the law must regulate in this field, and in related fields. What will the wider implications be for the relations between doctors and patients, husbands and wives, and so forth?[46] X cannot plausibly claim to be in the best moral position to evaluate these implications, and so, in killing Y, acts irresponsibly from the legal point of view, whether (apart from the law) she is morally justified in so doing or not.

[44] See Raz, n. 3 above, 62–5. See also Finnis, n. 11 above, 319.

[45] Griffin, n. 19 above, 100.

[46] These are clearly what have come to be known as 'slippery slope' considerations. For general discussion of slippery slopes, see F. Schauer, 'Slippery Slopes' (1985) 99 *Harvard LR* 361–83. For discussion in the euthanasia context, see e.g. R.G. Frey, 'The Fear of a Slippery Slope', in Dworkin, Frey, and Bok, n. 22 above, chap. 3.

AVOIDING 'SLIPPERY SLOPES' IN ADJUDICATION: RELYING ON LEGAL RATHER THAN MORAL GUIDANCE

I have been concentrating on defences fashioned by judges during many centuries of common law development. Our legal system remains one in which the development of relatively general justifications and excuses, outside special fields, is left to the process of a case-to-case adversarial system of adjudication. In such a system, judges are rightly bound to be reluctant to extend the scope of such defences into areas where they themselves—building on the point just made in the foregoing section—cannot properly assess the implications of so doing, in the case at hand. Recent developments have posed a serious challenge to this way of going about the development of defences. Consider the recent cases in which doctors have sought a court's backing for a decision to withdraw any form of treatment from a patient in a persistent vegetative state (PVS), to sterilize a mentally incompetent patient so that she can engage in sexual relations without fear of a pregnancy, or to force life-saving treatment on a patient who has irrationally refused to accept it voluntarily.[47] Some of these cases (e.g. the forced treatment of the gravely imperilled patient who irrationally refuses it) may involve the kind of one-off emergency to which the special considerations we have been analysing apply. The courts may have to be left to deal with such cases just as one-off cases, employing one of their primary roles as the ultimate authority in resolving disputes. With many such cases (PVS patients; surgical operations on mentally incompetent patients), however, a principled or policy-based approach is required, since the cases are much more likely to recur and to have wide-ranging ethical implications. One approach to such cases, which has tempted some judges, is to treat them as involving a new defence, 'acting in the best interests of the patient', that operates in much the same way as the traditional defences of necessity and self-defence. On this view, the law permits doctors to act on their sense of what is morally and professionally appropriate, as regards a particular patient, in the expectation that, by responsibly acting in this way, they will subsequently find that their conduct is covered by the relevant defence.[48] The analogy with the traditional defences comes from the fact that with these, too, defendants who successfully plead them will commonly have acted on a sense of the moral appropriateness of particular conduct, in the expectation that the law will clothe that conduct, *ex post facto*, with justificatory legitimacy.[49] The defect of this traditional approach, where the 'best interests of the patient' defence is concerned, is found in the very fact that the circumstances in which doctors will act are not 'one-off'. This means that doctors will inevitably be left to grapple with the moral dangers of 'slippery slopes' ahead. What nature and degree of surgical intervention is justified with mentally incompetent patients? Is the nature

[47] See, respectively, *Airedale NHS Trust* v. *Bland* [1993] 1 All ER 821 (HL); *F* v. *West Berkshire HA* [1989] 2 All ER 545 (HL); *Re C (Adult: Refusal of medical treatment)* [1994] 1 All ER 819.

[48] This approach was adopted by the majority in *F* v. *West Berkshire HA* [1989] 2 All ER 545 (HL).

[49] See Gardner, n. 3 above, 123–5.

and degree of such intervention related to the degree of the patient's mental incompetence? What is the relevance of relatives' views? And so forth.[50]

There is an alternative approach.[51] This approach requires medical authorities to act on *ex ante* legal instructions and advice, rather than relying *directly* on a sense of moral and professional appropriateness. In an important departure from the purely adversarial process, in cases concerning the withdrawal of treatment from a patient in a persistent vegetative state, the courts have provided highly specific legal guidance on which doctors must rely.[52] The importance of resolving such cases through legal guidance is that it can keep doctors away from the 'slippery slope' into full-scale euthanasia which reliance on moral guidance and professional judgement might require them to confront.[53] One should never underestimate the occasional usefulness of the law's ability to cut short moral debate, or to be insensitive to moral implications, by seeking to draw bright lines where none exist in morality. In situations that, considered as a type, are one-off emergencies, by way of contrast, the law can afford to be relatively open-ended and sensitive to moral nuances (e.g. by having a very broad view of what it is to act 'reasonably' in self-defence). The limited range of relevant ethical considerations bearing on such cases, means the law can now afford that luxury.

CONCLUSION: FROM NORMATIVE TO VALUE THEORY

I have been concerned with normative and ascriptive dimensions of criminal liability, but, as Raz argues, normative theory 'presupposes some value theory and derives from it the requirements which it imposes on the behaviour of individuals'.[54] The structure of criminal liability derives much from a concern for the values of moral and personal autonomy, and this is true of the defences.[55] Those who lack moral autonomy are shielded from criminal liability by defences such as insanity and diminished responsibility. Personal autonomy in its basic form of negative liberty (crudely, 'freedom from') is protected by the defences of self-defence and duress. The criminal law also does something to promote personal autonomy in its more complex form (crudely, 'freedom to') through the defence of consent, a defence which recognizes that causing harm to another can sometimes be intrinsic to a valuable, autonomy-enhancing activity. It is inevitable, however, that defences to criminal liability will be concerned with the complex form of personal autonomy only to a small degree. This

[50] For a helpful, brief discussion, see M. Brazier, *Medicine, Patients and the Law* (2nd edn., Penguin, London, 1992), 97–104.

[51] See the dissent of Lord Griffiths in *F* v. *West Berkshire HA* [1989] 2 All ER 545 (HL), and the views of Wood J in *T* v. *T* [1988] 1 All ER 613, at 625, discussed by Brazier, n. 50 above, 102–3.

[52] See *Practice Note* [1994] 2 All ER 413.

[53] On this, see Frey, n. 22 above; J. Finnis, '*Bland*: Crossing the Rubicon?' (1993) 109 *LQR* 329.

[54] Raz, n. 3 above, 11.

[55] For a comprehensive examination of the relevance of these values to the criminal law, see J. Gardner, 'On the General Part of the Criminal Law', in Duff (ed.), n. 6 above, 239–44.

is because it is just so rare that personal autonomy can be regarded as legitimately enhanced by deliberately causing harm; and that view has to be central to both collective and individual decision-making at all levels. It is, however, debatable whether the criminal law's concern for moral autonomy, and for the limited aspects of personal autonomy at issue in the defences, necessarily reflects only a liberal concern for those values over the broader terrain of political theory. That citizens have moral autonomy, and some degree of personal autonomy, would seem to be a necessary precondition for any political theory to flourish, and defences in the criminal law have their role to play in establishing such preconditions.[56]

[56] For further discussion, see Horder, n. 9 above, 172–7.

The Wrongness of Rape

John Gardner and Stephen Shute*

PHILOSOPHIZING RAPE

That rape is wrong, and seriously wrong at that, can scarcely be doubted. Arguably, rape is among those wrongs which are never excusable. Probably, it is among those wrongs which are never justifiable. Certainly, it is among those wrongs which ought to be forbidden and punished by the criminal law. Joel Feinberg is right to place it on his shortlist of wrongs which are crimes 'everywhere in the civilised world' and the decriminalization of which 'no reasonable person could advocate'.[1]

In view of all this, one might expect it to be obvious to every reasonable person *what* is wrong with rape. Many writers and commentators, including Feinberg, seem to imagine that this is indeed obvious, and do not give the question detailed attention. Some writers, for example, just take rape as a settled paradigm of wrongdoing in need of no explanation, and work towards the conclusion that certain other actions are wrong simply by pointing out their resemblance to rape. But unless we know what exactly is wrong with rape, how do we know whether such a resemblance is resemblance in a relevant respect—that is to say, in a respect which makes the rape-resembling action wrong too? Other writers concentrate on difficult test cases which seem to lie at or near the borderline of rape. Of a fascinating and burgeoning recent philosophical literature on rape, a very large proportion has been concerned with tricky issues about the precise demarcations of consent in rape, or the difficulties of relying on the concept of consent to settle particular classes of case (e.g. those involving false promises or emotional blackmail on the part of the alleged rapist).[2] Even if it were plausible to think that good philosophy could remove borderline cases of rape (or borderline cases of anything else) from their borderline—and we doubt that very much—it seems odd that anyone would try to settle such cases by studying the moral logic of consent without giving detailed thought to the prior questions whether and why consent matters to rape in the first place. And that depends, of course, on what exactly is wrong with rape.

* Stephen Shute would like to acknowledge the support of the Faculty of Law at the University of Birmingham, and the British Academy, for the research leave which made work on this project possible. The authors would also like to thank Tony Honoré, Nicola Lacey, and Timothy Macklem for detailed comments on earlier drafts.

[1] J. Feinberg, *Harm to Others* (Oxford University Press, New York, 1984) 10.

[2] e.g. David Archard, *Sexual Consent* (Westview Press, Boulder, Colo., 1998) 130ff., Likewise most of the contributions to the two special issues on 'Sex and Consent' in (1996) 2 *Legal Theory*. Another recent substantial philosophical contribution—Keith Burgess-Jackson's *Rape: A Philosophical Investigation* (Darmouth, Aldershot, 1996)—tries to proceed with various definitional or borderline questions while deliberately equivocating about what is wrong with rape (see his remarks at 58).

One can understand, of course, why there might be some reluctance to tackle this last question as a purely philosophical puzzle. Might a philosopher, starting from the professional presumption that nothing is quite as obvious as it appears, seem to be doubting that rape is wrong at all, or at any rate casting doubt on its seriousness? Might a philosopher, for whom no aspect of a subject can ultimately be left unspoken if the subject is chosen for study, be guilty of serious insensitivity in taking up the study of unspeakable experiences? Let us not forget that some victims of rape have had unspeakable experiences.[3] Some, like Lucretia, may even come to regard their lives after rape as not worth living. It may be said that the proper way to make such experiences morally vivid, and to bring out their moral significance, is not through intellectual dissection, in which the horror is reduced to the clinical banality of its component parts. Should it not instead be done through drama, poetry, sculpture, and other more purely expressive, as well as more effectively therapeutic, media? Or at least through study of a less abstract kind, led perhaps by the attempts of those who have experienced being raped to bring their experiences to life? This anti-philosophical line of thought is compounded, for male writers like us, by the fact that the experiences in question are often held to be paradigmatically, and are certainly preponderantly, the experiences of women rather than those of men. The resulting sense that the experiences in question are not even ours to dissect may make the subject seem philosophically uncomfortable, not to say unsafe.

But even in the confession of these anxieties one finds questionable philosophical assumptions. The most obvious is the assumed centrality of the *experience* of rape to an understanding of what makes rape wrong.[4] Consider, for example, Catharine MacKinnon's definition: '[p]olitically, I call it rape whenever a woman has sex and feels violated'.[5] Politically, maybe, but philosophically? Does the *feeling* of sexual violation capture what is wrong with rape? Or is it, rather, the violation itself? And if so what counts as 'violation' in the relevant sense? We can see at once that a focus on consent alone does not tell us the answer. It does not tell us what is wrong with rape *in particular*. Many other acts which would be wrong in the absence of consent are perfectly innocent in the presence of consent—handshaking, for example, or stripping someone's wallpaper while they are out at work. Why should rape be regarded as a different wrong from, say, non-consensual handshaking? Why should it be a *separate* entry on Feinberg's short list of crimes which nobody should decriminalize? Consent does not give the answer, since many other wrongs prohibited by the criminal law, such as vandalism, theft, and assault, might equally be defined in terms of absence of consent. Why are these not all handily collapsed into one crime of 'doing

[3] The word 'unspeakable' has been put to all sorts of uses by philosophers recently. All we mean by it is what it commonly means, namely the property which something might have of being so appalling that at least some rational agents might not be able to bring themselves to speak of it. On the very closely connected concept of 'unthinkability' see Harry Frankfurt, 'Rationality and the Unthinkable' in H. Frankfurt, *The Importance of What We Care About* (Cambridge University Press, Cambridge, 1988).

[4] But cf. John H. Bogart, 'Reconsidering Rape: Rethinking the Conceptual Foundations of Rape Law' (1995) 8 *Canadian Journal of Law and Jurisprudence* 159, 168–70.

[5] C. MacKinnon, *Feminism Unmodified* (Harvard University Press, Cambridge, Mass., 1987) 82.

to another that to which they do not consent'? Why are they not all just one and the same wrong? You may still think that the answer is obvious. Rape is a worse violation than mere vandalism, theft, and assault. We do not doubt that for a moment. But in what respect, in what dimension, is rape worse? Wherein does its 'worseness' lie? What exactly, in other words, is wrong with rape?

HARMLESS RAPE AS PURE RAPE

The view that associates rape with feelings of violation is one of a larger family of views which make the wrongfulness of rape a function of the harmfulness of rape. Such views are represented daily in the media through accounts of the trauma of rape and the sense of insecurity or loss of trust which the experience of it generates. These are harms because they change someone's life for the worse. Some unpleasant episodes in our lives are, by contrast, harmless. There is the pain and discomfort of being under the (competent) dentist's drill, or the fleeting but intense irritation of reading an objectionable letter from some foolish bigmouth in my local newspaper. We are not suggesting by these examples of harmless pain and offence that every pain or offence is necessarily harmless. The torturer uses pain to do a great deal of harm, often scarring his victims physically and psychologically, often breaking down his victims' sense of their own humanity, often forcing them into betrayals which undermine their lives. The buffoon who wields his smutty sense of humour around the office can be inflicting harm on the colleagues he offends by lessening their confidence, their self-esteem, or their sense of ease with their work and their working environment. In these examples the essential added feature on top of the pain, or offence as the case may be, is the diminution of someone's prospects, the change for the worse in his or her life, which the pain or offence brings with it.[6] That prospective dimension is the dimension of harm, and the first place people normally look for the wrongfulness of rape is in this dimension.

In focusing on the harmfulness of rape, liberal-minded lawyers have tended to make common cause with many of their radical feminist critics. In the case of the former, the focus on harm is a natural consequence of the application of the liberal 'harm principle', which forbids the attaching of legal sanctions to wrongdoing except to the extent that this is necessary to prevent harm and proportionate to the harm thereby prevented. Meanwhile, many of their radical feminist critics, politicians to the end, have tended to urge not that the harm principle is mistaken but that the list of harms to which the law and its liberal-minded defenders are typically sensitive, in thinking of rape and other offences mainly perpetrated against women, is a myopic, not to say facile, one.[7] The focus is too narrowly on physical harms, or on harms with a

[6] The main source of our view of the nature of harm is Joseph Raz, 'Autonomy, Toleration and the Harm Principle' in Ruth Gavison (ed.), *Issues in Contemporary Legal Philosophy* (Clarendon Press, Oxford, 1987).

[7] See e.g. MacKinnon, n. 5 above, 166; Burgess-Jackson, n. 2 above, 56–7.

medical diagnosis, and not enough on women's own experiences of rape—the way that a victim's life is changed *for her* by the fact of having been raped, or the way that women's lives are changed *for them* by the risk of being raped. No doubt these challenges to the narrow legalistic approach to harm have a great deal of merit. But they share with the views that they challenge a mistaken starting-point. The harm principle sets certain constraints on the legal proscription of wrongs, but it does not prevent the law from showing sensitivity to other features of those wrongs in defining or classifying them for legal purposes. It does not say that the only wrongfulness legal systems may attend to lies in harmfulness.[8] The law may proscribe breach of contract (whether by making it actionable in the civil courts or punishable in the criminal courts) and when it does so it complies, we think, with the harm principle. Breaches of contract tend to do harm even when they do not specifically harm the plaintiff by losing her the advantage (if any) of the contract, because even under those circumstances they tend to erode the practice of maintaining reliable voluntary obligations, thereby harming everyone who has reason, or might come to have reason, to enter into such obligations. But breach of contract is wrongful because it is the breach of a voluntary obligation, not because of these various harms which accompany the breach (including the damage to the practice). Focusing on the harms tends to occlude the wrongfulness of the act itself.

The same holds, in our view, for rape. It is possible, although unusual, for a rapist to do no harm. A victim may be forever oblivious to the fact that she was raped, if, say, she was drugged or drunk to the point of unconsciousness when the rape was committed, and the rapist wore a condom. To those who object that this is physiologically impossible—that the rape must involve damaging or painful force, which will inevitably bring it to light later—the answer is that this objection neglects the important fact that, as those who have drawn attention to the phenomenon of 'date-rape' have highlighted, one may be raped while sexually aroused, even while sexually aroused by the attentions of the rapist, and one may be sexually aroused, of course, while drunk or drugged. Then we have a victim of rape whose life is not changed for the worse, or at all, by the rape. She does not, in MacKinnon's phrase, 'feel violated'. She has no feelings about the incident, since she knows nothing of it. Indeed the story has no prospective dimension for the victim, except possibly a hangover in the morning; otherwise the victim's life goes on exactly as before. Not even, for that matter, a prospective dimension for others, who might be put in fear of midnight rape by tales of soporific victims taken unawares. Remember: in our example the incident never comes to light at all. (Let's add, for complete insulation, that the rapist, who told no-one of what he did, is run over by a bus as he leaves the house, and that this would have been no less likely to happen to him even if he had not perpetrated the rape, since that did not either delay or precipitate his leaving. So the rape makes no difference even to *his* prospects.)

[8] See further Stephen Shute and Jeremy Horder, 'Thieving and Deceiving: What is the Difference?' (1993) 56 *Modern Law Review* 548.

It is no objection that the question of the wrongfulness of this rape will never arise in any practical deliberation, such as the deliberation of a court, since *ex hypothesi* the rape will never come to light. We assume, what we hope will be ecumenically acceptable, that acts which never come to light are not rendered innocent by that fact alone. So we are left with the question of what is wrong with this particular rape. Its wrongfulness cannot lie in its harmfulness. For it does no harm. *Ex hypothesi* nobody's prospects are diminished, or indeed affected at all, by the rape. Yet this atypical, but absolutely unequivocal, feature does not in our view make any difference to the rape's being wrongful.

There are various ways to sideline the example, to regard its atypicality as making it philosophically hazardous to rely upon it. After all, we ourselves were the ones who raised doubts about the difference that philosophical argument can make at the borderline. Is this not just another borderline case? Not in our view. On the contrary, the case is, in the sense which matters here, the central case of rape. For it is the *pure* case, entirely stripped of distracting epiphenomena. In more typical cases, rape is of course harmful. Much of the harm is typically harm to the victim, and sometimes, as we already said, unspeakable harm. Some of it may be physical injury, but apart from that kind of injury any harm to the victim depends on the victim's evaluations of what has been done to her.[9] She may be traumatized, lose her trust in men, be deprived of her sense of her own security, suffer from a reduction in her self-esteem, feel humiliated and/or dirty, etc. All these reactions depend on the victim's own evaluation of her ordeal. Are we to regard all these evaluation-dependent harms as reflecting the victim's irrationality, her superstition, her oversensitivity, etc.? Are we to think of them as mere manifestations of her weakness?[10] Barring exceptional pathological cases, we think not. To avoid the consequence that these are irrational reactions on the victim's part one must explain what it is about the act of rape that gave the victim a reason to react this way. If nothing was wrong with being raped apart from the fact that one reacted badly afterwards, then one had no reason to react badly afterwards. So such reactions, to be rational, must be epiphenomenal, in the sense that they cannot constitute, but must shadow, the basic, or essential, wrongness of rape. This is not to deny that these reactions may count as grossly aggravating factors. We have no doubt that a rape is made worse, perhaps immeasurably worse, by the humiliation of its victim, by the fact that she blames herself, etc. We also agree that the rapist is more of a moral monster if he sets out to humiliate, or callously adds

[9] Psychiatric injury may be a borderline case. Arguably it is harm *to* the victim's evaluative powers rather than harm depending on her evaluations. This is not the place to explore this point.

[10] One reaction to this question may be to ask why irrationality is assumed to be a weakness. One strand in academic feminism, sympathetically critiqued in Genevieve Lloyd's *The Man of Reason* (Methuen, London, 1984), regards rationality itself—not just the following of particular reasons but the very idea of following reasons—as a 'male norm', and therefore questions whether the expectation that women should meet it is not itself an element of patriarchal oppression. We make no bones about rejecting this strand of feminism. In our view, the claim that women's reactions should not be judged by the simplest canon of rationality (i.e. should not be judged according to whether women have sufficient valid reasons for reacting as they do) plays straight into the hands of misogynists, and indeed rapists. See n. 36 below for further explanation.

to his victim's suffering by playing on her worst fears, etc. All we say is that what these (actual or intended) harms aggravate is the wrongfulness of rape, a wrongfulness which remains even in the absence of these harms. The alternative view, that these harms are what make rape wrong, turns the victim of rape, in a way, into a victim twice over: for she is now, in her reactions to the rape, additionally a victim of irrationality, a pathological case. She has no reason to react the way she does since, absent that reaction, she was not wronged by the rapist. Here we see the basic philosophical objection to MacKinnon's (admittedly 'political') proposal that rape occurs 'whenever a woman has sex and feels violated'. *Pace* MacKinnon, the victim's feeling of violation must be epiphenomenal to rape, or else there is nothing in rape to give her cause to feel violated. Presumably what there is in rape to give her cause to feel violated is the fact that, in some special way, she was violated by the rapist. And the crucial problem is to identify wherein exactly that violation lies, and hence to explain the (evaluation-dependent) harmful consequences of rape by first explaining what, exactly, is wrong with rape.

So our case of the utterly harmless rape—perpetrated on a sexually aroused but somatic victim and leaving no trace on her memory or her body (or indeed any other trace)—is the pure case because it strips out the epiphenomena. It strips out not only the physical injuries but also the victim's evaluation-dependent reactions to the rape. It is rape pure and simple. Those who accept the purity of the case, and hence the need to rehabilitate it into the centre of the moral terrain of rape even as it languishes at the statistical periphery, may feel moved to try adjusting their account of harm to include it. They may feel moved to devise a way in which the victim of our supposedly harmless rape is harmed after all, perhaps in the mere fact of her violation.[11] As a violated woman, some might say, she is somehow now a less than perfect specimen. The harm is that she has been defiled. We think that this conclusion, and indeed the urge to move towards it, has sinister affinity with older, and we hope long since discredited, views of female sexuality. The talk here—is it not?—is of fallen women. But beyond that moral question-mark which hangs over the search for a harm in the pure case, there lies the question of what would be the *gain* in adjusting our account of harm to transform this into a harmful rape. Why would one want this pure and simple rape to be accredited as harmful? Some might say that only in this way can the pure case pass through the filter of the liberal harm principle. We do not believe that the liberal harm principle excludes legal prohibition of rape in the pure case, and we will return to this point towards the end of this essay. But in any case, the question whether a certain wrong can properly be prohibited by law is a secondary question. We do not baulk at the possibility that there could be wrongs which are in general open to legal prohibition, but some morally significant instances of which cannot legitimately be prohibited by law. In such cases the moral considerations which bear on the wrongness of the action apart from the law do support legal prohibition, but additional moral considerations of an institutional character—including the harm

[11] Bogart speaks of this violation as a 'formal' or 'abstract' harm. We find this completely obscure. See Bogart, n. 4 above, 170 and 173. Similarly see H.E. Baber, 'How Bad is Rape?' (1987) 2 *Hypatia* 125.

principle—preclude prohibition as a legitimate means of eradicating the wrong. Perhaps, then, the case of rape that we described as the pure case is bound to be legally marginal. In fact, that is what one might expect, given that (*ex hypothesi*) the rape in this case is never detected and never prosecuted. For the law to focus on it might well be regarded as fatuous. But be it ever so legally marginal, the pure case we sketched remains morally central, for the reasons we have given. The alternative is to dismiss the outraged victims of more typical rapes as suffering pathological reactions. We regard this suggestion as literally adding insult to injury. In our view the wrongfulness of rape cannot, therefore, lie in the harmfulness of rape.

INFRINGING THE PROPRIETOR'S RIGHTS

One can say, of course, that the wrongfulness of rape lies in the violation of its victim's rights. But which rights? We might suggest, for a start, her right not to be raped. Since the victim has a right not to be raped if, and only if, raping her wrongs her, this introduction of the category of a right does not take us much further. It does have the virtue of introducing the thought that rape is not only a wrong but a wrong *against the person raped*, which means that it is based on her interest. That seems correct. But we are still left with the question of which interest of hers it is based on. And that question, it could be said, still represents little advance over the question with which we started, namely the question of what is wrong with rape. Phrasing the question in terms of rights and interests does, however, prompt a certain kind of more helpful, although we think nevertheless mistaken, reply to our original question. The wrongness of rape, according to this reply, comes of the fact that the victim of rape has a proprietary interest in, and derived from that a proprietary right over, her own body. It is her body, she owns it, nobody else may use it without her say-so. Rape is none other than the non-consensual 'borrowing of sexual organs'.[12] So the right not to be raped is, at base, a property right or an aspect of a property right.

What is our interest in property? Only some brief remarks are possible here. Those who focus on productivity are, fundamentally, on the right track—so long as 'productivity' is construed widely enough to include the provision of shelter, security, comfort, amusement, and other benefits to the property-holder. The importance of property lies basically in the valuable things we can do with that property that we cannot so easily do without it. This we will call its *use-value*.[13] Aspects of property rights

[12] G.A. Cohen, *Self-Ownership, Freedom and Equality* (Cambridge University Press, Cambridge, 1995) 244. Cohen comments that one may believe in ownership of the body while conceding that property rights might not provide the *whole* explanation of rape's wrongness. Nevertheless, his definition of rape as a 'borrowing' is as purely proprietarian a definition as one could conceive. For less equivocal renderings of the proprietarian approach, see Guido Calabresi and A. Douglas Melamed, 'Property Rules, Liability Rules, and Inalienability: One View of the Cathedral' (1972) 85 *Harvard Law Review* 1089, 1124–7; or else Donald A. Dripps, 'Beyond Rape: An Essay on the Difference between the Presence of Force and the Absence of Consent' (1992) 92 *Columbia Law Review* 1780.

[13] The mistake in many productivity accounts of the value of property-holding is to focus too narrowly on *further* productivity (i.e. the use of things with use-value for the production of *other* things with

other than the right to use property are basically derivative of the use-value of property. The value of being able to acquire and transfer property, for example, is basically the value of property's ending up where it can best be used. In conditions of global and indiscriminate abundance property rights may lose their basic moral purchase, because in these conditions everyone has more than they can use. The question whether something could best be used by a person other than the person who holds it is less prone to arise, for there is always plenty left to go round. But in times of scarcity or of merely local or discriminate abundance (i.e. abundance from which some are excluded, leaving them in conditions of scarcity) the question is always live: could this thing be better used by someone else? The idea of a property right to such things is that, up to a point, the question of where something is better used can least wastefully be settled by leaving the question to the person who already holds the thing. This means that, again up to a point, people are left free to hold property that they do not use. It is still theirs and cannot be taken without their say-so.[14] If others were to take it away from them this might yield a better use for it, but the suboptimal use of a particular thing is justified, up to a point, by the general gains in use-value that are made from a co-ordinating system based on consensual transactions.

We say 'up to a point', but the question on everybody's lips is: up to which point? In the long history of property rights the point has been located in different places by different civilizations and regimes. Some things have been regarded at some times and in some places as incapable of being subject to property rights, or incapable of being subject to certain kinds of strong property rights such as ownership. The tendency to wastefulness by property-holders, their refusal to let things be put to their best use, has often been regarded (no doubt sometimes rightly) as too high a price to pay for the avoidance of the costs associated with alternative methods of distribution and allocation. Some things, the value of which is basically their use-value, have therefore on occasions been taken out of a fully-fledged property regime. Thus, at some times and in some places, housing has been publicly provided for tenancy but not for ownership, TV stations or take-off slots at airports have not been capable of being owned, etc. Meanwhile, some things have been owned but with special regulation inhibiting their use and disposal, such as rent control legislation, restrictions on inheritance, rules against predatory pricing or monopolization, and official scrutiny of hostile takeovers. Since the basic value of property is instrumental, different policies and practices may serve that value more or less effectively at different times and places, depending on other prevailing conditions—for instance, the extent of the public ten-

use-value). This mistake lies at the heart, we think, of both Marx's and Locke's so-called 'labour theories' of property value, on the comparison of which see Cohen, n. 12 above, 165–94.

[14] Actually, the 'say-so' or consent condition does not strike us as a universally necessary element of respect for property rights. One can imagine a system in which things stay with the current holder unless complex bureaucratic measures are followed to secure a transfer. Even if these bureaucratic measures do not require the consent of the current holder, it is not misleading, in our view, to regard this holding as a kind of property right. However, for simplicity, we stick here to the familiar protective measure of requiring consent to transfers, which is common to most modern systems where the consideration mentioned in the next-but-one para. looms large.

dency towards decadence, the sluggishness of competition, the degree of scarcity, or the extent of globalization.

However, one observation that may be made regarding large parts of the inhabited world today is that property rights are tending to campaign, in a sense, for their own augmentation and deregulation. The rise of public faith in property-holding as a pat solution to the co-ordination problems associated with the use of things under conditions of scarcity, combined with people's increasing alienation from other human beings, leads people to attach great and ever-growing symbolic importance to the acquisition and holding of property. Increasingly, they come to identify with at least some things they hold as extensions of themselves, tokens of their own personality. The idea of 'sentimental value' has always highlighted this aspect of property holding. But it extends nowadays to much else besides the inherited keepsakes of the past or the gifts of friends and family. In fact, it is increasingly associated more with self-chosen than with other-chosen things. In so far as people regard themselves as autonomous beings, their own choice of property—which house to buy, which ties to wear, which CDs to collect—has an ever more important place in their self-expression. The result is the cultural condition which has come to be known as 'consumerism'. No doubt it has got wildly out of hand. But up to a point—and again the point cannot be settled out of local context—consumerism does effect the moral change which its participants seem to presuppose. They regard property as meaning more, as carrying more significance, than just the significance imported by its use-value. Their regarding it as carrying that significance actually endows it with that significance by changing its social meaning. People are increasingly *identifying* with what they have. So on top of its basic use-value, much more of what people hold now has what we might call *identification-value*. When property is taken away without the proper consensual process, it is not merely (or even) that the system of optimal use-value is disrupted. It is that people are metaphorically violated by the removal of a part of their extended selves.

Some think that identification-value, and particularly the value which comes of investing autonomous choice in property, suffices on its own to explain why property rights continue to reside in those who make suboptimal use of their property. But property rights can persist even when use-value and identification-value are *both* missing. Consider what might be regarded as the pure case of burglary. Suppose an estate agent who has keys to my house lets himself in while I am on holiday and takes a pile of my old clothes from the attic, passing them on to a charity shop. I had long since forgotten that the clothes were there, and I had no further use, anyway, for loon pants and kipper ties. The burglary goes forever undiscovered. (The estate agent, who told nobody of what he was doing, falls under a bus as he leaves the charity shop, as he would have done anyway even if my clothes had not been among those he delivered.) Yet my property right is violated. Why is this? After all, I have no interest in these old long-forgotten clothes that comes of *either* my use of them *or* my identification with them. But on top of that, as we already indicated, there is the co-ordinating value of property rights in securing use-value and identification-value *at large* (i.e. for people in general). My having this property right over my old clothes, which is violated by the intruding estate agent, does not come of any use-value or identification-value *to me* but of the contribution which my having such a property right makes to the perpetuation of a *system* of optimal use-value coupled, so far as possible, with optimal identification-value. So I have an interest in this property which is basically derivative of the public interest in my having such an interest. We call this the pure case for the same reason that we called the pure case of rape the pure case. It is the case of the wrong and nothing but the wrong.

The analogies between rape and burglary here are startling, and may seem to support the idea that rape is wrong because we own our own bodies. But in fact our remarks tend to undermine this view. Neither the use-value nor the identification-value which supports our proprietorial relations with things can apply straightforwardly to our relationship with our own bodies. We will come to the use-value in the next section. But the main point can be seen through the lens of the identification-value. The identification-value of property holding is the symbolic value of artificially extending oneself out into the world. But regarding our bodies there is no question of such an artificial self-extension. There is a longstanding tradition in western philosophy which diminishes the centrality of the body. The body becomes something like an arbitrary receptacle in which the real business of human life—that special inner thing called 'the self'—just happens to live.[15] This strikes us as an unintelligible view. People are, in part, their bodies and their relationship with their bodies cannot, barring strange pathological cases (schizophrenia?) or conceptually testing science-fiction (brains in vats?), be that of artificial self-extension. The embodied self is not the extended self; in the distinction between self and world the body already belongs to the 'self' side without any need for, or possibility of, self-extension into it. It is true that one may play with the boundaries of the body, deliberately blurring the line between the self and its extension into the world. Some kinds of body-piercing and tattooing fit this profile. They are ways of expressing a kind of continuity between self and world which can, under certain cultural conditions, be a symbol of rank or alternatively a symbol of individuality and even rebellion. But these boundary-blurring practices, and others, presuppose that the body is already part of the self and cannot, again barring pathological conditions or sci-fi fantasies, be alienated from it. It is not merely that the self cannot survive outside it, like a patient who cannot live without an artificial lung. It is that without the body there is no complete self to survive.

Some people nowadays say that the experience of being burgled was like that of being raped. Others may well resent this suggestion: have the people in question ever actually been raped? If not, how do they know that the experience of burglary was like

[15] We are thinking, of course, of the Cartesian tradition. But notice that one could follow Descartes' famous 'dualist' views about the *relations* between mind and body without adding that the body is the inferior partner. For two self-styled 'Cartesian friends of the body' taking this line, see the exchange between Sydney Shoemaker and Galen Strawson under the title 'Self and Body' in (1999) 73 *Proceedings of the Aristotelian Society Supplementary Volume* 287.

the experience of rape? The answer lies in the way in which property rights, particularly under modern conditions, and particularly in the immediate living environment, operate as self-extensions. Even someone who has not been raped but whose house has been burgled may experience a kind of violation of the self, because she understood her home as a projection of her identity, a kind of larger, more artificial body. The mistake comes in when one tries to reverse the analogy, when one tries to think of one's body as a kind of smaller, more natural house.[16] Anyone who had been raped and said it was like being burgled would be committing a serious travesty. It would show extraordinary moral insensitivity. This is not, or at any rate not merely, because they would be diminishing or trivializing their rape. It is primarily because property rights are necessarily the derivative or shadow case. One can analogize what happens to what one owns to what happens to oneself, because what one owns can be an extension of oneself. But one cannot in the same way analogize what happens to oneself to what happens to what one owns, because oneself cannot be an addition to what one owns. This is the first and major flaw in all self-ownership doctrines, including, but not restricted to, those that focus on ownership of one's own body. They render one's relationship to oneself contingent in such a way that there is no longer any self to do any owning, of itself or of anything else.

USE AND ABUSE

One consequence of the modern philosopher's alienation of the body from the self is to sever the value of the body from the value of the self. The body, like other tools and receptacles and artefacts, is basically use-valuable, its use-value augmented, in some cases, by the expressive value of the inhabiting self's contingent identification with it. Once the intelligibility of this latter expressive value is called in question, a question mark also appears above the idea that the body's value is mainly its use-value. Use-value for whom? Who is the user? The possibilities are self or others. If the body is part of the self then the idea that it is *used* by the self becomes harder to understand.[17] At any rate that cannot be its most basic value. In very rough terms, the explanation goes something like this. Use-value is value for people. Why should what is valuable for people be valuable *tout court*? The ultimate answer, although it may take a number of precise forms, cannot but include the premise that people are valuable. To avoid vicious circularity this further value cannot be use-value. So people may have their use-value, perhaps, but that cannot be the only, nor the most ultimate, value they have. To use people without at the same time respecting this further

16 The mistake is made, we think, by Michael Davis in 'Setting Penalties: What Does Rape Deserve?' (1984) 3 *Law and Philosophy* 61, 78.

17 This consideration is also at the basis of the account of rape's wrongness offered by Carolyn M. Shafer and Marilyn Frye, in their classic paper 'Rape and Respect' in Mary Vetterling-Braggin, Frederick Elliston, and Jane English (eds.), *Feminism and Philosophy* (Rowman & Littlefield, Totowa, NJ, 1977) 333, 337. Our position mirrors that of Shafer and Frye in many respects, but not in all. For the most important divergence see n. 22 below and accompanying text.

non-use value involves treating them as something other than people. It means treating them as things. In principle this applies as much to the use of the self as to the use of others. And because the (living) body is part of the self, part of the person, it applies equally to the use of (living) bodies.[18]

The most famous articulation of this argument is Kant's. In simple terms it shows that there is no value in objects unless there is some more ultimate value in subjects. It shows, therefore, that those who would tie the wrongness of rape to ownership of one's own body not only miss but positively invert the basic element of rape's wrongness. The value of the body becomes, in this view, basically its use-value. So what is the rapist doing wrong, in our pure case of rape, when he uses someone else's body for sexual pleasure? The answer may be that it is not his to use. But this answer, in a way, plays into the rapist's hands. It makes it intelligible for him to respond with the objection that he can make better use of this unconscious body than can the person whose body it is. After all, he is only harmlessly borrowing this body, or some of its components, while its regular user is not using it, or not using those components. Relative to that alternative non-use, this use optimizes use-value. On the proprietarian model one can resist this as a final answer by observing that owners still get to decide even when they decide against optimal use. Remember the clothes in the attic. But this resistance concedes to the rapist too much of the moral high ground. It concedes to him that in principle the body of a person is there to be used. This is a kind of use of a person, a kind of *objectification* of a subject. That a rapist objectifies his victim by treating her as a mere repository of use-value is, in our view, what is basically wrong with rape. In making arguments which ultimately rest on the sheer use-value of people and their bodies, the proprietarian approach not only fails to make sense of the wrongness of rape; it actually gives succour to rapists.

The claim that certain practices objectify women lies, as is well known, at the heart of Catharine MacKinnon's and Andrea Dworkin's joint critique of pornography. The critique has been subjected to searching philosophical study by Martha Nussbaum.[19] As Nussbaum shows, 'objectification' is a term which, in the work of MacKinnon and Dworkin, tends to equivocate between a cluster of related ideas: 1. the conversion of subjects into instruments or tools; 2. the denial of subjects' autonomy; 3. treating subjects as inert or inactive; 4. treating subjects as fungible (i.e. interchangeable with other subjects or objects); 5. breaking into subjects or breaking down the boundaries between subjects; 6. asserting ownership over subjects; and 7. refusing to regard subjects as beings with their own feelings and experiences (i.e. as subjective). While Nussbaum agrees that categories 2 to 7 can have their moral moment in the debate about sexual representation, she stresses category 1 (instrumentalization) as the crucial entry on the list, the one that best captures what objectification must be if it is to be generally objectionable.[20] We agree. We have added merely that category 1 is closely bound up with category 6 (ownership), and that those who base

[18] We put 'living' in parentheses so as not to prejudge the interesting question whether it can ever be demeaning, on the same grounds, to use someone's body after his or her death.

[19] M. Nussbaum, 'Objectification' (1995) 24 *Philosophy and Public Affairs* 249.

[20] Ibid. 265.

arguments against objectification on ownership or other property relations, including those who assert inalienable self-ownership, only encourage instrumentalization thereby.

The extension of this 'objectification' argument from pornography to rape helps to bring out what some feminists are getting at when they claim that pornography is bound up with rape irrespective of whether the consumption of pornography makes any causal contribution to the incidence of rape.[21] For our purposes, however, the main importance of the 'objectification' argument lies in the way that it begins to differentiate rape, or at any rate the pure case of rape, from other paradigms of criminal wrong, including paradigms of non-sexual criminal violence. There are interesting and no less problematic questions about what is wrong with murder, or with common assault, or with kidnapping, or with torture, or with threatening to kill, or with blackmail, etc. All are wrong in different ways, by virtue of different lines of argument. Arguably the wrongness of at least some of these wrongs is fully explicable only by invoking the Kantian argument somewhere along the line. But none of these wrongs instantiates the central moral importance of the Kantian argument so clearly and unequivocally as rape. Rape, in the pure case, is the sheer use of a person. In less pure, but statistically more typical, cases this use is accompanied by violence, terror, humiliation, etc. Our only point is that when someone feels humiliated by rape itself this feeling is justified. Rape is humiliating even when unaccompanied by further affronts, because the sheer use of a person, and in that sense the objectification of a person, is a denial of their personhood. It is literally dehumanizing.

DELIMITING RAPE

So all sheer use of human beings, all treatment of them merely as means, is *ab*use; and rape is the central case of such abuse. In our view, this is the line of thought that generates the basic distinction between rape and (most) non-sexual offences against the person (as well as some sexual offences). But does it fix, even approximately, the boundaries of rape? Does it help to explain the modern focus on *lack of consent* as the touchstone of rape? Does it help us to establish the focus on *penetrative* sexual abuse (or certain forms of penetrative sexual abuse) which is still typical of the law of rape in most jurisdictions which have retained the offence separately? And does our line of thought help us to settle how *mistakes* as to consent should be dealt with by the law of rape? Let's look at each of these familiar problems in turn.

[21] This is one sympathetic way to interpret Andrea Dworkin's remark in *Pornography: Men Possessing Women* (Women's Press, London, 1979) 137, that 'a rape [is] repeated each time the viewer consumes the [pornographic] photographs'. For more study of the point, see Deborah Cameron and Elizabeth Fraser, 'On the Question of Pornography and Sexual Violence: Moving Beyond Cause and Effect' in Catherine Itzin, *Pornography: Women, Violence and Civil Liberties* (Oxford University Press, Oxford, 1992).

(i) Lack of Consent

At the deepest level, the Kantian argument we echoed does not distinguish between use by self and use by others. It resists the objectification of subjects either by those subjects or by other subjects. In other words, the evil in question is *agent-neutral*: it consists in the use of people as a mere means, irrespective of which people are doing the using. So at the deepest level the Kantian argument makes no exception for self-abuse. *A fortiori* it makes no exception for self-licensed abuse by others. How, then, can consent make all the difference between the paradigmatic use of a person (rape) and the paradigmatic treating of a person as a person, which is the opposite of that use (sexual intercourse)? One suggestion is that only a subject can consent, and so, by being astute to another's consent, someone who has sexual intercourse with that other is not treating that other any more *merely* as a means, and hence is not objectifying her.[22] She may be treating herself as a mere means, but then again she is not the one accused of rape. This suggestion makes *astuteness to consent* of the essence. But in most familiar legal systems the first question about consent in a rape trial is not: was the accused astute to the complainant's consent? The first question is: did she actually consent? Only if the answer is 'no' does the further question arise (depending on the *mens rea* requirements for rape in that legal system) of how astute the accused was to whether the complainant consented. One may say that this is an institutional oddity, that the explanation lies in some technical consideration about the criminal process or the structure of criminal offences. But we suspect that it goes deeper.

If the argument from astuteness worked to show how consent comes to be pivotal in rape, it would do so only at the price of eliminating the accusation of objectification against consent-astute users of consenting subjects, including many clients of prostitutes and many consumers of pornography. To put the point crudely, it would deflect blame from clients to prostitutes, and from consumers of pornography to those appearing in it. Consenting prostitutes and pornographic performers would be objectifying themselves (objectionable), while their clients and consumers, assuming the latter were astute to the presence of consent, would be treating them as subjects (unobjectionable). In our view this conclusion lets clients of prostitutes and users of pornography slip too easily off the moral hook.

Two obvious ways of avoiding the conclusion have often been favoured by those who want to keep that moral hook in place, both of which have been adduced from time to time by MacKinnon and Dworkin. One way to keep the moral hook in place is to deny that the consent of workers in the sex industry is genuine. In denying that this kind of consent is genuine one may point to some other objectifier in the background—a pimp or a pornographer, say, or an insidious sex industry system, or indeed an insidious *sex* system—to mitigate the accusation of self-objectification against the prostitute or model. She was coerced or manipulated or exploited into

[22] This is roughly the line taken by Shafer and Frye in 'Rape and Respect', n. 17 above, and here we have the main point at which our position diverges from theirs.

submission by that other objectifier, and the client or consumer is complicitous because astute only to that submission, and not to any genuine consent.[23] This line of argument carries serious risks, not least the risk that one ultimately ends up accusing those prostitutes or models who *claim* to be genuinely consenting as suffering from a false consciousness, and hence as less than fully functional moral agents who can speak for themselves, and hence as not fully human. In other words, one risks objectifying sex industry workers oneself in order to make it seem to be the case that they are objectified by their consumers and clients and other participants in their industry. To avoid such risks one may alternatively regard the consent of women who participate in the sex industry as genuine, and hence as capable of forestalling the accusation that these women were *personally* objectified by their clients and consumers, while holding that women *in general* were objectified by being represented in that way.[24] This introduces Nussbaum's category 4 (fungibility) into the story, and requires us to show that the sex industry puts everywoman, and not only the women who work in it, under prurient, instrumentalizing gaze. This may well be so, but in our view the objectification element in the use of pornography or the resort to prostitutes does not depend on it. Nor do we need to show that women in the sex industry are not genuinely consenting in order to keep their clients and consumers on the moral hook. For the fact that women working in the sex industry may give their genuine and effective consent, and even the astuteness of their clients and consumers to that consent, does not make it the case that they are not personally objectified in the relevant sense by their clients and consumers.

In our view, such sex industry workers typically are being objectified by their clients and consumers, and this is indeed an attack on their humanity. They are being used purely for sexual gratification. But the sex workers' right to sexual autonomy, where their consent is genuine, serves to license the abuse.[25] The argument for drawing the line at consent is roughly the same regarding the right to sexual autonomy as it is regarding property rights. With property rights the argument was that even if, regarding a particular piece of property, use-value was in suboptimal combination with identification-value, the value of having a system in which people control by consent the uses of their own property optimally co-ordinates, within limits, the pursuit of use-value and identification-value. With the right to sexual autonomy the argument is that even if, in a particular sexual encounter, the ultimate value of a

[23] Robin West, 'A Comment on Sex, Consent and Rape' (1996) 2 *Legal Theory* 232, 242; MacKinnon, n. 5 above, 179–83; Dworkin, n. 21 above, 207.

[24] MacKinnon, n. 5 above, 170–4; Dworkin, n. 21 above, 224.

[25] Thanks to some familiar practices of pimps and pornographers it is likely that in many cases the consent is not freely given, in which case the considerations which follow do not apply. Nor of course do they apply to children. Our argument assumes only that sometimes consent is real enough and that on those occasions it matters. One reason, among many, why pimps and pornographers get away with practices that remove the reality of consent is that they inhabit a shady world of questionable legality in which employment protection etc. cannot be guaranteed. This creates an extra instrumental argument against the criminalization of aspects of the sex industry. But this argument is distinct from, and supplementary to, the one we pursue here.

person was denied (i.e. that person was used merely as a means), the value of having a system of sexual relations in which people control by consent the treatment of their own bodies secures optimally respect for the ultimate value of people. An obvious objection to this argument is that it depends on a contingency, namely the contingency of whether people generally grant their consent wisely (i.e. in ways that do not constitute self-abuse). The proliferation and permeation of sex-industry values in, for example, mainstream advertising may seem to show that this assumption cannot be upheld today. But it must be remembered that, in constructing and honouring people's rights, those people must be given a certain kind of moral credit. By much the same argument which condemns rapists, those of us who are discussing, legislating, implementing, and enforcing people's rights must also regard them as people, as beings with value other than use-value. In particular we must regard them as moral agents capable of understanding their own value and making up their own minds about their relationships with others. We must work on the assumption that they respect themselves or else we do not ourselves respect them. It follows that even when people betray that assumption they enjoy some latitude to do so. They have some moral space to go wrong and to permit others to go wrong with them.

This consideration is reinforced, in modern conditions, by the general value of personal autonomy which applies to all kinds of options, including, but not restricted to, sexual options, and pushes for avenues of experimentation to be opened up. But the value we have been describing is not the value of personal autonomy. It is the distinct value of allowing particular kinds of options to be pursued, including various sexual options, which may at first sight appear dehumanizing. The truth is that these options often *are* dehumanizing, and therefore to be avoided by the person who is confronted with them. But allowing people nevertheless to pursue them is, up to a point, rehumanizing, because it credits them with moral agency, without which credit their dehumanization is only compounded. This rehumanizing value combines with the general value of personal autonomy to yield a right to sexual autonomy. Rape, understood in the modern way as non-consensual sexual intercourse, is a wrong against the person raped because it is a violation of this right.[26] The resort to prostitutes and the use of pornography are also wrong, because they objectify the prostitute or model even when her consent is genuine. But when her consent is genuine such resort or use is not a violation of the prostitute's or model's right to sexual autonomy, and so not a wrong *against* the prostitute or model. Or at any rate it is not a wrong against the prostitute or model *under the same heading* as that under which rape is a wrong against its victim. For a person's consent is capable of licensing, in the name of sexual auton-

[26] This right is structurally different from a property right in that, regarding this right, the consent condition cannot be replaced with a condition licensing non-consensual access by bureaucratic procedures, of the type which we suggested may be consistent with property rights in n. 14 above. The marital rape exemption purported to do this—to by-pass the woman's say-so with a bureaucratic method for allocating sex—but it would be seriously misleading to present this as a protection of a married woman's rights, let alone her right to sexual autonomy. It was clearly a protection of a married man's rights against the sexual autonomy of his wife.

omy itself, some suboptimal sexual relationships, which in this case means depressingly dehumanizing relationships, relationships of objectification.[27]

(ii) Penetration

In many jurisdictions, including ours, what counts as sexual intercourse for the purposes of the crime of rape is limited to (one or another kind of) penetrative violation. Why is penetration so special? Does it count as a special way of using another person? The natural answer, of course, is that it counts as an especially humiliating way of using them. But again the special humiliation seems epiphenomenal. There was no special humiliation in the pure case because there was no humiliation at all in the pure case: the rape was never discovered. If, in more everyday cases, penetrative violations *are* particularly humiliating (or terrifying, confidence-sapping, etc.) in the eyes of those who experience them, then as usual we want to know the reason why. Why do violations of *this* kind have such special import for those who suffer them? One might say, of course, that the law itself contributes something to the special significance of penetration by historically reserving the name of 'rape' for that class of violations. Certainly there is something in that: the historic legal names of some criminal offences have gathered moral import with age, and often do contribute to structuring people's moral thinking. The thinking here goes: rape is (particularly) terrible; rape is non-consensual penetration; so non-consensual penetration is (particularly) terrible. But this cannot serve *by itself* to justify the law's maintaining its insistence on penetration. Perhaps the old focus on penetration was superstitious or corrupt and the modern law should now be doing its utmost to change the confused moral thinking which that old focus left in its wake. Some aspects of the law of rape or the practice of rape prosecution, such as the marital rape exemption and the institutional blindness to date-rape, as well as the accompanying interest in evidence of the victim's sexual history, are now widely acknowledged to have left a false trail, and hence a false understanding of rape, in public consciousness. Is not the penetration condition, with its crude phallocentrism, in the same camp? Does it not hang over from an era of obsession with female virginity and overbearing preoccupation with the sin of bearing illegitimate children, an era in which women were *officially* regarded as objects (chattels of their fathers and husbands) rather than subjects? So maybe we should dump this condition now? We do not think that the answer is quite so simple.

[27] You can see here why we favour the right to sexual autonomy over the alternative 'right to sexual *integrity*' advanced by Nicola Lacey in 'Unspeakable Subjects, Impossible Rights: Sexuality, Integrity and Criminal Law' (1989) 47 *Canadian Journal of Law and Jurisprudence* 47. The depressingly dehumanizing relationships we mentioned do not involve anything recognizable as integrity. They are self-betraying, and usually on both sides. Nevertheless, so long as there is mutual consent, those who engage in them have a right to do so under the heading of sexual autonomy. In spite of this disagreement, however, Lacey's paper is one which has influenced our own thinking greatly. We suspect that with the removal of unhappy Cartesian and Lockean overtones from the relevant idea of autonomy, the distance between us is considerably reduced.

What is true is that the justification of the penetration condition in the modern law of rape does involve some attention to social meaning. Some associate the Kantian argument we adopted above with a view of morality as a body of eternal verities which one abandons on pain of self-contradiction. In places this was how Kant himself presented the applications of the argument. But in fact the applications of the argument depend on many contingencies, including the social meaning of many actions. Which actions count as paradigms of sheer use-and-abuse of human beings varies, even though the Kantian argument against the sheer use-and-abuse of human beings has enduring force. Often the special symbolism of a particular act or class of acts is tied to the particular symbolism of acts which are regarded as their moral opposites. The special symbolism of penetrative violation is closely associated, in our culture, with the special symbolism of penetrative sexual activity. That latter symbolism may be over-romanticized. It may come of an aspiration to an impossible perfect union of two selves through two bodies, by making the two bodies, in a sense, just one (recall Shakespeare's 'beast with two backs'). Be that as it may, the fact that penetrative sex is regarded as having that significance actually endows it with that significance by changing its social meaning. The social meaning of the subversion of penetrative sex—its subversion in rape—tends to mirror the social meaning of penetrative sex. If the latter is thought of as a perfection of subject–subject relations—through the most complete and literal intertwining of selves—then the former may well come to represent a paradigm of subject-object relations. This is relevant to explaining and justifying the reactions even of those who do not share the aspiration to intertwine selves in this literal way (e.g. those who eschew or avoid penetrative sexual relationships, or those who see them as purely functional). The use of penetration can be a special weapon even against these people, perhaps *especially* against these people. It can become a peculiarly dramatic way of objectifying them, of turning them into mere things to be used, mere means to another's ends. That being so, there is reason for all those who suffer such violations to feel humiliated, whether or not they see particular value, or any value, in consensual penetrative sexual activity. The social meaning of consensual sexual penetration is not necessarily the meaning it has for them, and it is the social meaning of consensual sexual penetration which the rapist exploits by subverting it.

This is not a case against expanding the legal definition of rape to include some kinds of non-penetrative violations, or for discriminating among various kinds of penetration. In fact, it is not an argument for any particular legal definition of rape. It merely points out that the reactions of those who attach particular significance to penetrative violations, or to certain penetrative violations, need not be irrational. They may be supported by symbolic values. Much is left to law-makers and law-interpreters in deciding how best to embody and reflect such symbolic values in a given legal system. Social meanings are often ambiguous, and always have grey areas. Rarely do they set definite boundaries to moral wrongdoing without additional instrumental arguments, and instrumental argument also introduces many contingencies which can affect legal classifications. We showed this already in discussing the 'lack of consent' requirement. The instrumental question of what system of sexual relations would lead to the least use-and-abuse of human beings was an element of the argument. No doubt similar instrumental issues arise in the case of the penetration condition. The point is that although the mere use of people is a timeless evil, the elevation of penetrative non-consensual sexual violation to the status of special paradigm is a longstanding, but culturally conditioned application.

These remarks on the importance of social meaning merit the attention of those who are uneasy about the tendency to associate rape with sex, and in particular the tendency to think of it as a 'sexual offence'. Many campaigners and social researchers tell us that rape typically has nothing to do with sexual desire, and everything to do with a male desire for power over women. Surely it should be regarded as a crime of misogynist aggression, a hate-crime, rather than a sexual offence? We are uneasy about the essentialist view of sexual desire which this critique seems to harbour: Why, we wonder, cannot a misogynist desire to subordinate women be a sexual desire? (Is it because sex is wonderful and misogyny is vile?) But even if we grant the integrity of the assumed contrast between sexual desire and other kinds of desire, the main objection to this line of thought is that it assumes that 'sexual offences' are those offences which are differentiated by the offender's motivations. In our view, the real reason for thinking of rape as a sexual offence has nothing to do with the offender's motivations. It is that rape is a weapon against its victim which trades on the social meaning of sexual penetration. It is a way of taking a paradigm subject–subject relationship—a possibly over-romanticized conception of sexual intimacy—and turning it against someone to make a mere object of her.[28] This does not rule out, and indeed may well suggest, that the perpetrator hates the victim, or what she represents. It is not necessary to deny the connection between rape and sex in order to make this clear. On the contrary, if the connection with sex is dropped and rape is simply labelled as, say, 'aggravated assault', then it seems to us that (for better or worse) we have decided no longer to recognize in law what is *particularly* wrong with rape. True, a rape can *accurately* be labelled as a kind of assault (as the police often label it when conducting their investigations) since the unifying theme of assault crimes is invasion by one of another's personal space, and the rapist clearly does invade his victim's personal space. But this is a wrong incidental to, and usually rather trivial when placed alongside, the most fundamental element of wrongdoing in rape. So the description of rape as an assault, though accurate, is reductive and unrevealing.[29] That most fundamental

[28] Contrast the approach taken by Lois Pineau in her 'Date Rape: A Feminist Analysis' (1989) 8 *Law and Philosophy* 217. Pineau argues that sex should be understood, paradigmatically, as 'ongoing communication' and sex outside this paradigm should be understood as presumptively rape. Here Pineau *endorses* a particular idealized view of sex, and hence becomes what we just labelled an 'essentialist'. Our view, by contrast, is not essentialist about sex. It only trades on the mere fact that an idealized view of sex—which we did not endorse and which indeed may not be endorsed very widely nowadays—nevertheless still colours the social meaning of various actions, including, most notably, actions which appropriate and subvert that ideal.

[29] Contrast Michael Davis, n. 16 above, 79. Davis's reduction of rape to assault relies not only on the fact that rape must (incidentally) involve assault but also on the claim that all assault involves objectification. We do not see this. Someone who threateningly presses his face up to mine, or grabs me by the arm

element of wrongdoing in rape, which differentiates rape from (most) assaults and gives rape a separate theme from the family of assault crimes, is the *sheer use* of the person raped, whether that is how the rapist saw what he was doing or otherwise. To understand how rape counts as sheer use, the social meaning of sexual penetration has to be kept in focus.

Whatever the offender means by it, and indeed whatever it means to its victim, rape is a crime of sexual violation according to its social meaning; and that social meaning is the meaning which is at the heart of rape's wrongness. One may still insist that 'violence' would be a better word here than 'violation'. Would it not at least have more political bite? We doubt whether even this is true. Assimilation of rape to the category of 'violent crime' in the media and in public discussion of crime has, in our view, done more than almost anything else to maintain the public myth that rapists are strangers waiting in dark alleys who subdue their victims by force.[30] But rapists work by many more insidious methods than this and they still wrong their victims by non-consensual objectification of them. As our pure case of rape serves to remind us, and many more common kinds of case amply illustrate, the violation that is rape need not be associated with any kind of violence.[31] Nor are the worst rapes necessarily the most violent rapes. Rapes in breach of trust using subtle threats or surreptitiously administered drugs to forestall any resistance can, in some cases, represent an even more egregious abuse of the person raped and can therefore be worse *qua* rapes (and this still remains true, on our analysis, whether or not these are the rapes that involve the worst experiences for the person raped[32]).

to get my attention (both paradigm assaults), does not, by these moves alone, treat me as an object. An object, after all, does not respond to intimidation or to attention-grabbing. The wrongness of assault is only very indirectly related to the Kantian considerations we adduced, which lie at the heart of the wrongness of rape. (Davis also errs in thinking that an objectification argument like ours must rely on the rapist *seeing* his victim as an object. It does not. It is about his *treating* her as an object, however he may see her. He may see women as vulnerable child-like creatures in need of a masterly knight in shining armour to protect them. This is not seeing women as objects, but it is compatible with—and may well indeed be conducive to—treating them as such. That is one important lesson of the feminist critique of patriarchy: patriarchy is a *delusional* mode of oppression in which dehumanizing behaviour is often misconceived by its perpetrators as humanizing behaviour.)

[30] In 'Coercion and Rape: The State as a Male Protection Racket' in *Feminism and Philosophy*, n. 17 above, 360, 364, Susan Rae Peterson draws attention to a countervailing pragmatic consideration: classifying rape as a sexual offence may contribute to the shocking but still prevalent tendency to see a complainant's sexual history as relevant to the issue of consent, and indeed (even more outrageously) to the issue of her veracity on the issue of consent, in a rape trial. We think that this problem of 'the second rape in the courtroom'—in our view a rather apt metaphor, since such lines of questioning themselves make objectifying assumptions about female sexuality—should be addressed head-on, by making evidence of a complainant's sexual history inadmissible and by reforming and improving accessibility to the law of libel for those women who are represented in the press as 'asking for it'. Distorting the wrongness of rape to avoid the problem seems to us to mean throwing out the baby with the bathwater.

[31] Matters are made worse here by the confused assumption in much of the literature that assault is a crime of violence—so that, if rape is a kind of assault, then rape is by that token a crime of violence. See e.g. Susan Brownmiller, *Against Our Will* (Secker & Warburg, London, 1975) 377 or Robin West, n. 23 above, 242. On the differences between assaults and crimes of violence, see John Gardner, 'Rationality and the Rule of Law in Offences Against the Person' (1994) 53 *Cambridge Law Journal* 502.

[32] Cf. Alan Wertheimer, 'Consent and Sexual Relations' (1996) 2 *Legal Theory* 101, wherein the seriousness of a rape is regarded as a function of its harmfulness.

(iii) Mistakes as to Consent

Academic criminal lawyers often worry about the correct response, in the law of rape, to misunderstandings regarding consent. Should the defendant in a rape trial be given the benefit of his genuine mistakes as to consent? Or are there other conditions which need to be satisfied before mistakes as to consent will exonerate? We have already hinted at what we regard as the basic answer. The key, in our view, is the astuteness of the defendant to consent.[33] For the reasons we gave, being astute to consent is not a sufficient condition for avoiding the accusation of objectification. But it is nevertheless a necessary condition. Being astute to consent means not only paying attention to, but also taking seriously, the responses of another person to what one is doing to them. If one fails to pay attention to these responses or to take them seriously, it does not matter, so far as we can see, whether one's failure comes of malice, callousness, selfishness, misogyny, insensitivity, or sheer stupidity. We never cease to marvel at the extent to which criminal lawyers, in rape trials and elsewhere, are prepared to regard stupidity as exculpating rather than inculpating. Stupidity is a vice, not an excuse. Where risks are complex, some degrees of obliviousness to them may, of course, be excusable. It all depends on how much sophistication can reasonably be expected of human beings in general, without special expertise. But the risk that one is using another human being by sexual violation of them without their consent is not complex, does not call for special expertise, and attention to it can reasonably be expected of all adult human beings unless they are seriously mentally ill. That is why, as we said at the outset, rape is arguably inexcusable.[34] Barring serious mental illness, if one is not paying attention to the consensuality of some sexual activity one is embarking on then it is not hyperbolic to regard one as morally beyond the pale—an animal, as the tabloids might put it. Likewise if one is paying attention but, as in the famous *Morgan* case, one concludes or assumes that the protestations of one's victim are not to be taken seriously.[35] The *Morgan* defendants were animals *par excellence*. For, however they saw it themselves, they treated their sexual 'conquest' as something less than a subject, as something less than a self-respecting human being fit to decide and speak for herself when it came to her own sexuality.[36] She was just a sex-aid for their gratification. That is the clearest imaginable objectification of her. And since she did not in fact consent to the objectifying sexual penetration it was the clearest

[33] See 206 above.

[34] Serious mental illness is not an excuse. It eliminates the mentally ill person's responsibility for (some or all of) her actions and this means that there can be no requirement, and no possibility, for those actions to be justified or excused.

[35] *DPP* v. *Morgan* [1976] AC 182. Interestingly, the defendants' claim that this was the conclusion they drew was, according to the House of Lords, regarded as a 'pack of lies' by the jury.

[36] Here is where the consideration of women's rationality stressed in n. 10 above has its most important bite. Since women are rational agents, a woman who rejects sexual advances must be taken to have her reasons for doing so, and these reasons (thanks to the right to sexual autonomy) must be regarded by the person making the advances as sufficient reasons against persisting. It is not morally open to him to regard the word 'no' as rationally arbitrary (e.g. as a pathological reaction owed to sex-role conditioning) and therefore as presenting no rational obstacle to persistence.

imaginable way of violating her right to sexual autonomy, and the clearest imaginable case of rape.

These remarks, particularly those about stupidity, will likely be regarded by many criminal lawyers as supporting a rather radical form of 'objectivism' about *mens rea*. But in the face of this suggestion, three important caveats need to be entered right away.

First, as they stand our remarks bear only on the *mens rea* for the crime of rape. We are among those who believe that the question of what should be the *mens rea* for a particular crime is a question which calls, at least in the first instance, for a local answer specific to that crime. For it depends, as our foregoing remarks were meant to illustrate, on what exactly is wrong, or is supposed to be wrong, with perpetrating that particular crime. That what we called 'astuteness to consent' is a necessary condition of not being a rapist where there is non-consensual sexual intercourse comes of the fact that rape is, fundamentally, a crime of objectification, a crime of using a person as a thing. We do not claim or suggest that similar *mens rea* requirements would necessarily be suitable for other crimes which are wrong in other ways—that is to say, thanks to other arguments or other clusters of arguments.

Secondly, our remarks about mistakes as to consent are 'objectivist' only in the sense that they hold the defendant's mentality, as well as his conduct, up to the appropriate moral standard. Since morality governs reasons for action it governs not only what we do but also why we do it. Some criminal lawyers may wonder whether the criminal law has a role in requiring us to reason acceptably. The simple answer is that it does, if and when we proceed to *act* on the unacceptable reasons. Any *mens rea* standard in criminal law is, at base, a standard which bears on the reasoning by which certain actions may acceptably be performed. The one we suggested above is no exception. Thus ours is not an 'objectivist' proposal in the rather different sense, familiar from some corners of private law, of making nothing turn on the defendant's state of mind at the time of the offence. The defendant's attitude, the way he looks upon others, is at the heart of our approach to his mistakes.[37]

Finally, our remarks on astuteness to consent do not, strictly speaking, end the matter of what should be the *mens rea* for rape in law. There are some more general institutional considerations which need to be brought to bear before the task of specifying a suitable *mens rea* standard for rape can be completed. There may be many such considerations, and they are prone to vary from time to time and from jurisdiction to jurisdiction. They may include considerations relating to ease of explanation to and application by lay people who may be involved in certain kinds of trials, as well as considerations of statutory drafting, proof, precedent, procedure, etc. These considerations are such that different legal systems which include crimes of rape may go their different ways on this and other aspects of the definition of rape, especially at or

[37] For a similar approach to the *mens rea* of rape, see R.A. Duff, 'Recklessness and Rape' (1981) 3 *Liverpool Law Review* 49. In our view, Duff erred in generalizing his analysis of recklessness as to consent in rape to many other crimes without separate analysis of their moral structure: see his *Intention, Agency and Criminal Liability* (Blackwell, Oxford, 1990) 139ff.

near the borderlines. And some legal systems may be such that they have more than one acceptable way to go, especially at or near the borderlines. All we would add on this score is that there is one important institutional consideration which often bears on the specification of *mens rea* elements for crimes, but which has very little purchase in the law of rape. Quite apart from their independent moral salience, it is a further part of the job of *mens rea* requirements in the criminal law to help put potential defendants on notice that they are about to enter the realms of possible criminality. If it is a condition of criminal liability that one actually noticed what one was doing then, assuming one can be taken to know the law, one also knows whenever one is dicing with criminal liability. This supports a kind of 'subjectivist' twist in the *mens rea* for many crimes.[38] Not, however, in the case of rape. Barring bizarre conditions calling for the use of an insanity or automatism defence, it is hard to see how sexual penetration could be unwitting.[39] That being so, the institutional 'notice' requirement is fully satisfied in the requirement of sexual penetration, and there is no need for a further element of notice in shaping the law's attitude to mistakes regarding consent. Anyone who knows the law knows that when they embark on sexual penetration, lack of consent could carry them across the boundary into rape. And one can scarcely make a plausible defence of mistake of *law* in such a case, since (as we have shown) rape is *malum in se* rather than *malum prohibitum*. Morality itself—that is to say, the moral doctrine defended in this essay—puts one on notice.[40] Even if lack of consent did not turn sexual penetration into a crime in law, any tolerably morally sensitive adult realizes that lack of consent makes sexual penetration of another's body wrongful, because it amounts to the most straightforward breach of that other's right to sexual autonomy. It is morally unlicensed objectification.

THE ROLE OF THE LAW

You may say that it is enough, to justify the criminalization of rape, that it violates people's right to sexual autonomy, and enough to justify the criminalization of rape *as such* that it violates that right in a special symbolically significant way. Perhaps so. It is commonly thought, however, that justifying criminalization means, among other things, passing the test of the harm principle. Yet in no jurisdictions known to us is it true that rape is a crime only when harmful. Even the pure case is classified as rape, and criminally so. One could sideline it by saying that the harm principle is a rule of thumb, and tolerates some departures from its standard. One could also sideline the

[38] For fuller discussion see John Gardner, 'On the General Part of the Criminal Law' in R.A. Duff (ed.), *Philosophy and the Criminal Law: Principle and Critique* (Cambridge University Press, New York, 1998) 242–4.

[39] For a discussion of this issue and English law's approach to it, see Stephen White, 'Three Points on Pigg' [1989] *Criminal Law Review* 539.

[40] We have discussed this way of delimiting the scope for a 'mistake of law' defence to criminal charges in our introduction (with Jeremy Horder) to the volume the three of us jointly edited, *Action and Value in Criminal Law* (Clarendon Press, Oxford, 1994), 10–12.

pure case by observing that the harm principle's standard is met if the class of criminalized acts is a class of acts which *tend* to cause harm, and that is true of rape in spite of the possibility of the pure case. But, although we are not averse to these two qualifications, suitably refined, we think that the argument of this essay teaches a different lesson about the harm principle.

It is no objection under the harm principle that a harmless action was criminalized, nor even that an action with no tendency to cause harm was criminalized. It is enough to meet the demands of the harm principle that, if the action were not criminalized, *that* would be harmful. This test is passed by the pure case of rape with flying colours. If the act in this case were not criminalized then, assuming at least partial efficacy on the part of the law, people's rights to sexual autonomy would more often be violated. This would be a harm, not only to those people (if they were conscious and became aware of the rape), but also to a broader constituency of people (in our culture mainly women) whose lives would then be even more blighted than at present by violations of their right to sexual autonomy and, more pervasively still, by their justifiable *fear* of violations of their right to sexual autonomy.[41] These blights are harms which the legal prohibition on rape, if it is functioning properly, helps to reduce. For the purposes of the harm principle that is all that is needed. There is no need to show, in addition, that a given rape caused, or was likely to cause, harm.

These remarks yield two general conclusions about the moral scope and functions of the criminal law. Some have wanted to broaden the traditional interpretation of the harm principle to remove its instrumental cast. They have wanted to shift the focus of the principle away from the diminution of people's prospects, the change for the worse in their lives. They have thought this necessary to bring 'Kantian', non-instrumental wrongs, into the fold of the criminal law.[42] We believe, on the contrary, that the traditional instrumental reading of the harm principle is correct. But we also believe that non-instrumental wrongs, such as pure rapes and pure burglaries, can be brought under the umbrella of the harm principle. They are brought under that umbrella because the harm principle does not say that only harmful wrongs may be criminalized. It says that the criminalization of wrongs is justified only in order to prevent harm. Non-instrumental wrongs, even when they are perfectly harmless in themselves, can pass this test if their criminalization diminishes the occurrence of them, and the wider occurrence of them would detract from people's prospects—for example, by diminishing some public good, such as people's sense of ease with their living environment, the prospects for them to enjoy loving and trusting sexual rela-

[41] Thus Susan Rae Peterson is right, in our view, to emphasize the way that rape 'restrict[s] the freedom of bodily movement for women': n. 30 above, 360. But Peterson is wrong to regard this as what is primarily *wrong* with rape. It is because rape is anyway wrong that women justifiably fear it, and therefore become especially restricted in their use of some kinds of public transport, their access to certain neighbourhoods, and many other valuable options. This restriction is one of the key kinds of harm which makes it all right, according to the harm principle, to use the law to control the wrong of rape. But the wrongness of rape is independent of, and prior to, this harm.

[42] See e.g. R.A. Duff, n. 37 above, 111–12.

tionships, their ability to go out and enjoy themselves at night or in strange places, or the degree of mutual respect which prevails in public culture at large.

This brings us to the second conclusion. Some writers have thought that the criminal law could be characterized as a system of fundamentally public wrongs, in which the key interest is the interest of the public at large represented by the state, as opposed to private law in which the wrongs committed are fundamentally wrongs against individuals, who are therefore given the right to control enforcement and remedy.[43] Indirectly, we have attacked this view. If there is any fundamental difference between crimes and torts except for the procedures and remedies associated with them, then it is not the difference between a fundamentally public interest and a fundamentally private interest. Crimes and torts alike may protect or reflect similar mixtures of public and private interests. The wrong of rape is a wrong against the person raped, even when she is unaware of it and suffers no harm as a result. The criminal law protects her rights as an individual. Nevertheless, the criminal law may be, and often is, concerned with public goods. These include, for example, the public goods of property-holding and sexual autonomy, as well as those of tolerant co-existence, a clean and æsthetically acceptable environment, a decent social security system, etc. In some parts of the criminal law the harm to these public goods which is done by violations of the rights of an individual is the harm which justifies criminalization of those violations so far as the harm principle is concerned, even though the wrong done is a wrong against a particular individual right-holder. The same holds in the law of tort, which is equally subject to the requirements of the harm principle and may equally involve wrongs against particular people which are publicly harmful rather than harmful to those people. The law of trespass and the law of libel, as well as the law relating to breach of contract, take this form. The wrong in each case is against an individual but the wrong is actionable even when the individual wronged was not harmed by the wrong (in which case damages are nominal). In such cases the harm which justifies making the wrong actionable in law is the public harm of loss of respect for property, reputation, or voluntary undertaking, as the case may be. There may be differences between trespass, libel, and breach of contract on the one hand, and rape and burglary on the other, such that the former are nowadays normally actionable only in private law, and only the latter are crimes. But the difference does not lie in the difference between public and private interests in the subject-matter of the legal proceedings. In fact, these examples show that the contrast between public and private wrongs is, fundamentally, a misleading one. Many familiar individual rights, including those supported by these legal categories, are in large measure justified by the public good which is nurtured in their existence and recognition.[44] As we have endeavoured to show, the right to sexual autonomy, the right at the centre of the modern law of rape, is no exception.

[43] See e.g. Lawrence C. Becker, 'Criminal Attempt and the Theory of the Law of Crimes' (1974) 3 *Philosophy and Public Affairs* 262.

[44] On this broader point about rights see Joseph Raz, 'Rights and Individual Well-Being' in his *Ethics in the Public Domain* (Clarendon Press, Oxford, 1994).

On the Conceptual and Philosophical Foundations of Tort Law

Nicholas J. McBride

A. INTRODUCTION

In this essay I want to talk about the philosophical foundations of tort law. But perhaps I should start by making clear what branch of the law I am referring to when I use the term 'tort law'. It is necessary to do this because some lawyers use the term 'tort law' to refer to one branch of the law while other lawyers talk about a quite different branch of the law when they use the term 'tort law'. The reason for this is that not all lawyers use the term 'tort' in the same way.

1. The Traditional Use of the Term 'Tort'

Some lawyers, of a traditional bent, use the term 'tort' to refer to *conduct that breaches a non-equitable, non-contractual duty*[1] *owed to another to do something other than pay money to that other.*[2] So when these lawyers—let us call them 'traditionalists'—say that 'D committed a tort' they mean by saying that to say that 'D breached a non-contractual, non-equitable duty owed to another to do something other than pay money to that other'. Some of these terms need explanation before we can go on.

A duty is owed by one person to another if that other can release that person from that duty. So D owes a duty to V if V can release D from that duty by waiving its existence. This will only be the case if the duty that D is subject to is imposed for V's benefit. This is common sense. If D's duty were imposed, in whole or in part, for the benefit of people other than V, V's desire that D not be bound by that duty would have no effect on the existence of that duty. However, if D's duty were imposed for the sole benefit of V, then if V does not wish D to be bound by that duty there would seem to be no good reason why D should be bound by that duty—unless, of course, V is insane or immature and in no position to form rational wishes about how he should be treated by others.

Duties in English law are either statutory or judge-made. A duty is 'judge-made' if it is not statutory in nature—that is, if it does not owe its existence to the enactment of unrepealed legislation. Judge-made duties may be divided up into 'common law duties' and 'equitable duties'. An equitable duty is a judge-made duty that would only

[1] In this essay, for simplicity's sake, I use the term 'duty' when I mean to say 'legal duty'.

[2] Cf. P.B.H. Birks, 'The Concept of a Civil Wrong' in D. Owen (ed.), *The Philosophical Foundations of Tort Law* (Oxford, 1995).

have been enforced by the Court of Equity in the days when England maintained separate Courts of Equity and Courts of Law. A judge-made duty which would have been enforced by either court (the Court of Equity only enforcing the duty when the Courts of Law found themselves unable to do so effectively) is known as a common law duty—as, seemingly, is a judge-made duty which came into existence after the abolition of the distinction between courts of equity and courts of law. Common law duties are either 'contractual' or 'non-contractual' in nature. A common law duty is 'non-contractual' in nature if the person subject to that duty is not subject to it because he entered into a valid contract with another. So a duty is only non-contractual and non-equitable in nature if it is a statutory duty or if it is a non-contractual common law duty.

The point I am making here about how traditionalists use the term 'tort' can be restated by reference to Tables 1(a) and 1(b), below. Every duty recognized in English law can be placed in one of the sixteen shaded boxes on these tables; no duty can be placed in more than one of these boxes. Traditionalists, I am contending, use the term 'tort' in order to refer to conduct that breaches a duty whose place is in box 10 or box 12 on Table 1(b). Because traditionalists use the term 'tort' in this way, they use the term 'tort law' solely to refer to that branch of the law that determines what duties will be incurred by someone if he breaches a non-contractual, non-equitable duty owed to another to do something other than pay money to that other. So if a traditionalist were to write a book on 'tort law' he would write a book on what duties will be incurred by someone if he breaches a non-contractual, non-equitable duty owed to another to do something other than pay money to that other—in other words, he would write a book about what duties fall into box 6 on Table 1(a), below.[3] (All the duties that will be incurred by someone because he or she has breached a non-contractual, non-equitable duty owed to another to do something other than to pay money to that other are duties to pay money to another.)

2. The Modern Use of the Term 'Tort'

Other lawyers—let us call them 'modernists'—use the term 'tort' in a quite different way and, in consequence, refer to a quite different branch of the law when they use the term 'tort law'. When they say 'D committed a tort' they do not mean to say that D breached a non-contractual, non-equitable duty owed to another to do something other than pay money to that other; rather, they mean to say something like '*D caused another loss in circumstances which mean that D would normally as a result incur a duty or be held liable to compensate that other for that loss*'.

This leads modernists to say in some cases that a particular defendant committed a tort when a traditionalist would refuse to say this. Suppose, for example, that D manufactures—without fault on his part—a product that is unreasonably unsafe and

[3] I have on my shelves the 13th edn. of Sir Frederick Pollock's *The Law of Torts* (London, 1929), the full title of which reads: 'The Law of Torts: A Treatise On The Principles Of Obligations Arising From Civil Wrongs In The Common Law'.

Table 1(a). A table of duties to pay money to another

Duties to pay money to another							
Arising because the subject of the duty entered into a contract	Arising because the subject of the duty was unjustly enriched	Arising because the subject of the duty breached another duty to which he was subject					Arising from some other event
		Arising because the subject of the duty owed to another to pay money to that other	Arising because the subject of the duty breached a duty owed to another to do something other than pay money to that other			Arising because the subject of the duty breached a duty not owed to another	
			Arising because the subject of the duty breached a contratcual duty owed to another to do something other than pay money to that other	Arising because the subject of the duty breached an equitable duty owed to another to do something other than pay money to that other	Arising because the subject of the duty breached a non-contractual, non-equitable duty owed to another to do something other than pay money to that other		
1	2	3	4	5	6	7	8

Table 1(b). A table of duties to do something other than pay money to another

	Duties to do something other than pay money to another			
	Judge-made duties			Statutory duties
	Common law		Equitable	
	Contractual	Others		
Duties owed to another	9	10	11	12
Duties not owed to another	13	14	15	16

V suffers injury or serious damage to his personal property as a result. In such a case, a modernist would say that D has committed a tort—he has caused V loss and would normally be held liable to compensate V for that loss under the Consumer Protection Act 1987. In contrast, a traditionalist would not say that D has committed a tort as D did not breach any non-contractual, non-equitable duty in acting as he did—let alone a non-contractual, non-equitable duty owed to another.[4] Again, suppose D created a public nuisance with the result that V suffers special damage—that is, damage above and beyond that which is suffered by those who are generally adversely affected by the creation of the public nuisance. A modernist would say that D has committed a tort—D has caused V loss and would normally be held liable to compensate V for that loss. On the other hand, a traditionalist would not say here that D has committed a tort. True enough, D did breach a non-contractual, non-equitable duty in acting as he did. The duty breached by D in so acting was, at a very general level, a duty not to interfere with the existence of a public good—a good which, when it exists, can be enjoyed by everyone without exclusion.[5] That duty was not imposed on D for any one person's benefit but was, rather, imposed on D for the benefit of the community as a whole. That duty was therefore not owed to any one individual—no one person had the power to release D from that duty. Its place on Table 1(b) above was in box 14 or box 16—and not in box 10 or 12. Therefore, D, in acting as he did, did breach a non-contractual, non-equitable duty but he did not owe that duty to another. So a traditionalist, unlike a modernist, would not say that D committed a tort when he created a public nuisance with the result that V suffered special damage. Sometimes the differing ways in which they use the term 'tort' means that a traditionalist will say that a particular defendant has committed a tort when a modernist would not. For example, suppose D walks onto V's land and then off again without damaging anything of V's in doing so. A traditionalist would say that D has committed a tort in this case: D owed V a non-contractual, non-equitable duty not to trespass on V's land and breached that duty by walking onto V's land. A modernist would not say that D has committed a tort in this case. In acting as he did, D did not cause V to suffer any loss for which D would normally be held liable to compensate V.

[4] A manufacturer certainly has no *common law duty* to *ensure* that his products are not unreasonably dangerous to use or consume—he merely owes each person who, it can be foreseen, is likely to be injured if his products are unreasonably dangerous a common law duty to take reasonable care to ensure that his products are not unreasonably dangerous. Moreover a manufacturer does not have a *statutory duty* to ensure that his products are not unreasonably dangerous to use or consume. The Consumer Protection Act 1987 merely provides that a manufacturer who makes an unreasonably dangerous product shall be held liable to someone who suffers personal injury or serious damage to his personal property as a result. Contrast the language of the Protection from Harassment Act 1997, s.1(1): '[a] person *must not* pursue a course of conduct—(a) which amounts to harassment of another, and (b) which he knows or ought to know amounts to harassment of the other' (emphasis added).

[5] Examples of public nuisances include: obstructing a public highway or rendering it unsafe to travel along; obstructing passage along a navigable river by lowering it (*Tate & Lyle Industries* v. *GLC* [1983] 2 AC 509); disrupting the peace of the neighbourhood by throwing fireworks about in the street or by holding an 'acid house' party (*R.* v. *Shorrock* [1994] QB 279); and polluting a river with result that its fish are destroyed and its waters are rendered unfit to drink (*R.* v. *Medley* (1834) 6 C&P 292).

The way a modernist uses the term 'tort' has an effect on what branch of the law he refers to when he uses the term 'tort law'. A modernist uses the term 'tort law' to refer to that branch of the law that determines when one person will be held liable to compensate another for loss that he has caused that other to suffer. So if a modernist were to write a book on 'tort law' he would write a very different book from that which a traditionalist would write. A modernist's book on 'tort law' would detail all the situations when one person will be held liable to compensate another for loss that he has caused that other to suffer.

3. Taking Sides

I am a traditionalist. So, when I use the term 'tort' here and elsewhere, I use that term to refer to the breach of a non-contractual, non-equitable duty owed to another to do something other than pay money to that other and, correspondingly, when I use the term 'tort law' I mean by using that term to refer to that branch of the law that determines what duties will be incurred by someone if he breaches a non-contractual, non-equitable duty owed to another to do something other than pay money to that other.

4. What Understanding the Philosophical Foundations of Tort Law Involves

Those who attempt to understand the 'philosophical foundations of tort law' simply look at what duties will be incurred by someone who commits a tort and attempt to find out why someone who commits a tort will incur those duties. So, for me, as a traditionalist, we will understand the philosophical foundations of tort law if, knowing what duties will be incurred by someone who breaches a non-contractual, non-equitable duty owed to another[6]—that is, what duties fall within box 6 on Table 1(a), above—we can explain why someone who breaches a non-contractual, non-equitable duty owed to another will incur those duties.

In other words, we will understand the philosophical foundations of tort law if: (a) knowing what duties will be incurred by someone who breaches a *non-contractual common law duty* owed to another, we can explain why someone who breaches a non-contractual common law duty owed to another will incur those duties; and (b) knowing what duties will be incurred by someone who breaches a *statutory duty* owed to another, we can explain why someone who breaches a statutory duty will incur those duties. In this essay, I want to embark on an attempt to understand the philosophical foundations of tort law. I will begin by setting out what duties will be incurred by someone who breaches a non-contractual common law duty owed to another. I will then attempt to find out why someone who breaches a non-contractual common law duty owed to another will incur one of those duties.

[6] From now on, when I talk about a 'non-contractual common law duty owed to another' it should be taken as read that I mean only to refer to a non-contractual common law duty owed to another to do something other than pay money to that other.

B. THE DUTIES OF A TORTFEASOR

Someone who commits a tort by breaching a non-contractual common law duty owed to another to do something other than pay money to that other may incur one or more of six duties.

1. The Duty To Pay Compensatory Damages: I

If D owes V a non-contractual common law duty, that duty will have been imposed on D in order to help ensure that V does not suffer a certain kind of loss. Table 2 below makes the point. It lists a number of different non-contractual common law duties that might be owed by D to V and describes, in respect of each duty, what kind of loss the law aims to help ensure V will not suffer by imposing that duty on D.

Now—it is well established that if D breaches a non-contractual common law duty owed to V and V suffers loss L as a result[7] and the duty that D owed to V and breached was imposed on D in order to help ensure that V would not suffer that kind of loss, then D will incur a duty to pay V damages sufficient to compensate him for that loss L.[8] What is the position if D breaches a non-contractual common law duty owed to V with the result that V suffers loss K—but the duty D owed to V and breached was imposed on D in order to help ensure that V would not suffer loss L and was *not* imposed on D in order to help ensure that V would not suffer loss K? Will D have a duty to pay V damages sufficient to compensate V for the loss K he suffered as a result of D's breach? The law on this point is far from clear—but a number of different authorities and writers seem to testify that the answer to this question is probably 'no'.

(a) The builder of a house owes a future occupier of that house a non-contractual common law duty to take care to ensure that he does not build that house in such a way that that occupier will be exposed to an unreasonable risk of being injured. This duty is, of course, imposed on the builder of a house in order to help ensure that a future occupier of that house does not suffer personal injury. It is therefore well-established that if V is injured because D, in building the house V now lives in, breached the duty he owed V to take care to ensure that he did not build that house in such a way that V would be exposed to an unreasonable risk of being injured, D will incur a duty to pay damages to V sufficient to compensate V for the injury he suffered.[9] But what is the position if V suffers some loss other than personal injury because D, in building the house V now lives in, breached the non-contractual duty he owed V to take care to ensure that he did not build that house in such a way that V would be exposed to an unreasonable risk of being injured? For example, what is the position if D's breach of this duty forced V to spend money on repairing his house so as to make it safe to live in? The decision of the House of Lords in *Murphy* v. *Brentwood DC*[10] can be read as saying that in such a case D will as *a matter of principle* not incur a duty to pay damages to V sufficient to compensate him for the loss

Table 2. A table of non-contractual common law duties that might be owed by one person to another

Non-contractual common law duties that D might owe to V	The loss that the law seeks to help ensure V will not suffer by imposing this duty on D
A duty not to interfere unreasonably with V's reasonable use and enjoyment of land in his or her possession	Diminution of the use value of that land to V
A duty not to interfere with V's possession of land	V's being deprived of possession of that land
A duty to take care not to act in a way that, it can be reasonably foreseen, will expose V to an unreasonable risk of being injured	Personal injury
A duty to take care not to act in a way that, it can reasonably be foreseen, will expose V's property or possessions to an unreasonable risk of being damaged or destroyed	Damage or destruction to V's property or personal possessions
A duty to take care not to act in a way that, can reasonably be foreseen, will expose V to an unreasonable risk of developing a psychiatric illness	Mental illness
? A duty to take care not to act in a way that, it can be reasonably be foreseen, will expose V to an unreasonable risk of suffering devastating economic loss	Economic loss
A duty not to persuade a contracting partner of V's to act in a particular way in the knowledge that his or her acting in that way amounts to a breach of his or her contract with V	
A duty to take care to perform some task entrusted to D by V in the way V intended it to be performed	
A duty not to interfere with V's running a lawful business by acting unlawfully with the object of harming V's business	
A duty not to publish to another information that, if published to a right-thinking person, might cause him or her to shun and avoid V	Unjustified loss of reputation
A duty not to make, knowingly or recklessly, a misrepresentation to V with the object of inducing V to act on that representation	General detriment
?? A duty not to act with the sole object of harming V	

he suffered as a result of D's breach—that is, D will not incur such a duty irrespective of whether or not considerations of policy or fairness dictate that he should not incur such a duty.[11]

(b) Everyone owes someone who is in possession of land a non-contractual common law duty not to interfere unreasonably with that person's use and enjoyment of that land. So D will owe such a duty to V if V is in possession of Blackacre—he will owe V a duty not to interfere unreasonably with V's use and enjoyment of Blackacre. This duty of D's is, of course, imposed on D to help ensure that the use-value of Blackacre to V is not diminished. So it is well-established that if D breaches this duty by poisoning a well on Blackacre, thereby diminishing the use-value of Blackacre to V, D will incur a duty to pay damages to V sufficient to compensate V for the loss of the well. But what is the position if D breaches the duty he owes V not to interfere unreasonably with V's use and enjoyment of Blackacre by poisoning a well on Blackacre and this results not only in the use-value of Blackacre to V being diminished but also in V's falling ill—say because he takes a drink from the well, not knowing that it is poisoned? Will D incur a duty not only to pay damages to V sufficient to compensate V for the loss of his well but also to pay damages to V sufficient to compensate V for the illness he developed as a result of drinking from the well D poisoned? Many academics and judges are of the opinion that in the case just described D would *as a matter of principle* not have a duty to pay damages to V sufficient to compensate V for the personal injury he suffered as a result of D's breach of the duty he owed V not to interfere unreasonably with V's use and enjoyment of Blackacre—a duty, note, that was not imposed on D so as to help ensure that V would remain in good health.[12]

(c) In his classic and seminal paper, 'Negligence and Interest', Anthony Machin considered the following case: '[T] is carrying a parcel containing [V]'s fireworks, [V] standing fifty yards away, and [D] as he passes negligently knocks the parcel from [T]'s hands (being ignorant of its contents) and it explodes injuring [V]'.[13] What is the position? At all times, D will owe V a non-contractual common law duty to take care not to act in a way that, it can be reasonably foreseen, will expose V's property to an unreasonable risk of being destroyed or damaged. So at the time of the events described, D owed V a non-contractual common law duty to take reasonable care not to knock the parcel carried by T from T's hands—it being reasonably foreseeable that knocking the parcel containing V's fireworks from T's hands would expose those fire-

[10] [1991] 1 AC 398.

[11] Of course, the decision of their Lordships can be read as saying that, in the case described in the text, D *would* have a duty to pay damages to V sufficient to compensate V for the expense he was put to as a result of D's breach but for the fact that considerations of public policy dictate that D should not have such a duty: see e.g. R. Cooke, 'An Impossible Distinction' (1991) 107 *LQR* 46. However, this reading of the decision in *Murphy* is weakened by the fact that it is extraordinarily difficult to discover what these public policy concerns might be.

[12] See F.H. Newark, 'The Boundaries of Nuisance' (1949) 65 *LQR* 480 (though note he backtracks on his position in a hasty footnote: 490, n. 55); *Read* v. *J. Lyons & Co.* [1947] AC 156, 173, *per* Lord Macmillan; *Hunter* v. *Canary Wharf* [1997] 2 All ER 426, 442d, *per* Lord Lloyd, 452a, *per* Lord Hoffmann.

works to an unreasonable risk of being destroyed or damaged. This duty was, of course, imposed on D to help ensure that V's fireworks would not be damaged. So, V's fireworks having been damaged as a result of D's breaching this duty, it is well-established that D will have a duty to pay V damages sufficient to compensate V for the damage done to his fireworks as a result of D's breach. But V has also suffered personal injury because D breached the duty he owed V to take reasonable care not to knock V's package out of T's hands—a duty imposed on D, remember, to help ensure that V's fireworks would not be damaged and *not* imposed on D to help ensure that V would not suffer personal injury. Does D have a duty to pay V damages sufficient to compensate V for that injury? Machin thought that *as a matter of principle* D would have no such duty in the case discussed by him, saying that it would be 'contrary to common sense' to hold that D had a duty to pay damages to V to compensate him for the injuries he suffered.[14]

So here we have three cases in which D breaches a non-contractual common law duty owed to V with the result V suffers loss K, but where the duty D owed to V and breached was imposed on D in order to help ensure that V would not suffer loss L, and was *not* imposed on D in order to help ensure that V would not suffer loss K. In each case, there seems some support for saying that D will *as a matter of principle* not incur a duty to pay damages to V sufficient to compensate V for loss K—that is, D will not incur a duty to pay damages to V sufficient to compensate V for loss K, irrespective of whether or not considerations of policy or fairness require that D should not incur such a duty. This seems to indicate that if D breaches a non-contractual common law duty owed to V and V suffers loss L as a result, D will incur a duty to pay damages to V sufficient to compensate V for that loss L—but only if the duty D owed V that D breached was imposed on D, in whole or in part, so as to help ensure that V would not suffer loss L.

2. The Duty to Pay Restitutionary Damages: I

If D sells property belonging to V when he owed V a non-contractual common law duty not to do so, D will not have a duty to pay V damages sufficient to compensate V for the loss of his property, but will instead have a duty to pay V damages equal to the value of the money he received for V's property *if* V would prefer that D give him damages equal to the value of the money D received for V's property rather than damages sufficient to compensate him for the loss of his property. So in *Oughton* v. *Seppings*[15] the defendant was a sheriff who sold the plaintiff's pony for £81. 10s. when he owed the plaintiff a non-contractual, non-equitable duty not to do so. The defendant, it was held, would have a duty to pay the plaintiff damages equal to the value of the money he received for the pony if—as was the case—the plaintiff would prefer that the defendant paid her such damages than that the defendant paid her damages sufficient to compensate her for the loss of her pony.

[13] E.A. Machin, 'Negligence and Interest' (1954) 17 *MLR* 405, 410. [14] Ibid.

3. The Duty to Pay Restitutionary Damages: II

If D uses or retains property belonging to V when he owed V a non-contractual common law duty not to do so, D will not have a duty to pay V damages sufficient to compensate V for any loss V has suffered as a result of D's using or retaining V's property in the way he did but will instead have a duty to pay V damages equivalent to what a reasonable man would have paid V in order to use or retain V's property in the way D did *if* V would rather be paid damages of the latter kind as opposed to damages of the former kind. So, in *Strand Electric Engineering Co. Ltd.* v. *Brisford Entertainments*[16] Brisford allowed Bedford Theatre to take possession of a theatre which Brisford were negotiating to sell to Bedford. Bedford hired some electric switchboards from Strand Electric to control the stage lighting in the theatre and installed them in the theatre. The negotiations between Brisford and Bedford broke down and Brisford took possession of the theatre and its contents, including the switchboards. At the end of the hire period Strand Electric asked for the switchboards to be returned, but Brisford held onto them—even though they owed Strand Electric a non-contractual, non-equitable duty to return those switchboards to Strand Electric. Brisford, it was held, would have a duty to pay Strand Electric a reasonable sum for the time they had wrongfully held onto Strand Electric's switchboards if—as was the case—Strand Electric preferred that Brisford paid them such a sum rather than that Brisford compensated them for the loss they suffered as a result of their being deprived of their switchboards for the time Brisford held onto them.

4. The Duty to Pay Aggravated Damages

If D breaches a non-contractual common law duty owed to V in such a manner that V's feelings are outraged as a result, then D will incur a duty to pay damages to P sufficient to assuage P's feelings of outrage at the way D behaved.

5. The Duty to Pay Compensatory Damages: II

If D breaches a non-contractual common law duty owed to V and T, a third party, suffers loss as a result, D will rarely incur a duty to pay damages to T sufficient to compensate T for the loss he suffered as a result of D's breach. However, D will incur such a duty if: (i) D's breach caused V to die; (ii) T was a dependant of V's; and (iii) had V merely been injured by D's breach of the non-contractual common law duty that D owed him, D would have incurred a duty to pay V damages sufficient to compensate V for that injury. In such a case, D will have a duty under the Fatal Accidents Act 1976 to pay damages to T so as to compensate him for the loss of support he has suffered as a result of V's death.[17]

[15] (1830) 1 B & Ad. 241, 109 ER 776. [16] [1952] 2 QB 246.

6. The Duty to Pay Punitive Damages

If D breaches a non-contractual common law duty owed to V then the courts will sometimes impose a duty on D to pay V punitive damages—that is, a duty to pay V a sum payment of which by D to V will ensure that D is adequately punished for acting as he did. It is impossible to describe succinctly when the courts will impose a duty to pay punitive damages on someone who breaches a non-contractual common law duty owed to another to do something other than pay money to that other but *roughly speaking* the courts will impose such a duty on D if: (a) D breached that duty for financial gain or breached that duty in his capacity as a public servant, using his powers as a public servant in an oppressive way, and (b) the courts can punish breaches of the kind of duty breached by D by imposing a duty to pay punitive damages on someone who breaches that duty.

C. UNDERSTANDING TORT LAW: A BEGINNING

1. Introduction

Having outlined what duties will be incurred by someone who breaches a non-contractual common law duty owed to another, I now want to address the question: if D breaches a non-contractual common law duty owed to V and V suffers loss L as a result, why will D incur a duty to pay damages to V sufficient to compensate V for that loss L—but only if the duty D owed V and breached was imposed on D, in whole or in part, so as to help ensure that V would not suffer loss L?

2. A Principled Argument

It is sometimes easy enough to see why D will incur such a duty if he breaches a non-contractual common law duty owed to V. Suppose, again, that V is in possession of Blackacre. D will owe V a duty not to interfere unreasonably with V's use and enjoyment of Blackacre. Suppose that D breaches this duty by poisoning a well on Blackacre and V suffers personal injury as a result of the well being poisoned. Having poisoned the well on Blackacre, D's original duty not to interfere unreasonably with V's use and enjoyment of Blackacre will remain binding on D and will require him to do the best he can to restore the well on Blackacre that he poisoned to its original condition; so long as that well remains poisoned, V's use and enjoyment of Blackacre will be unreasonably interfered with as a result of D's actions. Instead of actually restoring the well on Blackacre to its original condition, it will be enough if D pays V the monetary equivalent of that well's being restored to its original condition—in other words, it will be enough if D pays damages to V sufficient to compensate V for the loss of his well. So, having poisoned the well on Blackacre, D's original duty not

[17] Fatal Accidents Act 1976, ss.1, 3.

to interfere unreasonably with V's use and enjoyment of Blackacre will remain binding on D and will require him to pay damages to V sufficient to compensate V for the loss of his well. But this duty will not require D to pay damages to V sufficient to compensate V for the personal injury he suffered as a result of his well being poisoned—D has no need to ensure that V is restored to his previous good health in order to comply with his original duty not to interfere unreasonably with V's use and enjoyment of Blackacre.

This is a *principled* argument as to why D—having poisoned a well on Blackacre—will incur a duty to pay damages to V, who possesses Blackacre, sufficient to compensate V for the loss of his well but not for any personal injury he suffers as a result of his well being poisoned. That is, the argument as to why the law treats D in this way does not rest on any idea that it would 'just' or 'fair' or in the public interest for D to be treated in this way—the law treats D in this way because *logic* dictates that it should treat him in this way. Speaking generally, if D owes V a non-contractual common law duty not to cause V to suffer loss L, and D breaches that duty with the result that V suffers loss L and a further loss K, we will always be able to use a principled argument to explain why in this situation, D *will* incur a duty to pay damages to V sufficient to compensate V for loss L but *will not* incur a duty to pay damages to V sufficient to compensate V for loss K. Unfortunately, outside such cases, it is hard to see how a principled argument could be mounted to account for why, when D breaches a non-contractual common law duty owed to V and V suffers loss L as a result, D will incur a duty to pay damages to V sufficient to compensate V for that loss—but only if the duty D owed V and breached was imposed on D, in whole or in part, so as to help ensure that V would not suffer loss L. For instance, to take an example already considered, if D breaches a duty he owes to V to take care not to knock a package containing V's fireworks from T's hands, with the result that V's fireworks are destroyed in the ensuing explosion, we know that D will incur a duty to pay damages sufficient to compensate V for the loss of his fireworks. But it is hard to see how one could argue that D's duty to compensate V for the loss of his fireworks arises as a matter of logic from the fact that D initially owed V a duty to take care not to knock a package containing those fireworks out of T's hands and then breached that duty. A different argument is needed to cope with these cases and explain why the law deals with them in the way it does.

3. A Concern to Satisfy Vindictive Feelings?

In his article 'The Inner Nature of the Tort Action'—rightly hailed by Peter Birks as 'an article which ought to be compulsory reading'[18]—John Kelly proposed that when D, having breached a non-contractual common law duty owed to V, incurs a duty to pay compensatory damages to V, the law imposes that duty on D to 'put [V] in possession of a sum of money which in the court's judgment ought to be enough to satisfy his vindictive feelings against [D]'.[19] Does this theory work to explain why, if D breaches a non-contractual common law duty owed to V and V suffers loss L as a result, D will incur a duty to pay damages to V sufficient to compensate V for that loss—but only if the duty D owed V and breached was imposed on D so as to help ensure that V would not suffer loss L? I do not think so.

(a) Suppose D inadvertently and without fault on his part breaches a non-contractual common law duty that he owes to V which is imposed on him in order to help ensure that V will not suffer loss L. Suppose further that V suffers loss L as a result. It must be counted as unlikely in such a case that D's doing what he did will cause V to harbour any vindictive feelings towards D at all. And yet D will still incur a duty to compensate V for the loss L that V suffered as a result of D's breach.

(b) Suppose D owes a non-contractual common law duty to V which is imposed on D so as to help ensure that V will not suffer loss L. Let us call this duty that D owes V 'duty C'. If D breaches duty C and V suffers loss L as a result, D will incur a duty to pay damages to V sufficient to compensate him for that loss L. If, on the other hand, D breaches duty C and V suffers loss K as a result, D will—if what is said in this essay is correct—not incur a duty to pay damages to V sufficient to compensate him for that loss K and will therefore not incur a duty to pay anything in the way of damages to V. (I am discounting the possibility that he might be liable to pay restitutionary or punitive damages to V.) Yet one would have thought that V would resent D just as much in the second of these two cases as he would in the first—that the vindictive feelings V would harbour towards D in these two cases would not vary depending on what kind of loss it was that D's breach caused V to suffer. So Kelly's theory cannot account for why, in the second of the two cases just described, D will not have a duty to pay damages to V sufficient to compensate him for the loss K that he suffered as a result of D's breach.

(c) Again, let us suppose that D owes a non-contractual common law duty to V that is imposed on D so as to help ensure that V will not suffer loss L—and, again, let us call this duty of D's 'duty C'. If D breaches duty C and V suffers loss L as a result, D will, of course, incur a duty to pay damages to V sufficient to compensate V for that loss L. But the law will allow someone else—usually D's insurer—to discharge this duty on D's behalf. This is surprising if D's duty to pay damages to V in this case is imposed on him so as to assuage the vindictive feelings that V will harbour

[18] P.B.H. Birks, *Harassment and Hubris: The Right to an Equality of Respect* (Dublin, 1996), 34.
[19] J.M. Kelly, 'The Inner Nature of the Tort Action' (1967) 2 *Ir. Jur. (NS)* 279, 287.

towards D because he has suffered loss L as a result of D's breach. Those feelings will not be assuaged if a third party is allowed to discharge D's duty to pay damages to V in this case—those feelings of resentment will only be assuaged if it is *D* who is made to pay damages to V sufficient to compensate V for the loss L he suffered as a result of D's breach.

These considerations lead me to think that Kelly's theory does not explain why, if D breaches a non-contractual common law duty owed to V and V suffers loss L as a result, D will incur a duty to pay damages to V sufficient to compensate V for that loss—but only if the duty D owed V and breached was imposed on D to help ensure that V would not suffer loss L. However, it *may* be possible to argue that the law, in imposing such a duty on D, seeks *not* to assuage any vindictive feelings that V will hold towards D as a result of what D did but, rather, to *prevent* V from developing such feelings towards D.

4. A Concern to Prevent Vindictive Feelings Arising?

i.

The following is true.

(a) If D intentionally did ϕ, knowing that he owed V a duty not to do ϕ, V will feel resentment towards D. In such a case the law will attempt to assuage that feeling of V's by imposing on D, not a duty to pay compensatory damages to V, but, rather, a duty to pay aggravated damages to V.

(b) The source of the resentment V will feel towards D in this case lies in the fact that D's duty not to do ϕ will have been imposed on D for V's benefit—say, to help ensure that V does not suffer loss L. The law will have judged, in imposing that duty on D, that V's not suffering loss L is so important that it is justified in imposing a duty on D not to do ϕ so as to help ensure that V will not suffer loss L. This judgment feeds into V's notions of self-worth; he will come to believe that it *is* important that he not suffer loss L and that the importance of his not suffering loss L is such that the law is justified in imposing a duty on D not to do ϕ so as to help ensure that V will not suffer loss L. Now—if D intentionally does ϕ even though he knows that he owes V a duty not to do ϕ, he implicitly asserts that the law was unjustified in imposing that duty not to do ϕ on him. In other words, he implicitly asserts either: (i) that it is not important that V not suffer loss L; or (ii) that it is not important enough that V not suffer loss L for the law to be justified in imposing a duty not to do ϕ on him. V, having been encouraged by the law to believe that the contrary is true, will feel belittled by that assertion—will feel that D, in making that assertion, fails to recognize his, V's, true worth. As a result, V will develop feelings of resentment towards D.

(c) Now let us suppose that D did ϕ when he owed V a duty not to do ϕ and that this duty of D's not to do ϕ was imposed on him so as to help ensure that V would not suffer loss L. V will find himself harbouring vindictive feelings towards D—even if D did not do ϕ intentionally or did not know that he owed V a duty not to do ϕ—if he thinks that D does not regret that he did ϕ when he owed V a duty not to do ϕ. The reason for this is that someone will regret doing something when he had a duty not to act in that way unless he thinks that the law was unjustified in imposing that duty on him. So—if D does not regret that he did ϕ when he owed V a duty not to do ϕ, imposed on him to help ensure that V would not suffer loss L, he will do so because he thinks that the law was unjustified in imposing that duty on him. But if he thinks that he must believe either: (i) that it is not important that V suffer loss L; or (ii) that it is not important enough that V not suffer loss L for the law to be justified in imposing a duty not to do ϕ on him. So if V thinks that D does not regret that he did ϕ when he owed V a duty not to do ϕ, V will think that D believes either (i) or (ii), above. As a result, V will feel belittled by D—having been encouraged by the law to believe that neither (i) nor (ii) above is true—and will as a result develop feelings of resentment towards D.

ii.

Is the following true?

(d) In our society, if A breaches a duty owed to B, imposed on A to help ensure that B would not suffer loss L, and A genuinely regrets having breached that duty, it is customary for A to attempt to assuage his regret—regret being something that needs to be assuaged by the person who feels it—by, one, attempting to ensure that B will not suffer loss L as a result of his breach and, two, in the case where B has suffered loss L as a result of A's breach, by compensating B for that loss L.

iii.

If (d) is true then the following is true:

(e) Suppose that D breached a non-contractual common law duty that he owed V not to do ϕ, imposed on him to help ensure that V would not suffer loss L, and V suffers loss K as a result. If D does not compensate V for that loss K, D's failure to pay such compensation to V will *not* lead V to think that D does not regret that he breached the duty he owed V not to do ϕ—given (d), V would not expect D to compensate him for the loss K he suffered as a result of D's breach even if D *did* regret that he committed that breach.

(f) Suppose that D breached a non-contractual common law duty that he owed V not to do ϕ, imposed on him to help ensure that V would not suffer loss L, and V suffers loss L and loss K as a result. If D does not compensate V for the loss L he suffered as a result of D's breach, V *will* think, given (d), that D does not regret that he breached the duty he owed V not to do ϕ—if D did feel such regret, V will think, D would have attempted to assuage it by compensating him for the loss L he suffered as a result of D's breach. So, in the situation we are discussing, if D does not compensate V for the loss L he suffered as a result of D's breach, V will develop feelings of resentment towards D. If, on the other hand, D *does* compensate V for the loss he suffered as a result of D's breach, V will not have occasion to develop feelings of resentment towards D. This is so even if D did not regret that he breached the duty he owed V not to do ϕ and compensated V for the loss L he suffered as a result of D's breach for some extraneous reason—for example, because a third party, T, forced him to do so. In such a case, V, not knowing the reason why D compensated him for the loss L he suffered as a result of D's breach, will not be able to tell that D did not regret that he breached the duty he owed V not to do ϕ and will therefore have no occasion to feel personally resentful of D.

(g) If, then, D breaches a non-contractual common law duty owed to V not to do ϕ and V suffers loss L as a result, V will feel resentment towards D if D does not compensate him for that loss—but only if the duty D owed V not to do ϕ was imposed on D to help ensure that V would not suffer loss L. And if D breaches a non-contractual common law duty owed to V not to do ϕ, imposed on him to help ensure that V will not suffer loss L, and V suffers loss L as a result, V will not feel personally resentful of D if D compensates him for that loss L—whatever D's reasons for paying him that sum.

iv.

If (g) is true *and* the law is concerned, among other things, to help prevent V becoming resentful of D, what would we expect the law to do if D breached a non-contractual common law duty owed to V with the result that V suffers loss L? We would expect the law to impose a duty on D to pay V a sum of money sufficient to compensate V for that loss L—but only if the duty D owed to V and breached were imposed on him to help ensure that V would not suffer loss L. And this is exactly what the law does do.

So if (g) is true, it is possible to argue that when D breaches a non-contractual common law duty owed to V and as a result incurs a duty to pay compensatory damages to V, the law imposes that duty on D to prevent V developing any feelings of resentment towards D. But is (g) true? This will depend on whether (d) above is true. I find it impossible, at this juncture, to say whether (d) is true or not. So I cannot claim that it *is* possible to argue that when D breaches a non-contractual common law duty owed to V and as a result incurs a duty to pay compensatory damages to V, the law imposes that duty on D to prevent V developing any feelings of resentment towards D. All that I can claim at this stage is that it *may* be possible to argue this—whether or not it *is* possible to argue this will depend on whether (d) above is true.

5. In Place of a Conclusion

Whether (d) is true or not is a question that needs further investigation. If it is true then we will be able to overcome the most substantial hurdle in the way of our fully understanding the philosophical foundations of tort law—we will be able to explain why, if D breaches a non-contractual common law duty owed to V, with the result that V suffers loss L, D will incur a duty to pay damages to V sufficient to compensate him for that loss L—but only if the duty D owed to V and breached was imposed on him to help ensure that V would not suffer loss L.

On the Relationship Between Corrective and Distributive Justice

Stephen R. Perry

Distributive justice is concerned with the just distribution of material resources, income, other forms of wealth, and perhaps certain other goods within a society. Corrective justice is concerned with the moral duty of repair, meaning the moral duty to pay compensation, that one individual can come to owe another as a result of having harmed him. In this essay, I inquire into the relationship between these two principles. More particularly, I ask whether corrective and distributive justice are independent principles, or whether they are related in either a conceptual or a normative sense.

One common view is that corrective justice requires a prior distribution of entitlements upon which to operate, and that its purpose or point is to maintain that distribution; for that reason, it is regarded as both conceptually and normatively ancillary to distributive justice. Another, less common, view holds that corrective and distributive justice operate on quite distinct kinds of entitlement, and hence are conceptually and normatively independent of one another. The position I defend is that corrective justice is a general moral principle that is concerned, not with maintaining a just distribution, but rather with repairing harm. Individuals can be harmed in a number of different ways, and corrective justice accordingly protects a number of different kinds of interest and entitlement. Distributive justice often contributes to the legitimacy of an entitlement that corrective justice protects, and in that sense there is a normative connection between the two. But corrective justice does not protect the entitlement *qua* distributive share, and its purpose is not to maintain or preserve a distributive scheme as such. Rather it protects a legitimate entitlement because interference with the entitlement harms the entitlement-holder. In that sense, corrective and distributive justice are conceptually independent.

It may be helpful to have a concrete theory of corrective justice in view as we proceed. To sketch briefly my own account of these matters,[1] the duty to repair in corrective justice depends on a more general concept of responsibility for outcomes which, following Tony Honoré, I call outcome-responsibility.[2] Outcome-responsibility, which is a fundamental aspect of our understanding of our own agency, requires that an agent have had control, in some appropriate sense, over the outcome that he caused. Different conceptions of outcome-responsibility involve different understandings of what it means to have control of this kind. The particular

[1] S.R. Perry, 'Responsibility for Outcomes, Risk, and the Law of Torts' in G. Postema (ed.), *Philosophy and the Law of Torts* (Cambridge University Press, Cambridge, forthcoming).

[2] T. Honoré, 'Responsibility and Luck' (1988) 104 *Law Quarterly Review* 530.

conception I defend conceives of control in terms of avoidability: a person is outcome-responsible for a harmful outcome to which she causally contributed if and only if she had the capacity to foresee that outcome and the ability and opportunity to take steps to avoid it. Outcome-responsibility in this sense means that a harmful outcome is properly attributable to someone's agency, but this is only a necessary and not a sufficient condition for the existence of a duty to repair in corrective justice. For such a duty to exist, it must also be possible to say that the harm in question belongs, in a moral sense, to the injurer rather than to the victim. I argue that a harm belongs to the injurer if she acted faultily in bringing the harm about, or if, in acting, she imposed certain kinds of unusual risks on the victim. In the former circumstance, a standard of intention or negligence is warranted; in the latter circumstance, strict liability is the appropriate approach.

The view just sketched is one understanding of corrective justice, but there are of course others.[3] Very little, if anything, in the argument I present below turns on the acceptance of this particular view. The argument should apply to any conception of corrective justice that understands it as a general moral principle giving rise to a duty to repair, and that does not involve either of the following two suppositions: first, that the function of corrective justice is by definition to protect distributive entitlements or, secondly, that there exist entitlements in corrective justice that are conceptually and normatively distinct from other kinds of entitlements, including in particular distributive entitlements. It also bears mention that the argument does not, for the most part, depend on any assumptions about the content of corrective justice—whether, for example, it involves a fault-based standard, a standard of strict liability, or some combination of the two.

Finally, I should note that corrective justice theorists are generally interested in corrective justice because they think that it constitutes the normative foundation of tort law. While I share that view, I make no attempt to defend it here. This essay is primarily concerned with the conceptual and normative relationship between two moral principles, rather than with the positive law that gives effect to those principles.

I

It might be suggested that corrective and distributive justice must be conceptually and normatively independent of one another just by virtue of being very different sorts of principles. Distributive justice is a matter of social justice. Since the concern is with the general distribution of goods throughout an entire society, it is plausible to think, with John Rawls, that the subject of distributive justice is the basic structure of society.[4] If distributive justice gives rise to reasons for action for individuals, as

[3] Three theories that meet the criteria stated in this para. are developed in the following works: J.L. Coleman, *Risks and Wrongs* (Cambridge University Press, Cambridge, 1992) 303–28; R.A. Epstein, 'A Theory of Strict Liability' (1973) 2 *Journal of Legal Studies* 151; G.P. Fletcher, 'Fairness and Utility in Tort Theory' (1972) 85 *Harvard L Rev.* 537.

[4] J. Rawls, *A Theory of Justice* (Harvard University Press, Cambridge, Mass., 1971) 7.

opposed to the state, they are presumably agent-general reasons. Corrective justice, on the other hand, appears to be a matter of personal or individual justice. The concern is with agent-relative obligations that one person owes to another as a result of a prior interaction between them. The basic subject of corrective justice is, we might say, not society but rather the individual. Given that distributive justice is most plausibly construed as social justice, whereas corrective justice is most plausibly construed as justice between individuals, why would the question of their relationship to one another even be thought to arise?

Corrective justice gives rise to a duty to repair when persons have harmed one another in certain ways. The phrase 'in certain ways' refers not only to the nature of the injurer's conduct (e.g. was the conduct negligent or subject to strict liability), but also to the type of harm suffered by the victim. It is plausible to think that the principle of corrective justice applies, like the law of torts, to harm of several different types. Put another way, corrective justice protects several different interests against interference by other persons. These need not be enumerated in full here, but they certainly include the interest an individual has in preserving her life and bodily security, on the one hand, and the interest she has in maintaining the physical integrity of her tangible property, on the other. The argument sketched in the preceding paragraph, to the effect that corrective and distributive justice are conceptually distinct principles that operate in separate normative spheres, has, in the case of the interest in life and bodily integrity, a certain plausibility. At least within non-consequentialist moral theory, it makes sense to think of this interest as morally fundamental, and hence as falling outside the purview of distributive justice; our physical persons belong to us from the outset, and are accordingly not subject to a social distribution of any kind. In so far as corrective justice concerns harm to the person, it appears to be both conceptually and normatively independent of distributive justice.

Matters arguably stand differently when it comes to damage to tangible property. For purposes of corrective justice, a person cannot have a cognizable interest in a particular material resource unless he has an entitlement to that resource. The law of torts necessarily concerns itself with legal entitlements, but at the level of corrective justice the entitlement must presumably be a moral one. Unless a person is morally, and not just legally, entitled to a particular thing that has been damaged, it is difficult to see how he could have the moral standing to claim compensation under what is, after all, supposed to be a principle of justice. It is plausible, moreover, to think that the moral legitimacy of an entitlement to a particular item of tangible property depends, at least in part, on its being held under a distributively just scheme of property rights. This suggests in turn that the point of corrective justice is to protect entitlements *qua* distributive shares, i.e. its point is to protect the just distribution as such. This is in fact a fairly common contemporary view of the relationship between corrective and distributive justice. Often, it is presented as an interpretation of Aristotle's original discussion of corrective and distributive justice in the *Nicomachean Ethics*.[5]

[5] Aristotle, *Nicomachean Ethics* (trans. M. Ostwald, Bobbs-Merrill, Indianapolis, Ind., 1962) Book V.

But several of the commentators defending this interpretation also suggest, either implicitly or explicitly, that this is also the correct understanding of the relationship between corrective and distributive justice. Since this view clearly regards distributive justice as conceptually and normatively prior to corrective justice, let me refer to it as the distributive priority view.

James Gordley and Wil Waluchow are two scholars who defend the distributive priority view both as an interpretation of Aristotle and, it would seem, as a correct understanding of the relationship between corrective and distributive justice. Gordley, after first noting that distributive justice is concerned with determining the shares of various goods that citizens are entitled to receive within a society, continues as follows:

> [Commutative, i.e. corrective, justice] is concerned not with sharing resources, but with preserving each citizen's share. Therefore, the party who has lost resources to another has a claim for the amount necessary to restore the original position. It is the mathematics of addition and subtraction, of balancing accounts.[6]

Waluchow's view is to the same effect. He suggests that distributive justice is concerned with 'a distribution flowing from state to citizen', whereas in corrective justice the aim 'is to correct an imbalance which has resulted from an unwarranted private transaction whose unwarranted status . . . is determined independently of corrective justice'.[7] Such transactions are unwarranted independently of corrective justice because, according to Waluchow, they involve a departure from the antecedently given just distribution:

> Corrective justice . . . is in a sense parasitic. It presupposes an independently definable just status quo; a status quo of equality in which each party has, by law, his due—his entitlements—and which owing to the actions of the defendant has been disturbed. Those actions introduce an imbalance which must be rectified.[8]

John Rawls arguably holds a similar view of the relationship between corrective and distributive justice, although it is also arguable that he holds a view closer to the one I will develop in section III.[9]

Leaving aside the question whether the distributive priority view is a plausible interpretation of Aristotle's original text,[10] the account it offers of the relationship between corrective and distributive justice is problematic in its own terms.[11] According to the distributive priority view, corrective justice is conceptually and normatively ancillary to distributive justice; the point of corrective justice, on this approach, is simply to regulate and maintain the antecedently-given just distribution.

[6] J. Gordley, 'Equality in Exchange' (1981) 69 *California L Rev.* 1587, 1589.

[7] W.J. Waluchow, 'Professor Weinrib on Corrective Justice' in S. Panagiotou, *Justice, Law and Method in Plato and Aristotle* (Academic Printing and Publishing, Edmonton, Alberta, 1987) 153, 155.

[8] Ibid. 156.

[9] Rawls, n. 4 above, 10–11.

[10] Gordley and Waluchow favour this interpretation. Opposing it are P. Benson, 'The Basis of Corrective Justice and Its Relation to Distributive Justice' (1992) 77 *Iowa L Rev.* 515, 529–49, and E.J. Weinrib, *The Idea of Private Law* (Harvard University Press, Cambridge, Mass., 1995) 76–80.

[11] S. Perry, 'The Moral Foundations of Tort Law' (1992) 77 *Iowa L Rev.* 449, 451–2.

From the Desk of
Professor Rhonda Magee Andrews

* sperry@law.upenn.edu

Won't be able to get to it before mid-November

(4) Will he review my article?

Questions for Perry:

(2) How can I frame as legitimate the effort to use Rawls as a guide for the discussion about the justice of particular laws, as opposed to systems of law? (Cite the O.P. piece...)

(3) What of my pt that one may view access to courts as a "good" or "resource" subject to distribution by the state? Any people I should cite to for that? (Haven't seen it anywhere...)

(3)

University of San Francisco School of Law
2130 Fulton Street • San Francisco, CA 94117-1080
(415) 422-5055 • Fax (415) 422-6433 • e-mail:andrewsr@usfca.edu

On that understanding, however, it is not clear that there is logical room for a principle of corrective justice that is in any way distinct from distributive justice; the latter concept is not merely ancillary to, but completely subsumed by, the former. Why not simply speak of maintaining the just distributive pattern, and leave aside misleading talk of a separate principle of justice? Corrective justice is, moreover, supposed to be concerned with rectifying departures from the antecedent pattern that were brought about by human agency operating in a certain way. By the phrase 'operating in a certain way', I mean to refer to an assessment of the agent's conduct in accordance with whatever standard of liability, fault-based or strict, that the best understanding of corrective justice determines to be applicable in the circumstances. But once the object of the exercise is taken to be the preservation of an existing distributive pattern, the limitations on achieving that object that are created, first, by the requirement that a certain standard of liability be met and, secondly, by the even more fundamental requirement that departures from the pattern must, to be rectifiable, flow from human agency, seem quite arbitrary. From the point of view of maintaining the pattern, why should it matter whether a given departure was brought about by human agency or by, say, natural disaster or the expenses associated with illness?

Gordley has argued that, on what I am calling the distributive priority view, corrective justice is in fact conceptually distinguishable from distributive justice. The idea is that a person responsible for undertaking a distribution 'would violate distributive justice if he disregarded the principle of proportionality that was supposed to guide the distribution. He would violate the arithmetic equality of corrective justice if he gave [someone] less than the amount that had been determined to be due to him.'[12] To do distributive justice, according to Gordley, a person must know what needs to be distributed, to whom, and on what basis, and then must be willing to apply the distributive principle even-handedly. To do corrective justice, '[o]ne has to be willing to pay what is owed'.[13] In other words, distributive justice involves calculating each person's share, whereas corrective justice involves handing those shares over. This would appear, however, simply to be a distinction between the deliberative and executive stages of distributive justice. It is possible, to be sure, to draw such a distinction, but it does not seem to have any theoretical significance, nor does there seem to be any basis for labelling the executive stage a separate principle of justice. It is thus not clear how this move is supposed to show that corrective justice is, after all, conceptually distinct from distributive justice.

If, moreover, we follow Gordley's suggestion and stipulatively define corrective justice as the executive stage of distributive justice, this understanding seems quite removed from corrective justice as traditionally understood. To see this, we need only revisit our earlier point about the arbitrariness, on the distributive priority view, of singling out distribution-preserving moves that are necessitated by human agency.

[12] J. Gordley, 'Tort Law in the Aristotelian Tradition' in D.G. Owen, *Philosophical Foundations of Tort Law* (Oxford University Press, Oxford, 1995) 131, 136.

[13] Ibid.

The executive stage of distributive justice would presumably include not just distribution-preserving moves of this kind, but also all initial allocations under the appropriate distributive scheme. This by itself goes well beyond the traditional understanding of corrective justice. In addition, the executive stage would presumably also include all subsequently required distribution-preserving moves, including those that were needed because, e.g., someone had suffered a loss due to natural disaster or disease. There does not appear to be any principled basis for singling out a more limited executive principle that applies only to deviations from the existing distribution that came about as a result of a human agent falling below a certain standard of liability. Traditionally, however, it is only cases of the latter sort that have been regarded as falling within the province of corrective justice.

On the point that the effects of natural events on distributive justice seem, on the distributive priority view, to be indistinguishable in principle from corrective justice, Gordley makes two arguments in response. The first takes as its starting-point the claim that the function of private property is, in the Aristotelian tradition, to provide an incentive to work and to prevent quarrels. Even if it were possible to distinguish chance gains and losses from those that were the result of labour and care, 'the attempt might lead to so many charges of arbitrariness as to give rise to the quarrels that a system of private property is supposed to prevent'.[14] Note first that this argument about the effect that natural events should or should not have on distributive justice depends on a more general claim about the function of private property. I discuss that claim below, where I suggest that it complicates our understanding of distributive justice in such a way as to render problematic the idea that corrective justice preserves antecedently-specified distributions. For now I will simply point out that it seems implausible to suppose that attributing this function to private property entails that distributive justice is impervious to all disastrous natural events. If any readjustments to a distributive pattern are ever required because, say, an unpredictably severe storm destroyed many people's property, those readjustments will fall under Gordley's definition of corrective justice (i.e. corrective justice understood as the executive stage of distributive justice). For the reasons already given, this seems problematic.

A similar point applies to Gordley's second response to the argument that the effect of natural events on distributive justice will, on the distributive priority view, be indistinguishable in principle from corrective justice. This response is that, if everyone were fully compensated when his property was destroyed through bad luck, people would be more willing than they should be to put their property at risk. Again, however, this argument does not establish that disastrous natural events should never affect distributive justice, since not all such events give rise to moral hazard problems. If a readjustment to a distribution is ever required because of a natural event—the unpredictably severe storm mentioned earlier, for example—that readjustment will, as already noted, fall under Gordley's definition of corrective justice. In addition,

[14] Ibid. 136–7.

Gordley's two responses to the disastrous-natural-event problem both seem misplaced, for the following reason. Both attempt to show that, for essentially practical reasons, natural events should not have any effect on distributive justice. If this claim is meant to be a generalization completely without exceptions, it seems highly implausible. Even if it were always true, however, that would still not address the conceptual difficulty that there does not seem to be anything special, on the distributive priority view, about corrective justice as traditionally understood (i.e. a principle that imposes a duty of repair on human agents who cause others losses). Even if, for practical reasons, natural events never affect allocations under distributive justice, the characterization of corrective justice as the executive stage of distributive justice still includes the possibility of such readjustments; for that reason it is, conceptually speaking, far too broad.

There are other problems with the distributive priority view in adddition to those just enumerated. Assume for the moment that distributive justice requires what Nozick calls a simple patterned distribution of goods, i.e. a more or less static distribution based on a fixed formula such as, 'to each in equal shares', 'to each in accordance with his moral virtue', etc.[15] Aristotle's discussion of these matters in the *Nicomachean Ethics* is plausibly interpreted as envisaging distributive justice as taking very much this form.[16] For the sake of simplicity, assume further that the relevant pattern is an equal distribution of material resources, that the society in question consists of four persons, and that each person has ten units of goods.[17] Suppose first that A takes four of B's units. The initial pattern can be restored, and equality reinstated, by taking those same four units (or perhaps some other four of equal quality) from A and giving them to B. Restitutionary cases of this kind appear, in fact, to be Aristotle's paradigm of corrective justice: '[a]s though there were a line divided into two unequal parts, [the judge] takes away the amount by which the larger part is greater than half the line and adds it to the smaller'.[18] It is with respect to such cases, moreover, that the distributive priority view seems to have most plausibility.

Suppose next that, instead of taking four of B's units, A causes their destruction. Assuming that the appropriate standard of liability applies to A's conduct, corrective justice would presumably require A to compensate B by giving her four units. Doing this will not, however, restore the original equal distribution. Equality can only be

[15] R. Nozick, *Anarchy, State, and Utopia* (Basic Books, New York, 1974) 155–60.

[16] I am neither advocating nor disavowing this interpretation of Aristotle, and nothing in my argument turns on whether or not it is correct. As we shall see later, Gordley's claim that the function of private property 'in the Aristotelian tradition' is to provide incentives and prevent quarrels is most plausibly understood as a denial that distributive justice should be understood in terms of simple patterned distributions. The fact remains that Aristotle is plausibly interpreted in this way, and many commentators have so interpreted him. Furthermore, many theorists discuss the theoretical question of the relationship between corrective and distributive justice on the assumption that distributive justice can be understood by reference to simple patterning. See, e.g., L. Alexander, 'Causation and Corrective Justice: Does Tort Law Make Sense?' (1987) 6 *Law & Phil.* 1, 6–7. Much of Nozick's critical discussion of distributive justice also makes this assumption, at least if we are to judge by his examples: Nozick, n. 15 above, 155–64. Thus, although I ultimately reject this understanding of distributive justice, there is reason to give it serious consideration.

[17] The example is taken from Alexander, n. 16 above, 6–7.

[18] Aristotle, n. 5 above, 1132a25–27.

restored if B receives one unit from each of the others in the society, thereby constituting a new distribution of nine units each.[19] There are a couple of points to be noted here. The first, which is specific to the Aristotelian restitutionary understanding of corrective justice, is that it is not clear how that approach can be extended to cover cases involving damage to or destruction of property. Quite apart from the normative difficulties that arise in trying to justify a duty to repair on the basis of restitutionary principles,[20] it is far from evident what the analogue of restitution would be in a case like this. In the example discussed in the preceding paragraph, A gained four units and B lost four. Corrective justice, on the restitutionary model, in effect required A to give the four units back; this wiped out both A's gain and B's loss and, in the process, restored the original pattern of distribution. In the case in which A destroys rather than takes four of B's units, however, the idea of giving something back seems inapplicable. A may well have incurred a gain in destroying B's units—perhaps he burned them to keep himself warm—but that gain is logically distinct from B's loss. Corrective justice, of course, focuses on the loss rather than on the gain. On a restitutionary model, however, it is not obvious why that should be so.

The second and more important point that is illustrated by the example of A destroying four of B's units pertains to the distributive priority view in general, and not just the Aristotelian restitutionary variant. The concern here is with the fact that if A compensates B for her loss, the original equal distribution is not thereby restored. In general, doing corrective justice between particular persons will not reinstate a formerly existing distributive pattern, and it might well have the effect of introducing new distributive distortions. (To take an example of Jules Coleman's, imagine that a very poor person negligently drives his ancient heap into the luxury vehicle of an extremely wealthy person, and that the former is then obligated to compensate the latter.[21]) The reason that doing corrective justice will not restore a distributive pattern is that the maintenance of such a pattern is a global problem, the solution to which requires taking account of the shares of all persons within the relevant group. But corrective justice rectifies loss on a local scale, between two persons. As a general matter, the local mechanism cannot respond satisfactorily to the global problem. Moreover, this deficiency of process reflects a deeper difficulty. The reasons for action arising from distributive justice are agent-general: they pertain to all persons within society (or to society as a whole). Corrective justice, on the other hand, is most plausibly thought to create agent-relative reasons for action: it gives the injurer alone a reason to compensate the victim.[22] For both these reasons—the local nature of corrective justice versus the global requirements of distributive justice, on the one hand, and the different structures of practical reasoning that pertain to each of the two forms of justice, on the other—corrective justice cannot plausibly be regarded as having the function of maintaining a just distribution of material resources.

[19] Cf. Alexander, n. 16 above, 6–7.

[20] Cf. Perry, n. 11 above, 452–61.

[21] Coleman, n. 3 above, 304.

[22] Cf. S.R. Perry, 'Comment on Coleman: Corrective Justice' (1992) 67 *Indiana LJ* 381, 389–90, 396–400; Coleman, n. 3 above, 319, 374.

Gordley offers a further defence of the distributive priority view, which takes issue with the premise that distributive justice should be understood in terms of simple patterned distributions of resources. According to Gordley, the Aristotelian tradition rejected this premise:

> Private property was supposed to prevent quarrels and to provide incentives to work. Consequently, a citizen cannot demand more resources in a democracy simply because he has less than someone else or in an aristocracy simply because he has the same amount as someone less virtuous. To obtain the advantages of a system of private property, a society will have to tolerate some deviations from the principle of distributive justice it regards as ideal.[23]

In assessing this defence of the distributive priority view, it is important to ask how seriously we should take Gordley's claim that 'a society will have to tolerate some deviations from the principle of distributive justice it regards as ideal'. On the most straightforward reading of this statement, Gordley is suggesting that the theoretical ideal of distributive justice is indeed a simple patterned distribution of resources, but that for various pragmatic reasons which are external to distributive justice this ideal cannot, and indeed should not, be attained in practice. If that is Gordley's argument, however, it is insufficient to save the distributive priority view. The various criticisms of that view that were offered in the preceding paragraphs were conceptual in nature, meaning they were offered precisely at the level of ideal theory. The general charge against the distributive priority view to which those criticisms point is that corrective justice cannot plausibly be understood as having the function of preserving just distributions of resources, if just distributions are taken to be simple patterned distributions. It is no answer to this charge to say that, even though distributive justice ideally calls for simple patterned distributions, these cannot be achieved in practice. Nor is it an answer to say that there are good moral reasons why such patterns should not be achieved—the need to create incentives, avoid quarrels, and so on—if those reasons are external to the theory of distributive justice.

Perhaps, then, Gordley should be understood as arguing, in the above-quoted passage, that distributive justice does not call for simple patterned distributions of resources even at the level of ideal theory. He is suggesting, rather, that because distributive justice must take account internally of such factors as the need to avoid quarrels and give people incentives to work, it must be conceived dynamically rather than statically. Although the particular factors of avoiding quarrels and creating incentives may not be the most important ones in a more complex conception of distributive justice—the desirability of permitting market exchanges seems much more significant, for example—the general claim that distributive justice is complex in this way is a very plausible one.

The most influential contemporary theories of distributive justice are dynamic rather than static. John Rawls, for example, explicitly rejects the idea of simple patterning, which he calls the allocative conception of justice.[24] Rawls' own theory takes distributive justice to be, within certain limits, a matter of pure procedural justice.

[23] Gordley, n. 12 above, 136. [24] Rawls, n. 4 above, 88.

This means that if certain institutions such as competitive markets, appropriate forms of taxation, and a reasonable social minimum are in place, and if together those institutions tend over time to satisfy the difference principle, then any particular distributive state that happens to emerge at a given point in time is acceptable.[25] There is no independent criterion for assessing the acceptability of such distributive states. Ronald Dworkin's theory of distributive justice holds that an equal share of resources should be devoted to the lives of each person, but it similarly rejects the idea that equality of resources is measured, in the manner of simple patterning, at particular moments of time.[26] Rather it is measured diachronically, across entire lives and against the background of such institutions as a free market and progressive taxation. Equality of resources is thus understood abstractly, in a way that is supposed to be unaffected by a person's talents but that takes account of choices that affect which resources are available to oneself and to others. These include choice of occupation, choice of how hard to work, choice of which risks to run, and choice of with whom to contract and on what terms. Robert Nozick's libertarian entitlement theory is very different from the egalitarian theories of Rawls and Dworkin, but by determining the legitimacy of entitlements on a purely historical basis it, too, embraces a dynamic rather than a static conception of justice in holdings.[27]

In so far as Gordley is saying that distributive justice must be understood dynamically rather than statically, he is undoubtedly correct. But that does not help his defence of the distributive priority view, since on a dynamic understanding of distributive justice it is no longer clear what it means to say that the point of corrective justice is to preserve a just distribution. The Rawlsian and Dworkinian conceptions of distributive justice operate through institutions and over time. Simple patterning is concerned directly with the holdings of individuals as these exist at particular moments in time. Let me call such patterns of holdings momentary distributive states. The Rawlsian and Dworkinian theories are properly called patterned, but the patterns are abstract and involve general tendencies that develop through time. So far as momentary distributive states are concerned, it is clear that both the Rawlsian and Dworkinian theories give rise to a great deal of indeterminacy; dynamic conceptions of distributive justice like these are compatible with many different such states.[28] While there are problems with the distributive priority view even as applied to simple patterning, we at least have some understanding of what it means to preserve or restore a momentary distributive state. What does it mean, though, to say that when an individual injurer complies with his duty to repair, this helps to preserve the abstract patterns associated with Dworkin's equality of resources or Rawls' difference principle? It is perhaps possible that content can be given to this notion, but surely the onus in this regard is on the person who wishes to defend the idea that the distributive priority view can be applied to a dynamic conception of distributive justice.

[25] Rawls, n. 4 above, 86–8.

[26] R. Dworkin, 'What is Equality? Part 2: Equality of Resources' (1981) 10 *Philosophy and Public Affairs* 283, 304–7.

[27] Nozick, n. 15 above, 150–3.

[28] Cf. Dworkin, n. 26 above, 334.

It is not enough to assert that the problems the distributive priority view faces on a simple patterned theory do not matter because distributive justice involves abstract patterns rather than simple ones. This is the starting-point for theorizing, not the end-point.

As for the Nozickian entitlement theory, it does not involve patterning of any kind, simple or abstract. Corrective justice is, in effect, built into the theory through Nozick's principles of rectification and justice in transfer. Since patterning plays no role in the theory it is not really about distributive justice at all, at least as that notion has traditionally been understood. (Nozick himself prefers the term 'justice in holdings'.) One is tempted to say that, on the entitlement theory, corrective justice comprises, together with the principle of justice in acquisition, all the justice there is. Such a view of justice in holdings is not likely to appeal to an Aristotelian like Gordley, but the distributive priority view clearly has no purchase on the entitlement theory in any event. If there is no patterning, then the idea of preserving or maintaining a pattern simply has no application. To put the point more bluntly, if there is no distributive justice, how can it take priority over anything?

There is one final point I would like to make about the distributive priority view, before moving on. As I mentioned at the beginning of this section, we tend to think of corrective justice as a general principle that protects a number of different interests against interference by other persons. In particular, corrective justice protects life and bodily security, on the one hand, and tangible property, on the other. Of these two interests, only tangible property is plausibly thought to be subject to distributive justice. Since the basic claim of the distributive priority view is that the point of corrective justice is to preserve just distributions, it faces a dilemma. Either it must say, in the face of strong intuitions to the contrary, that life and bodily integrity are, after all, subject to distributive justice. Or it must say, again contrary to strong intuitions, that corrective justice is not a single general principle but two, one of which protects the fundamental interest in life and bodily security, and the other of which protects just distributions of material resources.

II

In section III I will argue that, if we accept the premise that distributive justice is best understood dynamically rather than statically, corrective justice should be conceived as an independent moral principle that operates within the context of distributive justice, but not as a part of it. First, however, I would like to examine a different attempt to show that the moral duty of repair is, properly understood, a matter of distributive justice. The distributive priority view characterizes corrective justice as an instrument for preserving just distributions and, therefore, as a principle ancillary to distributive justice. In fact, a better characterization of that view would be that it tries to do away with the concept of corrective justice altogether, arguing that the moral duty to repair can be explained entirely in distributive terms. Ronald Dworkin has also attempted to explain the moral duty to repair in distributive terms.[29] The attempt is interesting for a couple of reasons. First, it explicitly begins with a dynamic conception of distributive justice which is, taken on its own terms, quite plausible and attractive. This is the theory of equality of resources that was sketched in the preceding section. Secondly, it looks upon the duty of repair not as a means for preserving or restoring an antecedently-given, determinate distribution of holdings—this being, of course, the approach of the distributive priority view—but rather as a means for refining or making concrete a set of initially abstract distributive entitlements.

Dworkin begins by considering situations in which there is a conflict between what he calls abstract rights in property. An example would be a dispute between A and B over their respective rights to use their neighbouring apartments as they wish: A wants to play his trumpet and B wants to study algebra. Another would involve a conflict between A's right to run a train on his land at the speed that he chooses and B's right to plant corn on his adjoining land, when sparks from the speeding train might ignite and burn the corn. Dworkin makes the assumption that A and B have roughly equal wealth in both the abstract sense of the theory of equality of resources, which is measured across entire lives, and the more limited sense of equal current holdings.[30] He also assumes that 'neither is handicapped or otherwise has special needs or requirements'.[31] Dworkin states that when A's and B's abstract rights conflict they must each act as if the concrete rights that they both cannot exercise had not yet been distributed between them, and that they must distribute these themselves as best they can, 'in the way equality of resources commends'.[32] If compromise is not possible then each must act 'so as to minimize the inequality of the distribution [they] achieve, and this means so that the loser loses less'.[33] Dworkin maintains that this principle of comparative harm calls for market-simulating behaviour, since, given the assumption of roughly equal wealth, this will provide a plausible measure of the relative respective importance to A and B of their two conflicting activities. Thus in the trumpet/algebra situation, for example, the conflict should be resolved in an all-or-nothing way by asking whether A would pay more for B to stop playing his trumpet than B would pay for the opportunity to play it.

Dworkin is thus looking at harmful interactions mainly from the point of view of a forward-looking distribution of rights, but it is clear that he regards the backward-looking moral and legal treatment of a loss as a question to be decided in light of how the parties ought to have applied the comparative harm principle. If A would not have paid as much for the opportunity to inflict the loss (or to impose the risk of the loss occurring) as B would have paid to engage in his activities unimpeded, then A has a moral duty of repair and B a correlative moral right. For the most part I shall only be considering here such criticisms of Dworkin's theory that call into question this explication of the duty of repair, although I shall also make incidental note of various ways in which the theory does not seem to provide a very good fit with the actual doctrines of tort law.

[29] R. Dworkin, *Law's Empire* (Harvard University Press, Cambridge, Mass., 1986) 276–312.
[30] Ibid. 302, 305. [31] Ibid. 302. [32] Ibid. [33] Ibid. 303.

The first point to be noticed is that Dworkin does not adequately take account of our strong pre-theoretical conviction that, absent special circumstances such as contributory fault or damages that are too remote, a moral duty of repair should make the victim whole and not just provide partial compensation. (This conviction, it should be noted, has always been reflected in the substantive doctrines of the law of torts.) Dworkin acknowledges that his approach seems to call for compromise among citizens, and remarks at one point that it is only 'practical circumstances' that force all-or-nothing decisions on citizens acting for themselves.[34] But if backward-looking allocations of loss ought to coincide with what citizens should have decided on a forward-looking basis, as Dworkin is apparently assuming, then he is simply ignoring our sense that a moral duty of repair ought to be an all-or-nothing affair. He is ignoring, that is to say, our sense that in ordinary circumstances either the plaintiff has a right to recover his entire loss or else the defendant does not have to pay anything. Moreover, whatever practical circumstances may force on citizens deciding these issues for themselves on a forward-looking basis, there does not seem to be any reason why judges, dealing with disputes *ex post facto*, cannot apportion a loss between plaintiff and defendant in such a way as to mirror the compromise that Dworkin says the parties should have reached if it had been practicable, and that better accords with the general principles of distributive justice to which he is ultimately appealing.

A second, related criticism of Dworkin's theory concerns the fact that distributive justice might not be best served by treating particular instances of conflicting rights as discrete cases to be considered in isolation from another. Dworkin recognizes that, ideally, individual decisions about the distribution of concrete rights should, on his approach, be treated as part of a continuing series of linked decisions that can be taken into account in a 'moral ledger'.[35] Once again, however, this runs counter to a strong pre-theoretical conviction that moral (and therefore legal) rights of repair should not directly depend on what else has transpired or will transpire between the parties, and that particular cases therefore ought to be treated in isolation from one another, at least so far as the determination of liability is concerned. (Set-off in the determination of damages is, of course, another matter.)

It is worth noting that the practical difficulties of treating individual decisions as linked do not, unlike the practical difficulties that are involved in allocating losses on an all-or-nothing basis, appear to be ones that can be overcome in the judicial context, since courts are presumably in no better a position than citizens to keep ongoing moral ledgers. (This is not to deny, of course, that on Dworkin's view they should nevertheless make the attempt.) Dworkin responds to the general impracticability of keeping ledgers by appealing to the hypothesis that 'if everyone treats [decisions that affect others generally, or a stranger only once] as isolated cases, this will work out roughly fairly for everyone in the long run'.[36] Such a hypothesis seems most plausible in situations involving regularly occurring, low-level nuisances of the sort represented by Dworkin's example of trumpet-playing versus algebra-studying.

[34] Ibid. 311. [35] Ibid. 305–6. [36] Ibid. 306.

However, as a generalization about the sorts of disputes that are dealt with by the law of torts as a whole, it is almost certainly untrue. For example, serious personal injuries, unlike low-level nuisances, occur randomly and relatively infrequently, so that any distributive injustice that results from the legal treatment of a single accident considered in isolation is unlikely to be offset, for the individual affected, by some future judgment in his favour. This aspect of Dworkin's theory is thus doubly problematic. First, in principle the theory calls for a linking of cases, where linking seems morally suspect in itself. Secondly, as a practical matter, the law of torts is incapable either of creating such links or mimicking their effects (by means, for example, of Dworkin's proposed hypothesis that everything will work out in the long run). This suggests that tort law is not a very efficient instrument for accomplishing the goal of refining or perfecting a scheme of distributive justice.

A third criticism of Dworkin's theory of moral rights and duties of repair focuses on the initial assumption that persons who find themselves in a situation requiring a decision about the distribution of concrete rights have roughly equal wealth, where neither is handicapped or otherwise has special requirements. Dworkin recognizes that this assumption will often not hold, but argues that because equality of resources is an abstract conception of distributive justice—i.e. it applies over lifetimes rather than simply looking to momentary distributive states—we should generally act on the assumption that people have equal resources in the abstract sense unless we have good reason to think this is not true. Recall, however, that Dworkin assumes that the parties have equal wealth both in the abstract sense and also in the sense of current holdings. The assumption that the parties have roughly equal current wealth would arguably yield information that is relevant and useful in the settlement of disputes. This is because what seems to be more appropriately compared in cases like that of the trumpet-player and the algebra-studier is the relative potential damage to the parties' specific conflicting projects, rather than the relative potential damage to their entire life-plans. Given an assumption of equal current wealth, knowing whether the trumpet-player would pay more to the algebra-studier or vice versa presumably tells us something about the relative strengths of their preferences for engaging in these particular activities, and that information is arguably relevant to settling the immediate dispute between them.

Equality of resources in the abstract sense, as measured over lifetimes, is the distributively ideal state of affairs within Dworkin's theory. The assumption that such a state of affairs obtains between two given persons is thus perhaps defensible,[37] at least in the absence of any evidence to the contrary. The same cannot be said, however, for the assumption of equal current holdings. Not only is it not a normative ideal of the theory that current holdings should be equal, but the expectation within the theory is very much to the contrary. Actual holdings are supposed to reflect various life-

[37] This is, however, subject to the argument of section III below, where I suggest that, on a plausible dynamic conception of distributive justice such as equality of resources, it may not even make sense to say of individual holdings that they embody distributive imbalances. Distributive disparities are, rather, necessarily systemic in character.

choices, which in the usual course of affairs will lead to different and possibly quite disparate levels of wealth among persons. In addition, the fact that two persons do or do not have equal current wealth is usually relatively easy to ascertain, at least as compared to the assumption of equal wealth in the abstract sense. There is thus neither a normative basis nor, ordinarily, an empirical one, for assuming of any two persons that they are even roughly equally wealthy. The assumption of equal current wealth, although it is arguably attractive because of what it reveals about the parties' preferences, is not warranted under Dworkin's theory and should not be made. According to the theory, persons' preferences should be reflected in their actual life choices and, ultimately, in the extent of their individual holdings. Unwarranted assumptions about the extent of their holdings should not be used to work backwards in order to ascertain their preferences.

Of the two assumptions we have been discussing, then, it is only the assumption of equal wealth in the abstract sense that can appropriately be made under Dworkin's theory. Such an assumption suggests, however, that the relevant conflict is one between entire life plans rather than immediate projects. Under that assumption, it does not matter that at the time of the simulated bargain the parties have unequal amounts of money in their pockets. The upshot is that the market simulation test might well penalize the algebra-studier, say, because he chose to devote his life to the not particularly lucrative career of a mathematics teacher. Suppose that, as a result of that decision, he is now less wealthy than the trumpet-player, who became a commercially successful jazz musician. Why should the resolution of the present dispute turn in any way on these past career decisions? It was presumably in order to avoid undesirable wealth effects of this kind that Dworkin assumed not just that the parties had equal resources in the abstract sense, but also that they had roughly equal funds at their disposal at the time of the simulated bargain. But an assumption of equal current wealth is, as we have seen, inappropriate under Dworkin's theory. The correct assumption, which is that the parties have equal resources only in the abstract sense, will inevitably create wealth effects of just this kind.

It is also important to remember that the assumption of equal wealth is, in the end, just an assumption. In particular circumstances, equality of wealth even in the abstract sense can be shown not to hold. Dworkin acknowledges that the appropriate distribution of concrete rights is in principle affected by the fact that one party has more than he should have, or that the other party has less than she should have, under the theory of equality of resources.[38] But he does not seem entirely comfortable with this conclusion when he states that 'it seems unjust that compensation to a victim should depend on the relative wealth of the actor, if for no other reason than the difficulty that would pose to someone anxious to insure against injury on sensible terms'.[39] The injustice in fact extends further than this observation suggests, since it

[38] Ibid. 305. Dworkin leaves open the question of what exactly citizens should do in situations of clear distributive injustice: ibid. 446, nn. 15, 18.

[39] Ibid. 308.

is highly implausible to think that, in principle, the manner in which I ought to act toward others in my daily life is in any way a function of my or their wealth. How I treat others should remain constant even against a range of different possible background schemes of distributive justice and, indeed, at least in certain sorts of cases, it should transcend membership in any particular political community. These intuitions are especially strong where personal injury is concerned. It surely cannot be correct that the degree of risk of death or bodily harm that I can permissibly impose on another person depends in any way on the wealth of either of us.

Dworkin does say that his general approach must be qualified to take account of individual rights that protect fundamental interests,[40] and at one point he suggests this would mean that 'threats to life' should not be dealt with in terms of the comparative harm principle.[41] However, he does not say how he thinks losses associated with such threats should then be handled. Differential treatment of property damage and personal injury cases would seem to be consistent with his assertion elsewhere that '[though a person's physical and mental] powers are resources, they should not be considered resources whose ownership is to be determined through politics in accordance with some interpretation of equality of resources'.[42] Thus while Dworkin regards the existence of a disability as a factor that should be taken into account in the distribution of resources, he does not think that distributive justice involves trying to make people equal in physical and mental terms: '[t]he problem is, rather, one of determining how far the ownership of independent material resources should be affected by differences that exist in physical and mental powers, and the response of our theory [of distributive justice] should speak in that vocabulary'.[43] This is surely correct, but the upshot would seem to be that an individual's interest in life and bodily integrity should not be treated as an 'abstract property right' of the sort with which Dworkin's theory of tort law primarily concerns itself. This suggests in turn, as does Dworkin's rather cryptic observation concerning threats to life, that he requires a separate account of moral (and therefore legal) rights and duties of repair where injury to the person is at issue.

The question that then arises is whether a moral theory that views rights and duties of repair as based on two distinct principles, one of which applies to the interest in life and bodily security and the other of which applies to interests in property, is a satisfactory one. (As was mentioned at the end of the preceding section, a similar difficulty seems to arise for the distributive priority view.) For the most part tort law itself does not determine liability differently in property and personal injury cases, and it seems implausible to think that such a distinction has any significant place in the general moral theory of rights and duties of repair. This is an issue to which I return in section III, where I argue that the most appropriate way to develop a unified general theory of corrective justice is to take the principle of repair that applies in personal injury cases as one's starting-point, and then inquire whether that principle can be extended to cases of property damage.

[40] Ibid. 307. [41] Ibid. 309. [42] Dworkin, n. 26 above, 301. [43] Ibid.

One final series of observations about Dworkin's assumption of equal wealth is in order here. As was mentioned earlier, Dworkin says that persons who have to distribute concrete rights between themselves should ordinarily assume, for practical reasons, that they each have available roughly equal resources for the pursuit of their respective projects in life. Whatever practicality may demand in everyday life, however, if Dworkin's account of rights and duties of repair were correct then there would be no reason why courts, when required in tort actions to distribute actual losses *ex post*, should not make an effort to ascertain the relative wealth of the litigants and then take that information into account, in the determination of both liability and the measure of damages, to try to realize as adequately as possible the abstract ideal of equality of resources. In fact the courts generally consistently refuse, as a matter of principle, to try to do anything like this. So far as plaintiffs are concerned, damages are assessed on the basis of actual losses suffered, without reference to whether the victim has more or less than he should have under an appropriate conception of distributive justice. So far as defendants are concerned, the law adopts objective standards, such as the standard of the reasonable person, the whole point of which is to make a great deal of specific information about the defendant irrelevant in principle. At least when it comes to information about wealth, however, the thrust of Dworkin's theory is exactly the opposite. In principle, the determination of liablity depends on specific facts about the relative holdings of the parties, and if that information is available it should, according to the theory, be employed. The theory only manages to approximate the courts' actual practices by relying on epistemic opacity, in the form of the the assumption of equal wealth. But something seems to have gone seriously wrong when such a wide gap between theory and practice has to be bridged in that manner.

III

In section I, I argued that the moral duty to repair cannot be understood as a means to preserve or maintain an antecedently-given, determinate scheme of distributive justice. In section II I argued that that duty cannot be understood as a means to refine or perfect an abstract and partially indeterminate scheme of distributive justice. The more general conclusion to which these arguments point is that a moral duty to repair cannot be justified in distributive terms. I have not fully established that conclusion, however, because I have not offered a comprehensive argument that a duty to repair cannot be justified within a dynamic conception of distributive justice. I have argued that Dworkin's particular attempt to offer such a justification, within the context of his own theory of equality of resources, does not succeed. I have also suggested that someone who wishes to combine the distributive priority view with a dynamic conception of distributive justice bears the onus of showing that this can be done. But I have not presented a general argument showing that such a combination is impossible, nor will I attempt to do so now. Instead, I will offer a general characterization of the principle of corrective justice—a characterization that is meant to apply to a number of more specific theories that can be found in the literature—and argue that corrective justice thus conceived is appropriately viewed as complementary to, although conceptually independent of, distributive justice. As we will see, this can only be true if distributive justice is understood in dynamic rather than in static terms, since no plausible conception of corrective justice can be reconciled with simple distributive patterning. The proper conclusion to be drawn from this is, so much the worse for simple patterning.

In what follows I will, in discussing abstractly patterned conceptions of distributive justice, leave aside Nozick's entitlement theory. The reason for doing so is that the entitlement theory is not, as was noted in section I, best conceived as an account of distributive justice to begin with. It is, in effect, a theory of corrective justice to which a principle of justice in acquisition has been appended. Dworkin and the distributive priority theorists might be described as attempting to get rid of the notion of corrective justice or, if not going quite that far, as at least attempting to subsume it, normatively and conceptually, within distributive justice. It is only a slight exaggeration to say that Nozick wants to do the reverse; he is attempting either to get rid of the notion of distributive justice or else to subsume it, normatively and conceptually, within corrective justice. I of course do not claim to have established that a theory of distributive justice in the strict sense—i.e. a theory based on simple or abstract patterning—is the correct theory of justice in holdings. But it is only on that assumption that the problem with which I am concerned in this essay is a genuine problem.

According to the general characterization I have in mind, then, corrective justice protects legitimate entitlements in tangible property, but it does not do so because such entitlements are distributively just shares. Nor does it do so in order either to preserve or to refine the distributive scheme itself. Rather, corrective justice protects legitimate entitlements simply because they are legitimate. It is perfectly true that, on most theories of private property (although not on the entitlement theory), considerations of distributive justice figure in the justification of entitlements to material resources. On the view of corrective justice I am sketching, however, once the moral legitimacy of an entitlement has been established, the justificatory role of distributive justice is no longer of central concern. The concern is rather this. Damage to a tangible object can harm someone who possesses or uses the object, and if the possessor or user has a morally legitimate entitlement to it then the harm is of moral significance. The moral focus of corrective justice is not on background distributive considerations but rather on harm to another person.

One might try to develop a general account of corrective justice along the lines suggested in the preceding paragraph in either of two different ways. One of these attempts to derive corrective justice from the concept of property, while the other begins with an independent moral principle of repair and tries to show why that principle is applicable to property interests. The first, property-based approach to corrective justice has sometimes been adopted by libertarians. Richard Epstein, for example, at one time argued that a moral duty to repair, based on a standard of strict liability, is directly entailed by the concept of property.[44] This is implausible, if only because there does not seem to be any contradiction in the idea of a property interest that is protected by a negligence standard or, for that matter, that is not protected by any liability rule at all. Epstein has also put forward a conceptual/normative argument that in effect makes the following two claims. First, a right of restitution is inherent in the concept of property and, secondly, a moral duty of repair is derivable from the right of restitution.[45] The first of these claims is plausible,[46] but, as I have argued elsewhere,[47] the second is not. The basic problem with the second step of the argument is that no analogue of restitution seems to apply when the gainer's gain is not equal to the loser's loss. (As we saw in section I, this is the same problem that is encountered by the Aristotelian restitutionary model of corrective justice.) There is in any event a more plausible libertarian conception of corrective justice, which begins not with the concept of property in the strict sense but rather with the looser notion of self-ownership.[48]

This brings us to the second possibility, which takes an independent moral principle of repair as its starting-point and tries to show why that principle is applicable to property interests. ('Independent' here means independent of distributive justice.) Since the underlying concern of such a theory is harm to other persons, let me call this the harm-based view of corrective justice. Particular theories of corrective justice that embody or are consistent with this view tend to invoke some conception of responsibility for the outcomes of one's actions. Jules Coleman equates such responsibility with a conception of objective fault.[49] The libertarian theory mentioned at the end of the preceding paragraph, which takes the notion of self-ownership as its starting-point, equates responsibility for outcomes with causation. I have argued

[44] R.A. Epstein, 'Causation and Corrective Justice: A Reply to Two Critics' (1979) 8 *Journal of Legal Studies* 477, 500–1. Notice that, if corrective justice is to be a general principle that applies to more than one interest and, in particular, to the interest in life and bodily security as well as to the interest in tangible property, this position requires that the libertarian language of self-ownership be taken more or less literally. Self-ownership must be construed as a property right identical in its incidents to the right of ownership one can have in a material resource. Epstein has at times seemed willing to bite this particular bullet. See ibid. 500. However, it is possible to characterize self-ownership somewhat more plausibly as a set of rights that in a loose sense are property-like and that give rise, because no one else besides me 'owns' my person and my powers, to a general right to liberty. This general right to liberty then serves as the basis for deriving property rights in the strict sense. See G.A. Cohen, *Self-Ownership, Freedom, and Equality* (Cambridge University Press, Cambridge, 1995), 69–89, 112–14; S.R. Perry, 'Libertarianism, Entitlement, and Responsibility' (1997) 26 *Philosophy and Public Affairs* 351, 358–63.

[45] R.A. Epstein, *Takings: Private Property and the Power of Eminent Domain* (Harvard University Press, Cambridge, Mass., 1985) 38.

[46] Cf. A.M. Honoré, 'Ownership' in A.G. Guest, *Oxford Essays in Jurisprudence* (1st series, Oxford University Press, Oxford, 1961) 107, 114.

[47] Perry, n. 11 above, 452–61.

[48] On the looser sense of self-ownership, see n. 44 above. On the more plausible libertarian conception of corrective justice, see Perry, n. 44 above, 363–73.

[49] Coleman, n. 3 above, 345–7, 486 n. 17. More recently, Coleman has argued that the concept of responsibility underlying corrective justice is 'political' in nature: J. Coleman and A. Ripstein, 'Mischief and Misfortune' (1995) 41 *McGill LJ* 91. This understanding of corrective justice, unlike the view presented in *Risks and Wrongs*, is in danger of collapsing into the distributive priority view. See S.R. Perry, 'The Distributive Turn: Mischief, Misfortune, and Tort Law' in B. Bix (ed.), *Analyzing Law: New Essays in Legal Theory* (Oxford University Press, Oxford, 1998) 141. Coleman responds in J.L. Coleman, 'Second Thoughts and Other First Impressions' in B. Bix (ed.), *Analyzing Law* 301–16.

elsewhere that the basis of this form of reponsibility is the fact that an outcome was both foreseeable and avoidable.[50] It would not, however, be to the present purpose to enter into the details of this debate. Instead, let me try to bring out some general points about the moral duty of repair by focusing on the paradigm case of intentional harm to the person.

If, intentionally and without justification, I cause you personal injury, I assume most people will agree that I have a moral duty to compensate you for the harm. Whatever the precise nature of the underlying responsibility here may be, notice that this duty is independent of distributive justice. If your interest in life and bodily integrity is properly called an entitlement, it is not an entitlement that is subject to distributive justice. Nor is my duty to compensate you sensitive to how wealthy I am.[51] This is enough to establish that there is an independent moral principle giving rise to an agent-relative duty of repair. The issue then becomes how general is this principle. There are two separate questions that arise in this regard. First, to what other conduct, besides intentional wrongdoing, can the duty be extended? Can it be extended, for example, to advertent negligence, inadvertent negligence, or non-faulty forms of conduct that would require a standard of strict liability? Secondly, to what other interests, besides the interest in life and bodily integrity, can the duty be extended? In the present context, it is the second of these questions that is of concern.

The main reason that personal injury constitutes harm is that it interferes with personal autonomy. It interferes, that is to say, with the set of opportunities and options from which one is able to choose what to do in one's life.[52] Interference with autonomy is not the only way that personal injury can adversely affect someone, of course; pain and suffering, for example, are separate types of harm. But there is no doubt that interference with autonomy is an exceptionally important category of harm, and the independent principle of repair clearly offers redress for having suffered it in inappropriate ways (in the paradigm case, by being intentionally injured). Notice next that the harm involved in damaging or destroying tangible property also constitutes an interference with autonomy. The use-value and the exchange-value of property both represent opportunities for the owner, and adversely affecting either type of value harms the owner precisely because it diminishes her opportunities.[53] If her entitlement to the property is morally legitimate, then the interference with autonomy is morally significant and a remedy against inappropriate instances should be provided

[50] Perry, n. 1 above.

[51] The *existence* of the duty does not depend on how wealthy I am, although the normative consequences of my inability to pay is a separate question. Perhaps, as was once suggested in a Seinfeld episode, if I cannot compensate you with money then I have a duty to become your butler. As this example suggests, compensation for harm need not be in the form of monetary payments or the transfer of property. The possibility of repair therefore does not depend on the existence of property rights. Of course, there are good reasons of liberal political theory, rooted in considerations of personal autonomy, why monetary compensation is preferable to any form of forced labour.

[52] Cf. J. Raz, *The Morality of Freedom* (Clarendon Press, Oxford, 1986) 413–14.

[53] Ibid. Interference with non-tangible forms of property, such as pure economic interests, also adversely affects autonomy. The law of torts has never offered extensive protection for such interests, however, and there are good reasons for this. See S.R. Perry, 'Protected Interests and Undertakings in the Law

by the independent principle of repair. Notice, finally, that while it is no doubt true that at least one of the aims of distributive justice is to ensure that everyone has enough material resources to be able to pursue an autonomous life, corrective justice is not best envisaged, in property damage cases, as either protecting entitlements because they are distributive shares or preserving a just distribution of resources for its own sake. Corrective justice applies in such cases because the owner of damaged property has suffered harm. She has, in fact, suffered the same general type of harm as she would have suffered had she been injured in her person. Because corrective justice focuses, even in property damage cases, on harm rather than on distributive considerations, it is properly regarded as conceptually independent of distributive justice.

It should be emphasized that the harm-based understanding of corrective justice can only be regarded as conceptually independent of distributive justice if distributive justice is conceived dynamically rather than statically, i.e. if it is conceived in terms of abstract rather than simple patterning. We saw in section I that the distributive priority view of corrective justice cannot be reconciled with a static conception of distributive justice, although that had as much to do with the problematic aspects of the distributive priority view as it had to do with anything about simple patterning. In fact, no plausible conception of corrective justice, including any grounded in the harm-based view, can be reconciled with a static conception of distributive justice. Let me return for a moment to the example of static patterning that I borrowed from Larry Alexander in section I. The relevant pattern is an equal distribution. The relevant society consists of four persons, and each person has 10 units of goods. Suppose that A intentionally destroys four of B's units. Any plausible conception of corrective justice will require A to compensate B by giving her four of his units. Alexander points out that this will upset the pattern of equality, which can only be restored if everyone other than B gives her one of their units. Alexander argues that this 'conflict' between corrective and distributive justice can only be resolved by jettisoning one or the other, and he concludes that it is corrective justice that has to go: '[s]ince distributive justice is logically prior to corrective justice—there must be a distribution relative to which loss and compensation are measured—the obvious principle to discard is that of corrective justice'.[54]

The obvious way to resolve this conflict, however, is not to discard either corrective or distributive justice, but to discard the idea that distributive justice is a matter of simple patterning. As we saw in section I, the most powerful and well-developed contemporary theories of distributive justice are dynamic rather than static. The difference between these two types of theory is qualitative, and not just a matter of degree. I will argue in what follows that the harm-based view of corrective justice is consistent with and complementary to, although it is conceptually independent of, an appropriate, abstractly-patterned theory of distributive justice. Alexander's

of Negligence' (1992) 42 *U Toronto LJ* 247, 262–70. It is an interesting question to which interests other than autonomy the principle of corrective justice can be extended, but it is a question beyond the scope of the present essay.

[54] Alexander, n. 16 above, 6.

example, based as it is on a static pattern, in no way calls this conclusion into question. His argument is, in many ways, reminiscent of Nozick's famous Wilt Chamberlain example,[55] which also begins with a static distributive pattern. Nozick observes that a significant deviation from the pattern will occur if a large number of individuals voluntarily choose to give Chamberlain a certain proportion of their distributive shares to watch him play basketball. From this Nozick concludes that liberty upsets patterns, but all that he is really entitled to conclude is that liberty upsets simple patterns. The example tells us nothing about the role of liberty in any plausible dynamic theory of distributive justice, for example those of Rawls and Dworkin.

The general approach to corrective justice that is exemplifed by the harm-based view has not gone unchallenged. Although he does not address that view directly, Peter Benson has in effect argued that any understanding of corrective justice that possesses the following two characteristics will inevitably collapse into what I earlier called the distributive priority view: (1) it views corrective justice as protecting legitimate entitlements; and (2) it views the legitimacy of entitlements as determined by distributive justice. Benson argues that if distributive justice is postulated as the ground of the entitlements that corrective justice is supposed to protect, then there is nothing to preclude the injurer from claiming that his infringement of the entitlement is, from a distributive point of view, actually an improvement:

> If the injuring party can coherently frame the dispute in this way, the correction of the infringement should also properly be characterized as an act of distributive justice, seeing that it can be viewed as a decision made between two competing distributive claims. In short, once the initial entitlement is grounded in distributive justice, there is no reason why the violation of the entitlement as well as its correction should not be construed from the same distributive standpoint. It follows that there is no need to introduce, and indeed no basis for referring to, a second, genuinely distinct form of justice such as corrective justice. . . . The distinctiveness of corrective justice is not made out.[56]

Benson goes on to argue that the understanding of corrective justice he is criticizing can only hope to distinguish corrective from distributive justice by treating the background distribution, and hence the injured party's holdings, as presumptively just. But, he continues, since there is no particular reason to think that the distributive arrangement that existed before the parties harmfully interacted was more just than the arrangement that came into existence afterwards, such a presumption preserves the distinctiveness of corrective justice at the cost of its being a principle of justice.[57] According to Benson, corrective justice can only be understood as truly distinct from distributive justice if it operates with respect to a structure of entitlement that is completely independent of the structure of distributive entitlement. His own, Hegelian theory of corrective justice adopts the following principle: '[a] person

[55] Nozick, n. 15 above, 160–4.

[56] Benson, n. 10 above, 530–1.

[57] Ibid. 531–2. For similar arguments, see also J.W. Neyers, 'The Inconsistencies of Aristotle's Theory of Corrective Justice' (1998) 11 *Can. J of Law & Juris.* 311, 315–19. Neyers, unlike Benson, thinks that Aristotle's original account of corrective justice cannot accommodate a Kantian/Hegelian interpretation and is, for that reason, defective.

who, through an external manifestation of will, has brought something under his or her present and exclusive control prior to others is, relative to those others, entitled to it in corrective justice'.[58] Since such entitlements can either coincide with or be at odds with distributive entitlements, this view of corrective justice treats the notion as both conceptually and normatively independent of distributive justice. Each form of justice exists in its own self-contained normative sphere.

Benson's Hegelian theory of corrective justice is subtle and complex, and it is beyond the scope of the present essay to offer a critique of it here. Instead, I will try to show that his objections to such conceptions of corrective justice as the harm-based view are not well-founded. The first point to be made in this regard is that Benson seems to beg the question by implicitly assuming that the position he is criticizing incorporates the distributive priority view. Benson suggests that, if the initial entitlement is grounded in distributive justice, then the injuring party can argue that his infringement of the entitlement is a distributive improvement. Even if the injurer can make such an argument, however, he is, on an understanding of corrective justice like the harm-based view, at best making a normative claim that is dissimilar from, and in competition with, the victim's claim. The moral focus of the victim's claim is the harm she has suffered. She is saying: you harmed me, and therefore you have a moral obligation to compensate me. The injurer responds with the argument that, distributively speaking, it would be better if he did not have to pay compensation.[59] At most, we have two distinct kinds of moral claims which must be balanced against one another. Yet according to Benson, the decision whether or not to correct the infringement involves a choice 'between two competing distributive claims'. There is, however, simply no basis for treating the victim's as well as the injurer's claim as distributive in nature, unless one has implicitly rejected anything resembling the harm-based view and assumed instead that a non-Hegelian theory of corrective justice must adopt the distributive priority view.

The second and more serious problem with Benson's argument is that he seems to be assuming that the legitimacy of so-called 'distributive' entitlements is determined solely by considerations of distributive justice. Benson clearly conceives of distributive justice in terms of patterning, and he appears to allow for the possibility that patterns can be abstract as well as simple.[60] Even so, he apparently does not think that there can be any normative 'play' between the distributive justification of an entitlement and its ultimate moral legitimacy. While this might very well be true of a simple patterned theory, there are strong grounds for thinking that it will not be true of any plausible dynamic conception of distributive justice. An important obser-

[58] Benson, n. 10 above, 543. Ernest Weinrib holds a roughly similar view of corrective justice and of its relationship to distributive justice. See Weinrib, n. 10 above, 80–3, 104, 128–9.

[59] As we shall see below, there is a difference between a set of entitlements being morally legitimate and its being distributively ideal. Perhaps the injurer might be understood as saying that the victim did not even have a morally legitimate entitlement to the damaged property. That is different from arguing that leaving the victim uncompensated is a distributive improvement. The claim is, in effect, that the victim was not harmed, or at least that her harm was not of significant moral concern.

[60] Benson, n. 10 above, 537.

vation by Jules Coleman is relevant in this regard.[61] Coleman points out that there are very good reasons, in addition to considerations of distributive justice, for having a system of private property rights, and this suggests that a set of entitlements that is not distributively ideal—Coleman speaks of a set of 'second best' entitlements—may nonetheless be morally legitimate and worth protecting. He mentions in particular the importance of property rights to sustaining markets, since markets contribute to overall social welfare in well-known ways, but there are many other, similarly consequentialist concerns that come into play here. Gordley's points about giving people incentives to work and preventing quarrels are examples.[62] As Coleman observes, 'within limits, the rights in place may help to sustain an institution that generally improves individual well-being and social stability, and that does so in ways that encourage individual fulfillment, initiative, and self-respect. Those rights would then be worthy of respect even if they did not exactly coincide with the best or most just distribution of resources.'[63]

To this point Benson might reply that, just because an entitlement is morally legitimate, it does not follow that the courts, say, should not take advantage of a tort action to make distributive improvements. Why should legitimacy be thought to confer immunity from morally-required redistribution? Perhaps the degree of protection that even a morally legitimate entitlement should receive from corrective justice and tort law is dependent on the status of the entitlement in distributive justice. This might mean, to revert to an earlier example, that an extremely poor person who negligently collides with the Mercedes of an exceptionally wealthy person does not have to pay the Mercedes' owner compensation, even though the latter is morally entitled to her car. Benson's counter-argument would then conclude that the existence of 'play' between the distributive justification of an entitlement and its moral legitimacy does not prevent the collapse of the harm-based view of corrective justice into the distributive priority view (or, more accurately, into distributive justice *tout court*).

This is where the dynamic nature of distributive justice enters the picture. On a dynamic, abstractly-patterned theory based on, e.g. Rawls' difference principle or Dworkin's notion of equality of resources, distributive justice does not operate at the level of momentary distributive states, let alone at the level of individual holdings. These theories are dynamic and abstractly-patterned precisely in order to allow people to enter into contracts, make gifts, and so on, without thereby creating distributive disparities. The result is that such theories are highly indeterminate with respect to momentary distributive states and the extent of individual holdings. It is possible, for example, for some individuals to become very wealthy without disrupting abstract equality or the difference principle. Who ends up at any given moment with which resources and how much wealth is, as Rawls says, a matter of pure proce-

[61] Coleman, n. 3 above, 350–4.

[62] The formulation 'preventing quarrels' understates the significance of Gordley's point, which is perhaps better captured by saying that the existence of property rights contributes to preventing social chaos.

[63] Coleman, n. 3 above, 354.

dural justice. Coleman's point tells us that the overall system of private property rights can be morally legitimate even if it is not ideally distributively just. The moral legitimacy of the system will presumably be transmitted to individual entitlements. It is far from clear, however, that it even makes sense to say of individual holdings that they embody distributive imbalances, or at least that they do so in such a way that would justify *ad hoc* adjustments by a judge in a tort action.

Consider the case of someone who has acquired vast wealth in business but who has always played by the rules; she has always observed applicable market norms, paid exactly what she owes in income tax, never stolen from anyone, and so on. No doubt it is possible to say of such a person that she is too wealthy, but notice what this does and does not mean under a dynamic conception of distributive justice. As the Coleman point makes clear, it does not mean, or at least it does not necessarily mean, that her holdings are morally illegitimate (although if the entire system is too askew distributively, that is at least a possibility). It does not mean that she has too much under the existing, perhaps less-than-ideal, scheme of distributive justice. (How could she, since by hypothesis she played by all the rules, including in particular the redistributive rules embodied in the taxation scheme?) It might mean that she has too much wealth to be justified under any plausible conception of distributive justice, in which case the extent of her holdings might well be morally illegitimate. What it probably means to say that she is too wealthy, though, is that her vast wealth is symptomatic of systemic distributive problems in the property regime as a whole. Systemic deficiencies must be dealt with systemically: perhaps anti-trust law must be tightened up, or the marginal tax rates increased, or the social minimum raised. Contrary to what Benson suggests, however, it is not possible to do distributive justice in any meaningful way by tinkering with individual levels of holdings on a case-by-case basis, through, say, tort law.[64] As was noted earlier, it is not clear that this notion even makes sense. This is a normative point, and perhaps a conceptual point, about dynamic theories of distributive justice; it is not just a matter of practicality. Part of the point of such theories is to enhance people's liberty by creating stable and enduring entitlements to property that are not subject to continuous, ongoing, or *ad hoc* redistribution.

The harm-based view of corrective justice operates at the level of individual entitlements that have been subjected to interference by another person. By contrast, dynamic conceptions of distributive justice operate systemically, institutionally, and over time. Such conceptions are, as we have seen, highly indeterminate with respect to momentary distributive states and the extent of individual holdings as these exist at any given time, and this creates the logical space within which corrective justice is able to function. Thus when impoverished A negligently rams the Mercedes of extremely wealthy B, then so long as B's entitlement to her Mercedes is morally legitimate, A owes B compensation for the damage.[65] The reason is that A has harmed B

[64] The core problem with Dworkin's theory of rights of repair might be expressed by saying that he tries to combine a dynamic conception of distributive justice with the fundamentally incompatible idea that distributive adjustments can be made at the level of individual entitlements.

in an inappropriate way. Of course, neither the legitimacy of B's specific entitlement, nor the justifiability of the property system as a whole (this being the most likely source of legitimacy for the specific entitlement), entails that the system is ideally distributively just. Thus it might well be the case that welfare payments should be raised, which would benefit A. Perhaps it is also true that marginal tax rates should be increased, which would hurt B. None of this alters the fact that, right now, A has a moral duty to hand money over to B which is unaffected by the great disparity in wealth between them.

According to Benson's Hegelian theory of corrective justice, corrective and distributive justice operate on distinct kinds of entitlement, and for that reason they are, in both a conceptual and a normative sense, completely independent of one another. The harm-based view looks upon corrective justice as conceptually distinct from distributive justice, and also in large measure as normatively distinct, because the two principles have different normative functions. One is concerned with the just distribution of resources, while the other is concerned with remedying harmful interactions between persons. But that does not mean there are no normative connections between the two principles; they are not, as on Benson's view, completely independent from one another. Despite the possibility of a shortfall between moral legitimacy and ideal distributive justice, a system of private property rights will generally only be morally legitimate if it is distributively just to at least some minimum degree. Thus, in the case of property interests, corrective justice generally operates on what we might loosely call distributive entitlements ('loosely', because of the possibility of shortfall). To that extent, corrective and distributive justice are normatively connected.

Benson argues that if there is a normative connection between corrective and distributive justice of the kind just discussed, then corrective justice can only be regarded as independent from distributive justice if the former adopts a presumption that the existing set of holdings is distributively just. But that seems to be wrong. The conceptual independence of corrective and distributive justice, as well as their partial normative independence, results not from any such presumption but from the fact that the two principles have different normative functions. Benson further suggests that there is no reason in any event to presume that a given set of holdings is distributively just. This is in a sense correct, but irrelevant. If Benson means that no property system in, say, any existing liberal democratic state is ideally distributively just, he is undoubtedly right. From the point of view of corrective justice, however, what matters is not ideal distributive justice but moral legitimacy. Given Coleman's point about the possible discrepancy between the two, it is by no means outlandish to suppose that the property systems in many liberal democratic states are in fact morally justified.[66] Even if that were not true, however, it would not follow that corrective

[65] Corrective justice, as a moral principle, presumably only operates on morally legitimate entitlements. Tort law is another matter, since it is plausible to think that the law must either refuse to look past the fact of legal entitlement, or else must incorporate a very strong and perhaps irrebuttable presumption that legal entitlements are always also moral entitlements.

and distributive justice are not conceptually independent. It would just mean that the principle of corrective justice would have no applicability to property interests.[67]

My defence of the independence of corrective from distributive justice might, finally, be challenged from a different quarter. Even if a proponent of Dworkin's theory of equality of resources were to acknowledge the problems with the comparative harm principle that were discussed in section II, he might nonetheless wish to argue that the harm-based view of corrective justice is not independent of distributive justice for the following reason. Even though corrective justice operates at the level of individual entitlements rather than at a systemic level, it does so in such a way as to preserve equality of resources in the abstract sense. In this respect corrective justice resembles the role in Dworkin's theory of market transactions and decisions involving so-called option luck, i.e., deliberate or calculated decisions to run certain risks. Dworkin argues, quite plausibly, that individuals should, against the background of general redistributive institutions, both take the benefits and bear the costs of market transactions and other kinds of calculated gambles. Equality of resources in the abstract sense is thus unaffected by such events, regardless of the outcome. The same would seem to be true of the operation of corrective justice, which might perhaps be regarded as just a special case of option luck. Since corrective justice preserves equality of resources in this way, the argument concludes, it is best conceived as one element of the larger distributive theory.

The phrase, 'corrective justice preserves equality of resources', is ambiguous. On one reading, it suggests that the function of corrective justice is to preserve equality of resources, in very much the same way that the function of corrective justice is taken to be, on the distributive priority view, to preserve determinate just distributions. On another reading, however, the phrase simply means that the abstract pattern of equality is unaffected by the operation of corrective justice. Corrective justice is, so to speak, transparent to distributive justice. In the present context, it is clearly the second meaning of the phrase that is relevant. The function of corrective justice has nothing to do with distributive justice, even though it sometimes operates on distributive entitlements, as these were loosely defined above. The function of corrective justice is, rather, to provide a remedy to persons who have been harmed in certain ways by other persons. While it is an interesting and perhaps theoretically significant fact that corrective justice is transparent to distributive justice, it is one that seems to confirm rather than to call into question the conceptual independence of the former principle from the latter.

[66] Cf. Coleman, n. 3 above, 354.

[67] It would still apply, of course, to the interest in life and bodily integrity.

Index